I0457931

José Antonio, Fascist

José Antonio, Fascist

José Luis Jerez Riesco

ANTELOPE HILL PUBLISHING

English Translation copyright © 2025 Antelope Hill Publishing
Copyright © 2003 José Luis Jerez Riesco

All rights reserved

Originally published in 2003 as *José Antonio, Fascista* by
Ediciones Nueva Republica

First Antelope Hill edition, first printing 2025

Translated by Giammarco Simonelli, 2025

Cover art by Swifty
Edited by Tom Simpson and Harlan Wallace
Proofread by Sebastian Durant
Interior formatting by S. Alexander

Antelope Hill Publishing | antelopehillpublishing.com

Paperback ISBN: 978-1-953730-33-6
Ebook ISBN: 978-1-953730-34-3

Table of Contents

Original Publisher's Foreword   xi

Introduction   xiii

Dedication   xv

Essential Considerations   xvii

1. Fascism in the Conception and Development of the Spanish Falange   1

2. October 29th: A (Fascist) Flag Is Symbolically Raised   37

3. Spanish Fascists in *La Nueva Catolicidad*   51

4. Falange Española is Born   57

5. The (Fascist) General Staff of José Antonio   73

6. F.E., An Unequivocally Fascist Newspaper   103

7. Foreword to Benito   187

8. José Antonio Visits Adolf Hitler   195

9. What Chances Do You Believe Fascism Has in Spain?   205

10. Fascist Confessions of José Antonio   209

11. José Antonio, Founding Member of the CAUR   217

12. Fascist Programs   241

13. *¡Arriba España!*, A Unique Journal of Fascist Memories   253

14. The Weekly Newspaper *Arriba*   263

15. Haz: University Students Contribute to the Movement   287

16. Mussolini's Aid to José Antonio   289

17. A Recommendation from José Antonio: La Riqueza en el Régimen   297
Liberal, Comunista y Fascista [Wealth in the Liberal, Communist, and
Fascist Regimes]

18. José Antonio and the European Fascist Leaders   303

19. No Importa: "The Fascist is not the one who has the desire, but the   325
one who has the ability"

20. German Logistical Support for the Liberation of José Antonio   339

Original Publisher's Foreword

EDICIONES NUEVA REPÚBLICA could not better commemorate the founder of the Falange on the centenary of his birth than through the pen of José Luis Jerez Riesco.

There was a time when one could openly speak the truth anywhere. Today, on the contrary, the truth has become politically incorrect, something that is widely opposed.

Jerez Riesco approaches the unique figure of José Antonio Primo de Rivera with a very well documented and detailed book that will displease not only the thought police, but also those who, by attempting to find a little corner inside the walls of the System, have distorted the image of an authentic Fascist leader with deceitful and naive tricks, in order to appease weak souls.

For those of us who believe that confronting falsehoods is always a revolutionary act, we are confident that Jerez Riesco has produced a text that will make people think, one that will be impossible to ignore, and, of course, one that will spark debate.

Juan Antonio Llopart
Barcelona, April 24th, 2003

Introduction

The relentless pursuit of the elusive trail of truth is a rather difficult task. Furthermore, many times it endangers the daring person who seeks to unveil, against all odds, the secrets behind the blurred shapes of the unified truth that has been shattered, broken down into minimal truths, and defended by the prejudices of those who selfishly seek to exploit these truths for ideological purposes rather than for enlightening all seekers.

This is particularly clear in matters of opinion and those things which affect the political course of our society, as well as the experiences, more or less transcendental, that shape the underlying history upon which the future of the Fatherland will be constructed.

Before these facts, each of which carries its own subtext or hidden truth, the men who will analyze them and who will therefore make history adopt very different positions. Many times, sticking to the *politically correct* (which is so much in vogue nowadays), they do not care about the search for truth and its acquisition in order to subsequently disseminate it, but they frame the facts that determine it so that their hidden implications will satisfy the political system on which they depend and with which they generally coexist in a symbiosis that is mutually profitable. There are many examples of this in the political episodes of the Fatherland today.

Opposing them, unfortunately less numerous, are those men who passionately maintain the truth, offering in that search, even more than their proven intelligence, the affectivity that ennobles the clean expression of their word, of their transmitting speech, demonstrating before the court of their own conscience that they know what the word, oral or written, signifies and stands for. They are those who struggle to prevent their intellectual vocation from being drowned in the maddeningly economic utilitarianism of contemporary politics.

I am proud to be friends with one of these men. His name is José Luis Jerez Riesco, a man who, as an intellectual in his prime, speaks what he thinks, shouts it out, and writes it down, never being satisfied with just keeping these matters for his own meditation. He aspires to bring his vision to others and, therefore, to be heard and listened to.

José Luis Jerez Riesco has approached José Antonio Primo de Rivera as he should be approached, with loyalty and respect. What he says, with sincerity and fairness, may be admired by some and despised by others, but it will certainly not be indifferent or obvious to anyone.

My only request, as the master Adolfo Muñoz Alonso used to say, is that the Manicheans of culture and the Jansenists of salvation do not "storm the square" with the unsheathed weapons provided by the official armory of the kingdom.

Dr. Luis Teigell Cea
Old Guard of the Falange, Former National President of the Brotherhood of the
Blue Division, Chief of the Medical Guard of the Caudillo

Dedication

To José Antonio, on the centenary of his birth.

To the thousands of Blackshirts, Italian Fascist volunteers fallen in the lands of Spain during our Liberation Crusade, who sealed with courage and youthful, copious, generous blood the pact of fidelity and honor with their comrades of the Falange, immolated in the same trenches.

To the heroes of the German Condor Legion.

To the comrades and brother Viriatos and Blueshirts of Portuguese National Syndicalism, who fought with nobility.

To the Irish Blueshirts of General O'Duffy.

To the martyrs Ion Motza and Vasile Marin, of the Romanian Iron Guard, whose fatal sacrifice is an example, and whose memory is preserved under the sky of Castile where there is, in Majadahonda, a cross of granite and a perennial triumphal arch that symbolize their deeds for God, Spain, and its National Syndicalist Revolution.

Essential Considerations

The meaning of the term *Fascist* is currently understood according to the malicious meaning given to it by its hardened enemies and detractors, the official antifascists, who have demonized the word to the point of making it a slanderous insult, a word to be thrown like a poisoned dart by anyone who wants to vilify his most hated neighbor. The curious thing is that all political zealots, whatever their political affiliation, label their opponents with this word, which from their point of view is the most denigratory one they can utter. The conclusion to be reached is that, reducing to absurdity the invectives used by the politicians, in the end they are all, paradoxically, "Fascists" in the eyes of each other, which they do not want to be, and cannot avoid being called, ungenerously and with total verbal incontinence, by their dissenters and adversaries.

Evidently, *Fascism* does not actually accord with the pejorative interpretation applied to it by its many visceral detractors, who are often bad people trying to propagandize, with a great irrational willfulness, with the intent of hurting feelings rather than reasoning thoughtfully. The loudmouths of obstinate defamation always clash with reality. In the end, truth prevails.

Fascism, which in contemporary language is an insult employed by the fraudsters of truth, in the 1930s represented the new and revolutionary political doctrine of hope against a world in ruins, gripped by materialism, whether communist or capitalist. Fascism attracted followers, enthusiasm, sympathy, hope, and jealousy. It was what, at that time, was *politically correct*, ethically right, and factually necessary.

Fascism can be calmly understood, in an orthodox way, as the political regime that was in effect in Italy from 1922 to 1945, under the rule of the Duce Benito Mussolini, founder of the Fasces, who, in 1922, was appointed prime minister after the March on Rome, and whom the Catholic Church referred to as "the man of providence," a man who gave dignity and greatness to his Fatherland in a righteous and social way.

The terms *Fascism* or *Fascist* can also be applied to a related event or phenomenon in world history. As Ramiro Ledesma Ramos points out,

> It is evident that an investigation of Fascism, an examination of it, not as a specific regime of a given country but as a world concept in operation, is a legitimate and achievable task. We can, as a matter of fact, list a series of characteristics, profiles, purposes, and dreams that provide us with an accurate picture of Fascism as a world phenomenon. In this sense and only in it, it is possible to speak of Fascism outside Italy; that is to say, this word acquires a universalist meaning. [Therefore,] it cannot be surprising that the victory of Italian Fascism—its fortunate search for a new state, emerging from the very entrails of that age, in the face of its essential difficulties and appealing to the strongest values: national distress, the need for order and discipline, the concern for the historical and economic destiny of *all* the people—would polarize the world's attention.[1]

In identifying, legitimately and validly, the word *Fascist* with both an era in Italian political life as well as the extrapolation and dissemination of its principles into a global, ecumenical political doctrine, Fascism turns out to be the most advanced and progressive political theory of the twentieth century, overcoming the two sides of the same false Judaic coin: on the one hand liberal capitalism, selfish and ruthless, managed by the worshippers of the golden calf, and on the other hand communism, criminal and heartless, which arose in the nineteenth century from the minds of Marx and Engels and was put into practice, for the most part, by bloodthirsty and despotic Jewish revolutionaries or the like, with results and consequences that we know all too well.

As Manuel Pastor writes, on page 33 of his essay "Los orígenes del Fascismo en España,"

> one should not mistake the term *Fascism*, applied to the Italian political movement and regime, which, undoubtedly, gathered its own specific and unrepeatable characteristics, and the term *Fascism* as a generic concept,

---

[1] Ramiro Ledesma Ramos, *¿Fascismo En España?* (Barcelona: Ediciones Ariel, 1968), 45–46.

understood as a historical political phenomenon that can be observed in different stages of development in various European political societies, starting from the 1920s.

This idea is further developed by Ernst Nolte in his work *Three Faces of Fascism*, in which he claims that,

> it is absurd to deny the unity of a phenomenon so deeply rooted in the basic elements of the era as a unit and, as a unit, so passionately disputed. In actual fact the proposal to limit the term *Fascism* to Mussolini's party never succeeded.[2]

Fascism went from being a typically Italian phenomenon to becoming, in essence, a universal phenomenon, even if its realization had to be inevitably adapted to the specific situation and context of each country.

It is clear that there is no such thing as a *single and universal Fascism*, nor is it possible to assign to this concept a singular definition without distinctions. In any case, what is evident is the possibility of establishing a common and unitary basis for the nationalist and revolutionary movements that arose in Europe in the interwar period, inspired by the same common spirit of mutual camaraderie.

In opposition to liberal-capitalist or Bolshevik-communist materialism, the Fascist idea arose as a movement to save and regenerate the peoples from the oppressive Judaic grasp, whose cancerous growth threatened to devour the healthy social body that still remained in the traditions and the genes of the civilized peoples.

Fascism put values of superior quality in place of the old values, so that its strategy managed to enter the international scene—bearing in mind that its *internationalization* entailed, precisely, the national essence of each people, the most deeply rooted sign of the identity of each nation, and the most authentic, genuine, and profound being of each historical mission shared in collective unity and hopefulness for the Fatherland, bound together with a sense of integration and scope. Fascism is, therefore, a moral, political, and economic *commitment to life*.

It is not possible, therefore, when speaking of Fascism, to credit imitation or egalitarian standards, nor the theory of communicating vessels, as an explanation; rather, one must consider originality as the creative force and peculiarity as the guiding reference in each case.

Fascism stems from natural principles of universal value, from common and firm axioms, but the design which is applied to each sovereign entity is the result

---

[2] Ernst Nolte, *Three Faces of Fascism*, 567.

of pure genius, is traditional, and is emblematic of the values of the respective paradigms. Fascism is therefore a widespread, far-reaching, universal phenomenon that, stemming from the political genius of Mussolini (which is of an essentially popular character), represents the genuine and legitimate aspirations of the people, giving it a universal character and justifying its ecumenical triumph "since it is not just another political doctrine, but a genial and effective way of solving the powerful problems that torment the peoples."[3]

Fascism is national revolution, national spirit, national sentiment, united with justice and social mysticism, taking root wherever it is embraced as a bastion and organizing principle of the natural and spiritual conception of life and history. Fascism is about being, not merely existing.

---

[3] *Fascismo régimen del pueblo para el pueblo* (Valldolid: Imprenta Castellana, 1937), 40.

1.

Fascism in the Conception and Development of the Spanish Falange

Germany, 1933

On January 30th, 1933, at 11 o'clock in the morning, with Germanic discipline, Adolf Hitler was received by the elderly Marshal von Hindenburg to be entrusted with the Chancellery of the Reich. A thin mantle of snow covered the sidewalks and roads of Berlin. Hitler reached such a high position, entrusted to him by popular will through the majority vote of the German people, fairly. That day at the end of January would lead German destiny into a new historical phase. Hitler's rise to power shaped the twentieth century. The eagerly awaited hour had arrived after fourteen years of bitter struggle, almost fifteen years of renunciations and sufferings, during which the new chancellor had demonstrated and proven, with eloquence and unquestionable authority, his outstanding leadership qualities as a man of thought and action. This herculean effort raised him to the top, even in a democratic system where elections were called and controlled by the very enemies of National Socialism.

The joy of the crowd was overwhelming. People poured into the streets. They wanted to cheer, acclaim, and salute their new leader. The snow melted under their feet. The roar and bursts of applause followed one after the other like uninterrupted fireworks along the length and breadth of the Wilhelmstrasse. The news of the accomplishment spread all over the world. Alongside the German national anthem,

"Deutschland Über Alles," chanted in unison by the crowd, a new hymn was hummed and sung with eyes filled with emotion. This was soon to become popular throughout Europe: the "Horst Wessel Lied," the National Socialist anthem.

A few hours later, that excited and joyful crowd marched in an orderly and martial manner, carrying torches, down the avenue of the Tiergarten under the gaze of the charioteer atop the Brandenburg Gate, in a new form, in perfect order, in a triumphal procession, with drumrolls and marching bands following banners. It appeared like a flow of glowing magma, emerging from the most traditional and genuine roots of the earth, clad in brown and saluting with their raised arms the new Europe.

Italy

Benito Mussolini, founder of Fascism, raised on October 29th, 1922, following the March on Rome, the flag of Fascism. Fascism was the new nationalist and revolutionary ideology that was to overcome the contradictions of both liberalism and Marxism. Fascism carried with it a fresh, youthful atmosphere of camaraderie. It represented a totalitarian and unifying movement that placed the common good over private self-interest.

Mussolini was a tribune of the people to whom he delivered the message, loud and clear, that wealth should be subjected to national interest rather than vice versa. Italian Fascism was a popular and social movement, a movement based on action and not on mere promises. Mussolini, the blacksmith's son born in Predappio, began his political career as a Marxist militant, diverging from this initial trajectory by introducing a national character (as opposed to internationalist principles) into his political thought, together with a more social character that was a far cry from the stale rhetoric of nineteenth-century socialism.

Fascism was a rallying cry of hope. It was the new alternative. In opposition to materialism, idealism, it proposed a moral, political and economic commitment to life. This spirit and feeling was shared by the European youth, tired of Marxist dialectics and obsolete economic materialism. Fascism was a movement aimed at overcoming class struggle and was meant to be the spearhead of the struggle against the cult of the power of money embodied in liberal capitalism. For this reason, since its advent, it has attracted a large number of detractors. Fascism was about the integration of all social classes into a strong and powerful state, a state in which everything would serve one mission.

The characteristics that made the Italian Fascist revolution innovative can be summarized, in an informative but inconclusive way, by the following:

- mystical and ascetic understanding of life and politics;
- spiritualist, idealist, or voluntaristic thought;

- cyclical view of history;
- denial of Marxist materialism;
- version to selfish and unbridled individualism;
- aversion to democratic liberalism;
- ritique of the bourgeoisie;
- establishing of the organic, structured, and hierarchical militant community, totalitarian and communitarian;
- exaltation of the hero, the martyr, the genius, the athlete, the worker, the leader;
- the search for a new value of aristocracy, for a new nobility, the nobility of work and a new elite founded on merit;
- authority by example;
- aspiration toward a nobler and superior society;
- creation of a new ruling class drawn from the petty and middle bourgeoisie and from the working class;
- glorification of youth—the National Fascist Party's very own anthem was called, not by coincidence, "Giovinezza";
- promotion of culture, art, and science;
- moral rearmament involving values such as honor or heroism;
- spiritual idea of empire;
- assertion of traditional values;
- adoption of new technology;
- fusion of nationalism and socialism;
- supremacy of political sovereignty over international finance;
- defense of private property that is subject to the common and public good;
- a taste for what is rural;
- protection of the family;
- unionism and corporatism;
- separation and respect between the Church and state. And, in relation to women, femininity rather than feminism.

The word *fascio* derives from the sheaf or bundle of wooden rods with an axe emerging from it that accompanied the lictor, the representative and symbol of justice in the Roman Republic. The color of the shirt that Mussolini adopted was black—a liturgical, ceremonial, and revolutionary color, a synthesis of mourning and elegance, of etiquette and struggle.

Mussolini brought the Fascist revolution to power without any bloodshed. It was a call for order in the midst of chaos, for the stability of government in the midst of a permanent crisis, and, as the Duce himself would clarify,

I affirm that the idea, doctrine, and spirit of Fascism are universal. It is Italian in its particular institutions, but it is universal in spirit; nor could it be otherwise, for spirit is universal by its very nature. It is therefore possible to foresee a Fascist Europe that will model its institutions on Fascist doctrine and practice, a Europe that will solve in a Fascist way the problems of the modern twentieth-century state.[4]

Four years after this declaration, rethinking and analyzing the circumstances confirmed in March 1934, Mussolini stated the following: "From 1929 to today, Fascism has passed from being an Italian phenomenon to a universal phenomenon . . . . In a decade, Europe will be Fascist or fascistized!"

The Spanish Fascio

Felipe Ximénez de Sandoval, university classmate, friend, and passionate biographer of José Antonio, offers a series of keen insights in his magnificent and apologetic work on the life of the founder of the Falange.[5] He establishes an initial parallelism between José Antonio and Benito Mussolini, with an anecdotal revelation regarding a literary event held on November 27th, 1929, at the Ritz Hotel in Madrid to celebrate the great success of Manuel and Antonio Machado's Andalusian poem, "La Lola se va a los puertos":

> It is curious that this first performance of José Antonio in the arena of public oratory coincides with the first one of Benito Mussolini. Both had to hone their skills in oratory by discussing poetry or music. The son of the blacksmith of Dovia, at that time a teacher in the Giosuè Carducci school at Forlimpopoli, achieved his first success at the age of seventeen, when he commemorated in the local theater the death of the great composer Giuseppe Verdi. The son of the general of Jerez speaks of poetry. Both their fathers are moved when they see their boys—who study fervently and compose poetry—confident of the great destiny that awaits them. "History will have a lot to say about this boy," prophesied José Antonio's father. "You will be the Crispi of tomorrow," said Alessandro Mussolini, the crude socialist blacksmith, to Benito. Humanity and history have their coincidences beyond time, space, classes, and peoples.[6]

---

[4] Benito Mussolini, Speech in Rome, October 27th, 1930, delivered from the balcony of Palazzo Venezia in Rome, quoted by Eduardo Núñez in *80 Aniversario de la Marcha sobre Roma* (Madrid: S.O.S. Libros, 2002), 7–8.

[5] Felipe Ximénez de Sandoval, *José Antonio, Biografía apasionada* (Madrid: Editorial Fuerza Nueva, 1976).

[6] Ibid., 59–60.

With regard to his education and his political readings, José Antonio's biographer shares with us the following confidence:

> He did not neglect the improvement of his political ideas . . . . The Mussolinian creation has already been in existence for ten years and has already developed into a doctrine, largely expressed in the volumes of the Duce's speeches. Adolf Hitler's *Mein Kampf* had already traveled the world before January 30th, 1933. All these books, alongside those of Rosenberg, Farinacci, Malaparte, Trotsky, Lenin, and other theoreticians of the new regimes, had their place on José Antonio's desk. Next to them were those of the Spanish thinkers.[7]

José Antonio had already read and meditated on the books of Giménez Caballero, such as *Circuito Imperial* (1929), the book in the Spanish version by Curzio Malaparte *En torno al casticismo de Italia*, with a long foreword by GeCé, published with the title *Carta a un compañero de la Joven España* (1929), *Genio de España: Exaltaciones a una resurrección nacional y del mundo* (1932), and *La Nueva Catolicidad: Teoría General sobre el Fascismo en Europa: en España* (1933); he had let himself be seduced by the fine prose and the sensitive and profound rhetoric of Rafael Sánchez Mazas, who, as a correspondent of *ABC* in Rome, greeted with his enthusiastic articles the new awakening of "Italy with Graceful Steps" during the dawn of the new European revolution. It was Rafael Sánchez Mazas who, facing the subsequent Falangist martyrdom, would write the "Oración por los muertos de la Falange," a funeral piece of poetic and mystical inspiration. José Antonio enjoyed reading the writings of Eugenio Montes, in accordance with the German and Italian situations of the time. He was also well aware of the Fascist literature that was published in Italy and in other European countries and that was translated into Spanish by a friend of José Antonio, such as the book by O. Scheid, *Hitler y el Nacionalsocialismo* (1933),[8] which was commented upon and translated by Juan Vidal Salvó in 1933, who witnessed with interest and hope how in Germany, Hitler and his National Socialists came to power. Vidal himself was an admirer of Fascism and National Socialism who would join Primo de Rivera from the start.[9] According to Carlos de Arce, "it was Georges Sorel, and above all his famous book *Reflections on Violence*, published around 1908, that served as the inspiration for some of the principles of José Antonio's militant movement."[10]

---

[7] Ibid., 80.

[8] Julio Gil Pecharromán, *José Antonio Primo de Rivera, retrato de un visionario* (Madrid: Temas de Hoy, 1996), 161.

[9] Joan Maria Thomás, *Lo que fue la Falange* (Barcelona: Plaza & Janés, 1999).

[10] Carlos de Arce, *José Antonio. Biografía* (Barcelona: Editorial ARE, 1983), 61.

Likewise, Felipe Ximénez de Sandoval depicts a similar picture of the situation. We find ourselves in 1933, among the Fascist revolutions that are emerging throughout Europe and with a power vacuum in Spain. With nostalgia and yearning, like the passenger who witnesses how the train departs and is left behind by the rhythm of the times:

> Outside of Spain, following the example of Italy, Germany established a totalitarian regime, proclaimed by Adolf Hitler and his phalanxes of Brownshirts, that scraped democratic liberalism, social democracy, Marxism, and Freemasonry off of the Third Reich. The swastika and the fasces, over the German and Italian skies, heralded a new era against the hammer and sickle victorious over the skies of Moscow, and against the permanent democratic limbo suffered by other empires, kingdoms, and republics . . . . The old capitalist order, which dominated Europe, was threatened by the tremendous disorder of those marching on at a martial and youthful pace, with songs of war and love, with vigorous cries, with faith and joy. In Spain, a right-wing republic was still thought possible. In Germany and Italy, the certainty of empire was palpable, sounded in trumpets and burning throats, to the tune of the "Horst Wessel Lied" and of "Giovinezza."[11]

In the opinion of Arnaud Imatz—the pseudonym of the French writer Alain Couartou, who in the 1970s wrote *José Antonio et la Phalange Espagnole*,

> the study of contemporary social phenomena and the most recent literary works slowly persuaded José Antonio that only Fascism and a regime of public health could save Spain. He then firmly adhered to this approach. He publicly presents himself as a "Fascist" by participating on the editorial staff of the weekly magazine *El Fascio*, which, after causing a lot of rumors throughout Spain, was suspended before even being published.[12]

José Antonio thus declares himself a Fascist, and despite his subsequent efforts to mark the originality of his positions, this label, which did not yet carry its insulting connotation, would remain tied to his person until his death.

Antonio Medrano, the great Spanish philosopher of perennialism, remarked:

> 1933 was a key year in the life of José Antonio. It marked his definitive appearance in the political arena, to which he would devote all his energy

---

[11] Ximénez de Sandoval, *José Antonio (Biografía apasionada)*, 89.

[12] Arnaud Imatz, pseudonym of Alain Couartou, *José Antonio et la Phalange Espágnole* (Paris: Editions Albatros, 1981), 101–2.

and even his own life. He began to organize what would later become the Falangist Movement with a series of unrefined attempts, such as the Frente Español, the Fascismo Español, or the Movimiento Español Sindicalista.[13]

On February 23rd, 1933, at the home of Ernesto Giménez Caballero, located at 41 Calle Canarias in Madrid, where his editorial printing offices were also located, a gathering occurred: a long-time close collaborator of José Antonio's father, Manuel Delgado Barreto, met with the director of the weekly magazine *Gracia y Justicia* and the newspaper *La Nación*, Ramiro Ledesma Ramos (founder and central figure of the JONS with Rafael Sánchez Mazas and Juan Aparicio López, secretary of the JONS and literary collaborator of *El Debate*), along with José Antonio himself, representing the Spanish side. Also present at that meeting was the Italian ambassador, Raffaele Guariglia, and a German press correspondent of the *Telegraphen Union*. This was to be the initial staff, the founding core, of the future weekly magazine *El Fascio*, which was already shaping into a reality at that very meeting.

Guariglia, during his diplomatic mission as Italian ambassador in Spain, was charged to encourage, help, and stimulate Fascist movements abroad. In February of that same year, he initiated a program of action and distinctly Fascist propaganda with the opening of an information center located in the Casa d'Italia, where recent books and magazines on the social achievements of Italian Fascism, together with photographic material, informative brochures, and the press in general, could be consulted.

Meetings were also held in order to establish contacts with Juan Pujol, director of the evening newspaper *Informaciones*; Alfonso García Valdecasas, head of the small party Frente Español; and with the Italian journalist and militant of the National Fascist Party, Cesare A. Gullino, a good friend of the commander Emilio Rodríguez Tarduchy, a close and dear supporter of José Antonio.

A month and a half after Hitler's rise to the Reich Chancellery, in Spain, that intellectual initiative, the launching of a political weekly magazine under the title *El Fascio*, would be ultimately foiled, despite the indomitable will of its promoters and the optimistic expectations of a large part of the Spanish public.

José Antonio, with this initiative, did not intend to copy, imitate, or plagiarize the Italian National Fascist Party or German National Socialism, but to dive deeply into the native Spanish essence, into its identity, into the most genuine and authentic aspects of Spain—but, of course, in harmony and camaraderie with his European counterparts, who were exploring what was their own. He was not unaware of the legacy his father left when, on November 22nd, 1923, shortly after taking over the charge of the Military Directory, during his

---

13 Antonio Medrano, "José Antonio Primo de Rivera, el fundador de la Phalange," from the magazine *Totalité*, no. 13, 51.

visit to the headquarters of Fascism in Rome, he wrote in his own handwriting: "In memory of my visit to the Headquarters of Fascism in Rome and in enthusiastic recognition of its high doctrine and the purity with which it is professed by its leaders."

In 1939, the first biographical document of real importance was published: *José Antonio, el hombre, el Jefe, el camarada,* written by Francisco Bravo, an early member of the JONS and, later, provincial chief of the Falange in Salamanca, who dedicates a chapter of his work to the "Evolution of José Antonio toward Fascism," in which he informs us:

> on March 16th, 1933, José Antonio was to publicly show himself as a "Fascist" collaborating in the writing of a weekly magazine that failed to be published and that, nevertheless, caused a lot of rumors all over Spain. We are referring to *El Fascio*—Spanish fasces . . . which was undoubtedly an exclusive initiative of the National Syndicalist Movement, destined not to come to fruition due to its prematurity.[14]

Bravo argues that in the articles written by José Antonio in *El Fascio*, his spiritual evolution, influenced by the currents of spiritual renewal that were spreading in the West, can be observed, perfectly defined. He adds to justify José Antonio's evolution toward Fascism that "he was a Spanish man of his generation and of his time" who "sought the atmosphere of struggle, the promising youth of the new movements, capable of merging the national and the social."[15]

Juan Aparicio, an early secretary of the JONS, wrote this:

> Great surprise and immense joy were brought to us by the following news and announcement: José Antonio decided to intervene in the public life of Spain. Don Manuel Delgado Barreto would be the director of a political weekly where José Antonio would collaborate, and we were invited to participate. *La Nación* was about to announce the first issue of *El Fascio*.[16]

Concerning who the person behind the idea was, Felipe Ximénez de Sandoval formulates and develops the following thought:

> Who told whom to launch this newspaper? Delgado Barreto to José Antonio, or José Antonio to Delgado Barreto? Who suggested to the director of *La*

---

[14] Francisco Bravo, *José Antonio, el hombre, el jefe, el camarada* (Madrid: Ed. Españolas, 1939), 23.

[15] Ibid., 24.

[16] Ximenez de Sandoval, *José Antonio*, 90.

Nación the names of the leaders of the JONS? It would be very interesting—and I am sure of this—if it was José Antonio who, in the initial conversations with the founder of *El Fascio*, made him realize the advantages of having, instead of the old front men of the right-wing intelligentsia, that youthful and revolutionary group that launched so many slogans for the future from the pages of his little newspaper, sterile due to a lack of encouragement and vital space.[17]

Saz, in his book *Mussolini contra la II República*, similarly points to José Antonio as the author of the initiative, based on a report sent to his superiors by an Italian agent at that time.[18]

Maximiano García Venero, in his work *Falange en la guerra: la Unificación y Hedilla*, argues that "it is probable that the journalist [Delgado Barreto] submitted the weekly project to Primo de Rivera and that from him came the command that certain writers and members of the JONS were required."[19]

Ramiro Ledesma Ramos reports instead, in his own account, that the idea of founding *El Fascio* "is entirely Delgado Barreto's . . . . It naturally came to him in view of Hitler's triumph, when the great Spanish masses, which were starting to be hostile to the Azaña government, watched in admiration the deeds of German Fascism," although later on he clarifies the obvious:

> Undoubtedly, behind Barreto was José Antonio Primo de Rivera. The ties of Delgado Barreto with the General should not be forgotten. And now, in the face of the Fascist project, he operated in accordance with the political purposes of his son, José Antonio, who at that time began to dream of a Fascist party of which he would be the leader.[20]

El Fascio aroused great expectation throughout Spain. The marketing of the time predicted an initial print run of one hundred thousand copies, which would be distributed widely in the most densely populated areas of Madrid and in the main provincial capitals. It was a very risky gamble, an all-or-nothing bet. It seemed that success was on the side of the promoters, thanks to the famous Fascist domino effect. The restless Spanish youth wanted to know firsthand the authentic version of the new currents of Fascist thought, rather than having them interpreted for them by the poisonous and distorted reading of their enemies and detractors.

---

[17] Ibid.

[18] *Mussolini contra la II República* (Valencia, 1986), 105, note 40, quoted by Julio Gil Pecharromán in *José Antonio Primo de Rivera, retrato de un visionario*, 165.

[19] Maximiano García Venero, *Falange en la guerra: la Unificación y Hedilla*, 37.

[20] Ledesma Ramos, *¿Fascismo en España?*, 105.

Prior to the formation of the editorial team of *El Fascio*, José Antonio wanted to get in contact with the JONS, and for this purpose, he sent his assistant Sarrión, who had previously been in contact with the weekly magazine *La Conquista del Estado*, as an intermediary.[21] With the agreement of his intern on the positive disposition of the JONS to the project, José Antonio "takes the tragic step toward public life and shares his assistant's heroic resolution with La Cuerda, his secretary, and some of his close friends."[22]

Ángel Alcázar de Velasco has left us the following testimony of that situation:

El Fascio: the newspaper that was destined to have the shortest run in the history of the press in this century. *El Fascio* was issued when José Antonio had already defined himself as a totalitarian and was still lingering, like the others, around the movement that was about to be formed and which, after scrawling many titles "among friends," was called Movimiento Español Sindicalista, that is, MES, which Ledesma Ramos found simply "humorous." *El Fascio* was too Italian a name for it not to hurt the national pride for which they were beginning to fight; this led them to add a subtitle with the same meaning, but in Spanish: *Haz*, employing Unamuno's translation.[23]

The editorial staff of *El Fascio* consisted of its director, Delgado Barreto, José Antonio Primo de Rivera, Ernesto Giménez Caballero, Rafael Sánchez Mazas, Ramiro Ledesma Ramos, and Juan Aparicio, the latter two being the leader and the secretary of the JONS, respectively. Juan Aparicio recalled, in 1972, that the collaborators had met for the launch of *El Fascio* "in the office of José Antonio, at number 8 Calle Alcalá Galiano. We drafted the first issue of the newspaper, which would then be seized by the Guardias de Asalto and the police under the orders of the Marxists, along with Don Manuel Delgado Barreto himself, at his home in Carabanchel."[24] Along with the four editors, the meetings and discussions held in José Antonio's office were attended by Julio Ruiz de Alda, Alfonso García Valdecasas, Carlos Rivas (a young Galician man who had recently left the leadership position he held in the Communist Party), and a son of the Duke of Hijar, who attended the meetings as a delegate of José María Albiñana.[25] On some occasions, Juan Pujol attended the editorial board.[26]

Onésimo Redondo, one of the other leaders of the JONS, was in exile in

---

[21] Joaquín Arrarás, *Historia de la Cruzada Española* (Madrid: Ed. Españolas, 1939), 595.

[22] Ibid., 595.

[23] Ángel Alcázar de Velasco, *La Unificación de Falange Española* (Mieres: Ediciones de las Termas de Hista, 1988).

[24] *En Pie*, no. 314, February 1972.

[25] Arrarás, *Historia de la Cruzada Española*, 595.

[26] Gil Pecharromán, *José Antonio Primo de Rivera*, 165.

Portugal, and the newspaper included a very special message for him, as follows:

> Logically, the Spanish city that proved to be more readily receptive to the national spirit of the JONS was Valladolid, the city of renaissance and imperial memories.
>
> For months now, the national youth of Valladolid have been wielding the flag of the JONS as a symbol of triumph. They have been mobilizing enthusiastically against the anti-Spanish statute during these magnificent days of struggle. And there they are, bundled in their strong and optimistic fasces, with their discipline and their style. Their coordinator, Redondo Ortega, a comrade of quality, has been following, step by step, from Oporto—where he has been exiled from Spain for six months—the hopes of those young people who, like us, remember and acclaim him.[27]

Subsequently, in the weekly newspaper *F.E.*, dated February 22nd, 1934, a brief historical overview of *El Fascio* was given, taking for granted that the core of the editorial board "presented a brilliant record of service to the national and social movement of the Fascist type."

As Ian Gibson observes, "both the title and the content of *El Fascio: Haz Hispano* demonstrate that, in the view of its editors, the only hope for the 'salvation' of Spain lies in the implementation of a system similar to that of Mussolini."[28]

Rafael Sánchez Mazas was in Rome as a correspondent for *ABC* when, in 1922, the March on Rome and the subsequent advent of Fascism took place, and he felt drawn to it. The columns that he regularly sent from Rome to the newspaper in Madrid convey his enthusiasm and fervor for the Blackshirts' revolution. Undoubtedly, Sánchez Mazas was one of the greatest propagandists in Spain of the historical phenomenon of Fascism, drinking from its original and genuine springs.

The first appearance of *El Fascio*, a new weekly paper of Fascist ideology and thought, was announced by three heralds of journalism. The magazine *Bromas y veras*, which as early as February 16th had already predicted in a headline that "Spain can only be saved by a Spanish Fascism," repeated on February 23rd, "Fascism is the union of all those who feel the pains of the Fatherland and want to heal them," and, lastly, in the issue of March 2nd, even bid farewell to its readers, announcing the publication of *El Fascio* originally planned for March 9th, which had to be delayed until the 16th. The newspaper *La Nación* also advertised the event in advance, as did the magazine *Gracia y Justicia*, which, on March 11th, five days before the appearance of *El Fascio*, wrote on page eleven:

---

[27] *El Fascio*, no. 1, March 16th, 1933, 15.

[28] Ian Gibson, *En busca de José Antonio* (Barcelona: Planeta, 1980), 49.

The country stands on its feet. Raising the arm, with a gesture of sincere salutation, of enthusiastic acclamation, and of manly threat.

The man raises his vigorous arm; the woman, her beautiful arm; the old man, his trembling arm; the child, his small rosy arm. And the lion of Spain raises his paw.

Marxism is leprosy, as is Zionism.

Freemasonry: thieves that run away to their cowardly hideout.

It is the self-preservation instinct. The true army of salvation.

Hitler is a musician; he is the Bismarck of the people.

The advertising prior to the launch of *El Fascio* stated in the following unequivocal terms:

Next Thursday, March 9th, the first issue of the weekly magazine *El Fascio* will be published. All Spaniards who feel the sorrows of their fatherland, all citizens who aspire to a better state, all men who, contemplating the national misfortunes, believe that only a tight bundle of determined wills can bring forth the reconstitution of this people, great in the past and worthy of being so again, must read and propagate *El Fascio*, upholder and disseminator of the Fascist ideas and methods that are prevailing throughout the world as the only force capable of saving civilizations from the avalanche of destructive barbarism that affects all classes of society— starting from capital, which is necessary for the progress of the economy, to manual labor, without which the economy could not develop.

Fascism, belonging neither to the right nor to the left, welcomes all national elements who, in discipline, yearn for the unity and independence of their homeland, free from all international interference and free from the tyranny of secret associations. It requires everyone to take part.

El Fascio will explain how this is to be achieved, and in its pages, writers qualified in the matter will be setting forth the theories and tactics of this movement that, among the great peoples, has served as a dam against the Marxist wave.

It will be sold for fifteen cents throughout Spain.

Before next Thursday, correspondents and organizations that are interested, along with the subscribers, can place their orders with the administrator of *El Fascio* at Post Office Box 546, Madrid.[29]

The magazine *La Epoca* included, in its March 13th issue, an interesting article written by C. Fernández Cuenca under the title "Nueva política: Hacia un fascismo

---

[29] *Bromas y veras*, February 22nd, 1933, 13.

español" [New Politics: Toward a Spanish Fascism], in which the following can be read:

> It seems that there will finally be Spanish Fascism. It is a matter of bringing together in a single group, which will rapidly increase in size, all the great and small groups and isolated elements that aspire to, or at least identify with, Fascism as the only formula for national salvation. Naturally, it has already been announced that the immediate appearance of a magazine spokesman for the new doctrine will be organized for its most effective function . . . . The existence of an organized plan for Spanish Fascism, or rather, for a Fascism of Spanish character, fills me with healthy jubilation.

March 16th, the date of the publication of *El Fascio*, coincided, and not by mere chance, with the third anniversary of Miguel Primo de Rivera's death in Paris, in the Port Royal Hotel, "executed," according to Mauricio Carlavilla (one of the best Spanish experts on Judeo-Masonic plots of the twentieth century), by Freemasons. Carlavilla blamed the death on Dr. Bandelac de Pariente and the transnational lodges.

That same day, in the chapel of St. Isidore Cemetery, at eleven in the morning, José Antonio attended, with his relatives and closest friends, a memorial Mass. Once the ceremony was over, they proceeded to pray at the tomb of his father, buried in a simple grave at ground level in the churchyard. Manuel Delgado Barreto, the director of *El Fascio*, was present at the ceremony, next to José Antonio. Several troublemakers tried to disrupt, with their insults and provocations, the intimate and dear commemoration in honor of Don Miguel Primo de Rivera held by his loved ones. The police charged the mob. One officer, José Román, was wounded in the back. Six communists and a monarchist who vigorously rebuked the harassers were arrested. Several shots were fired by the leftists in the vicinity of the cemetery; these were driven away by the forces of law and order. In the evening, José Antonio was taken to the police station, accompanied by General Antonio Losada Ortega, with the pretext of having given "approval to Fascism" during the memorial ceremony. His deposition was taken, and he was immediately released, according to the press reports that appeared in the following day's newspapers.

A professor at the University of Louvain, V. A. Marcotte, in his work *L'Espagne Nationale-Syndicaliste*, commenting on the publication of *El Fascio* on March 16th, 1933, affirms that "in it, for the first time, José Antonio Primo de Rivera, who would become the undisputed leader of all the national and Fascist movements [in Spain], took a stand,"[30] and as the renowned professor reminds us, all his aspirations could be condensed into a single word: *unity*.

---

30 V.A. Marcotte, *L'Espágne Nationale-Syndicaliste* (Augusto Puvrez S. Bruselas, 1943), 62.

Joaquín Arrarás gives a detailed account of the event and comments that:

The genuinely Fascist group is planning a journalistic campaign with a weekly magazine entitled *El Fascio*, with the subtitle *Haz Hispano*. The director of *La Nación*, Mr. Manuel Delgado Barreto, with his sharp professional instinct, perceived the certain success, even economically, of a weekly newspaper that could awaken in Spanish people a curiosity and interest in Fascism.[31]

The author of the *Crónica de la Cruzada Española* concluded that the attempt, although unsuccessful, had the positive effect of bringing in new members to the original group—such as Ruiz de Alda—and establishing a relationship with the military supporters of Primo de Rivera that Emilio Rodriguez Tarduchy had brought together.

The word *fascio* was an Italianism. The term was not included in the dictionary of the Royal Spanish Academy. The closest word was *fasces*, which referred to the insignia of the Roman consul. *Fascio*, as a single word, could be translated loosely as "bundle" or "sheaf." In order to clarify the uncertainties, it was decided to add to the title of the weekly *El Fascio* a subtitle that left no room for doubt: *Haz Hispano* [Spanish sheaf]. By inspiration of the members of the JONS, the emblem of the Catholic monarchs was also adopted: the yoke and arrows.

In a footnote added to the second edition of his work *Genio de España* (1934), Ernesto Giménez Caballero states that it was he who first perceived and proclaimed the kinship between Mussolini's Fascism and the yoke and arrows of the royal heraldry of Ferdinand and Isabella, unitary monarchs par excellence. As he already pointed out in 1929 in his letter to a companion of the young Spain, this would be the national symbol of the future.

José Antonio contributed two articles. In the one titled "Distingos Necesarios" [Necessary Distinctions] he writes:

Those who, referring to Italy, believe that Fascism is linked to the life of Mussolini do not know what Fascism is, nor have they bothered to find out what corporatism entails. The Fascist state, which owes so much to the resolute will of the Duce, will outlive its inspirer because it constitutes an unshakable and firm organization.[32]

In this article, José Antonio clarifies the purpose and aspirations of the founding group:

---

[31] Joaquín Arrarás, *Historia de la Cruzada Española*, 595.

[32] *El Fascio,* no. 1, March 16th, 1933.

What we seek is the full and definitive conquest of the state, not for a few years but forever. The last supporters of democracy, defeated and in crisis, try, with the bad intention that is to be expected and in order to defend their crumbling bastions, to bring confusion to the people's minds. We are here to prevent the deception of all those who do not want to be deceived. We do not advocate a dictatorship that achieves the calking of the sinking ship, that cures the ills of a passing period, and that involves only a solution of continuity in the systems and in the practices of disastrous liberalism. On the contrary, we march toward a permanent national organization, toward a strong state, truly Spanish, with an executive power that governs and a chamber of corporations that embodies the true national realities. We do not aim at the transitoriness of a dictatorship, but at the establishment and permanence of a system.[33]

The second of José Antonio's articles published in *El Fascio* is signed with the capital letter "E," which indicated his Spanish noble rank of marquis—Marquis of Estella—and in it he presents a brief summary of the ideas that, months later, he would develop in the masterful speech he delivered at the Teatro de la Comedia on October 29th the same year. The title of the article is "Orientaciones hacia un nuevo Estado" [Guidelines toward a New State], in which he draws the conclusion that:

all the aspirations of the new state can be summed up in one word: *unity*. The Fatherland is a historical totality in which we all merge, superior to each one of our separate groups. In homage to this unity, classes and individuals have to bow down. The construction of this unity shall be based on these two principles: 1) In its purpose, the state must be an instrument placed at the service of that unity, in which it must firmly believe. Nothing that opposes such an intrinsic, transcendent unity must be received as good, whether there are many or few who proclaim it. 2) As for its form, the state can only be a regime of national solidarity founded on a spirit of fraternal and courageous cooperation. Class struggle and the bitter conflict among political parties are incompatible with the vision of the state.[34]

The presentation of the magazine is reflected in an editorial article on the front page of the newspaper, in which the birth of the new publication was supported by these arguments:

This magazine is born under the sign and name of *El Fascio*.

---

[33] Ibid.

[34] Ibid.

At first, we wanted to give up this name, which, although foreign in its origins, has now become universal and is an international point of reference. After all, the *fascio* is the bundle of rods with the lictorial axe, which Rome used to establish and consolidate its Pax Romana, the *orbis romanus*, the first united and civilized Europe in history.

Everyone instinctively knows what this sign of salvation is meant to symbolize, as opposed to those that represent dissolution. It stands against the hammer and sickle of communism and against the triangle and compass of Freemasonry.

Through this magazine, we seek to inform our people and propagate to them the meaning of the *fascio* as doctrine, as politics, as action, and as the salvation of the world—and above all, as the way to rescue Spain from all the dissolving dangers that threaten to crush it.

Fascio in Spanish means *haz*, which is a popular, rural, and historical word. For it includes everything from the sheaf of wheat—our daily bread—to the symbolic bundle of arrows with which our Catholic monarchs achieved the unity of Spain in the Renaissance.

When our readers have familiarized themselves with the content of *El Fascio*, there will be no problem nationalizing this word and adopting our Castilian word *haz*.

Haz will mean not only the gathering of the genuine Spanish people in a defensive and offensive coalition against the enemies of Spain. It will also be the imperative that the Spanish need most: the imperative to "do." *¡Haz!*

This editorial was not forgotten by José Antonio when, two years later, in 1935, as he was founding the combat magazine of the Spanish University Union, he chose for it the name *Haz*.

The issue, in journalistic terms, was a thorough and comprehensive piece of work. In addition to the editorial that justified the print run and the two articles by José Antonio, one could read an interview by Giménez Caballero with Captain Julio Ruiz de Alda, one of the crew members of the famous *Plus Ultra* flight, and the "Puntos de Partida" ["Starting Points"], which were Fascist programmatic points, extracted verbatim from the last chapter of the fourth part of his book *La Nueva Catolicidad*, which had just been published.[35] One could also read "El Genio romano de Mussolini" ["The Roman Genius of Mussolini"], an excerpt from another one of his books, *Genio de España*, which he himself considered—and so it was advertised in the magazine—a basic book for the foundation of Spanish Fascism. It also included an interview by journalist Julio Fuertes with the writer Federico García Sanchiz. Among the other spare articles, some by Manuel Delgado and others by Giménez Caballero, we can find titles such as "El sentido

---

[35] Ibid., 3. Quoted by Ernesto Giménez Caballero in *La Nueva Catolicidad: Plan de una resurrección nacional para España*, 173–182.

social del fascismo" ["The Social Meaning of Fascism"], "La recia figura de Hitler" ["The Strong Figure of Hitler"], a transcription of paragraphs from Hitler's book *Mein Kampf* under the heading "Hablan los triunfadores: Mi primera propaganda" ["The Victors Speak: My First Propaganda"], or the review of Italo Balbo's published diary. Juan Aparicio wrote an eloquent article on "La camisa negra" ["The Black Shirt"] and another one on "El emblema de las JONS" ["The Emblem of the JONS"]. Ramiro Ledesma contributed with a detailed explanatory article on the Spanish JONS movement, "Qué son las JONS" ["What Are the JONS"] in which he also indicated his address in Madrid: 16 Calle Acuerdo. Sánchez Mazas published the excerpt of a conference held in Santander and which had been published by the *Boletín* [*Official Bulletin*] of the Menéndez y Pelayo Library of 1927, titled "Haz y Yugo," headed with the emblem of the seven arrows bundled together by a yoke. Of course, there was no shortage of news and commentary on the aggression suffered by the sixteen-year-old student, Antonio Mendoza, who was beaten and injured by the mobs for shouting "*Viva el Fascio!*" for which he was honored as "the first wounded Fascist" in Spain.[36] The issue also attacks Freemasonry, which it considers an extension of Judaism.

The loose notes interlaced between the articles do not leave any room for doubt concerning the intentions of the publication:

Page 2: "Fascism regards every man as a necessary piece essential for the collective well-being, rather than as a steppingstone for another to climb."

Page 4: "*El Fascio* declares its absolute incompatibility with entities, groups, or individuals who do not act within the laws and in the light of day. It does not want to hear of surreptitious maneuvers, secret activities, or hidden agendas. Fascism is, in its entirety, about clarity and responsibility."

"OWNERS: Your properties will not be spared from the onslaught of the red barbarity if you do not come to an agreement with those who help you to maintain and increase them by allowing them to become sharers of your wealth. This agreement, human and Christian, is one of the foundations of the Fascist state and a main source of national well-being."

Page 6: "SPANISH PEOPLE OF ALL VIEWPOINTS: Learn what Fascism is; look at the examples of Italy and Germany, and when you are convinced that in the face of the destructive avalanche there are no other doctrines that can rescue you and no other efficient procedures but those advocated and put into practice by Mussolini and Hitler, spread them, convince your own people, and advise them to convince those around them. Tie up, Spaniard, your *fascio*, your small *fascio*, your bundle, and bring it at once to the Spanish

---

36 José Luis Jerez Riesco: *Falange Imperial, crónica de la Falange toledana* (Madrid: Fuerza Nueva Editorial, 1998), 36.

bundle of salvation."

Page 7: "Fascism is not reaction, but salvation. At most, it is the reaction that life produces in a sick body in order to save it from death. It is a reaction against deadly bacteria. It is a victory against the clutches of socialist tuberculosis!"

Page 8: "Either the Spanish right wing will be filled with social sense, or the social consciousness of Spain will leave the Spanish right empty."

Page 9: "Capital can only find rescue from the snares of Marxism by offering itself generously to the Fascist cause, which will protect it in the new state, ensuring that it will produce with great efficiency for the advantage of the poor and for its own profit."

Page 12: "*Farmer*: only in a corporate state like the Fascist one will you feel fully represented and protected. The firmest foundation of the Fascist economic regime is the production of the national soil. Its greatest efforts are directed toward intensifying it. Encourage those around you to contribute to the triumph of Fascism."

Page 15: "Fascism, whether for employers or workers, will firmly be the guarantee of capital and labor because it is the guarantee of social tranquility."

Page 16: "Against the Marxist poison that destroys, there is no other antidote than Fascism, which creates."

"Fascism is the bundle of men fit to make their fatherland great."

According to another biographer of José Antonio, Carlos de Arce, in the magazine *El Fascio* he made his first appearance in the political arena as a supporter of Fascism, and "in the magazine the guidelines for a Spanish Fascism were presented."[37]

The legal headquarters was located at 18 Avenida de Pi y Margall—a section of the current Gran Vía in Madrid—and the postal address was Post Office Box 546 in the capital. The selling price of a copy was fifteen cents. It was printed in the workshops of the newspaper *La Nación*, from where the police seized, in a preventive operation, 24,000 copies.

On the eve of the date of the publication of the Fascist newspaper, at ten o'clock in the evening, a meeting was held at the Madrid Socialist Group, between the Committees

---

[37] De Arce, *José Antonio, biografía*, 167.

of the Socialist Youth and the Administrative Board of the Casa del Pueblo [House of the People], to try to prevent the distribution of *El Fascio*. On the 18th, forty-eight hours after its failed publication, the Casa del Pueblo declared that "the management of the printing press had also agreed that its affiliates should not publish *El Fascio*."

The newspaper was outlawed and seized. Only a few shipments sent out to the various provinces were able to reach their destination. The police gathered ten thousand copies from various towns in the north—Tolosa, Eibar, Irún, Pasajes, among others. A local newspaper seller, who kept several copies, was assaulted in the Cuatro Caminos neighborhood of Madrid, a leftist area of the capital, by a group of communists who beat the man, snatched the copies he was carrying, and made a bonfire out of them. In Calle de Alcalá and Calle del Sol, fights broke out between supporters—members of the JONS—and detractors of the publication. With this authoritarian and antidemocratic measure, the Republic wanted to repress, with extreme intolerance, any openness in Spain to the new currents and the latest generation of authentically European movements. The shutdown, confiscation, seizure, and dismissal of the magazine led José Antonio to spontaneously write a strong protest note that same day, March 16th, in the evening newspaper *La Nación*, which reads as follows:

> This morning, before even a single issue appeared on the street, the complete edition of *El Fascio* was seized by the police, without any court order.
>
> It is a purely doctrinal magazine that propagates the ideas that prevail today in nations friendly to Spain and which are making their way throughout the world.
>
> There was not a single line in our newspaper that alluded to the government or fought against the regime, because *El Fascio* came to fight for something greater, something permanent: the formation of a new state, which would be organized, unionized, corporative, and capable of conciliating production and labor, with enough seriousness in its structure and in the masses to contain the advance of the propaganda and dissolving processes that, in our opinion, represent Marxism in all its forms, as all now see in Spain.
>
> *El Fascio* declared that its concern was not the regime but the state.
>
> As far as can be seen, socialism sees the spread of these doctrines as a huge threat to its already precarious situation, which is threatened on one side by unionists and communists and on the other by conservative elements within the Republic itself, which agreed, in a meeting held by its representatives, that *El Fascio* should not reach the public, resorting to any means available to prevent it.[38]

Cáceres, where the project of *El Fascio* had the greatest impact in periodical

---

[38] *La Nación*, March 16th, 1933.

publications, was the city that saw the publication of a magazine called *Decimos*, which had been launched in June 1933, directed by Francisco Maderal, and which eventually would become an official branch of the Falange in 1934. In issue number 16, dated September 14th, there is an article signed by Arnaldo with the title "Que se nos aclare: ¡Hay fascistas en España!" [Let's Be Clear: There are Fascists in Spain!], which, among other matters, stated:

> In Spain, a fertile ground for Fascism's growth, the yet-to-be established Fascist system was declared illegal, and the publication of *El Fascio*, a newspaper that tried to spread Fascist ideology, was forbidden. Since then, there has been constant talk of Fascism, of the Fascist organization, of a considerable number of Fascist supporters.
>
> And with this resounding claim, Fascism, which began as a curiosity, is now an obsession, and Fascist ideas have become so widespread that one hears the most outlandish claims about the new system. Wouldn't it be better to allow freedom of information so that everyone knows what this is all really about? They say there is a danger that it would immediately pull in the masses and establish its dominance. If this were the case, it would be undeniable proof that it responds to what the country needs. And in democratic terms, it is not legitimate to deny Spain what it wants.

Epistolary Polemic

On March 17th, the day after the seizure and confiscation by the government of *El Fascio*, the monarchist newspaper *ABC* published a letter from its director, Juan Ignacio Luca de Tena, in which, on the one hand, he criticized the socialist government for censoring the publication, which represented a threat to the freedom of opinion, and, on the other hand, he expressed a series of reproaches to Fascism that hurt José Antonio's political sensibility, who answered him in a letter published in the monarchist newspaper on March 22nd, where, among other remarks about Fascism in Europe, he argues:

> As a student who has spent many hours researching the Fascist phenomenon, it pains me that *ABC*—your admirable newspaper— addresses its concern about Fascism through only a few unpleasant sentences, which display a superficial understanding of it. I request to be given space in the columns of *ABC* to provide some clarifications. What matters the least in the movement that now announces its great tide in Europe is the tactics of force (merely accessory, circumstantial, perhaps, in some countries, unnecessary); rather the deep thinking that drives it is

worthy of a more profound study.

Fascism is not a tactic—violence; it is an idea—unity—as opposed to Marxism, which affirms as dogma the class struggle, and as opposed to liberalism, which requires the mechanism of struggle among parties. Fascism affirms that there is something above the parties and above the classes, something of a permanent, transcendent, supreme nature: the historical unity called the fatherland. The fatherland is not merely the territory where several rival parties seek to reach power, tearing each other to pieces—even if only with the weapons of insult. Furthermore, it is not an insignificant arena for the ongoing conflict between the bourgeoisie, which seeks to exploit the proletariat, and the proletariat, which seeks to tyrannize the bourgeoisie. It is instead the intimate unity of everyone at the service of a historical mission, of a supreme common destiny, which assigns to each one his task, his rights, and his sacrifices. In a Fascist state neither the strongest class, nor the most numerous faction triumph (for, despite what universal suffrage says, numbers do not equate to correctness); rather what triumphs is the orderly principle that is common to everybody, the constant national thought, the institution of which is the state.

The liberal state does not believe in anything, not even in itself. It stands idly by and watches, with its arms crossed, all kinds of experiments, even those aimed at the destruction of the state itself. It is sufficient that everything is done in accordance with certain regulatory procedures . . . . The time for this sterile attitude is over. It is necessary to believe in something. When has anything ever been achieved with a liberal attitude? Frankly speaking, the only successful examples of politics that I am aware of are based on belief, in one form or another.

In order to kindle a faith—not of the right, which ultimately aspires to preserve everything, even what is unjust, nor of the left, which eventually aspires to destroy everything, even what is good—a collective, conciliatory, national faith, Fascism was born. In its faith lies its fruitfulness, against which persecution will be powerless. Those who profit from discord are well aware of this. That is why they can only dare to resort to slander. They attempt to present it to the workers as a movement of gentlemen, when there is nothing more distant from the idle gentleman, a guest in a life in which he fulfills no function, than the citizen of the Fascist state, to whom no right is recognized except by virtue of the service he offers to his country. If anything truly deserves to be called a workers' state, it is the Fascist state. For this reason, in the Fascist state—and the workers will soon come to know this, no matter who may disagree—the workers' unions are elevated to the direct dignity of organs of the state.

Finally, I close this letter not with a Roman salute, but with a Spanish embrace. With it comes my hope that your spirit—so favorable to noble passion and so opposed by nature to the dull and cold climate of liberalism, which believes in nothing—be kindled in the flame of this new civil faith, capable of giving us a strong, industrious, and united country, a great Spain.

José Antonio Primo de Rivera.

Luca de Tena responded to what he called José Antonio's "warm Fascist apology" in his reply. "By what means, by what procedures does the nascent Spanish *El Fascio* intend to seize power?" he wondered, before launching into a fiery defense of liberalism. The reply of *ABC*'s director provoked a rejoinder from José Antonio, published as an open letter in the newspaper *La Nación*, which was also included in the March 23rd issue of *ABC*, wherein José Antonio declared:

You keep on thinking about what is instrumental and not about what is profound. Conversely, I am not outraged because the dissemination of Fascist ideas is restricted; I am outraged because it is restricted in compliance with a "class" or "group" principle. Socialism, by definition, is not a national party, nor does it aim to be one. It is a party of class struggle. To be oppressed by the victors of a civil war humiliates me, but to be limited in the power to pay my respects to a conciliating totalitarian national principle makes me proud. Human dignity is only achieved when we serve. He alone is great who plays his part in the undertaking of a great task.

Luca de Tena, that same day, with a new letter, brought to an end the open polemic, thereby preventing his newspaper (because of José Antonio's expressive and argumentative lucidity on Fascism) from becoming the disseminator of the very ideas that the editor himself opposed. The exchange of opinions, the dialectical struggle, did not end in a tie score, but was clearly and irresistibly in favor of the new argument, in opposition to Marxism and liberalism, that Primo de Rivera advanced and defended.

Clarifications on José Antonio's thinking, in relation to some questions raised about *El Fascio* by his cousin Julián Pemartín, are contained in a long, clarifying, and calm letter, dated April 2nd, replying to José Antonio, in which he writes:

Trying to address the objections against Fascism that you mention in your letter to me:

1. "It has no other means than violence to seize power."

Firstly, this is historically false. There is the example of Germany, where National Socialism triumphed in an election. But even if there were no other means than violence, would it matter? Every system has been implemented violently, even delicate liberalism (the guillotine of 1793 is responsible for many more deaths than Mussolini and Hitler combined).

Violence is not systematically reprehensible. It is only so when committed against justice. But even St. Thomas, in extreme cases, would allow rebellion against the tyrant. So, then, if violence is used against a triumphant sect, sower of discord, denier of national continuity, and at the service of foreign agendas (the Amsterdam International, Freemasonry, etc.), why should one discredit the violence that would overturn such a system?

2. "Its idea and its leadership must emerge from the people."

The first part is wrong. The idea can in no way originate from the people. It is "made," and those who are aware of it are not usually men of the people. Now, giving force to that idea is probably something that is fated for a man of the people. To be a caudillo has something to do with being a prophet; it requires a dose of faith, of health, of enthusiasm, and of anger that is not compatible with middle-class refinement. As for me, I would be better suited for anything other than being a Fascist caudillo. The attitude of doubt and the ironic sense, which never leave those of us who have had, more or less, any intellectual curiosity, inhibit us from making the unhesitating and robust affirmations that are required of mass leaders.

3. "It had a reasonable cause to exist in the countries in which it succeeded."

Is this not the case of Spain? There may not be a justification for warfare. That is why, as I stated in my letter to Luca de Tena, Fascism in this country is unlikely to be violent. Is the loss of unity (territorial, spiritual, and historical) perhaps less pronounced here than elsewhere? In any case, it may be necessary to wait until things get worse. But what is the benefit of waiting until things are desperate if it is possible to act sooner? Especially when a socialist dictatorship is being planned by those in authority—which, if successful, would plunge Spain into a predicament that would be very challenging to reverse.

4. "It is anti-Catholic."

This argument is very typical of our country, where everyone is more Catholic than the pope. While the Lateran Treaty is being signed in Rome, we label Fascism as anti-Catholic—Fascism, which has, after ninety years of liberal Freemasonry, brought back the crucifix and religious teaching in the schools of Italy. I understand the concern in Protestant countries, where there could be a conflict between the national religious tradition and the Catholic zeal of a minority. But in Spain, what can the exaltation of national authenticity lead to if not finding the Catholic values of our mission in the world?

As you will see, almost none of the objections against Fascism are raised in good faith. In them there is a hidden desire to provide an ideological excuse for laziness or cowardice, if not for the national defect par excellence: envy, which is capable of spoiling the greatest things in order not to give to the other an opportunity to shine.

The Movimiento Español Sindicalista–Fascismo Español

El Fascio's hopeful but thwarted initiative was not wasted, nor did it leave the political arena sterile; on the contrary, the widespread publicity and resonance of the event fertilized it. Unjust as it was, the restriction served as a wake-up call for a sizable portion of Spanish youth interested in the Fascist movement and unwilling to get left behind. Furthermore, the subscriptions and letters of support and encouragement received by its promoters served as a powerful unifying force among previously unconnected and dispersed groups and individuals across Spain. *El Fascio* was like the stone that is thrown into a calm pond, sinking but producing on the surface of the waters, from that tiny and circular epicenter, increasingly large, sweeping, and unstoppable waves that reach all the corners of the vast pond.

El Fascio was more than just an experiment; it was the embodiment of firm and well-considered ideas that sought to find expression through this magazine. The small group of young people who had gathered around the idea knew that the defeat inflicted on them by the seizure, prohibition, and closure of the magazine had been transformed into a great victory because of the enormous enthusiasm that had been aroused and because of the large number of people who offered to carry on with the effort to forge a Fascist mass movement in Spain.

The first meetings to draft a structure for the political movement took place in April. The meeting place was, mainly, the professional office of José Antonio, at 8 Calle Alcalá Galiano, and, occasionally, in the office of the director of *La Nación*, as Manuel Valdés Larrañaga recalls. Julio Ruiz de Alda, who had been interviewed by Giménez Caballero for the unpublished magazine and who had the opportunity to meet José Antonio and the rest of the editorial team, attended the meetings. In the office, helping in the preparation of the political foundations, together with its owner, were assistants Manuel Sarrión and Andrés de la Cuerda. There, in the afternoons, went Rafael Sánchez Mazas, dreaming for Spain the same images that so impressed him in Rome. Also present was José Moreno Herrera, Marquis de la Eliseda, a national-catholic who had been charmed by Fascism. Around José Antonio gathered admirers and ardent supporters. Commanders Emilio Rodríguez Tarduchy and Emilio Alvargonzález, both close collaborators of General Primo de Rivera and the Patriotic Union, were among them. Giménez Caballero brought his creativity and wit to the gatherings. Raimundo Fernández-Cuesta was there, as were his cousins from Jerez de la Frontera, Julián Pemartín and Sancho Dávila, on their occasional visits to the capital. The office was a hive of correspondence, phone calls, visits, meetings, telegrams, and pent-up concerns. Contacts were also established with Alfonso García Valdecasas and Elíseo García del Moral, who were then members of a group called Frente Español [Spanish Front].

In the words of García del Moral, "García Valdecasas and José Antonio swiftly reached an agreement. The Spanish Front had a legal organization but lacked the means of struggle; on the other hand, F.E.—Fascismo Español—had a certain size and resources for struggle but lacked a legal organization."[39]

In his book *La Rebelión de los estudiantes*, David Jato writes that:

> the activity at 8 Alcalá Galiano, office of José Antonio in Madrid, was by no means sterile; on the contrary, it contributed to the maturation of the definitive launch. The Movimiento Español Sindicalista (MES) reached a provincial level; in Oviedo, it even gave public signs of life by distributing cyclostyled propaganda leaflets, and at a farmers' gathering in the Paseo del Bombí, seven students were arrested, including Eugenio Miñón, José Esteban, Antonio Pérez Campoamor, and García Cernuda. In other places, small groups began to operate without any connection to Madrid, assuming what needed to be done. This was the case in Seville, where two students, Narciso Perales and Juan Domínguez, obtained the first student subscriptions.[40]

Meanwhile, José Antonio attended other literary circles, such as the gathering of La Ballena Alegre, in the Calle de Alcalá in Madrid, opposite the post office, in the basement of the Café Lyon, where a group of literary artists articulated a classically infused modernism. Its members were Pedro Mourlane Michelena, Eugenio Montes, Agustín de Foxá, Víctor de la Serna, José María Alfaro from Burgos, Jacinto Miquelarena, Samuel Ros, and a slew of journalists, writers, poets, and dreamers, for a total of twenty-three individuals who, assiduously or sporadically, frequented that meaningful and florid gathering. One could feel the pulse of Fascism on their conversing lips and tongues.

---

[39] Elíseo García del Moral, quoted by Ian Gibson, 60.

[40] David Jato, *La rebelión de los estudiantes* (Madrid, 1953), 54.

On May 2nd, José Antonio wrote a small leaflet, which he read to the faithful members of his office; it was a warning cry of rebellion. A group of teenagers, high school students, such as a young boy from Toledo named Espejo, were in charge of the distribution throughout the surrounding areas of San Bernardo, Eduardo Dato, and Pi y Margall, and in the environs of the Plaza del Callao. The first printed leaflet was signed in capital letters by an unknown "MOVIMIENTO ESPAÑOL SINDICALISTA (Fascismo Español)." The flyer read:

SPAIN IN DANGER! MAY 2ND

On May 2nd, 1808, Spain was apparently stripped of its dignity.

Its ruling and governing classes, devoted to the power and culture of the foreign.

Anarchy and misery reigned supreme.

Its possessions and colonies, some lost and others on the verge of being lost.

Everything indicated that Spain would succumb to an invasion by an armed and powerful country that had won wars against other peoples.

But the population was neither corrupt nor for sale. It rose up as a single hero. It defeated the invincible.

May the memory of May 2nd not be erased as some want to erase it, Spaniards!

The mayor of Móstoles shouted: *Spain is in danger! Come and save her!*

This is the cry of those Spaniards who dream of a strong and unanimous popular movement against the defeat of the Spanish nation: Spain is in danger! Spaniards! Come and save her! Just as your forebears did on May 2nd!

SPANISH SYNDICALIST MOVEMENT (Fascismo Español)[41]

On May 26th, the police were still rounding up in Madrid these flyers.

That summer, Rafael Sánchez Mazas, José Bergamín (whose magazine *Cruz y Raya* had begun its literary journey on April 15th of that same year), and José Antonio all met in the Plaza de Santa Bárbara in Madrid. In the words of José Bergamín, "José Antonio told me then of his plan to establish a Spanish Fascist party and offered me a position in it."[42]

Contacts spread to the provinces. The organization operated in complete secrecy. Rodriguez Tarduchy and Alvargonzález, soldiers and former supporters of

---

[41] Private archive of the author.

[42] Ian Gibson's interview with José Bergamín in Madrid, 62.

Primo de Rivera, were in charge of spreading the MES through a large amount of correspondence. The government became concerned about the rise of Fascism. All we had at that moment was hearsay, table talk, rumors, and gossip. There was only one single leaflet. In Spain, a new political current embracing Fascist positions was forming. It was a Fascism of Spanish style which, from its first pamphlet, did not appear as a party but as a "movement," which carried, in its name, the word "syndicalist" along with its organization and, naturally, proclaimed its Spanishness, although it did not reject the original idea that drove it, and that is why it presented itself publicly, without concealment or ambiguity, as "Fascismo Español."

On May 27th, the first declaration—the first manifesto—which outlined the principles that Spanish Fascism upheld and the goals it sought to achieve, was published. In Madrid, it spread like wildfire. In the following days, it was distributed in clubs and on the streets of major cities in the provinces. In Seville, it appeared on the first day of July.

The first manifesto was a sheet with two columns written on both sides; the turned side is not written completely. In its declaration, it was emphasized that it is the first proclamation of the Spanish Syndicalist Movement. The words "FASCISMO ESPAÑOL" were written in the heading of the manifesto in bold letters, using the largest typeface available. In the document, which was written by José Antonio and signed by Rafael Sánchez Mazas, Julio Ruiz de Alda, M. Sarrión, Emilio Alvargonzález, Rodríguez Tarduchy, Alfonso García Valdecasas, and Elíseo García del Moral, one reads:

> Spanish Fascism desires that the strength, the unity, the popularity, and the authority of Spain accomplish in the world our destiny as great people . . . . Spanish Fascism is the furious desire to create a virile, harmonious, totalitarian state, worthy of the men of Spain . . . . We arrive with the chivalrous, hard, humane violence that all surgical interventions demand . . . . More than being a program—although we do have one precisely outlined—Spanish Fascism is a new way of being Spanish: new but very ancient, because the name of Spain has been created, elevated, and supported by this youthful spirit of warfare . . . . The power of our idea is both national and overwhelmingly universal. Our party is the genuinely Spanish expression of what is already a common crusade in the great countries to pull Europe, the fatherlands of Europe, out of the spiritual degradation and material ruin into which the poisonous and anti-national leftists and the spineless, obtuse, and selfish right-wing parties have plunged it.
>
> Our program is known by its fundamentals: unity and power of the Fatherland, popular unionism, hierarchy, harmony of the classes, discipline, anti-liberalism, rurality, militarism, culture, national statism, and justice— which, by giving to each his own, does not consent to the anarchic excesses of workers nor to the predatory excesses of employers . . . . These are the principles that are being called upon to restore in all countries of great lineage the

strongest forms of European civilization, in harmony with those great traditions of universality and patriotism, of family spirit and guild spirit, of religiosity and noble civil character, of tradition and modernity, that have ennobled the sacramental unity of Europe . . . . Spain calls upon us. It urges us to restore, before everything else, the pride, the drive, and the virility that come from being Spanish, and to channel this refreshing flow into the discipline of service and sacrifice . . . . All proposals of freedom or authority are prison songs until we bring into being a free Spain—one which can face the world, one which is organized, armed, powerful, capable of trading, of reaching agreements, of making demands, of asserting itself among the peoples in order to bring forward its spiritual and material wealth, to save itself at all times from usury and foreign competition, to live finally without the supervision of the foreign institutions organized either by socialism, or by the banks, or by the international powers, or by Freemasonry, or by whoever it may be—always those who can never have the greatness of Spain as their ultimate goal . . . . *¡Arriba España, una, indivisible y eterna!* [Up with Spain, one, indivisible, and eternal!][43]

The First Proclamation of the MES–Fascismo Español sealed its statement with the new cry of "*¡Arriba España!*"

According to historian José Luis Jiménez "it is, thus, an initiative that combines the efforts of declared Fascists and a part of the supporters of the so-called Frente Español."[44]

Maximiano García Venero believes that "the embryo of the successive Falange was something called Movimiento Español Sindicalista."

David Jato writes:

Propaganda leaflets began to be distributed by groups led by José Antonio Primo de Rivera and Julio Ruiz de Alda; the flyers were marked with the initials F.E., which used to be indistinctly interpreted by their distributors as Fascismo Español, Frente Español, or Fe Española [Spanish Faith]. Despite the fact that it had already been used in *La Conquista del Estado*, no one associated the letter "F" with the term *Falange*. The general director of safety, Andrés Casaux, concocted a plot in order to put an end to the "Fascist" groups and, at the same time, to the F.A.I. [Iberian Anarchist Federation].[45]

---

[43] Private archive of the author.

[44] José Luis Rodríguez Jiménez, *Historia de Falange Española de las J.O.N.S.* (Madrid: Alianza Editorial, 2000), 128.

[45] Jato, *La rebelión de los estudiantes*, 56.

The fuse was lit. The manifesto was passed from hand to hand in streets and squares, boulevards and promenades, café entrances and university campuses. The enterprising spirits of the militants, with youthful energy and morale, remained high. The government saw ghosts everywhere. It attempted to achieve by force what it could not with reason. It sought to eradicate all traces of Fascism. From July 19th to July 22nd, it gave the order to carry out operations against any sort of action by Fascists and against any suspicious activity. There were searches and arrests. They took shots in the dark. Entire districts and neighborhoods were searched, arresting anyone they thought might have ties to the newly emerging Fascism. With frontpage headlines like "A Plot Against the Government Is Feared at Dawn," or with the metaphorical disclosure, like "The Failed Plot," the state-owned media ginned up public fear.

Ramiro Ledesma Ramos reported in his book *¿Fascismo en España?* that more than three thousand arrests were carried out throughout Spain from July 19th to July 22nd. The headlines of those days were characterized by great social alarm:

> On the 23rd: "Is a Plot Against the Government Coming at Dawn?"
> On the 25th: "The Failed Plot."
> On the 26th: "Apparently, the Goal Is to Destroy a Fascist-Type Organization at Its Inception."
> Most of the people arrested were taken to Ocaña Prison, around ninety in total.
> Among these, forty-one were anarchists, the social democratic Christian Fr. Gafo, and the rest a conglomerate of monarchists, Primo de Rivera's Fascists, and the JONS group . . . . About twelve of them belonged to the organization that Primo de Rivera was then trying to establish under the name of MES (Movimiento Español Sindicalista) . . . . Among the men of Primo de Rivera was José Gómez, the general's former trusted chauffeur.[46]

The former bullfighter Marquina, a collaborator of the MES, was also imprisoned.

The MES–Fascismo Español then reorganized itself. Its struggle was joyful and youthful. It did not fear the threats or the persecution of the government. They knew very well that ideas can only be defeated by persuasion, and what they were convinced of was that Fascism was a radically new and revolutionary idea that could overcome the political squalor of the moment. After the "imaginary plot" which existed only in the timorous minds of the government, the Fascists printed a new leaflet in two colors. In an intense red, printed in the upper left and thickly marked, were two identifying initials: "F.E.," with the following printed in black ink:

---

[46] Ledesma Ramos, *¿Fascismo en España?*, 119–120.

TO THE MILITANTS:

Governmental terror and police incompetence have combined to produce the grotesque discovery of a new plot, and for several days they have shaken the tranquility of the citizens.

We stand firm in the face of the nervous authorities. The organization has remained unaffected. The blind stabs in the dark of the directorate of security have not hit a single one of our vital points. The vast majority of the detainees are strangers to us, but their solidarity with some of our own in the persecution already qualifies them as future comrades. In any case, you all know that, whether the leaders are imprisoned or dead, those who must succeed them have already been appointed and are ready to take their place.

The *fascio* will not forget a single one of our fallen comrades. None of the traitors will sleep peacefully at night. And from this trial, we will draw new courage and new conviction that the pseudo-democratic and socialist state is uninhabitable. All of their tyrannical nonsense is like a dying gasp that announces the coming demise and the triumphal advent of the Fascist State.

LONG LIVE SPAIN![47]

Due to the attack the government had launched on the MES–Fascismo Español, José Antonio led the group with the utmost caution and discretion. Those were intense days. A destiny was being forged. He read constantly, held meetings, debated in groups, responded to letters, broadened his circle of friends, and got along with and became intimate with some of those close to him, such as Julio Ruiz de Alda. He combined his social life with his growing political involvement.

In the month of July, another new leaflet written by José Antonio, with the mark "F.E." framed in red in its upper right margin, contained this message to the Spanish people:

FASCISMO ESPAÑOL will fight until its triumph:

For the sacred unity of the Fatherland.

For the integration of all classes in a just and strong hierarchical harmony.

To elevate labor to the highest level of civil dignity.

For the corporative state, which liberates the destiny of the country from the political oligarchies.

To return to Spain the universal significance of its history.[48]

The leaflet would be published in its entirety almost a year later, on May 24th, 1934, in the local weekly magazine of Càceres, *Decimos*.

---

[47] Private archive of the author.

[48] Private archive of the author.

On August 1st, José Antonio wrote a letter to Tomás Dehesa, who lived in Santander, in which he informed him: "It is probable that this summer I will be visiting Santander. If that won't be possible, I intend to spend my vacation studying the Fascist political and intellectual movement in greater depth."[49] That same day, the student Rafael Vera de Castro, who was twenty-two years old, and the mechanic Pedro Ollazo, twenty-three years old, were arrested for shouting "Long live Fascism!" in the Casa del Pueblo.

In an interview with José Antonio for the newspaper *La Nación*, on August 24th, he declared that it was a matter of adapting "the magnificent Italian model to the needs of Spain."

During the last days of August, Ramiro Ledesma Ramos traveled, in the company of the then-radical JONSist José María de Areilza, to San Sebastián, where José Antonio was on summer vacation "trying to organize a Fascist force," according to Ramiro's own recollection. They held a long interview with Primo de Rivera, Ruiz de Alda, and García Valdecasas, who attended the meeting, but the meeting concluded without any positive result.

The last MES pamphlet to appear was dated September 1933, with the title "Consignas de depuración fascista" ["Instructions for Fascist Purification"]. It was written on one side of a two-column page. In the heading the emblem, the anagram, and the initials of Spanish Fascism, "F.E.," were outlined inside a black frame. The text tried to dispel any doubt as to who the genuine representatives and exponents of Spanish Fascism were. It was written by José Antonio, who claims for himself the legitimacy of Fascist origin and practice. It reads as follows:

Those who fear the power of our truth are persecuting Fascist propaganda. The enemies of Fascism know that as soon as the doctrine we advocate reaches the real population, hundreds of Spaniards in whom national feeling is not dead will join our ranks. The suppression of our propaganda will not stifle the Fascist movement. However, it might result in the possibility that, in the absence of true propaganda of genuine Fascist principles, various vile distortions could appear.

This serious danger imposes, above every other duty, the one duty of keeping pure, intact, and unequivocal the Fascist meaning of our movement. The initial success attained has sparked an appetite for speculation on the word *Fascism* by many elements that are completely unrelated to us. Let us all be on the lookout for these impostors! Bad company is to be feared more than loneliness. Therefore, only those who have been approved by this organization should be regarded as legitimate Fascist organizations, and only that which has been approved by our commanders should be propagated as good Fascist

---

[49] Private archive of the author.

doctrine. Additionally, we must exert every effort to prevent the masses who are inclined to join us from becoming confused by self-serving pseudo-fascisms.

Spanish Fascism is not a movement at the service of the conservative classes or groups deposed from power by the revolution of 1931. If Fascism finds the present occupation of Spain by international sectarian leaders disastrous, it also wants nothing to do with a return to the old, lethargic schemes that made the surrender possible. May those who aspire to a reconstruction of what has been demolished lose all hope of taking advantage of us. We will never be the spearhead of their return. And if this will take support away from us and make our mission of conquest harder, we will draw out of this hardship that fortitude of spirit with which victories are won.

Spanish Fascism does not aspire to anything other than the complete establishment of the Fascist state. That is to say, a state led in its core by the Spanish genius that authoritatively indicates to all, both groups and individuals, their mission to achieve the resurrection of a great national historical destiny. Fascism sees the fatherland as a fundamental unit called upon to carry out, as in previous centuries, universal undertakings in the world. For this reason, Fascism subordinates the efforts of all to the well-being of the fatherland and does not allow propaganda or freedoms that are contrary to the destiny of the fatherland itself. And that is why the Fascist state (which is not the property of a triumphant party or of a stronger class) can, like no other regime, impose social justice from its undisputed authority. There are the magnificent examples of Italy and Germany, two states that do not owe their strength to any oligarchy because they are the bearers of a deep and absolute patriotic will that successfully elevated the workers to a condition of dignity, freedom, and welfare never achieved by the destructive path of class struggle.

The Fascist movement aspires to this and nothing else. Soon, you will all be given a detailed ideological program. But, in the meantime, continue to be vigilant, as you have been entrusted to do here. Take as a clue the spirit that emerges through their statements in order to distinguish the real Fascists from the impostors. He is a false Fascist who gives signs of his aspiration to regain privileges and comforts. The authentic Fascist is the one who is ready to give up everything, even privileges and vanities in our ranks, in order to serve the glorious cause that drives us.

September 1933[50]

In the weekly newspaper *Decimos*, distributed in Cáceres, which was close to the political alignment of the MES, an article signed by Arnaldo with the title "Socialismo y corporativismo" [Socialism and Corporatism] was published on

---

[50] Private archive of the author.

October 12th. It reads: "How are the workers and farmers in Italy? We can state unequivocally that in no country, bourgeois or democratic, socialist or socialist-leaning, do the most vulnerable have such a privileged position as they do in Italy today."

On October 19th, Benito Mussolini received José Antonio at Palazzo Venezia in Rome. It was the approval to embark on his Falangist mission. The meeting, which lasted a little more than half an hour, was arranged by his friend, the Italian ambassador in Madrid, Raffaele Guariglia, the same one who on February 23rd of that year met with José Antonio at Giménez Caballero's residence, at 41 Calle Canarias, to shape up and give life to the idea of the weekly *El Fascio*. The ambassador delivered to him a letter of invitation for the appointment with the Duce. The time for the appointment was 6:30 in the evening. José Antonio was accompanied on that trip by his close friend Rafael Sánchez Mazas and by the Italian journalist Manlio Barelli, who recalled that José Antonio confessed to him before the interview with the Duce: "I feel like a student who is going to meet the master." On that occasion, José Antonio also had the opportunity to establish contact in Rome with the vice-secretary of the National Fascist Party, Marpicarti, who also accompanied the Spanish guests in the visit they made to several branches of the party to explore its functioning and organization.

The encounter with Benito Mussolini was narrated, as if it were an Impressionist oil painting, by José Antonio in his prologue to Benito Mussolini's book *El Fascismo*, which was published on April 15th, 1934, with an afterword by Julio Ruiz de Alda. The title of the prologue evokes the nostalgia of an unforgettable evening, "En una tarde de octubre,"[51] and it begins with José Antonio stating:

> Man is the system, and this is one of the profound human truths which Fascism has brought to light again . . . . I have seen Mussolini twice: one afternoon in October 1933, at the Palazzo Venezia in Rome, when he sought to make me understand Italian Fascism in ways beyond what I could learn from books . . . . I had seen him before, years ago, at a formal audience, when I was received together with a number of students from Madrid University . . . . We talked for about half an hour . . . . When the two of us reached the door, he said to me with paternal calm, without the slightest emphasis: "I wish you the very best, for yourself and for Spain." . . . What kind of a government apparatus, what system of weights and scales, councils and assemblies, can possibly replace that image of the hero become father, watching beside a perpetually glimmering lamp over the toil and slumber of his people?

---

[51] Translator: "On an October Afternoon." Translation from *Selected Writings of José Antonio Primo de Rivera* by Hugh Thomas.

As a memento of that visit, Mussolini gave him a large official photograph with a very special dedication. It was displayed with the utmost honor and dignity in José Antonio's private office, on the white marble fireplace, beneath an oil painting of his father.

During that memorable meeting, which preceded the formation of Falange Española, José Antonio presented to the Duce his political vision for Spain. The meeting at the Teatro de la Comedia in Madrid was already planned when José Antonio met with Mussolini. José Antonio attended the appointment with enthusiasm. He wished to convey his desire for Fascism to its founder, to the "hero become father."

Years later, remembering that interview, Mussolini himself would remark to José Antonio's sister, Pilar Primo de Rivera, that "José Antonio was one of the most beautiful spirits he had ever known."[52] This opinion was personally confirmed to the author of this book by Rachele Mussolini, the Duce's wife, in Predappio, during a recorded interview conducted in an atmosphere of cordial camaraderie and affectionate sympathy. That encounter represented:

> the dialogue of two brilliant men, kindred in race and sentiment—one at the summit of glory and the other preparing the tools with which to climb it—who fully understood and admired each other. To us Falangists who blindly followed our *jefe* [leader], Mussolini's words, while not telling us something that we did not already know in our souls, fill us with a deep sense of satisfaction and pride for having done so with enthusiastic loyalty, when so few people were aware of him.[53]

According to the documentation that Professor Gil Pecharromán collected from his colleague Ismael Saz in his book *Mussolini contra la II República*, and from the Italian records of the time, José Antonio justified his trip to the Fascist authorities on the grounds of "obtaining informative material on Italian Fascism and on the achievements of the regime," as well as for "advice in the organization of an analogous movement in Spain."

In the opinion of Felipe Ximénez de Sandoval, the prelude to the Spanish Syndicalist Movement "is the most intense stage in the gestation of the Falange, which has not yet been born and does not yet have a name."[54]

A week before the famous speech of October 29th at the Teatro de la Comedia in Madrid, José Antonio published in the newspaper *La Nación* an

---

[52] Ximénez de Sandoval, *José Antonio, Biografía apasionada* (Madrid: Editorial Fuerza Nueva, 1976), 98.

[53] Ibid., 99.

[54] Ximénez de Sandoval, *José Antonio*, 102.

article with the following title: "¿Moda extranjera el fascismo?" ["Is Fascism a Foreign Fad?"]. In it, he writes:

> Fascism is not only an Italian movement; it is a total, universal way of understanding life. Italy was the first to implement it . . . . What is universal in Fascism is the reinvigoration of all peoples; that attitude of energetic delving into their own innermost selves. With Fascist spirit, the Italians have found Italy. We Spaniards, with the same spirit, will find Spain. Fascism is an injection that has the ability to revive: the injection might be the same for all, but each one would resuscitate as it was before.[55]

The event at the Teatro de la Comedia, the foundational act of the Spanish Falange, took place on October 29th, 1933, which was also the eleventh anniversary of the March on Rome. The event was called by the leading Italian Fascist newspaper—*Il Popolo d'Italia*—"the first propaganda rally of the Spanish Fascist movement."[56]

---

[55] *La Nación*, October 20th, 1933.

[56] *Il Popolo d'Italia*, October 31st, 1933.

2.

October 29th: A (Fascist) Flag Is Symbolically Raised

On the 29th of October, the favorite month of poets because of its rain, its mild weather, the fall of the leaves, and the favorable conditions for sowing, marks the date on which Italian Fascism commemorates the anniversary of the March on Rome, which brought Mussolini to the top of the pole. For Spanish Fascism, it is also a historic date. After the initial steps with *El Fascio* and the solid foundations of the MES, which signed its public statements with the initials "F.E.," and after the thrilling and instructive visit of José Antonio to Benito Mussolini, a few days before what would be called the "foundational rally," the public presentation would take place one Sunday morning at the Teatro de la Comedia in Madrid, with the hoisting of a symbolic flag.

According to the Italian documentation, José Antonio justified his trip to Rome to the Fascist authorities as a means of "obtaining informative material on Italian Fascism and on the achievements of the Italian regime," as well as advice for the organization of an "analogous movement in Spain." For this purpose, he met, as we have already noted, with the vice-secretary of the National Fascist Party, Arturo Marpicati, and visited several branches of the Italian Fascist organization.[57] In his book *Semblanza de José Antonio joven*, Serrano Suñer writes, for the purpose of

---

[57] Julio Gil Pecharromán, *José Antonio Primo de Rivera, retrato de un visionario* (Madrid: Temas de Hoy, 1996), 195.

corroboration: "José Antonio greatly admired Mussolini, but upon returning from his trip to Fascist Italy, he commented: 'I would have liked to feel the mood of other people, elevated in the planes of thought, culture, and conduct, to get to know how they judged the system.'" [58] The visit was too brief to sate José Antonio's thirst for knowledge.

José Antonio had met Mussolini before. He met him shortly after his father Miguel Primo de Rivera took power in Spain as head of the military directorate in 1923; later, when he visited Rome with a group of students from the University of Madrid, his classmates from the law faculty, in 1926, he was also received by the Duce, although this interview falls within the framework of formal hospitality. Pilar Primo de Rivera, his sister and future national delegate of the Women's Section of the Falange, writes in her memoir *Recuerdos de una vida* that José Antonio felt great admiration for Mussolini: "We all felt admiration for Mussolini, and José Antonio was the first to express it."[59]

Alfonso Martínez Carrasco wrote in the middle of 1934 a political essay entitled *Fascismo en España*,[60] the first serious and interpretive monograph on this political phenomenon, which is a sociological work divided into two parts. The first one is devoted to the study, examination, and *a priori* considerations, in search of the precursors and the circumstances and causes that made its advent possible, discovering its furthest traces in the dictatorship of General Primo de Rivera, with his militias and the Patriotic Union, Martinez Anido, the Legionnaires of Albiñana, and the events that made it possible, among which he cites the policies of Azaña—the burning of convents, the Statute of Catalonia, and the governorship of Lerroux. In the second part, the author continues with his analysis "Fascismo: La Falange Española," in which he concludes that:

> Spanish Fascism takes shape and begins on October 29th, 1933. In the Teatro de la Comedia of Madrid the birth of Falange Española takes place. A notable indifference, and even more, some journalistic mockery, greeted this transcendental birth. Undoubtedly, Spanish public opinion, always slow to recognize universal realities, did not want to fully realize that on that day a movement that would prevail in the world in the immediate future took form . . . . The real importance of that birth was the work of José Antonio Primo de Rivera, who explained all its programmatic basis, even more important because it was his very own, since it is known that José Antonio Primo de Rivera is going to be the leader of Spanish Fascism.[61]

---

[58]Serrano Suñer, *Semblanza de José Antonio joven*, 58.

[59] Pilar Primo de Rivera, *Recuerdos de una vida* (Madrid: Ediciones Dyrsa, 1983), 60 and 102.

[60] Alfonso Martínez Carrasco, *Fascismo en España*, with comments by José Antonio Primo de Rivera. (Madrid-Barcelona: Ed. Júpiter, 1934)

[61] Ibid., 56–57.

What was the purpose of José Antonio's visit to Rome in October 1933 to meet with the Duce? This is what the first biographer, friend, comrade, and classmate of José Antonio in the law faculty wonders. The answer is clear and straightforward:

> He went to Rome to see the man. That is, the master. José Antonio knew all the biographies that have been written about the Duce. He had thoroughly read his articles and speeches. He is shaken before his tremendous personal situation and needs to talk to him to take encouragement from his voice . . . . José Antonio had learned a lot from Mussolini, who is both a peer and a good friend of his father. What about him was so special that he felt the need to learn from him? Let us not forget that José Antonio's great vocation was that of a student. To learn and learn without ceasing. Why would he overlook Mussolini's invaluable lesson? He already knew him through his works and his biographies; he knew him by listening to the conversations of General Primo de Rivera. But he knew he needed an intimate conversation that would provide him with "the image of the hero made father."[62]

According to his passionate biographer, José Antonio needed to study his secret.

Eduardo García-Reboredo González, a chief of the Galician Falange, delivered a speech in the headquarters of the Falange Española de las JONS in Villagarcía on November 21st, 1936, when the blood of José Antonio had not yet finished coagulating and freezing after his assassination in the prison of Alicante. He concluded with these words, recalling the events of October 29th and the speech of José Antonio:

> As we move forward with a firm step toward the formation of the National Syndicalist state, let us turn our gaze to the past without forgetting the present. For this to have a real and positive existence, the three conditions that Mussolini outlined in his speech of September 14th, 1933, are required: that is, one single national party, which allows for the action of political and economic discipline, and which must be placed above all other conflicting interests; it must be a bond that brings everyone together under the same faith. Secondly, a totalitarian state that shall incorporate in itself all the demands, interests, and hopes of a people in order to give them strength, and shape the people, ultimately, to a high degree of ideological fervor.
>
> And these words of the Duce were supported by our Caesar José Antonio in his speech of October 29th, 1933, when he said: "May all

---

[62] Ximénez de Sandoval, *José Antonio, Biografía apasionada* (Madrid: Fuerza Nueva Editorial, 3rd edition, 1976), 97–98.

peoples, however diverse they may be, feel themselves in harmony and united in an irrevocable destiny. May all political parties disappear, for since we were all born into a family, we are all neighbors of a community, and we all work hard at our jobs." If therefore our natural units are the family, the community, and the corporation, which is what we really live in, why do we need political parties, which, in order to unite us in artificial groups, begin to separate us within our authentic relations?[63]

In Madrid, at that time, an organization had taken shape based on a triumvirate, led by Commander Emilio R. Tarduchy and backed by his comrades in arms, Infantry Commander Luis Arredondo and General Staff Commander Román Ayza, Baron of Tormoye. The three were in close contact with José Antonio, who, according to Tarduchy's words,

On one occasion wanted to assess our strength and our numbers, asking us to make a demonstration in the street on the occasion of the famous crisis of the lion and the snake. That night, in the vicinity of the Puerta del Sol, a large crowd greeted José Antonio with raised arms for the first time. Following that public demonstration, what would later be the Falange Española began to take shape. And we began the celebration of a public act that would announce, to all corners of the country, the appearance of the movement.[64]

José Antonio set out at ten o'clock that night from the Café Lyon D'Or—later renamed Lepanto and then Nebraska—at 18 Calle de Alcalá, along with Tarduchy and Ruiz de Alda. That was the first parade of the "imaginary militias of Tarduchy," as José Antonio affectionately referred to them.

Commander Tarduchy proposed holding the rally in Burgos, the Cabeza de Castilla, in order to evoke resonant historical memories.[65] José Antonio gave his consent and ordered that the necessary arrangements be made for this occasion. Commander Tarduchy and José Mara Alfaro, who was from that province and knew his countrymen well, traveled to that city to survey the field and make preparations. Both were accompanied on the preparatory visit to Burgos by Dr. Florentino Martinez, a militant of the movement of the Legionnaires of Spain, led by Dr. Albiñana. The date they had initially chosen for the celebration of the event was October 7th, a date that was marked in the calendar as the anniversary of the Battle

---

[63] Eduardo García-Reboredo González, *Unidad de pensamiento y de fe*, stenographic text of the meeting held in the afternoon of November 21st, 1936, in the headquarters of the Falange Española de las JONS, 14.

[64] *Juventud*, October 27th, 1949, "Emilio R. Tarduchy nos habla del 29 de octubre de 1933."

[65] [Translator: the Cabeza de Castilla is the zone in which the Reign of Castile was founded.]

of Lepanto against the Turks, which would serve as a pretext to request, underhandedly, the corresponding governmental permission for the "commemorative act of the Battle of Lepanto," and which request would be submitted by the National Front of Alfonso García Valdecasas, in agreement with José Antonio. The chosen speakers for that hypothetical day that would mark the beginning of the Fascist movement would be, as agreed, the writer and journalist Eugenio Montes, the ideologist of the Spanish Syndicalist Movement; the Fascist poet Rafael Sánchez Mazas; and José Antonio, who would speak last. The required enthusiasm was not found among the small groups of sympathizers in the Castilian city, but rather a mixture of apathy and reserve. The civil governor, on the other hand, prevented the celebration's authorization. The initial idea of the event in Burgos was eventually discarded by its promoters.

On October 11th, Román Ayza, García Valdecasas, García del Moral, Rodríguez Tarduchy, and Peláez met in Madrid at Julio Ruiz de Alda's apartment to discuss and decide the name of the movement that was to be officially announced on October 29th. Hence, with the approval of all those gathered, the name *Falange Española* was adopted for the first time among the various suggested names; it coincided with the initials of Fascismo Español, which had been used in the propaganda of flyers, leaflets, and the manifesto of the MES, and also with the initials of the Frente Español of Alfonso García Valdecasas. Of this party—which was already formally authorized— the statutes for the future Falange Española were copied by García del Moral, in order to avoid legal, bureaucratic, and administrative problems. This simple sophistication cleared up the hypothetical contradiction that the governmental authority might be tempted to incur by denying statutes whose articles had been previously approved, in accordance with the law in force at the time, for the Spanish Front in 1932.

Professor Joan Maria Thomás remarks that in the months prior to the event at the Comedia, José Antonio had been placing himself "publicly, more and more in the role of future Fascist leader, replacing—but not giving up—the main role he had carried out until then: that of defender of the memory of his father, whose figure and work he had felt obliged to defend from the many attacks directed at him in the first years of the Republic."[66]

The Comedia theater on Madrid's famous Calle del Príncipe was chosen because it provided the best conditions for the rally's celebration. Its owner, Mr. Tirso Escudero, although aware of the inconveniences and troubles that such an assignment could entail, did not hesitate in accepting the offer. On the night of October 27th, the play *El Creso de Burgos*, by Jacinto Capella and José de Lucio, a light and humorous play in three acts written in prose, premiered on the stage of the Comedia.

---

[66] Joan Maria Thomás, *Lo que fue la Falange* (Barcelona: Plaza & Janés, 1999), 27.

Mr. Tirso Escudero was an unconditional admirer of José Antonio's father, Miguel Primo de Rivera. He selflessly provided his theater for free. The preparations were completed quickly, fueled by the euphoric spirit of the legendary aviator Julio Ruiz de Alda, who had fought so valiantly in the MES. Invitations on red cardboard printed in black ink were distributed to the group of names listed in the file that was jealously guarded in Emilio Rodríguez Tarduchy's private home after the first appearance of *El Fascio*. The rally at the Comedia was planned from his home office. The tickets from the theater's own box office were used as entrance tickets.

Two military men, Captains Luis López Pando and Claudio Rivera Macías— laureate of San Fernando—under the direction of Julio Ruté de Alda and Manolo Valdés (José Antonio's swimming teacher and trusted advisor during his difficult times, in charge of keeping order in the hall)—were responsible for organizing the event and commanding the first militias. From the start, they relied on the enthusiastic cooperation of three interns from José Antonio's law firm—Andrés de la Cuerda, Sarrión, and Rafael Garcerán—who, alongside the typists and employees of the firm, were in charge of distributing the invitation cards.

That public act was advertised as a "Spanish affirmation" rally. The event was staged and disguised within the electoral landscape in the midst of the electoral campaign of Diego Martinez Barrio, president of the Spanish Grand Orient and a 33rd degree Mason. Joaquín Airarás explains that "there was hardly any written graphic propaganda; but on the other hand, the version spread by word of mouth was that it would be a Fascist rally, and this aroused lively curiosity."[67] The organizers had received word the night before that leftists would attempt to violently disrupt the meeting, which did not occur, though the usual scuffles came at the theater's exit.

The government, in order to prevent disorder, dispatched police and assault corps to deter any potential riots. Forces of order could be seen flanking the arched doors of the theater; some assault cars were in the vicinity, and at the ends of the street, in the squares of Santa Ana and Canillejas, mounted guards were present. Officers in civilian clothes could be seen on the sidewalks, blending in with the crowds.

The event was broadcast by Unión Radio Madrid. The Dean of the University of Salamanca, Miguel de Unamuno, listened to it through the receiver, in the casino of the city, where Francisco Bravo, a member of the JONS, was also present.

When the curtain went up, just a few minutes after eleven o'clock in the morning that Sunday, Mr. Narciso Martínez Cabezas—tall and skinny—an old militant of the MES who had distinguished himself in organizing the preparations

---

[67] Quoted by Carlos Arce, *José Antonio*, 184.

for the convocation, personally requesting the necessary permission from the General Directorate of Security, introduced the three speakers, characterizing the act as a rally of "Spanish affirmation." Manuel Valdés says of him that,

> Narciso was the most representative type of the genuine Spaniard, a Castilian of pure lineage, a constant in the best pages of our history because of his simplicity and austerity; a tall, lanky man, like the stalk of wheat of Castile, who, from his distant youth, had felt the call to the service of Spain, first in the call of the Maurist youth, then, in his maturity, as councilman and deputy mayor in the City Council of Madrid, in the days of General Primo de Rivera, and, finally, in his old age, joining the Falange, prior to the Act of the Comedia.[68]

Tomás Borrás, a writer and journalist present at the event, describes it as follows:

> On the stage, there is the table that will be chaired by Narciso Martínez Cabezas. A bare, simple, checkroom table, covered in dark canvas. The footlights were lit; a scenographic light fell on the table.
>
> José Antonio has arrived in his car. Pilar and Carmen, his sisters, arrive with him and move to a balcony. The car remains parked in Santa Ana, guarded by the watchmen of the MES. The four actors of the historical drama take their place. Narciso has by his side the police chief; Valdecasas, boyish face, small, nervous; Ruiz de Alda, carved in muscular stone, wide, solid, smiling; and next to Valdecasas, José Antonio, youthful, elegant, slender, with thoughtful eyes.[69]

Alfonso García Valdecasas, born on May 14th, 1904, in Granada, studied law in his hometown, specializing in civil law. He later studied at the University of Freiburg and completed his legal training as a collegiate of San Clemente de los Españoles at the University of Bologna, where he obtained his doctorate in 1925. He was appointed professor of civil law at the University of Salamanca in 1924, then at the University of Granada, and finally he was nominated professor of higher studies of private law at the University of Madrid and, subsequently, professor of civil law at the same university. He served as a member of the Constituent Courts of the Republic. He was also a disillusioned member of the Association for the Service of the Republic, which he left in March 1932 to form a political party called Frente Español, which had a small, almost non-existent membership, and which, in 1933, had a doctrinal crisis between the followers of the Republican regime and those in

---

[68] Manuel Valdés Larrañaga, *De la Falange al Movimiento (1936–1952)* (Madrid: Fundación Nacional Francisco Franco, 1994), 203–204.

[69] Tomás Borrás, *Ramiro Ledesma Ramos* (Madrid: Editora Nacional, 1971), 439.

favor of transforming the state along Fascist lines. García Valdecasas was a member of the group in favor of "embracing Fascism as a doctrinal principle" and of the establishment in Spain of a corporative state. Professor Gil Pecharromán confirms that "at the beginning of the summer, García Valdecasas joined the MES, with Bouthelier and García del Moral."[70]

On that cold morning, García Valdecasas was the first to begin the session of speeches. He was greeted with the Fascist salute, which he reciprocated by raising both arms vertically. These were his words:

> It has been said that this is a Fascist rally, and I say that, since it is Spanish to the core, they can call it whatever they want. We may share all our affinities and points of agreement with Italian Fascism, which is a foreign thing, but we Spaniards do not want to live under foreign systems.

The audience, which crowded the theater, greeted the speakers, standing up, with the Roman salute: a forest of raised arms, firm and straight, each of them at a right angle. When it was Julio Ruiz de Alda's turn to speak, he stepped forward "to perform the Roman salute that put everyone on their feet. Many thousands of arms were raised. Unquestionably, Ruiz de Alda is the Spanish Balbo."[71] According to Ximénez de Sandoval, Julio "lacked a well-defined political orientation, despite his Fascist flirtations and having appeared last summer in one of the imaginary 'plots' in which Casares Quiroga's republican fantasy took so much delight."[72] Before beginning his speech, José Antonio also greeted the audience with his arm outstretched, in a Roman, Fascist manner, as can be read in the newspaper *El Heraldo de Madrid*, in the October 30th issue.

His first sentence was resounding, successful, categorical, and firm, although pronounced with a certain timidity: "There will not be an entire paragraph of thanks. As befits the military laconicism of our style, just a brief 'thank you.'" Military laconicism and militarism as the Fascist style and the Fascist way. These preliminary phrases of his speech were an initial confirmation of the order, hierarchy, discipline, service, and sacrifice that were brought together in the movement, which regarded them as both rule and style.

And then, the resounding affirmation of an imperial and righteous will expressed in desires to make clear his aspirations:

> We want all the peoples of Spain, however diverse they may be, to feel themselves in harmony, in an irrevocable unity of destiny . . . . We want less

---

[70] Gil Pecharromán, *José Antonio Primo de Rivera*, 96.

[71] *Decimos*, November 2nd, 1933: "Del mitin de la Comedia. Impresiones de un fascista."

[72] Ximénez de Sandoval, *José Antonio*, 104.

liberal talk and more respect for the profound freedom of man . . . . We want everyone to feel that they are members of a serious and complete community . . . . We want to stop the blathering about individual rights that cannot be fulfilled in the homes of the hungry . . . . We want the religious spirit, the key to the best historical achievements of our history, to be respected and protected as it deserves . . . . We want Spain to resolutely reclaim the universal destiny of its culture and its history . . . . And lastly, if this is to be achieved in any case by violence, we do not stop before violence . . . . Our place is in the open air, under the clear night, with a weapon in hand and the stars above us. Let the others go on with their banquets. We remain outside, in tense, fervent, and confident alertness; we already sense the rising of dawn in our guts.

Vicente Gaceo joined Matías Montero and Ruiz de la Hermosa on the stage of the theater. Ramiro Ledesma Ramos and a few brave early JONS members were in another section of the audience.[73] Ramiro would later write: "A few days after the meeting, its organizers announced the foundation of F.E., Falange Española. It is easy to see in this denomination their intention of not abandoning the initials F.E., which for months before they had already been using as initials of Spanish Fascism in their propaganda leaflets."[74] Also present at the meeting was the former deputy Royo Villanova, who occupied a seat in the front rows. Among the audience, dressed in civilian clothes, were some young military men. Also present was General Varela, one of the chiefs of the army.

A large contingent of the Albiñana Legionnaires was there. Dr. Albiñana was unable to attend the event in person because he had been ill in bed for several months. Confronted with this eventuality, on October 28th he had a leaflet printed urgently, on both sides, in the graphic workshops of the V. Huerta printing house a 7 Calle del Nuncio, Madrid, in which, on one side, under the Cross of Santiago, the symbol of his Spanish Nationalist Party, is reproduced "España Inmortal," the hymn of his party, whose four verses were written by Albiñana himself, with each ending "*¡Sobre España inmortal, sólo Dios!*" ["Above Immortal Spain, only God!"]. On the other side it read:

Endorsement of Doctor Albiñana to the meeting of Spanish Affirmation.

Mr. José Antonio Primo de Rivera, Marquis of Estella.

---

[73] A magnificent introduction to the JONS and to the main ideologues of this radical group of the early days of Spanish fascism is the book by Erik Norling: *Las JONS revolucionarias. Compañeros de Ramiro Ledesma: los otros jonsistas. Semblanzas y textos* (Barcelona: Ediciones Nueva Repúblia, 2002).

[74] Ledesma Ramos, *¿Fascismo en España?*, 135.

My dearest friend:

The unconditional support of the Spanish Nationalist Party, whose intangible Spanishness is the sole reason for its existence, is required for this act of Spanish affirmation, which you have brilliantly organized.

For this reason, from my bed of pain, where I have been lying for five weeks, liquidating with a terrible surgical operation the criminal confinement of fifteen months to which the sinister government of Casas Viejas sentenced me, I send you the enthusiastic endorsement of Spanish Nationalism and my personal endorsement. Both have the merit of corresponding to entities and individuals who have never given up and who have known how to confess and maintain their faith in martyrdom.

The painful conditions in which I find myself prevent me from attending the event with my blue shirt on.

With the victorious Cross of the Patron Saint of Spain, and proclaiming the desire for a Spanish Front exclusively devoted to the salvation of our poor fatherland, so forgotten by the traitorous leftists and by some selfish rightists, who fled the dangers of struggle and rushed to share the comfortable loot of laws and vanities, eliminating those who, tortured, knew how to encourage with their example of integrity the Spanish masses, subjected to the terror of a criminal government.

Wishing that God may restore my health so I can offer it in struggle for the good of our beloved Spain, your good friend and companion sends you a strong embrace and shakes your hand.

Dr. José María Albiñana.
Madrid, October 28, 1933.[75]

The leaflet was tossed by handfuls from the highest seats of the theater, creating a minor murmur and confusion, initially perceived as an act of sabotage by the left, until the content of the leaflet that was initially ignored was known, and with it the origin of those pages that fell gently from above, like snowflakes on the crowded stalls.

Among the women who attended the inaugural meeting were José Antonio's sisters, Pilar and Carmen Primo de Rivera, and his cousins Inés and Dolores, accompanied by María Luisa Aramburu.

Several people from Barcelona came to the event, including J. Vidal Salvó, who had contributed significantly to spreading National Socialist ideas in Spain. He had even translated the book *Hitler and National Socialism* into Spanish, which was published in Barcelona by the printing house J. Horta a few months prior to the rally at the Comedia,

---

[75] Private archive of the author. This previously unpublished document from the event's bibliography is being reproduced here for the first time.

which he had attended with Carlos López Manduley (the head of the Spanish Nationalist Party in Barcelona), Giumet, and José Parés, the latter arriving from Badalona.

Few journalists covered the event. Two tables were set up on the stage, with only six reporters present. From Salamanca, Ismael Herráiz, Santos Alcocer, and Alberto F. attended on behalf of *El Debate* and the news agency Logos. Luis Muñoz Lorente attended the event in his role as editor of *La Nación*. The agency Mencheta was represented by Borrás Vidaola —these two were the ones who, although not being stenographers, recorded on paper the copy of the speeches. Julio Fuertes stood almost the entire time in an aisle of the theater.

The main attractions for those groups more favorable to Fascism—writes Joan Maria Thomás—were the fervent nationalism and the demand for the construction of a new type of state, at once conciliatory and totalitarian, which would put an end to the divisions between political parties and social classes, fight separatism, and constitute a bulwark against the Marxist revolution.[76]

Julio Fuertes also reminds us that an attentive reader would be able find in the work that José Antonio outlined in his *Puntos iniciales* for the weekly *El Fascio* everything that would be later included in the programmatic points of the Falange.[77] The event at the Teatro de la Comedia was arranged in September, with a series of meetings and appointments held by José Antonio in his professional office at 8 Calle Alcalá Galiano, with Julio Ruiz de Alda, Alfonso García Valdecasas, Commander Rodríguez Tarduchy, Ernesto Giménez Caballero, Rafael Sánchez Mazas, José María Alfaro, Manuel Valdés, Claudio Rivera Macías, Luis López Pando, and Narciso Martínez Cabezas, all of them leading figures of the MES.

Carlos de Arce, José Antonio's biographer, clarifies that "it is undeniable that Falange Española resembled a Fascist party, and it would always be considered as such. However, it was a unique kind of Fascism that did not fit its description exactly."[78]

The day culminated with a meal at the Amaya on the Carrera de San Jeronimo, not far from the theater. José Antonio instructed Tarduchy to avoid making speeches after the dessert because "everything had already been said." Not for anything in the world did he want the event to turn into just another banquet, with endless verbosity of toasts and stale speeches. The only one who intervened, addressing the guests, was Commander Tarduchy, with these brief words:

Now, with this triumvirate encouraging and commanding us, it is up to us to obey with humility, which will be the sign of our utmost greatness; with abnegation and precision; with conscious and iron discipline.[79]

---

[76] Maria Thomás, *Lo que fue la Falange*, 19.

[77] *Arriba*, October 29th, 1940, 2.

[78] De Arce, *José Antonio*, 188.

[79] *Juventud*, October 27th, 1949, "Emilio R. Tarduchy nos habla del 29 de octubre de 1933."

The press covered the rally in an unusual manner. The left-wing newspapers either did not talk about the event—as did *El Socialista*—or published false articles full of bitterness, as did *El Sol* and *El Liberal*. The so-called right-wing newspapers, with the exception of *La Nación*, which bravely dedicated the front page to the speech, and *ABC*, which also published it and provided a fair amount of coverage, seemed unaware of the significance of the event.

There was a general agreement among the media to characterize the event as "Fascist,"

> - *La Nación*—closely associated with José Antonio—(October 30th): "The first act of Fascist character dispels the misconceptions with which they tried to deceive the people." That edition published the full text of the speeches and described the event as "one of the three most important national events of the present century." The other two, according to the newspaper, were the dictatorship of Don Miguel Primo de Rivera and the political action of Antonio Maura. In the section entitled "Quisicosas políticas" [Political Riddles] of the October 30th edition, one can read: "Falange Española is born. F.E. is born and the Fatherland is reborn!"
>
> - *Informaciones* (October 30th): "Messrs. Valdecasas, Ruiz de Alda, and Primo de Rivera raise the Fascist flag. Great turnout and enormous enthusiasm. Yesterday at the Comedia, with the theater full of an enthusiastic public, a rally organized by Fascist elements was held. They did not call themselves so, although they would have every right to do so. Whatever the savages who want to stifle the free expression of other people may think, they support ideals inspired by the organization of the Italian state."
>
> - *Decimos*—Subsequently, in February 1934, the organ of the Falange Española in the province of Cáceres (November 2nd): "The first and great Spanish Fascist rally."
>
> - *Acción Española*, in its fortieth issue, on November 1st, published the complete text of José Antonio's speech under the headline "Bandera que se alza" [A Flag Rises], and an introduction to the text written by Eugenio Vegas Latapié.
>
> - *El Sol* (October 29th): This influential liberal newspaper described it as "a poetic movement, which we reject because it wants to be Fascism . . . and not because it is a deep and authentic Fascism."

The patrons of the event collected the following days, in a four-page large-format sheet, the complete texts of their speeches and an article by Sánchez Mazas that concluded the booklet with the title "Conclusión," in which the home address of 10 Calle Eduardo Dato was provided, serving as the contact address for the new national movement.

In Italy, the rally at the Comedia was celebrated with official jubilation under the headline "The First Propaganda Act of the Spanish Fascist Movement" in the newspaper *Il Popolo d'Italia* (October 31st), Mussolini's daily paper, which wrote:

> With the participation of 1,500 people, the first propaganda event of the Fascist movement, organized by the Frente Español, which is born today with a purely anti-electoral program exclusively valorizing traditional and national corporatist factors, has taken place, arousing fervent enthusiasm in the audience.
>
> The former deputy to the Constituent Cortes, Professor García Valdecasas, spoke of the deviation of Spain from its historical destiny as a consequence of the adoption of exotic ideologies contrary to the peculiar characteristics of the (Spanish) race. He defended the adjective *Fascist* applied to the renovating movement, which, basing itself on national values, is inspired by the example of other countries, eliciting from the audience cheers for Italy.

Bernd Nellessen, in his work *La rivoluzione proibita*,[80] focuses on two details regarding the "foundational" act. First of all, he does not ignore José Antonio's visit to Mussolini on October 19th, ten days before the event at the Comedia, believing that "with this meeting he underlined his unequivocal commitment to Fascism." Regarding the chosen date, he comments: "Just as we cannot consider it a coincidence that the anniversary of the death of General Primo de Rivera occurred on the same date as the publication of *El Fascio*, neither can we consider the choice of the founding date of the Falange to be a coincidence: the March on Rome had taken place on October 28th."

According to the newspaper *Völkischer Beobachter*, the official publication of the National Socialist Party in Germany, the founding of the Falange marked the entry of the "Fascist movement into the public life of Spain." Even the old newspaper of the Catholic Center Party, *Germania*, covered the founding of a "new Fascist party in Spain" in its November 14th edition.

---

[80] Bernd Nellesen, *La rivoluzione proibita (ascesa e tramonto della Falange)* (Rome: Volpe Editore, 1965), 84.

3.

Spanish Fascists in La Nueva Catolicidad

Ernesto Giménez Caballero would publish, in November 1933 (just a few weeks after the founding of the Spanish Falange), the second edition of his work *La Nueva Catolicidad—teoría general sobre el fascismo en Europa: en España*. The first edition of the book had been published that same year, and, in just over three weeks, it was sold out, which led the author to comment: "This indicates—more than anything else in my favor—the support that today's Spanish people are capable of granting to Fascist theories presented with a national character."[81]

The second edition was a reproduction of the first, enriched with an additional chapter on "Los fascistas españoles" ["The Spanish Fascists"]. In the "Note regarding the second edition" added by the author, one can read:

> This second edition includes corrections and notes on events that occurred after the first. But this edition contains something that particularly enriches it in comparison with the previous: an additional chapter on "Los fascistas españoles," which can be very useful and valuable as a guide to explore the Fascist movements in our country from 1923 to the present.
>
> Madrid, November 1933.

---

[81] Ernesto Giménez Caballero, *La Nueva Catolicidad*, 2nd ed. (Madrid: Ediciones de La Gaceta Literaria, 1933).

The book, after its general introduction entitled "Roma cita a Europa" [Rome Meets Europe], consists of an essay on the ideas and contributions discussed at the Volta Congress of the Academy of Italy (which took place in Rome between November 14th and 22nd, 1932), in which Ernesto Giménez Caballero participated, and where the new emerging intelligentsia took a position as a true European force, adopting a Fascist and redemptive perspective.

The Volta Congress started from the premise of defining and establishing the terms of the conceptual framework, like pillars of a new political architecture, beginning by trying to answer, from the new perspective, the question "What is Europe?" After this, it focused on the European dreams of unity and peace, achievable and embodied in the heroic figure of Mussolini, Duce and mentor of the a new, ultimate, revolutionary social doctrine of historical regeneration and national resurrection.

The book, after a review of the dense Volta Congress, outlines a "Plan para la resurrección nacional y para España" [Plan for the national resurrection and for Spain], the same that Giménez Caballero drafted for publication in the weekly *El Fascio* which served as the major guidelines of the subsequent doctrinal program, from which José Antonio gained insight.

The master plan designed by Giménez Caballero, published in *El Fascio*, in its single and unborn copy before being seized and removed from circulation by the Republican governmental authority, emphasized that "the first and last objective of a national movement is to make or remake in history a great people, a great nation."[82]

The roots that would produce this great nation had to be sought in "the secret of a brilliant past": for Italy it was the Roman imperial past, under the sign of the *fascio littorio* of the Caesars; for Hitler's Germany, the Germanic empire, under the sign of the Aryan swastika; and in Spain it was necessary to seek greatness through its internal unity—which assured autonomy and independence—and its expansion in the world, under the sign of unity, at the service of universal ideals, represented by the bundle of arrows of the Spanish Renaissance.

The young people called on for this undertaking should, as a premise, accept the inescapable and stoic motto "that life is struggle," understanding life as warfare, both civic and spiritual, calling for the formation of a "new state," the overcoming of the liberal state in order to implement the Fascist and corporative state, and bringing together capital and labor in a harmonious and creative peace, where authority would be integrated with freedom, with a syndicalist parliament.

The most powerful ideas put forward in the plan were those of unity—political, religious, military, social, and cultural—and of empire. "Fascism is today the new catholicity of the world," since "Fascism is not a doctrine exclusive to Italians nor to

---

[82] *El Fascio*, March 16th, 1933, "Puntos de partida," and Ernesto Giménez Caballero, *La Nueva Catolicidad*, 173 ff.

Germans, but to Roman Europe."[83]

The brief summary of the program was synthesized with the words "unity" and "universal idea." An "upright and active" Spain at the service of the new crusade "against the East and the West," against communism and individualism.

For the national revolution, Giménez Caballero called upon the poets in their role as active propagators.

In the chapter of the book on the Spanish Fascists, he starts with the premise "that Fascism represents the best channel through which the genius of Spain can flow again generously," which is crucial for the future of Spain. That is why, when "José Antonio Primo de Rivera gave a beautiful meeting at the Comedia and some friends offered him a banquet, the sensible Spanish opinion did not hesitate: Fascism must already be that!"[84]

He then proceeds listing all the possible *caudillos* of Fascism and examining, one by one, the pretenders, starting with Dr. Albiñana, continuing with the Republicans Lerroux and Maura, the generals Sanjurjo, Goded, and Franco, the populist Gil Robles, and the monarchist Calvo Sotelo; he then moves to the younger *caudillos,* such as Ramiro Ledesma Ramos and, at the top, on the apex of Spanish Fascism, José Antonio:

> I saved the most recent Fascist contender to appear on the Spanish political scene for last. The last and the one who has most rapidly achieved an atmosphere of sympathy and romantic hopes: José Antonio Primo de Rivera, the eldest son of the dictator of Spain, Don Miguel. José Antonio made his appearance with a simple rally speech in a theater in Madrid on a Sunday morning in October. His speech was precise, energetic, cultured, and full of Spanish sensibility. Really promising. Just enough for the people who were still longing—more and more expressly—to see a new Primo de Rivera appear on the horizon, with the same kindness and sympathy as the general, and with something that the general could not have: youth. José Antonio was in his thirties. With a temperament, whose characteristics are kindness, courage, and a keen intelligence, sharpened, honed, and refined by the exercise of his profession as a lawyer, he is one of the best in Madrid. The fact that this young man was a friend of intellectuals and leftist politicians and was politically opposed to his father's dictatorship has earned him a certain degree of benevolence from the liberal press. Perhaps because of this, and not for being too concerned about surrounding himself with some elements with no proven Fascist fervor and control, the right wing and some other authentic Fascists have cooled their enthusiasm for

---

[83] Giménez Caballero, *La Nueva Catolicidad*, 181.

[84] Ibid., 190.

him. And it should be noted that I am speaking on behalf of no one in particular—even less on behalf of his ambitious assistant, the aviator Ruiz de Alda, perhaps our future Balbo or Goering (the workers still see in this Second First—Secundus Primus—just another "señorito" [rich kid]).

José Antonio finds himself in a very delicate and perhaps decisive moment for his future as a caudillo. He has enough tact, courage, finesse, and patience to come out on top. But I would like to render him a service that only we poets are capable of when it comes to offering a *reloj de príncipes*.[85] I seek to place before your eyes—without the intention to dazzle—a historical reflection of haunting resemblance: The case of the young Octavian in Rome, Augustus.

José Antonio Primo de Rivera could very well be in a future Fascist Spain something like what Augustus, the young Octavian, was in Rome (with all due respect to the differences between an imperial Rome and a Spain as modest as the contemporary one) . . . . José Antonio Primo de Rivera could find himself in Octavian's situation in Rome.

For Spain, the Fascist leadership could correspond to the Octavian princedom. It would not be necessary for the caudillo to come from a working-class family, as in Italy and Germany. (An authentic aristocrat is always of pure descent).

We must not forget the precedent—may it be better or worse—of Fascism in Spain: that of General Primo de Rivera, vilely overthrown one day. The Spanish people, who have endured two years of suffering, disarray, and national tragedies, yearn more and more each day for the image of that good and simple man who preserved peace and prosperity for six years.

Why should they not accept faithfully the heirloom of that natural king in the person of his son? It would not be a difficult task. The doctrine and system are becoming more and more suitable for implementation as a result of the Fascist experiences in Italy, Germany, and General Primo's own experiences.

The problems of Spain are, in the end, the same ones that the deposed general addressed so well. They are now slightly worsened, but essentially the same: the social question, the economic question, the separatist question. Why not continue and bring to a successful conclusion a failed work interrupted by death?

José Antonio Primo de Rivera has almost all the winning cards in his hand. May he know how to play them with success. I wish him well, as a Fascist and as a friend.

---

[85] Translator: the *Reloj de Príncipes* or *Dial of Princes* is a book written in 1529 by Antonio de Guevara; it is a pseudo-historical book of incidents and letters from the life of Marcus Aurelius, and a guide for princes.

And now—to conclude—a remembrance of great importance in the formation of the nascent Fascism in Spain: the poets.[86]

He then cited the poets who made possible the Fascist revolution in Spain: Eugenio Montes, José María Alfaro, Rafael Sánchez Mazas, José María Pemán, and others.

José Antonio, in his role as director and owner of the weekly *F.E.*, from the first issue (December 7th, 1933), promoted the diffusion of Ernesto Giménez Caballero's book *La Nueva Catolicidad*. On the fourth page of that first issue, the final paragraph of Giménez Caballero's book is published, with the addition of the following comment: "An excellent guide to Fascism in Europe and Spain," celebrating the fact that the first edition had quickly sold out and the second was about to appear. As if the reproduction and the commentary on page four of the newspaper *F.E.* were not enough to identify with the contents of the book *La Nueva Catolicidad*, on page 10, the book in question was expressly recommended to the newspaper's readers. The release of the second edition was promoted in the third issue of *F.E.* (January 18th, 1934), with an insert informing the reader that it was already on sale in all bookstores. The book advertisement appeared several times in the magazine over the course of its run.

José Antonio adopted from *La Nueva Catolicidad* his general theory on Fascism in Europe and in Spain, as the subtitle of the work itself indicates.

---

[86] Ibid., 206–210.

4.

Falange Española is Born

The speeches at the Teatro de la Comedia represented the beginning of a new political movement that was consolidating between the followers of the Spanish Syndicalist Movement, the MES, led by José Antonio Primo de Rivera and Julio Ruiz de Alda (who presented themselves to the public in their propaganda leaflets as "Fascismo Español"), and a dissident minority group of the Frente Español, which had emerged in 1932, headed by Alfonso García Valdecasas. The three most prominent figures were, in fact, the heralds of the Comedia meeting, which was regarded as the foundational meeting.

Barely four days had passed since the meeting when the founders met again, on November 2nd, 1933, on the main floor of the building at 46 Calle de Torrijos—today Conde de Peñalver—in Madrid, to formalize the act of constitution of the new movement they were building. For this purpose, Elíseo del Moral assumed the role of secretary of the meeting, drafting the following document:

> In Madrid, on November 2nd, 1933, the founding members of "Falange Española" gathered at the headquarters of said entity, at 46 Calle de Torrijos, building A, and having passed the period of eight days determined in Article 4 of the Law of Associations of June 30th, 1887, the said members agreed to the following: First, to constitute the entity Falange Española. Second, to appoint the following Governing Board:
>
> Board of Command—Don Julio Ruiz de Alda, Don Alfonso García Valdecasas, and Don José Antonio Primo de Rivera

Study Representative—Don Rafael Sánchez Mazas
Representative of Local Organization—Don Julio Martínez Cabezas Secretary
—Don Eliseo García del Moral y Bujalance
Treasurer—Don Román Ayza
Chairmen—Don Agustín Escudero, Don Antonio Bouthelier Espesa and Don
Mariano García

Signature of the Secretary— Eliseo del Moral
Read and approved. On behalf of the Board of Command as Chairman:
Julio Ruiz de Alda[87]

On the same day, a member of the JONS, José Ruiz de la Hermosa, was stabbed to death by socialists in Daimiel (Ciudad Real), his birthplace. He had attended the act of Spanish affirmation at the Teatro de la Comedia and the successive dinner held after the speeches at the Amaya, approaching José Antonio during the dessert to express his support and to congratulate him enthusiastically. The tragic and criminal event took place outside a socialist meeting in the Ayala Theater in the town of Daimiel, when Ruiz de la Hermosa, with patriotic expressions, rebuked the speaker Antonio Cabrera and reminded the parliamentary secretary, the socialist Cañizares, of the massacre of Casas Viejas, at which point several socialists, in a mob, rushed at him and struck him with clubs and knives, stabbing him everywhere on his body until he succumbed to the wounds. From that moment on, the name of Ruiz de la Hermosa would be at the top of the honor list of the Telón de los Caídos [Curtain of the Fallen] of the Falange. It was a baptism of blood for the new movement.

On November 6th, Julio Ruiz de Alda submitted the new party's statutes and founding document, which complied with the Law of Associations (in effect since the nineteenth century), to the general directorate of security's registry.

Alfonso García Valdecasas, who at the rally at the Teatro de la Comedia had declared "it has been said that this is a Fascist rally, and I say that, since it is Spanish to the core, they can call it whatever they want," was a professor at the Central University. His first occasional political dealings were in opposition to the dictatorship of Miguel Primo de Rivera, and he resigned from his professorship in the spring of 1929 due to the firmness of the regime against the leftist student movement FUE. He was a pupil of the great philosopher José Ortega y Gasset. He had run and was elected for the district of Granada as a representative for the party Agrupación al Servicio de la República in the Constituent Cortes in 1931. In 1932, with some friends and colleagues, he wrote a manifesto and launched a political party under the name of Frente Español—using initials identical to those of the later Fascismo Español and Falange Española. The party's leadership was represented by, among others, Juan Antonio Maravall, Antonio

---

[87] Private archive of the author.

Garrigues, Salvador Lisasarrague, Antonio Riaño, Justino Azcárate, Elíseo García del Moral, María Zambrano, Antonio Bouthelier, and Antonio Sacristán, working under the watchful eye of the master Ortega y Gasset.

A few months after the formation of the Frente Español, its members, faced with the growing Fascist phenomenon, followed two very distinct paths. Alfonso García Valdecasas was the first to approach Fascism, influenced by the current trend, and was followed by Elíseo García del Moral, Antonio Bouthelier, and Riaño. Suffering a lack of resources, branches, and channels of expression, they sought an agreement with José Antonio, who, in the spring of 1933, was politically busy after the aborted attempt to publish *El Fascio*. Valdecasas had attended some meetings with him, as well as being present at the launching and establishment of the Movimiento Español Sindicalista–Fascismo Español. As García del Moral recounts:

> The Frente Español had a legal organization, but it lacked the means of struggle; on the other hand, F.E. (Fascismo Español) had a certain strength and means of struggle but lacked legal organization. Because the initials coincided, the propaganda already carried out by one group could be advantageously used by the other. A change of leadership was agreed upon, and a triumvirate formed by José Antonio, Ruiz de Alda, and Valdecasas was established at the head of the new organization.[88]

Ramiro Ledesma Ramos, when trying to identify the features of the new political organization Falange Española, characterizes the inspiration behind it as "openly Fascist; that is to say, the organization aimed to achieve in Spain a victory analogous to those of Italy and Germany,"[89] reminding us that "the first enlistments to the Falange, which arrived in considerable numbers, were not to the Falange itself, but were to Fascism, which in that year, 1933, was of interest to a large part of Spanish public opinion."[90] Falange Española embodied "the ideas, the rites, and the label of Fascism."[91]

In August 1933, García Valdecasas, José Antonio, and Ruiz de Alda met with Ramiro Ledesma Ramos in the presence of José María de Areilza and discussed with him the initiative of "organizing a Fascist force," according to Ramiro's account in his book *¿Fascismo en España?* Although this meeting with Ramiro ended without an agreement, one would be reached half a year later, on February 13th, between the already constituted Falange Española and the *older*—they had begun their political

---

[88] Eliseo García del Moral, "Cómo conocí a José Antonio," in *José Antonio, fundador y primer Jefe de la Falange*, 144–145.

[89] Ledesma Ramos, *¿Fascismo en España?*, 137.

[90] Ibid., 142.

[91] Ibid.

odyssey in 1931, a few weeks before the proclamation of the Second Republic—JONS.

Valdecasas had already pointed out, on October 8th, to his fellow member of the Frente, García del Moral, that for the new political organization in the making, it was necessary to find a proper name, whose initials would have had to coincide with those of the Frente. Taking a look at the dictionary, García found several words with political significance whose first letters matched the ones necessary. On October 11th, after dinner, they met at the residence of the aviator Julio Ruiz de Alda, with José Antonio, Commander Rodríguez Tarduchy, Manuel Valdés, and Román Ayza y Peláez. At first, they all seemed to be in favor of the already registered name of Frente Español, but when a new possibility was proposed to combine the term Falange with the denomination of Española, the name was unanimously adopted, and the congregation raised a glass of cognac in toast. The solution proved to be both fortuitous and fortunate. Falange Española coincided with the predecessors Frente Español and Fascismo Español and was the Catholic expression of the sublime belief, of eternal faith. García del Moral, originally a member of the Frente Español, was the commissioner in charge of managing the bureaucratic and administrative procedures of the party whose name had just been coined. To avoid inconveniences, they resorted to the stratagem of using the text of the statutes of the already existing and authorized Frente Español, changing the names and other significant details, which were typewritten in a private school located in Calle Esparteros in Madrid. The initials "F.E.," which originally meant Fascismo Español, could not be employed at the time, since the Republic prohibited the use of the word "Fascism" in the name of political parties and trade unions. It was not the only term that was prohibited by the repressive Republican legislation; the use of the word "national" in political denominations was also forbidden, and, for this reason, the Catholic right-wing group Acción Nacional of Angel Herrera was forced to change its name to Acción Popular.

The word *falange* harkened back to ancient warfare, to correct and orderly military training, and to a military way of life. The term had been used in the manifesto launched in 1931 by the original group who worked on the weekly newspaper *La Conquista del Estado*, directed by Ramiro Ledesma, in which he already spoke of "brave and steadfast phalanxes," and the same idea appeared again in some of the writings published in that same magazine when, in the July 27th issue, the following question was posed: "Is it not, then, legitimate, the formation of steadfast phalanxes, which would represent at this time a pledge to Spanishness?" In that same issue, readers were encouraged to join "the combat phalanxes of *La Conquista del Estado*." Even the hymn of the JONS was labeled "Of Our Combat Phalanxes." Likewise, the Fascist writer Giménez Caballero made use of the word *phalanx* in his book *Genio de España* in four instances:

With a precise Fascist sense, one of them when speaking about Mussolini and reproducing a section of his speeches, to praise the saints and the genius as divine phalanxes, to refer to the troops and militias led by the hero in triumphal march, like the clouds in the sky.

José Antonio ran for the legislative elections, as an independent candidate in alliance with the conservative and monarchist Unión Agraria y Ciudadana [Agrarian and Citizens Union], for the province of Cádiz, whose candidate list also included Francisco Moreno Herrera, Marquis of Eliseda, from Jerez, who supported Fascism, and the monarchist poet José María Pemán, among others. He had to leave Madrid immediately, to join the election campaign held between November 5th and 17th, which was not free from incidents. He succeeded in obtaining a seat for himself and Herrera in the new Cortes. Thus, the Falange obtained two seats. José Antonio reached second place, just behind José María Pemán.

On November 18th, an article appeared in the *ABC* newspaper of Madrid, written by Fernández Flórez, mocking José Antonio for the lack of retaliation for the attacks against the new movement:

To add to the absurdity, they make Fascism swallow ricin here.
The leading figure at the rally in the theater of the Cortes in San Fernando was the young organizer of the Spanish fascio. It is fair to assume that there were Fascists there. And it is known that Fascists, in Italy and in Germany, did not exactly use reason to calm the irascibility of their adversaries.

Well then: a criminal discharged his magazine on the crowd. And they allowed him to leave calmly and with impunity, while the naïve leader asked for his verbal protest to be put on record. If Fascism repays two corpses with verbal protests, then it is not Fascism: it is Franciscanism.

José Antonio, upon his return to the capital and having received the news of this disrespectful and vile article, gave through the newspaper *ABC* of Seville, in the issue of November 23rd, the following unappealable reply:

On my return from my election campaign in Cádiz, I was informed that *ABC* published a signed article a few days ago in which Fascism was ridiculed on the occasion of the tragic event that took place in San Fernando on Sunday, the 12th. It seems that the author of the article, with delicate taste, drew from the horrendous event and the mourning and distress of several families the comic effect of comparing it to a dose of ricin administered to Spanish Fascism.

Truth and justice were not served in that article for the following reasons:

Firstly: The rally in San Fernando was not a Fascist rally, but a propaganda rally for an electoral coalition; nor was the aggression directed against any Fascist; nor was there a Fascist organization in San Fernando; nor did Fascism have anything to do with the organization of the rally, nor with the security.

Secondly: The author of the crime fired on the public and not on the stage.

Thirdly: It has not been possible to determine the identity of the people behind the crime, who, if known, could have been appropriately punished. With this, public truth is hereby restored. As for the rest, the Spanish Fascists, without boasting, will take care of demonstrating that they do not accept, even symbolically, the smallest dose of ricin.

José Antonio Primo de Rivera.

On November 19th, Manuel Valdés Larrañaga presented the Statutes of the Sindicato Español Universitario to the General Directorate of Security for its approval, without mentioning its dependence on and affiliation with Falange Española. The statutes had been drafted by Valdés with the collaboration of Alejandro Allanegui and Matías Montero. It was initially rejected due to clerical errors that, once corrected, with the tenacity and vigorous persistence of the students, were finally approved and legalized on March 5th, 1934, when Falange already constituted a single movement with the JONS.

On December 4th, the harassment and attempts to overthrow the new movement by the authorities began, with the first confiscation of the newly opened branch of Falange Española, located in the center of Madrid at 10 Calle Eduardo Dato, on the third floor. The second closing order, by decision of the civil governor, would be carried out on December 29th, lasting until January 11th, 1934.

On December 15th, 1933, the German ambassador in Madrid, Count Welczeck, sent his government a report—"Faschismus in Spanien"—analyzing the Spanish political situation after the results of the November elections and taking the opportunity to analyze the active Fascist forces, among which he included the Falange, which was "only a few weeks old and under the leadership of Primo de Rivera's eldest son. The young Primo de Rivera is about thirty years old, a lawyer, intelligent, and a fine speaker . . . . Primo de Rivera has openly proclaimed himself a Fascist during the last elections."[92]

The December 15th report received a follow-up on January 29th of the following year, also titled "Faschismus in Spanien," in which he added:

The most valuable element in the organization of F.E. is the young Víctor D'Ors, who has studied in Heidelberg, speaks perfect German, and is the son

[92] Angel Viñas, *La Alemania Nazi y el 18 de Julio*, 2nd ed. (Madrid: 1977), 122–123.

of the well-known intellectual Eugenio D'Ors.

José Antonio Primo de Rivera, Marquis of Estella, plans to visit Germany soon, as previously reported. I would be very glad if he could be offered the opportunity to contact important party leaders, be received by the chancellor, his lieutenant, the prime minister of Prussia, and the minister of propaganda, and become acquainted with the organization of the party, the SA, and the SS, particularly in Berlin and Munich. Primo de Rivera already considers our Führer as his master and strives to transfer the ideological foundations of the National Socialist Party to the Spanish situation and condition.[93]

The structural core of the new Falange organization was under the responsibility of Julio Ruiz de Alda and his military team formed by Lieutenant Colonel Emilio Alvargonzález, in charge of the correspondence with the provincial units; the head and instructor of militias being Major Luis Arredondo, closely linked to Millán Astray, the founder of the Legion, who was assisted by his fellow soldiers, Lieutenant Colonel Ricardo Rada and Colonel Román Ayza, who took as their model the Italian paramilitary units. The person in charge of propaganda was Lieutenant Colonel Emilio Rodríguez Tarduchy, owing to his skill as both a journalist and as a military man; he had previously been the director of the publication *La Correspondencia Militar*. The three men involved had been active members of the Partido de la Unión Patriótica [Patriotic Union Party], a political keystone of Primo de Rivera's government, and ardent supporters of their comrade-in-arms Don Miguel, all of them concerned with the safety of his son José Antonio, the great promise of nascent Spanish Fascism.

José Antonio appointed a person in charge of the new organization in Catalonia, Juan Vidal Salvó, a seasoned man who, in 1933, had translated, commented on, and distributed O. Scheid's pro-Nazi propaganda work *Hitler y el Nacionalsocialismo*, a book that José Antonio read immediately after its publication. Vidal Salvó began his political career with the Lliga Regionalista, a conservative Catalanist party, and later joined the Unión Patriótica. He was a great admirer of Fascism and National Socialism. Vidal Salvó was eventually succeeded by lawyer Roberto Bassas Figa.

Luys Santa Marina, in his work *Hacia José Antonio*, writes: "We always called him that way [with his own first name], in the Roman way. There was no one who bore his simple, almost familiar name, now ennobled, like him. No surnames, no titles, like the ancient consuls and emperors of the legions: Fabius Maximus, Paul Emilius, Publius Cornelius, Caecilius Metellus. It was him, and no one else; it could not be anyone else."[94]

93 Ibid., 411.

94 Luys Santa Marina, *Hacia José Antoni* (Barcelona: Editorial AHR, 1958), 72.

The poet Dionisio Ridruejo, in his essay *Escrito en España*, leaves the following considerations: "Summarily, but justly, a historian will have to define Falangism as one of the variants or replicas of the Fascist phenomenon that flourished in other European countries."[95] In 1939, the Fascist Ridruejo wrote the following sonnet "A Benito Mussolini" ["To Benito Mussolini"] (*Vértice*, June 1939):

Estatua de tu propio pensamiento
[Statue of your own thought]

Roma de piedra firme y enrasada
[Rome of firm and flush stone]

Sobre el calor del alma edificada,
[Built upon the warmth of the soul,]

Dura al reposo y noble al movimiento.
[Enduring at rest and noble in motion.]

Pulso, atadura, corazón y aliento
[Pulse, union, heart and breath]

Que vuelves a la Italia levantada,
[Which you restore to the now-risen Italy,]

La majestad ardiente de la espada,
[The fiery majesty of the sword,]
La luz del trigo, y la sazón del viento.
[The light of the wheat, and the taste of the wind.]

Salvaste las columnas del olvido,
[You saved the pillars from oblivion,]

Tierras y tiempo dilató tu suerte
[Lands and time dilated your fate]

Donde aprende la historia su sentido
[Whither history learns its meaning.]
Vértice de tus días, roca fuerte
[Stronghold, apex of your days]

---

[95] Dionisio Ridruejo, *Escrito en España* (Buenos Aires: 1962), 79.

Y sangre fraternal, donde ha vencido
[And fraternal blood, where it prevailed]

La apariencia del mármol a la muerte.
[The semblance of marble over death.]

For his part, Ernst Nolte says that "it is necessary to consider the Falange as a Fascist movement" and adds a personal clarification, stating that "José Antonio's thought was inspired by the Catholic tradition." Stanley G. Payne, professor of contemporary history at the University of Wisconsin, considers the Falange to be the "Spanish version of European Fascism."[96]

The Italian Fascist writer, Nello Enriquez, is bolder in his evaluation, and believes that "Primo de Rivera grafted to his party veins of Fascist faith and veins of Hitlerian ardor. The two movements emerging from the reborn Europe gave life to the Falange." To transcribe what follows: "We are Fascists—says José Antonio—because we find our origins in the principles of Mussolini; we are Hitlerians because our faith and our doctrine resonate with the National Socialist doctrine. But above all, we are Spanish. The National Syndicalist state, corporative and totalitarian, is typically Spanish. It is not a building block of Italian or German origin. It is a Spanish creation."[97]

According to Professor Manfred Böcker, "the Fascism of the Falange and of its preceding organizations leaves no room for doubt. The Fascist nature of the style and ideology of the Falange is unquestionable."[98] He further asserts that "both in Spain and in Fascist Europe, the Fascist character of the new organization was undeniable."

This idea is also corroborated by the professor Santiago Montero Díaz—affiliated with the JONS—when he writes:

The Spanish movement has arisen from the depths of our people . . . but it is an answer to the same historical demands, to the same universal conditions, to the same objective requirements as Italian Fascism and German National Socialism. History, in its supreme universal unity, generates, through different channels, analogous political structures in the various national situations. Hence the city-state in the ancient world. Hence the Hellenistic monarchy after Alexander, or the centralized states of the Renaissance, or the absolute monarchies of Enlightenment despotism, or the liberal movements

---

[96] Stanley G. Payne, "Intrigas falangistas contra Franco," in *Historia*, vol. I, no. 8, (December 1976), 36.

[97] Nello Enriquez, *La Spagna Risorge* (Milan: La Prora., 1937), 165.

[98] Manfred Böcker, "¿Nacionalsindicalismo o fascismo? El fascismo español de la Segunda República y su relación con los movimientos fascistas en el extranjero," in Albert Mechthild (ed.): *Vencer no es convencer. Literatura e ideología del fascismo español* (Vervuert, 1998), 15 and 20.

of the last century. Also, the new forms of revolutionary nationalism acquired a generalization imposed by the universality of historical events, although each movement is aware of the particular characteristics of its own nation.[99]

That is why, in another of his lectures, he reminds us that "National Syndicalism was born with a generous and combative solidarity, established peer to peer, comrade to comrade, with Germany and Fascist Italy."[100] Professor Montero Díaz insisted on clarifying that it was "affinity, not identity."

Bernd Nellesen shares the same opinion, commenting:

> The Falange has never left any doubt that it regards itself as the bearer of the 'permanent values of Fascism.' Their reference to the ideas and external forms of Italian Fascism and National Socialism is evident. The totalitarian state they are creating, the ideology they want to base it on, proves the agreement in principle. The Falange stands and professes its allegiance to its foreign references.[101]

Nellesen justifies this affinity of the Falange with the ruling European Fascist models with the observation that, during its brief historical period of existence within the legal framework, no substantial criticism or discrediting censure was made of these regimes and doctrines, and for the double reason that, while the Fascist regimes in Italy and Germany were developing and achieving unprecedented social successes, Spain was simultaneously going downhill toward its gravest decadence. As a result, the Falange saw copying what was good and denouncing what was bad as acts of distinct intelligence, as well as faithfulness and coherence.

Ramón Serrano Suñer, Primo de Rivera's friend and, in November 1933, candidate for the right-wing Unión de Derechas [Union of the Right] in Zaragoza, has written that José Antonio created the Falange "under the pressure of those who wished to promote in Spain a reproduction of the Italian Fascist movement."[102] Several years later, in 1940, Minister José Luis Aírese, Old Guard of the Falange, with the proviso that the Falange had its own original peculiarities with respect to other fascisms, wrote in his work *La revolución social del nacionalsindicalismo*: "Fascism, National Socialism, and National Syndicalism are children of the same

---

[99] Santiago Montero Díaz, *Mussolini 1919–1944*, lecture delivered at the Central University on March 23rd, 1944, 43.

[100] Santiago Montero Díaz, *Idea del Imperio*, lecture delivered by Montero Díaz at the event organized by the Directorate of the School of Formation and Training of the Old Guard of Madrid in July 1943, 23.

[101] Bernd Nellesen, *La rivoluzione proibita (ascesa e tramonto della Falange)* (Rome: Volpe, 1965), 141.

[102] Ramón Serrano Suñer, *Memorias*, 473.

mother; therefore brothers, twin brothers if you will, but not Siamese twins."[103]

With hindsight, history professor Ricardo de la Cierva, in his voluminous book *La Historia se confiesa*, writes that "José Antonio already recognizes his Fascist ties, name, and talent." And he wonders: "If he was not a Fascist, what was he?"[104]

From the very moment of the rally at the Comedia, the form of greeting of recognition and affection, which was chosen by José Antonio, was the Roman salute —a raised arm, the same as that of all the European Fascist movements.

A month had passed since the presentation of the Falange Statutes to the registry for approval when the press organ of the new organization was published: the weekly *F.E.*, whose directorship was under the personal responsibility of José Antonio, who was also the owner of the newspaper.

On December 27th, an interview with José Antonio conducted by journalist Cecilio Garcirrubio was published in Toledo in the Catholic conservative newspaper *El Castellano*:

> For quite some time now, Fascism has been manifesting itself throughout Spain, adopting in each town and place a different name. They all had the same ambitions, although their tactics were different. They longed for a strong state, a firm authority capable of putting an end to social struggles and fratricidal extremism. Fascism was born here and there spontaneously, without any planning or preparation. That Fascism was a natural product of the land; it was Hispanicism irked by the anti-Spanishness of the political parties; it was the reaction to direct or subtle action; it was the consequence of Fascism.
>
> Those small groups, sometimes timorous and hesitant, sometimes courageous and daring, walked without direction or coordination, without cohesion or discipline. Persecuted like vermin by some, despised by others, they could not find a direction that matched the aspirations of all. There was the need for a leader, an intelligent mind, an austere, virile, self-sacrificing man; a leader was required to mold and lead that young, ductile, and at the same time rebellious mass.
>
> No one with sufficient capacity would step in at that time to take on the leadership of that national movement. Some of them were subtly showing their inclination toward the corporative or trade union state, but without openly committing themselves to it. This noble, gallant, and brave action had to come from the firstborn child of that great soldier and patriot who, in trying times for Spain, knew how to take admirable and, despite all his critics, rescuing measures. It had to be Don José Antonio Primo de

---

[103] Ramón Alfonso Lazo, *La iglesia, la falange y el fascismo*, 14, note.

[104] Ricardo de la Cierva, *La Historia se confiesa*, vol. I, 280.

Rivera—talent, youth, and energy—who, on October 29th, together with Ruiz de Alda and Valdecasas, assumed the leadership of the Spanish fascio in a public act.

Since that day, the Fascists have had their caudillo; since that day, their caudillo, although not with my support, has my sympathies.

Cecilio Garcirrubio: "What experiences are there to assert that the corporate state is better than parliamentarianism?"

José Antonio: "In terms of practical experience, nothing is more meaningful than that of Italy. But please note that I do not like to call the Italian model a 'corporative' state. The corporative regime is but one of the instruments that Fascism uses to achieve its great purpose of national unity; with it, it overcomes the class struggle and avoids the existence of political parties. But Fascism is much more than a corporative regime. It is, above all, the faith of a people in its collective destiny, the consciousness that forms an entity superior to all class or group differences."

C.G.: "From which political parties or classes will Spanish Fascism mainly draw its support?"

J.A.: "As for the parties and classes from which our Spanish movement will probably be supported, I will only say that, because of its totalitarian character, it can be equally embraced by everyone. Perhaps it will be the middle class that will understand it earlier, but it will not be long before it will also earn the trust and the enthusiasm of the workers. The upper classes will have to endure some sacrifices in the new state; but they will surely know how to accept them with an elevated national spirit and with the reward of the regime of order and security inherent to political organizations such as the one we defend."

C.G.: "To what extent is Spanish Fascism related to Italian and German Fascism, and what does it borrow from each of them?"

J.A.: "Our Spanish movement (which is *not* called Fascism) has in common with Italian Fascism the faith in the fundamental principles which I mentioned a moment ago. They are characteristic of everything that is characteristic of Spanish reality, which, in contact with those universal principles, will produce its own reactions and never an imitation. Thus, the application of Fascist principles to Spain will not produce the same effect as in Germany. Catholic Spain, that is to say, *universal* Spain, could never be racist, for example."

C.G.: "What about those political parties that sympathize with Fascism? Will they eventually join it?"

J.A.: "These organizations are brimming with goodwill and have admirable members. Ours has been fortunate to arrive at the right time and achieve the best results in the shortest time. However, given our shared principles, complete unification without humiliation for anyone will not be difficult to achieve in the near future. I strongly desire it, and I will never put the smallest obstacle in the way of it."

C.G.: "What fundamental social, political, and religious points constitute the program of the Spanish fascio?"

J.A.: "Regarding the social aspect: collaboration between the classes in the interest of national production; therefore, no struggle, which always leads to the oppression of the weakest class. Politically: consideration of the Fatherland as a unit of destiny with its own universal aims, and the establishment of the state as an instrument at the service of this destiny, above all group interests. Regarding religion, a Catholic conception of life that distinguishes clearly between the objectives of the Church and the state. I refer to the speech I delivered at the Comedia and to the 'Initial Points,' published in the first issue of *F.E.*"

C.G.: "The Spanish character—will it lend itself to the movement you are advocating for?"

J.A.: "Why should it not? Spain has carried out magnificent works, works of discipline. There are still many Spaniards whose lives are examples of self-sacrifice and productivity. The fact that we have experienced Spain in its worst moments of skepticism, laziness, and slyness does not allow us to consider it definitively decomposed."

C.G.: "Fascism can be generated by the reaction of another Fascism, by social struggles, and by the decomposition and ruin of peoples. If a moderate government were to provide a solution to all the conflicts and problems that Spain is facing, would there be any reason for the existence of Fascism?"

J.A.: "Almost every political movement arose out of necessity and has been generalized for the sake of convenience. That which in the original people is produced by tragic circumstances in other peoples can enter without the need for tragedy, perhaps precisely because of its effectiveness in avoiding the same tragedy. Specifically, Spain has a history of adopting political transformations almost reflexively, without any need for great turmoil. That is why I am confident that the new state we want will soon arrive. Apart from that, there is no possible solution; that is why imagining that it would adopt another political tendency seems to me to be, simply, a dialectical game."

C.G.: "Many people are afraid of Fascism because they believe it represents the absolute negation of freedom and of the individual."

J.A.: "Those who do not understand the idea are frightened. It surpasses all other political structures in its profound respect for human freedom and its role as the guardian of eternal values. The affirmation of the individual spirit will be not only permitted but encouraged. What is inadmissible is this misconception of political freedom that allows everyone to freely enjoy the activity of undermining the foundations of public coexistence. There can be no freedom for blasphemy, for treason, nor for the poisoning of the people."[105]

The Falange was born with Fascist style and symbols. Fascist was its salute, the Roman salute, with a raised arm: a solar and imperial salute. Fascist would be its uniform, the blue denim shirt, which, from October 6th, 1934, was adopted as the clothing of the militants and the shroud of their fallen. Fascist was its revolutionary flag, raised defiantly, red and black. Fascist were the arrows and the yoke, the emblem and the insignia, embroidered in red next to the beating hearts of the militants. Fascist were its slogans, its rules, its order, its respect, its conduct, its style, and its way of being. Fascist were its militias of blood and effort, of reunion and protection, of defense and combat. Fascist were its rallies, its framing, its alignment, its centuries, its phalanxes, and its squadrons. Fascist was the cult of the fallen, the cry that rang like thunder reverberating in the sky, the final voice of contained rage, of lasting remembrance, of shared militancy. The Italian Fascists, just as those of the Romanian Iron Guard, also bid farewell to their dead when their names were called, with the cry "Present!" Fascist was its conception of a totalitarian state. Fascist were its principles, the foundation of its doctrine. Fascist were its pamphlets. Fascist was its press. Fascist were its hymns, marches, and songs. Fascist was its mysticism. Fascist was its dialectics. Fascist was its sense of mission. Fascist was its service and sacrifice, offered on the altar of the fatherland. Fascist were its European comrades—and antifascist its enemies.

---

[105] José Luis Jerez Riesco, *Falange Imperial (Crónica de la Falange Toledana)* (Madrid: Fuerza Nueva Editorial, 1998), 74ff.

As the poet sings:

Y si Roma impusiera sus dictados
[And if Rome were to impose its decrees]

Y el ímpetu sin par de sus legiones
[And the unparalleled strength of its legions]

Sus más brillantes héroes y soldados
[Its greatest heroes and soldiers]

Llevaron, por designio de los hados.
[Bore, by the design of fate.]

Nombre español e hispanos corazones
[Spanish names and Hispanic hearts]

Y las piedras que dicen de su fama
[And the stones that testify to their fame]

Y el estro magistral de sus cantores
[And the masterful inspiration of its cantors]

Tomaron esplendores en la llama
[Shone forth in the flame]

De la España inmortal, que hoy se proclama
[Of the immortal Spain, which today proclaims itself]

Imperial, por romana en sus albores.
[Imperial, for it was Roman in its beginnings.][106]

---

[106] Eduardo de Santiago, *Cuando España renace* (Burgos: 1939), 83.

5.

The (Fascist) General Staff of José Antonio

José Antonio received political support from his closest collaborators. They were a compact, cohesive group of young people. Writers, intellectuals, and poets; dreamers; cheerful and committed military men. They were the *top brass*, the mentors of the movement. They were his advisors and friends, his most devoted comrades, his trusted people, his confidants. They were unwavering. They were cultured. They formed a generational intelligentsia of smooth speech and swift pen. They were young men who responded to the call of the revolution, thoughtful in their candlelit solitary places. A literary court of writers and aesthetes in the Italic style, all of them were fascinated by the nascent Fascism: Ernesto Giménez Caballero, Rafael Sánchez Mazas, José María Alfaro, Dionisio Ridruejo, Francisco Moreno, Agustín de Foxá, Eugenio Montes.

José Antonio's guard was made up, on the other hand, of military men loyal to the memory of their comrade-in-arms, Miguel Primo de Rivera. They were men of war with a strong sense of honor. They had collaborated in the Patriotic Union during the military directory headed by José Antonio's father. They were patriots. Filled with love for Spain, they came from the previous generation. Good and noble, tough and legionary, Africanists all. Chiefs and officers of the Spanish Army, they were repressed and expelled by the Azaña legislature. Lovers of order, of rigid hierarchy, they were disciplined, militant, concise, of impeccable neatness and strict morals. All were men of faith. They were always ready to step forward for any mission, be it risky or difficult: Emilio Rodríguez Tarduchy, Emilio Alvargonzález, Román Ayza, and so many others.

Let us proceed to give some brief biographical notes on the inner circle of José Antonio, which will lead us to a better understanding of the human environment around the national leader of the Spanish Falange, his squad of poets and his platoon of soldiers, all united in a single phalanx.

Ernesto Giménez Caballero (Gecé) (1899–1988)

He advanced the cause of Fascism in Spain. He always claimed, with pride, to be the first to introduce Fascist ideas in Spain. José Antonio awarded him card number 5 of the founders of the movement as a proof of his invaluable ideological and intellectual contributions.

He was born in Madrid on August 2nd, 1899, in 7 Calle Duque de Rivas. He earned his doctorate in philosophy and literature. In 1920, when he was twenty-one, he began working as an assistant lecturer of Spanish language and literature at the University of Strasbourg, where he met the young woman he would later marry in 1925, a girl from Florence, sister of the Italian diplomat in Strasbourg. At a very young age, he obtained the professorship of Spanish language and literature. His literary concerns led him to found and direct a biweekly cultural magazine, *La Gaceta Literaria* (1927–1931), an avant-garde publication featuring contributions from, among others, Rafael Alberti, who entered the editorial office with a Roman salute, and Ramiro Ledesma Ramos, who was introduced to him by César Muñoz Arconada. There they met in the same crypt where, in January 1930, during a dinner in homage to Giménez Caballero, and in the presence of the Italian Fascist playwright Bagaglia, the communist Antonio Espina placed a wooden gun on the table during the toast, lamenting that a representative of Fascist Italy was present at the banquet with the young Spaniards, which caused Ramiro Ledesma to pull out a gun and shout, while throwing a Roman salute, "*¡Viva España! ¡Viva Italia! ¡Arriba los valores hispanos!*" ["Long live Spanish values!"]. The magazine *La Gaceta Literaria* was published for over a hundred issues and played an important role in the introduction of avant-garde literary, political, and artistic trends in Spain, clearly orienting itself toward Fascism in its final stage. It should not be left out that "future Spanish Fascists such as Ramiro Ledesma Ramos, Francisco Guillén Salaya, Luys Santa Marina, and Juan Aparicio" all collaborated with Giménez Caballero in the magazine.[107]

"Out of the Gaceta Literaria," wrote Giménez Caballero in his work *Genio de España*, emerged the two spiritual groups that would shape the future of Spain: the communists and the Fascists."[108]

---

[107] José Luis Rodríguez Giménez, *Historia de Falange Española de las JONS* (Madrid: Alianza Editorial, 2000), 56.

[108] Ernesto Giménez Caballero, *Genio de España* (Madrid: Ediciones FR, 1932), 7.

He was a prolific writer, imaginative, enthusiastic, joyous, and restless. He was also a seminal poet, a dreamer.

He grasped prematurely the essence of Fascism, delved into its roots, embraced it with the passion of a poet, and took on the personal challenge of spreading it in Spain as the herald of good news. As he himself recognizes, "the most important thing for me was, perhaps, the contact with Rome."[109]

The Italian writer Nello Enriquez considered him a "most faithful friend of Fascism," and also interviewed him in Rome at the Regina Carlton Hotel at ten o'clock in the evening on January 22nd, 1937. Giménez Caballero had visited Rome to meet the Duce seven times since their initial meeting in 1927. He grew more and more fascinated by Rome; he was "in love with Rome." "Your doctrine captivates me; your principles and your revolution are the object of my continuous admiration," he told the journalist conversing with him, who commented: "By listening to him speak, I am more and more moved by how Fascism and love for Italy can be found in each one of his words."[110]

The first manifesto in support of Fascism he wrote on February 15th, 1929, titled "Carta a un compañero de la Joven España":

> The sheaf: That is, in our fifteenth century, the emblem of our Catholic and Spanish kings, the reunion of all our Hispanic sheaves, without admixtures of Austrians or Bourbons, of Germany, England, or France; with Cortes, but without parliamentarianism; with liberties, but without liberalism; with holy brotherhoods, but without a somatén.[111]

And he anticipated the coming Fascist and Peninsular dream: "Our Spanish spirit, arch-Spanish, of *hacistas*, of future *comuneros*, is already vigilant and will not die. It will be magnificently resurrected in future generations, in a future that is once again ecumenical and humane."[112] In his prologue, Giménez Caballero "invited all the young spirits of our country to prepare the Spanish resurgence—our renaissance—drawing upon all the authentic forces of the past and the future" and wanted his writing to serve—and so he concludes—"as a comprehensive Magna Carta for the young Spanish boys who want to feed their conscience with it, early in the morning."

That same year, in his book *Circuito Imperial* (1929), he recounts how he was impressed by Fascist Italy:

---

[109] Interview with Ernesto Giménez Caballero by Alfonso Paso in *El Alcázar*, September 22nd, 1976.

[110] Enriquez, *La Spagna Risorge*, 136.

[111] Curzio Malaparte, *En torno al casticismo de Italia* (Madrid: January 1929), X.

[112] Ibid., XXIII.

When the Fascist phenomenon burst into my consciousness after my endearing acquaintance with Rome, I found myself at a loss. I had to admit it unbiasedly. Like a family mandate, like an imperious gaze of obedience.

For me, the Fascist was no longer the abstract entity of a transitory political category, out of time and space, but a substitute for the normal everyday life in Rome.

His black shirt—the black of the imperial eagle, the black of the clergyman in the Middle Ages, and the black of the doublet of the Renaissance. It was the ecumenical, catholic, all-encompassing black.[113]

In that journey of 7,644 miles, he happens to meet in Rome Sánchez Mazas, who lived there, describing him in his *Circuito* as follows:

I could not be more glad to be friends with the baroque and fervent Sánchez Mazas, a man overflowing with literature, poetic leisure, and ideas as sharp as daggers. Along with his great character, he was somewhere between a cleric, a Florentine, and a sailor.[114]

According to Ernesto's personal account, Rafael would be the one he would discuss the Italy–Spain comparison with as part of his Fascist solution to the new political situation.

In this book, he conceives of Mussolini "as a Cisneros in the new Italy,"[115] whom he does not hesitate to call "Caesar," reaching the conclusion that "the population that does not find in itself a formula for Fascism true to its own is a controlled population, without character and without a backbone."[116]

Giménez Caballero was acquainted with the European intelligentsia of the young and promising movement. He often conversed with Curzio Malaparte— pseudonym of Kurt Eric Suckett—whom he considered "his Virgil." It was Malaparte who, in 1924, founded the magazine *La Conquista dello Stato*. Ernesto had exchanges of opinions with the poet and futurist Marinetti, dialogues with Cario Boselli, and interacted with Giuseppe Bottai, Minister of Corporations and founder and director of the magazine *Critica Fascista*. He was also received with cordiality by Benito Mussolini, Giovanni Gentile, Puccini, and Zuani.

Gumersindo Montes Agudo, a veteran Falangist, published in 1939 the first

---

[113] Ernesto Giménez Caballero, *Circuito imperial* (Madrid: La Gaceta Literaria, 1929), 49.

[114] Ibid., 51.

[115] [Translator: Francisco Jiménez de Cisneros (1436–1517) was a Spanish cardinal and statesman. He attained a great deal of power despite his humble origins, becoming a religious reformer, the regent of Spain twice, a notable cardinal and grand inquisitor, founder of the Alcalá University, and an enthusiast for the Crusades in North Africa.]

[116] Ibid., 55.

book on the history of the Falange with the title *Vieja Guardia*, which contains a prologue by Giménez Caballero and an epilogue by Rafael Sánchez Mazas, the two ideological aesthetes of the Spanish Fascist movement. In it, Ernesto is described in his role as a proponent of Spanish Fascism:

> Ernesto Giménez Caballero brought from Rome a Fascist emotion, a heroic warmth, that those rescued people managed to transmit to him. His Roman, imperial, Caesarean cry opened a wide path to the dream, and his Fascist salute with the raised arm and open hand was the first spark that awakened the Spanish youth from its lethargy.[117]

On March 14th, 1931, Giménez Caballero was among the signers of the manifesto published in *La Conquista del Estado*, "a typically Fascist proclamation,"[118] together with Ramiro Ledesma, Roberto Escribano (the illustrator who gave the definitive straight and vertical shape to the yoked arrows that later became the emblem of the JONS), Juan Aparicio, and Souto Vilas. Giménez Caballero was one of those *gallos de marzo* [March roosters] crowing in the new Fascist dawn.

In 1932, he published the book *Genio de España*, the book that foretold Spanish Fascism and would become José Antonio's main ideological point of reference, as he told his comrades. In it he wrote that "the secret of Fascism was the eternal secret of Rome: The Universe of Rome. The sole universe of the world. It was a new universality. An ecumenism. A catholicity."[119] In this book, which had a fundamental influence on Spanish Fascist thought, the following is stated:

> Mussolini believes at first that to be a Fascist is simply to consolidate the political unity of Italy, a purely "nationalist" affair.
> That is why he said, in his first years of power, that "Fascism is not an export commodity."
> But by saying that, he was not appropriately serving the spirit of Rome.
> Mussolini had a better idea than to act with "genial" humility, and he recognized that Fascism was spreading throughout the world with a force he had not anticipated.
> Rome was on its feet once again. "And when Rome stands up, the whole world stands up," as an ancient medieval chronicler once said.

---

[117] Gumersindo Montes Agudo, *Vieja Guardia* (Madrid: M Aguilar, 1939), 28. Among Montes Agudo's cited works are *Hacia un Orden Nuevo* (1937) and *Fundamentos de una revolución: Arquitectura del Imperio,* with a foreword by Angel María Pascual and a letter from His Excellency the Ambassador of Italy (1938).

[118] Manuel Pastor, *Los orígenes del fascismo en España* (Madrid: Tucar Ediciones, 1975), 77.

[119] Ibid., 188.

In the face of communism and liberalism, in the face of the negation of the individual and the overvaluation of the individual, Rome has once again synthesized in history its eternal tradition—the Eternal City—its spirit of integration, of corporatism, of hierarchy, and freedom. Civilization, *between* East and West: Christian, European, that is, universally Catholic.

This was the supreme mission of Fascism. That was the spirit he had to serve.

And Mussolini, after straightening up the weapons of battle, began to bend the souls of an entire historical humanity: the newborn Rome. The spirit of Rome, Mussolini.[120]

In his book *Genio de España*, he tries to solve that enigma, wondering:

What was—then—the magic secret of Fascism? Of course, the eternal one of Rome:

1. In terms of the economy, a corporative, integrating system. Neither pure capitalism (West) nor pure laborism (East). No leftism on the one hand and no rightism on the other. Only capital *and* labor, united in a superior unit: the state. Eternal synthesis of Rome! Europe and the world will not be able to live on the principle of exploiters or on the backs of the exploited. Neither a right wing nor a left wing. Neither East nor West: Rome. Sum and synthesis of the West and the East, of capitalism and Marxism: Rome.
2. Politically, Fascism represented freedom against Bolshevism, and hierarchy in opposition to capitalism. It defended the world from the monsters: the ego of capital, arrogant and implacable—the spirit of the West. And the mass of the proletariat, haughty and irreconcilable—the Spirit of the East.
3. Socially, it represented the eradication of all modern illegitimacies.

   a) The Caesar would no longer be a Jewish banker or a cigar smoker; the Caesar would no longer be a burgher, nor a sort of operetta kaiser, nor a Republican president dressed in tails, nor a medieval king out of a movie. The Caesar would be a hero—a battle-hardened superior human—a commander of troops and militias, of organized and spirited phalanxes.
   b) God would no longer be a bank check. Money is filthy and vile and deserves no more respect than all things which are pitiful and unavoidable.

---

120 Ibid., 136–137.

c) Man would no longer be a conceited, culture-obsessed ape, boasting of his superiority. He would be a man with a sense of his limits and dependencies. Neither socialism nor liberalism. No more bastardizing the sacred essence of work and technique, but a return to guilds, to the religious sense of technique and work. Everything in its place: hierarchy. And a place for everything: harmony, system.[121]

In his digression on "España y el Fascismo" he notes:

For Spain, the banner of Fascism is not the fasces, but Rome.

In Spain, the fasces existed before being pinned to the hat of an Italo Balbo. Our Catholic monarchs had it on their coat of arms: their bundle of arrows, instead of military and lictorial stakes. We do not need to borrow symbols.[122]

Ernesto Giménez Caballero considers Fascism a political movement of universal influence. The historian Southworth categorically writes in his book *Antifalange* that "it can be affirmed without hesitation that Giménez Caballero was the first promoter of Fascism in Spain. He knew what Fascism was, and in his works he achieved one of the clearest presentations of this doctrine."[123] Stanley G. Payne considers him "the first intellectual to espouse directly Fascist ideas in Spain," although "if Gecé was the first clear-cut Spanish Fascist intellectual, Ledesma was the first intellectual to define a relatively clear-cut Spanish Fascism."[124] He met José Antonio "dressed in a tuxedo, at the Ritz Hotel during a banquet with Pemán in 1932."[125]

In 1933, his book *La Nueva Catolicidad* was published, in which he gives a summary of the Volta Congress, which he personally attended, held in Rome in November 1932, and in which he unconditionally opts for universal Fascism, even outlining a plan for the national resurrection of Spain under the following premises:

1. A great nation: internal unity and expansion in the world at the service of an elevated and necessary undertaking of human, social, and universal character.

---

[121] Ibid., 185–188.

[122] Ibid., 226.

[123] Herbert Rutledge Southworth, *Antifalang* (Paris: Ruedo Ibérico, 1967), 63.

[124] Stanley G. Payne, *Fascism in Spain, 1923–1977* (Madison: University of Wisconsin Press, 1999), 51 and 55.

[125] Interview with Ernesto Giménez Caballero by Alfonso Paso, in *El Alcázar*, September 22nd, 1976.

2. A new state: corporative, which integrates authority with freedom, with a trade union parliament, for the benefit of production and work.
3. Unity: political, religious, military, social, and cultural.
4. Tactics and institutions: Every movement must have a leader.
5. Possible organization: stoic and Jesuitical movement. Life as military service.
6. Empire: corporative and international, which seeks the triumph of justice in the world by bringing together capital and labor in a harmonious and creative peace (Rome).

In the weekly *F.E.*, directed by José Antonio (from December 1933 to July 1934), he wrote a series of articles, installments in a larger essay, "España y Roma," in which he sings the praises of Fascism as an imperial and regenerative idea for the world.

When, in May 1934, the inspector of the Committees of Action for the Universality of Rome— CAUR—Dr. Guido Ferruccio Cabalzar, visited Spain in order to establish the Madrid branch of the CAUR, Giménez Caballero was appointed "representative of the Committee, with the task of keeping contacts with Rome both for the formation and for the operation of the Committee itself."[126] The Italian ambassador noted in his report that Gecé was "one hundred percent Fascist, very loyal to Italy and to the Duce." The Italian journalist Cesare A. Gullino was appointed trustee coordinator of the CAUR in Madrid.

In that year, the monthly magazine *Roma Universa*, the official publication of the CAUR, in issue 9/10, published an article by Giménez Caballero with the title "Fascismo español, José Antonio Primo de Rivera," which was also incorporated into the chapter of the second edition of his work *La Nueva Catolicidad*, published in November 1933.

Being unable to attend the meeting of the Congress in Montreux (December 16th and 17th, 1934) organized by the CAUR, to which he was personally invited, he sent a written statement of his "support for the work of the Congress." It was Giménez Caballero who said: "to the astonishment of Europe, Spain raises its hand to salute Rome."

In February 1935, when the Spanish Nobel laureate for literature Jacinto Benavente was appointed to occupy the honorary presidency of the CAUR, Giménez Caballero took over the General Secretariat of the CAUR in Madrid.

In his book *Arte y Estado* (1935), perhaps without intending to do so, he gives us some interpretive keys to his contribution to the Fascist ideology, stating that there has been no Christ without his St. John the Baptist, only for the world and history to forget the Baptist and leave to the Redeemer alone the absolute paternity:

---

[126] Ambassador Guariglia in his "Appunto sulla missione Cabalzar in Spagna" ["Note on the Cabalzar Mission in Spain"], June 23rd, 1934. A.C.S. Minculpop, 423.

And in the beginning was the Word. The herald. The Baptist. The Word.

The Baptist is the water of life. He is the fire of life. The elemental.

Bound to these two primordial elements of the world—water and fire —is the symbol of the Baptist . . . . St. John the Baptist was one of those solitary, hallucinating visionaries, with his girded and lean flanks of an ascetic, whose nourishment was locusts and whose dress was the hides of a wandering shepherd. He was preaching a new world, a golden age, a messianic era: a savior.[127]

Giménez Caballero was, without a doubt, the herald, the water, the fire, the hermit, the Robinson Crusoe, the visionary, the poet of Fascism as a new coinage, as an ideological revelation, as an idea-force, as spirituality, and as an unveiled secret.

On March 11th, 1935, the provincial chief in Salamanca of the Falange Española de las JONS sent four letters to José Antonio: "To urge on your authorization in order to organize a lecture by Giménez Caballero on Sunday the 24th, arranged by the SEU, together with the screening of the film *Camisas Negras* [*Blackshirts*]. I personally consider it beneficial for the movement." José Antonio's response did not take long, and on March 13th, by letter, the reply of the national chief was received in Salamanca: "There is no objection to the screening of the film *Camisas Negras*, along with Giménez Caballero's lecture."[128]

In the last months of his life, José Antonio sent to him from the prison in Alicante a letter dated July 12th, 1936, in which he expressed his fears concerning the implantation in Spain of a "false conservative Fascism," reflected in the following paragraph: "Another falsification that I fear is that of the implantation by violent means of a false conservative Fascism, without revolutionary courage or youthful blood. Of course, this cannot attain power; but what if power is given to it?"[129] José Antonio detested this "false conservative Fascism" because he unambiguously advocated a genuine and truly revolutionary and youthful Fascism.

In the words of Giménez Caballero, Fascism "was the true revolution of modernity, but also the genuine expression of a Latin and Catholic people that transcended materialism and artificiality, elevating popular culture and national atmosphere to a violent and transcendental mission."[130]

---

[127] Ernesto Giménez Caballero, *Arte y Estado* (Madrid, 1935), 188–189.

[128] Bravo, *José Antonio, El hombre, el Jefe, el camarada*, 228 and 230. The letters from Francisco Bravo to José Antonio on March 11th, 1935, and his reply on March 13th, 1935, are reproduced in their entirety in the book.

[129] Ibid., 136. It reproduces in its entirety the letter sent by José Antonio to Ernesto Giménez Caballero from the Alicante Prison on July 12th, 1936.

[130] Payne, *Fascism in Spain, 1923–1977*, 53.

Rafael Sánchez Mazas (1894–1966)

His was membership card number 4 of Falange Española de las JONS. He was born in Madrid in 1894 and died there in 1966. A poet of extraordinary discoveries, a classicist, he was endowed with a proverbial inspiration and a sensibility translated into words. He was a master of Spanish letters, an intellectual of great stature; he had the gift of the written word—exact, vibrant, poetic, and intoxicating.

He spent his youth in the Basque country, studying with the Jesuits of Orduña. He was part of the so-called Escuela Romana del Pirineo [Roman School of the Pyrenees], a creation of Ramón de Basterra, which formed around the magazine *Hermes*, published in Bilbao (1915–1922). He later graduated with a degree in law from the University of El Escorial.

In his role as correspondent for *ABC* in Rome, he was the spearhead of Italian Fascism in Spain. From there, he sent enthusiastic reports of the new dawn in Italy and the Duce that he titled "Italia a paso Gentil" [Italy at a Gentle Pace] (1923), displaying without reserve his most overt sympathies for the Fascist doctrine and regime. He was captivated by Fascist ideology from the start. His columns were literary, vibrant, and emotional. The newspaper *ABC*, on August 16th, 1922, published the column "Mussolini con el fascio de Roma" [Mussolini with the Fasces of Rome], in which he writes:

> The Duce stands up to speak. The polemic speech, sharp and precise, and the transfiguring and canonizing fit of images in the style of d'Annunzio are not unfamiliar to him . . . . Listeners remain inebriated and immersed in an ancient illusion. The leader does not deliver cold and predictable orders. The leader, against a background of spears and funeral banners, has come to rekindle in its mournful men the glory of a "plus ultra" of fire.

In another of his columns, he went on to say about Fascism: "In the heart and in the program of the party is written in Catholic letters the name of God."[131] In the opinion of Sánchez Mazas, the Italian Duce was certainly "the most original and interesting politician of this time. His revolution and his dictatorship are a model" (*ABC*, April 15th, 1923).

His first book, published in April 1932, bears the title *La política religiosa: España-Vaticano, Encuentros con el capuchino*, written under the pseudonym of Persiles. In it, he gives testimony of Fascism's seizure of power in Italy; it was withdrawn from sale by order of the ecclesial hierarchy.

Sánchez Mazas can be considered one of the closest and most intimate friends of José Antonio, whom he accompanied during his trips to Italy and introduced to

---

[131] *ABC*, January 7th, 1923.

the Italian representatives. José Antonio regards him as "the first intellectual" of the movement. Eugenio Montes would say of him in a letter dated February 14th, 1939, upon learning of his passing due to being executed by the reds:

> The first in theory had to be also the first in the accomplishments of suffering, risking, and fortitude; it had to be one hardened by sun, rain, dew, and adversities that would have put an end to anyone who had been anything less than a real man, like him.
>
> He was in the Madrid prison with José Antonio, who had him by his side when the Falange was not even yet born, when we were still looking for a name for what was then a mere platonic idea, an archetype, a scheme. In the prison of Madrid, the two inseparable friends, Romulus and Remus of the new, eternal, Roman spirit of Spain, collaborated to complete the doctrine of the Falange, in which he was the one who contributed the most, apart from José Antonio.[132]

Sánchez Mazas participated in the project of *El Fascio* in 1933, being part of its editorial board, as well as being active and diligent in the political struggles of the MES–F.E., suggesting to José Antonio, in the manifesto of the MES, the closing line with the slogan *Arriba España*, which would become, later, the motto of the Falange.

A founder of Falange Española, he was appointed on the day of its constitution, November 2nd, 1933, as study representative on the board of directors, in recognition of his role as the ideologue of the new political movement, as well as the bringer of the most exquisite and refined rhetoric to the Falange Española. As acknowledged by the historian José Luis Rodríguez, Sánchez Mazas "was constantly present in the party, always by Primo de Rivera's side, of whom he became the main ideological mentor. Secondly, he really identified himself with the Fascist currents, and with the Falangist press he set himself the task of shaping the images and attitudes of a Catholic and agrarian Fascism."[133] He was a member of the board of command of the Falange.

For the newspaper *F.E.*, he was in charge of preparing and editing the front page of the weekly, writing most of the editorials and the "Guiones," the two-sided columns that served as political guidelines and outlined the main slogans and lines of thought for the movement. In the first issue he writes under the title "Consigna" the following:

> This publication, under the sign of F.E., is the only publication of our

---

[132] Eugenio Montes (Burgos: February 14th, 1939). Reproduced in *Fundación, Hermandad y Destino*, XIII–XIV.

[133] Rodríguez Jiménez, *Historia de Falange Española de las JONS*, 159.

movement authorized by the command. It is important to underline this . . . . In our movement, where technique, economy, doctrine, and social discipline matter greatly, the first word has been of poetry, but poetry understood as the crude mother of heroism and satire to achieve a civilized and classic apex of edification and irony: eternal poetry of Spain, which today throbs and sings in us with its tumultuous rhythm of genesis, and which will not stop until it solidifies in a national architecture and becomes fluid in a resounding river of patriotic emotion—like the Tagus in Toledo —that plays his music belt around the walls . . . . And now, arms up and onward. *¡Arriba España!*[134]

In the first issue of *F.E.*, in order to explain that Falange Española was a movement of its time based on Fascism, he wrote a column under the title of "El más ignaro" ["The Most Ignorant"], published on the first page, to dispel any kind of doubt; he showed up the stupidity of those accusing the Falange of copying "foreign models" with arguments that did not leave any room for replies or rejoinders:

Also, "foreign models" would have included the plans of the cathedrals of Compostela, Burgos, León, and Seville; "foreign models" would have included the first sonnet "made in the Italic way," and the joyful arrival of the Renaissance in music from the lute of Italy through the battlements of Salamanca. "Foreign models" would include—according to the most narrow-minded communist nationalism—the magnificent conception of the empire and the seafaring charts of the explorers. "Foreign models" would have been in St. Quentin at Breda—to Manuel Filiberto of Savoy and Ambrosio Spinola—the battle plans of many generals in the service of Spain; "foreign models" would have included the rhythmic prose of Cervantes, or the philosophy of Vives.

A foreign model, according to the vulgar idolatry of the local "pagan" countrymen, would be the apostolic preaching, and as it would also be a "foreign model" for these people who do not want to hear about the Roman Empire, one day the Latin language and the local councils and another day the laws of Partida. *O mentes amentes!* ["Oh mindless minds"], as St. Augustine used to say.[135]

He thus presented himself not as a son of his place but as a son of his age—the age of Fascism.

It is curious to observe how the spirit and essence of Rafael Sánchez Mazas'

---

[134] *F.E.*, no. 1, December 7th, 1933.

[135] Ibid.

thought have been manipulated, replacing the term "Fascism" in his writings with "Falangism." A single instance will do as a demonstration. The weekly *F.E.*, issue number 5, dated February 1st, 1934, opened, as usual, with Rafael's "Guiones." The first of them referred to "Nuestros enemigos" ["Our Enemies"] and began as follows: "Antifascism is divided into two large groups. The first group is made up of those who say that Fascism exists and is an enormous danger, so all the security forces and police of the state must mobilize against it." In Rafael Sánchez Mazas' *Fundación, Hermandad y Destino*, edited by the Movimiento Nacional in 1957, they replaced the word "Fascism" with the word "Falangism," which is shameful. Rafael wrote what he wrote, without any complex or false syndromes. Rafael was a Fascist and, therefore, a Falangist, but attempting to erase what can be easily proven with evidence is an aberration. Subsequent censorship not only changed names but also cut parts out, as in the "Guión" titled "Agrarios" (*F.E.*, January 25th, 1934), which ended with the sentence "the countryside has given back to Italy and Germany the great virtues." It became, in the *Ediciones del Movimiento*, "the countryside has given back to the nations—since Virgil—the great virtues."

In the second issue of *F.E.*, he responded to those who criticized the Falange for following "foreign models" with a striking dialectic by saying:

> In times of great national trials, the best method, wherever it may come from, is the one that best serves the demands of necessity. And it was precisely the greatest precursor of Italian Fascism—the one whom Mussolini exalted in his famous thesis—who at the end of his *Art of War* implored, through the example of the first phalanx in history, the need to save the freedom and unity of the Italian fatherland against the barbarians by imitating under the banners of Florence, the doctrine and discipline of the people of the Spanish empire, which is for us, at the top of our own history, what is exemplary and our very own.[136]

On January 25th, he provided a summary of the "morals of the classic phalanx," which he summarized in three commandments: 1. Utmost vigor in tight order; 2. Utmost readiness and precision in all types of movements; 3. Utmost discipline maintained by utmost austerity. He claimed that the three principles of the classic phalanx could be summed up in one "unity of command," using Mussolini as an example: "Distrust of the rich parties. The Duce of Italy has been seen, in the cold autumn that preceded the March on Rome, wearing a worn-out summer suit. The Fascists were always poor but disciplined, like the men of the classic Falange."[137]

On Thursday, March 1st, 1934, in the eighth issue of the weekly *F.E.*, on the

---

[136] *F.E.*, no. 2, January 11th, 1934.

[137] *F.E.*, no. 4, January 25th, 1934.

front page, he published the following defense of Fascism:

> The pope has never condemned Fascism in Italy. He has referred to Mussolini as the "man given to Italy by Divine Providence." He has assigned chaplains to each legion of the Blackshirts. He has celebrated the social and religious benefits of Fascist legislation, from the return of the crucifix in schools to the moral elevation of Italy in all aspects of life. But Fascism has been condemned as anti-Catholic in *El Heraldo* by the young gentleman Gil Robles, who was nervous precisely after the unanimous emotion aroused by the Christian honors paid to one of our dead. The gentleman Gil Robles must understand that the anathemas of Holy Mother Church can never come from below or from such a low position.
>
> Between *El Heraldo* and the *Acta Apostolicae Sedis*, there is more or less the same distance as between the anathema of Mr. Gil Robles and the anathema of the Vicar of Christ.[138]

He was the author of the *Oración por los muertos de la Falange* [*Prayer for the Fallen of the Falange*] (*F.E.*, number 7, February 22nd, 1934, and *Haz*, October 12th, 1935), a dirge to be read as a funeral epitaph for the fallen martyrs of Spanish Fascism. It was also Rafael who drafted the oath to be sworn to the Falange.

He was part of the group of poets who composed the lyrics of the Hymn of the Falange, "Cara al Sol" ["Facing the Sun"], on December 3rd, 1935, in the Orkompón café, which would later be intoned for the first time in public during the rally at the Cine Europa in Calle Bravo Murillo, Madrid, on February 2nd, 1936, and, subsequently, in all the events of the Falange. Its music was composed by Maestro Tellería.

The symbol adopted by the Falange, the yoke and arrows, was an idea that came from Rafael Sánchez Mazas. In a conference given at the Ateneo de Santander on January 24th, 1927, on the theme "Some Images of the Renaissance and the Empire," he alluded to the impression produced in him by his discovery—in a square in Palermo, Sicily, in the tower of Castellamare—of the yoked arrows crest of the Catholic monarchs. "It evoked in him a series of meditations on the Spanish empire and the 'balance' of the pastoral (yoke) and the epic (arrows), considered as an ideal national goal by the lecturer."[139]

The text of the lecture was published in the *Bulletin* of the Menéndez y Pelayo Library (IX, n. 1, January–March 1927). "Virgilian shield of Queen Isabel! Let us fly, let us press on, let us plough, let us bend the bow with marksmanship, let us spur on the yoke and the flight, let us have a daily awareness of the furrow and the trajectory.

---

[138] Sánchez Mazas, *Fundación, Hermandad y Destino*, 92 (*F.E.*, no. 8, March 1st, 1934).

[139] Ian Gibson, *En busca de José Antonio* (Barcelona: Editorial Planeta, 1980), 38.

Among the yoke of the ox and the bundle of arrows, may you become our sundial, waiting for noon."

On November 19th, 1936, the day before his assassination in Alicante, José Antonio, already sentenced to death and awaiting martyrdom in prison, wrote a letter to Sánchez Mazas:

Dear Rafael,

I am only going to write a few letters, but one of them has to be to you. Our communication has been cut off since we parted ways, because while I received letters from you, I don't believe any of the two I wrote to you made it into your hands. May this one tie up that loose end and leave it knotted for eternity.

I confess that the thought of dying struck down by a hail of bullets, under the sad sun of the executions, in front of unknown faces, and doing a macabre pirouette, horrifies me. I would have rather died slowly, in my own house and bed, surrounded by familiar faces and breathing the religious aroma of sacraments and recommendations of the soul—that is to say, with all the rites and tenderness of traditional death.

But this death cannot be chosen; perhaps God wills this to end differently. May He receive my soul (which I prepared yesterday with a good confession) and sustain me so that the decorous deference with which I die does not contradict the sacrifice of so many new and generous deaths that you and I have commemorated together. And may God give you, Liliana, and your children the greatest things. I send you a strong embrace, Rafael.

José Antonio.[140]

As one of Primo de Rivera's closest and dearest comrades, he carried the coffin on his shoulders at the start of the funeral procession as the body of José Antonio was transported from the cemetery in Alicante to the monastery in El Escorial.

He delivered the following speech in Italian at a radio conference in April 1939, just after the end of the National Liberation Crusade, entitled "Oración a Roma" [Prayer to Rome]:

Rome, Rome, Rome: we greet you with a triple greeting as our mother, teacher, and heroine. Everything speaks of you in our homeland. Aqueducts, arches, and columns of Roman, Lusitanian, or Tarraconensis Spain; names of cities and mountains, of seas and rivers . . . . It was the young Rome, now revived by the Duce, that, in Italy and outside Italy, in

---

[140] Sánchez Mazas, *Fundación, Hermandad y Destino*, IX–X.

Eastern Europe, in Ethiopia, and in Spain, has turned into fresh and living matter the classicism of Caesar's style . . . . We see you joyful, young Rome, eternal and victorious, carrying on your infallible path. For the king of the empire, for Italy, for the Duce, the voice of Spain also cries: *Eia Eia, Eia! Alalá.*[141]

After the Liberation Crusade in 1939, he was appointed national delegate of the Falange Exterior (May 1939), minister without portfolio (August 1939), and national advisor of the movement. He later became a member of the Spanish Royal Academy (1940) and president, beginning in 1950, of the Patronage of the Prado Museum.

Julio Ruiz De Alda Miqueleiz (1897–1936)

He was born in the town of Estella, Navarre, on October 7th, 1897, at 1 Calle de la Zapatería, to a noble family. He studied the first three years of high school with the Escolapios Fathers in his hometown and moved to Logroño to continue his secondary education while preparing for admission to the military academy. He was an athlete, of noble beliefs, austere and formal.

At the age of fifteen, he moved to Madrid to prepare for a military career at the Iriarte Academy. He applied in Segovia at the first announcement and was accepted into the Academia del Real Cuerpo de Artillería [Royal Artillery Corps Academy]. He was first in his class and was promoted, entering on September 1st, 1913.

Lieutenant Ruiz de Alda was assigned to the Second Mountain Artillery Regiment, garrisoned in Vitoria, where he was stationed for a year. His second assignment was to the Mixed Regiment of Tétouan, where he assisted in the operations of Ben Arous and in the capture of Chefchaouen, the Muslim holy city, which was forbidden to non-Muslims. Lieutenant Ruiz de Alda's unit was the first to reach the fortified walls of the forbidden city. Among his notable actions as a soldier were his interventions on the battlefields of Mura-Tahar, where the battle devolved into hand-to-hand combat after fierce engagements.

He was promoted to captain in 1921 at the age of twenty-four. He worked with civil engineer Guinea on the construction of a waterfall in the Loukkos River, which was commissioned by Electras Tetuanies. That same year, he joined the air force, the most romantic and risky military force of the time, where aces defied the laws of physics. He earned the title of observer at the Academy of Los Alcazares, and later, in Tétouan, he was in charge of the airfield's organization, serving as the head of its workshops. He earned his pilot's license at the Getafe Academy.

---

[141]*Arriba España*, April 12th, 1939, reproduced in Julio Rodríguez Puértolas, *Literatura fascista española* [*Spanish Fascist Literature*], vol. I, 717.

With the assistance of Captain Aguirre, he began participating in photogrammetric work in 1922, drawing up plans of areas occupied by Kabylian rebels. In 1924, he provided aerial support and provisions to the encircled positions near Chefchaouen.

Julio Ruiz de Alda went down in the history of Spanish aviation for his participation in the famous *Plus Ultra*'s flight, an event of global significance. There were four Spaniards—the aviator Commander Ramón Franco, the mechanic Pablo Rada, the navy lieutenant Juan Manuel Durán, and the pilot Captain Ruiz de Alda —who, aboard the seaplane *Plus Ultra*, accomplished the feat of following the Colombian route from the air, crossing the Atlantic Ocean, and making the flight from Palos, in Huelva, to the waters of the Plata, in Argentina, establishing an air bridge between their homeland and Latin America in a flight without precedent, an adventure defying the winds and the waves. The heroic flight made all of Spain thrill.

At 7:55 in the morning on January 22nd, they started their engines and flew along the magnetic heading marked by Julio, making their first stopover in Las Palmas, after covering eight hundred miles in eight hours at an average cruising speed of a hundred miles per hour. On the 26th, the *Plus Ultra* took off on the second phase of its journey toward the archipelago of Cape Verde, covering the 1,100 miles that separated this island from the archipelago of the Canary Islands. On the 31st, they took off again, without Durán, crossing the 1,500 miles that separated them from the American continent, landing in the vicinity of Noronha in Brazilian territorial waters. The next stopover was in Pernambuco, 330 miles away. On February 4th, they departed from Pernambuco for Rio de Janeiro, where all the ships and aircraft in the area were waiting to welcome them. On the 6th they made the jump from Rio to Montevideo, where the crew was greeted enthusiastically by the crowd. Finally, on February 7th, they took flight for their last trip, from Montevideo to Buenos Aires, where the reception was overwhelming. They returned by ship, aboard the Argentine cruiser *Buenos Aires*. In Spain, the crew members of the Spain–Argentina flight were decorated with the recently instituted Medalla Aérea by King Alfonso XIII on February 16th at the airfield of Cuatro-Vientos, during the same ceremony in which General Primo de Rivera was awarded the Gran Cruz Laureada de San Fernando.

In 1928, he was promoted to chief of the Aviation Group, a rank in the aviation hierarchy similar to that of commander. He also served as president of the International Aeronautical Federation in Spain. He attended the International Congress of Aviators in Rome, presenting several papers that were approved and later decorated with the Commendation of St. Gregory the Great by the Fascist government.

In October 1931, he married Amelia Azaróla, whom he met while studying medicine in Madrid.

Ruiz de Alda felt great admiration for Fascism. As his uncle Pablo Alda writes:

In his soul the purpose of establishing a national totalitarian movement of a deeply ingrained popular character had emerged already . . . . During 1932, the most informed were already whispering that 'they knew for certain' that the aviator Ruiz de Alda was the head of Fascism in Spain.[142]

In 1933, he was interviewed by Giménez Caballero for his deeds as the legendary hero of the *Plus Ultra* by *El Fascio*:

The Heroic Spain

Julio Ruiz de Alda and his sentiment of what is Spanish.

Interesting statements on the present and future of Spain.

Giménez Caballero: "Do you think it is possible for the Spanish people to return to a national state that would truly unite them?"

Ruiz de Alda: "I believe it to be possible, though it will be a difficult, self-sacrificing, and laborious task. The people are still disoriented, and it will be arduous to restore their awareness of their true identity."

G.C.: "What potential strategy do you envision for this resurgence of national consciousness?"

R.A.: "An enthusiastic and violent movement, directed to the new generations and with widespread social support, bringing together workers and intellectuals. A movement led by determined spirits, willing to sacrifice themselves, so that it does not turn out to be a simple act of class defense or cowardly capitalism."[143]

El Fascio presented the perfect opportunity for Julio and José Antonio to meet. An unconditional friendship and fraternal affection grew between them, and José Antonio always referred to him as "my dear brother Julio." Ruiz de Alda was enthusiastic about the project of the MES–F.E., and in the Teatro de la Comedia on October 29th, he was one of the speakers.

On November 2nd, 1933, at the founding act of Falange Española, he was present, together with Primo de Rivera and Valdecasas, as a member of the Command Committee of the new organization, signing the act together with the secretary, in his role as president.

Raimundo Fernández Cuesta revealed, in 1939, a little secret:

Julio, everyone knows, was one of its founders, but what is perhaps not so

---

[142] Pablo Alda, "Su vida" ["His Life"], in Julio Ruiz de Alda, *Obra completa*, 27.

[143] *El Fascio*, March 16th, 1933, 13.

well known is how much he did for it, starting with the name, which he proposed to José Antonio, who enthusiastically accepted it because of the military connotations it carried, in combination with the use of the initials of the words that made it up, to form the one that expressed the absolute F.E. triumphantly . . . . It was also Julio who suggested the idea of organizing the historic demonstration (on October 7th, 1934), which, led by José Antonio, would drag the people of Madrid in front of the Ministry of the Interior the following day, to ask the government not to waste the opportunity it had to save Spain . . . . Julio was nobility made flesh . . . . His contagious optimism, his unwavering determination, his boundless generosity, and his open character of affectionate rudeness made Julio a favorite comrade and one to be dearly remembered for the rest of our lives.[144]

Ramiro Ledesma described Julio Ruiz de Alda as: "A leader of magnificent excellence. For a number of reasons—his profession, his popular sense, his serene fearlessness—he embodied a human type that everywhere has given to the triumphant Fascist movements the best contributions."[145]

In the first issue of the magazine *F.E.*, published on December 7th, 1933, Julio wrote: "We have succeeded in fostering a pre-Fascist environment in Spain thanks to the mistakes and conduct of the previous rulers. The rally at the Comedia embodied this. And now we are organizing the elements that have answered our call."

On February 12th, 1934, when the fusion of the F.E. with the JONS took place, Julio was part of the triumvirate of the new unified movement, together with José Antonio and Ramiro Ledesma. He was given card number 3 of the new Falange; number 1 went to Ramiro, and number 2 was assigned to José Antonio.

After the first national council, the decision was made to establish the one-person leadership of the Falange, under the command of José Antonio. Assuming the second position in the movement's top hierarchy, Julio Ruiz de Alda was appointed president of the political board.

He wrote an eloquent afterword for Benito Mussolini's work *Il Fascismo*, which appeared in April 1934, wherein, among other things, he affirms:

Primarily, Fascism is, above all, faith in the nation and faith in ourselves, and this whole, complete, and absolute faith is what ennobles men in their qualities of sacrifice and heroism. For this faith, we fight, we work, and, what is more sacred and more important, we die . . . . Fascism is too serious

---

144 Raimundo Fernández Cuesta, "Estampa," in Julio Ruiz de Alda, *Obra completa* (Ediciones FE, 1939), 6–8.

145 Ledesma Ramos, *¿Fascismo en España?*, reproduced in Pablo Alda, "Su vida," in Julio Ruiz de Alda, *Obra completa*, 34.

and profound; we may not agree with it, but we must recognize its human eagerness to overcome and its generous spirit.[146]

On March 14th, 1936, he was imprisoned, tried, and acquitted, although the government detained him anyway. While in prison, he wrote for the underground newspaper *No Importa* the article "La Justificacion de la Violencia" ["The Justification of Violence"], which was published on the first page of issue 2, on June 6th, 1936. The costs of publishing *No Importa* during the days of his persecution amounted to six hundred pesetas, which were paid by Amelia Azaróla, Julio's wife, who was arrested on her way out of a visit to the Cárcel Modelo after meeting her husband on July 28th, 1936; she was detained in the red jails.

Julio Ruiz de Alda was assassinated on August 22nd, 1936, when the Marxist mobs stormed the Cárcel Modelo in Madrid, where they proceeded to free the common prisoners and gathered in the courtyard of the prison the political prisoners, who were interned in the main cell block, massacring them like cattle with machine guns from the top of the walls of the penitentiary enclosure. The most important ones were gathered in a room until a militiaman read the eighteen names of those who would accompany him. He led them to the basement, and there a discharge of rifles finished them off; among them were Julio Ruiz de Alda and Fernando Primo de Rivera, José Antonio's brother.

Emilio Rodríguez Tarduchy (1879–1964)

He was born in Seville on November 4th, 1879. Julio and Emilia were his parents' names. His career was in the military, where he reached the rank of colonel. His house in Madrid was located at 3 Calle Marqués de Cubas, on the main floor.

He was part of the secretariat of General Fernando Primo de Rivera y Orbaneja, with whom he collaborated closely. In 1929 he published the book *Psicología del Dictador (Caracteres mas salientes, sociales, morales y políticos de la Dictadura Española) [Psychology of the Dictator (Most Salient, Social, Moral, and Political Characters of the Spanish Dictatorship)]*, which was dedicated "to my children, as an example" and published by the Board of Patriotic and Citizen Propaganda, of which he was part, and which had its headquarters at 52 Calle de Alcalá, in Madrid. The book was an exaltation of the life and work of Miguel Primo de Rivera, for whom faith in God, in his fatherland, and in himself stood alongside the two sentiments that most characterized him: his great humanity and his love for justice, with a reputable honesty and a kindness recognized by all. The work won a national award. The ten thousand copies of the first edition sold out

---

[146] Julio Ruiz de Alda, *Obra complete*, 212–214.

in less than a year, which prompted, in 1930, the appearance of a second edition, although this only contained the first part of the complete work. He met José Antonio when he assumed, upon his father's death, the presidency of the Propaganda Board of the General's Work, of which Emilio R. Tarduchy was also a member. "Since then I established relations with him, we sympathized, I adhered to his personal politics, and I never left his side for a moment."[147]

The journalist Julio Fuertes recalls that, between August 1932 and February 1933, Rodríguez Tarduchy organized a social gathering that took place in the Café de Recoletos, which was attended by the journalist César González Ruano, Giménez Millas, the García Noblejas brothers, the Triana brothers, Castro, del Rivero, Salvide, Captains Rivera and López Pando, Carlos Rivas, Samuel Ros, Fernando de la Cuadra, and the journalist Julio Fuertes, all of whom also collaborated with the director of the newspaper *La Nación*, Manuel Delgado Barreto.

In 1933, he published yet another of his books, the biography *Sanjurjo: Una vida española del novecientos*, written in collaboration with *ABC* journalist César González Ruano, whose dedication proclaimed:

> To the Spanish people, who loved, praised, and abandoned General Sanjurjo. To the Spanish children who on one day, far from the great beast of rancor, will sing the romance of the general among the prickly pears and the general behind bars. To the Spaniards of all political climates who fight against the opposing targets of opposing convictions, we offer this brief book on the life of one who, at the time of writing, is only a convict, who, like those unhappy lovers that are ruined and crushed by what they have loved most, was humiliated and imprisoned by Spain herself, perhaps so that behind bars he could love her better and more dramatically.[148]

He was José Antonio's military defendant in the case that ensued against him for "insulting a superior."

He was one of the organizers and leaders of the pre-Falangist groups of the MES–F.E. The underground organization operated from his home at 3 Calle Marqués de Cubas, where all those who knew about the new group went, some personally sent by José Antonio, others brought by friends and sympathizers:

> We followed the method of the triangle to get in communication with our people. Due to our clandestineness, it was impossible to know for

---

[147] Colonel Tarduchy interviewed by Santiago Córdoba in *Pueblo*, October 29th, 1953.

[148] César González-Ruano and Emilio R. Tarduchy, *Sanjurjo (Una vida española del novecientos)* (Madrid: Acción Española, 1933), 5.

sure the exact number we had. I assumed that it was a considerable number, while José Antonio humorously called them the "imaginary militias of Tarduchy."[149]

The secret meetings of Fascismo Español were held in his home, and José Antonio attened them as well. The idea of these initials was owed to Colonel Tarduchy, and its meaning, "*fascio español*" [Spanish fasces], was an expression of the unifying and totalitarian ambition of the rising movement.[150] It was Tarduchy who appointed several triumvirates in the provinces. He later recalled:

I remember that one day, before the rally at the Comedia, I told him how organized groups were increasing in Madrid and in the provinces and how they had a desire for violent action against the anti-Spanish and anti-Christian political system that was leading us to the total loss of our fatherland, so that I believed that he was the one called to lead them, to be their leader. I urged him to do something because I feared that if the movement started without a leader, its strength would weaken and it would be fragmented into isolated groups. He responded that he needed to first carefully study the experiences of other countries—Italy and Germany—and concluded that the system used in those countries would be suitable for Spain; this would always have to be original and adapted to our character and authentic tradition.[151]

He made arrangements on behalf of José Antonio for the founding act to be held in Burgos on October 7th, but eventually this idea fell through.

He was in charge of the organization of the rally at the Comedia and was responsible for the security of the event. All the provincial representatives of the MES–F.E. who collaborated with Rodriguez Tarduchy in the pre-Falangist period were present at the event. They came from Asturias, Barcelona, Seville, Granada, Lérida, and Burgos, for a total of twenty-two people. Because of the snow, a large group of Asturians who traveled by road were unable to reach Madrid. At the dinner that followed the rally, held at the Amaya restaurant, in the Carrera de San Jerónimo, it was Tarduchy who, by order of José Antonio, stood up during the dessert to speak, affirming that there would be no toasts or speeches "because everything had already been said by the men who were eloquently present at the meal, faithfully interpreting the emotion of everyone within the limits of the sublime," ending with a short phrase,

---

[149] *El Noticiero de Zaragoza*, October 29th, 1942.

[150] *Arriba*, November 20th, 1942, 8.

[151] Emilio Tarduchy, "Aquel 29 de Octubre" ["That 29th of October"], *La Tarde de Málaga*, October 29th, 1941.

expressing with his final words something that would become the norm in the Falange: "Now," he said "that we have this triumvirate that encourages and leads us, it is only up to us to obey with humility, which will be the symbol of our utmost greatness; with abnegation and exactitude; with a conscious and iron discipline."[152]

He was head of the first militias, and always first in line; José Antonio appointed him head of Social Assistance as soon as the Falange was constituted and included him among the members of the first political board, where he assisted in the work of the first national council. José Antonio issued him membership card number 8.

As a journalist, while directing the publication *La Correspondencia Militar*, he was persecuted, prosecuted, and fined by the Republican government. Under the pseudonym Marcos de Ysaba, with his writer's pen he spread a thousand ideas, which flew with wings across the four winds to reach the disoriented people of Spain. He was the founder of the Press Association, holding card number 19. Azaña officially declared him "undesirable," and the police carried out several raids on his home. On a few occasions, when these arbitrary actions took place, the partisan police proceeded to arrest some of his sons. He was assistant manager, with the prior consent of José Antonio, of the traditionalist newspaper *El Siglo Futuro*, from January 1st, 1935, to July 16th, 1936.

He was a member of the board of directors of the Unión Militar Española (U.M.E.) [Spanish Military Union], to which Arredondo and Rada also belonged. He informed José Antonio of the attempted uprisings in the military ranks from his privileged position in the shadow of this organization.

The war took him by surprise in Madrid, where he took refuge in the Chilean embassy from October 10th, 1936, to March 7th, 1939. Three of his four sons were killed the same day in the vicinity of his home, in the first months of the war. When she was freed, his honorable wife Soledad de la Puente, who had taken refuge with him in the Chilean embassy, was unable to get over the loss of her three sons, who had been brutally murdered, and passed away from anguish, sorrow, and pain. Years later, Emilio got married again to another exemplary woman and great patriot, the nurse Amelia Pozuelo Villarreal.

In a conference on "Nociones del arte de Mandar aplicadas a la Falange" [Notions on the Art of Command Applied to the Falange], the infantry colonel and comrade Tarduchy stated:

Before the March on Rome, Mussolini, in a statement to the Neapolitan paper *Il Mattino*, affirmed: "Fascism is something else—there is no difference between the party member of the past and the political soldier of today; there is an abyss. The members are, above all, soldiers for fighting and not for arguing." According to a German publication, "the National Socialist Party

---

[152] Julio Fuertes, "Apuntes para la historia de la Falange" ["Notes for the History of the Falange"], *Jornada*, October 28th, 1941.

gives the impression of being a troop; this is what definitively distinguishes it from any other party. The troop is a community of soldiers. The military foundation has been very active in this party since its inception."

Our José Antonio appeared to be filled with this military spirit through all the events of his political life, which came to override the influences that his profession as a lawyer exerted on his mind, leading him to the comforts of a sedentary life. Thus, he declared one day that "the religious and the military are the only two complete and serious ways of understanding life." "We must adopt a human, profound, and complete attitude before life in its entirety," he said when founding the Falange. "This attitude is the spirit of service and sacrifice; the ascetic and military sense of life."[153]

After the war, he subsequently became associated with the orthodox Falangist group, and some meetings of the underground organization Falange Española Auténtica were held in his house, although his loyalty to Franco remained unimpeachable. He held various positions of responsibility, such as head of the National Broadcasting Network (1944), national secretary of the National Delegation of Press and Propaganda (1947), and, from 1952, secretary of the board of directors of that delegation; senior chief inspector of Administration of the Ministry of Information and Tourism (1953); *ex officio* member of the national board of the Old Guard (1962); national advisor of the Movement (1955, 1958, 1961, and 1964); and member of the Cortes.

On January 13th, 1948, in the name of the Old Falange, he attended the inauguration in Majadahonda of a stone cross with the names of Ion Motza and Vasile Marín, comrades of the Romanian Iron Guard, who had fallen on January 13th, 1937, in the Siege of Madrid. The Falange and the Iron Guard were two European Fascist movements that, although geographically distant, were united by their ideals and by their blood.

In an interview with Manuel Pimentel, journalist of the newspaper *Pueblo* in 1961, responding to the question "What traits characterized the personality of José Antonio?" Tarduchy answered resolutely and spontaneously:

I must tell you that José Antonio never turned his back on the political and ideological currents of his time . . . . Of Fascism, for example, he primarily embraced its sense of national unity. The fact that Fascist politics had defeated regionalism in Italy appealed to him in a unique way.[154]

Rodríguez Tarduchy passed away in Madrid on August 29th, 1964.

---

[153] "Nociones del Arte de mandar aplicado a la Falange," lecture delivered by Colonel Tarduchy on May 18th, 1942, at the Provincial Delegation of Educación Popular, 8.

[154] *Pueblo* October 30th, 1961, "Declaraciones de Emilio R. Tarduchy," interview by Manuel Pimentel.

Ángel Alcázar De Velasco (1909–2001)

The first winner of the Palma de Plata [Silver Palm] of the Falange in Madrid, he was born on October 2nd, 1909, in the town of Mondéjar (Guadalajara). At the age of nine, he moved to Madrid, where he worked in a tavern and was able to attend the School of Arts and Crafts, located on Calle Marqués de Cubas, where he completed his primary education.

He had a great talent for writing, and all his youthful efforts were toward his studies. Because he lacked the financial means to continue his education, he became a bullfighter, joining a gang of gypsies who used to hang out at the tavern and even performing in the bullring under the name Gitanillo de Madrid. The help he received from Don Miguel Primo de Rivera allowed him to alternate his bullfighting with his studies. In 1932, he obtained a degree in philosophy and letters from the University of Salamanca, and that same year, he abandoned bullfighting.

In 1933, he joined José Antonio, Sánchez Mazas, Eugenio Montes, and the Count of Montarco to form the Falange Española, where he quickly distinguished himself as a very active and courageous member of the squad.

He was one of the first Falangists to become, in 1934, a member of the CAUR, the Committees of Action for the Universality of Rome.

In the middle of August 1934, in response to the rumor that a revolution was being forged in Asturias, José Antonio asked him to travel to the principality to keep him updated on what was true about the subversive movement's preparations. He arrived in Oviedo at the end of the month and was soon able to confirm to the national leader not only information about the uprising preparations but also that ammunition boxes and explosives were being stockpiled in the mines.

In Mieres, he disguised himself as a poet in the Athenaeum in order to be able to slip in among the rioters who were already on the move at the sound of gunpowder and dynamite. At the recital, he was able to report that weapons and ammunition had arrived at the port of San Esteban de Pravia in large quantities for the terrorist attack, finding out that they were stored in the warehouse of the funeral parlor in western Mieres, as well as how they were being delivered to the mining towns using coffins. He sneaked into the premises and discovered the whole operation of the revolutionary machine. On October 2nd, he left Mieres for Oviedo, where he sent a detailed report to José Antonio on all his findings.

When the uprising began, he went to the infantry barracks, where he volunteered and was assigned to guard the city's water storage tanks. His group was attacked with gunfire, forcing them to flee to Oviedo, a city that the reds had already half conquered. He reached the home of the Falange's territorial leader, Leopoldo Panizo, whom he found with the secretary and member of the national council, Professor Francisco Yela, and the three of them marched toward the headquarters of the civil government under a hail of crossfire. When they arrived at the government building, they were entrusted with its defense, taking up positions in a nearby house where the

Center for Castilian Studies was located, next to the Jovellanos Cinema, where they took up shooting positions to carry out their mission. In the midst of the storm of bullets, they spent the night of October 4th and October 5th repelling the attackers. He then reached two other soldiers, who took position on the Jovellanos Cinema's terrace, where they set up a mounted machine gun. There, he witnessed the two soldiers who formed the machine gun post drop dead. Being left alone to defend the site, he prevented anyone from leaving the entrance of the Estación del Vasco with the bursts of his machine gun, allowing the immediate storming of the civil government building. There he held out, in a demonstration of bravery and heroism, until López Ochoa's forces arrived and restored order.

The Falange prepared the documentation for the awarding of the Palma de Plata, the highest decoration for valor, bestowed upon him by José Antonio on October 19th, 1935, thus joining the honor roll of the Falange as the first Palma de Plata in Madrid. The awarding of such a high decoration was reported in the weekly *Arriba*, issue number 17, dated October 31st, 1935, with some errors that were corrected in the following issue, dated November 7th. It includes a detailed description of the facts and the decision to confer this high honor:

Roll of honor. Asturias. Dossier number 4.

The award results from the proceedings in this file:

I.   I. That, during the revolutionary events that occurred in Asturias during the month of October 1934, the comrades of the JONS of Oviedo, Juan Francisco Yela, Manuel Gutiérrez, Ulpiano Cervero, Ángel Alcázar, Juan Junquera, Fernando Cobián, Enrique Rodríguez Cuesta, Amadeo Álvarez , Primitivo Vallina, Salvador López de Rodas, and Celso García Tuñón, under the command of the then local chief Leopoldo Panizo, bravely cooperated with the authorities in the defense of the city invaded by the rebels, and they held out for several days, without faltering, at critically dangerous posts.

II. II. That the leader Leopoldo Panizo not only deserved the highest praise for the serenity and firmness with which he exercised his command at all times, but also, together with Ulpiano Cervero, he carried out under enemy fire the very dangerous task of driving trucks, occupying, together with Juan Francisco Yela and Ángel Alcázar, the Casa del Centro Castellano, in Calle de Jovellanos, during the fiercest moments of combat that were taking place in that site and held it from the seventh to the thirteenth of October with the two comrades mentioned above, under a relentless siege that did not discourage them from making several sorties in order to gather supplies and ammunition.

In light of this, and in accordance with the provisions of Articles 11 and 5 of the Rewards Regulations, the Palma de Plata is awarded to comrades Leopoldo Panizo, Juan Francisco Yela, Ulpiano Cervero, and Ángel Alcázar.

Early in November 1935, José Antonio himself awarded him this prestigious honor, personally pinning it to his left arm just below the shoulder.

He collaborated closely with the Falange in Madrid, and José Antonio appointed him national advisor of press and propaganda of the Falange Española de las JONS.

On July 18th, he was imprisoned in the Rinaga Prison in Bilbao, from which he managed to escape and reach Nationalist-controlled territory in the first days of August 1936, collaborating with several newspapers in liberated Spain and being one of the founders of the leading Falangist newspaper during the war: *Unidad*, based in San Sebastián.

During the events that took place in Salamanca, in the days prior to the Unification Decree, when the body of comrade Goya was being laid to rest, Ángel Alcázar placed on his coffin the Palma de Plata that he wore on the shoulder of his blue shirt, which had been pinned on him by José Antonio.

Together with Pepe Sainz (Territorial Chief of Castilla la Nueva), Vicente Cadenas, Vicente Gaceo, and other national councilors, he dissented against the dissolution of the Falange Española de las JONS mandated by the Decree of Unification of April 19th, 1937, and for this he was condemned to death on June 5th, 1937, after an extremely brief court martial. On July 18th, that same year, his sentence was commuted to life imprisonment in the Fortress of San Cristóbal and, later, in the Burgos Prison, where he was released after two years and three days after being pardoned.

Among the duties he filled after the war were those of head of State Press Control and founding member of the Institute of Political Studies, of which he was head of the press office.

He cooperated with the German secret services of the Third Reich while employed as a press attaché at the Spanish embassy in London during World War II. After World War II, he moved to Buenos Aires, where he arrived in 1947 as a correspondent for the newspaper *La Tarde*. He was part of the entourage of Eva Perón during her trip to Spain. He worked as a correspondent for the Pyresa news agency. He went by many pseudonyms, among them Adrián de España and Paul Walton.

He was decorated with the Order of Isabella the Catholic. He wrote twenty-four books, among them *Papeles de un falangista* (1936), *José Antonio hacia el sepulcro de la Fe* (1939), *Serrano Suñer en la Falange*, with a foreword by Antonio Tovar (1941), *Los 7 días de Salamanca* (1976), *La gran fuga* (1977), and *Memorias de un agente secreto* (1979).

Ángel Alcázar never concealed his close relationship with his Fascist and National Socialist comrades, neither in public nor in private. In his home office, he always kept a photograph of Adolf Hitler.

He was fully aware of the Jewish question, knew of their attempts to rule the world, and also was attuned to the hidden side of Freemasonry.

He wrote:

As Marxism failed to achieve a higher form of life, Fascism was born to provide a solution to society's and the spirit's fundamental problems—an effective, comprehensive, harmonious solution.

Fascism believes in sanctity and heroism, that is, in actions that have no economic motive, either distant or immediate. It rejects historical materialism, according to which men would be no more than mere spear carriers in history, appearing or disappearing on the surface of the waves while, in the background, the real guiding forces are at work; it also rejects class struggle, immutable and irreparable, which is the natural consequence of that economic understanding of history. Above all, it rejects the notion that class struggle is the predominant agent of social transformation.

Fascism, therefore, is a spiritual conception that emerged as a general reaction of the present century against the materialistic and degenerate positivism of the eighteenth century. That is why it is also opposed to democracy, which confuses the entire population with the majority and elevates them to the same level. It rejects the notion that a number, simply because it is the largest number, can direct society and govern through a periodic consultation at the ballot box.[155]

Ángel Alcázar de Velasco was a brave, valiant man, a Palma de Plata of the Falange, a poet, a sincere writer, and a Fascist filled with pride, as he writes:

Since the European war, two political systems have appeared in the world that had been subjected to a long and protracted gestation process: Fascism, Italian in its institutions and its origins, was universal in its principles and its spirit; and communism, which was born in Europe and took root in a people different from the European one, and which, placed at the service of Judaism, threatens to invade Europe, not only with its doctrines, to which several populations are already enslaved, but, what is more serious and alarming, with its political and social procedures and practices.[156]

When Mussolini and Hitler sounded the alarm, warning their peoples

---

[155] Ángel Alcázar de Velasco, *Serrano Suñer en la Falange* (Madrid: Ediciones Patria, 1941), 22 and 23.

[156] Ibid., 27.

of the incoming disaster and showing them that the catastrophe was so monstrous that if it were not avoided, the world would succumb to its own viciousness, they fulfilled a providential destiny and saved the eternal values of Western culture, which were in danger of perishing.

On October 28th, 1922, in Rome, the conquest of the world began, and not only for Rome but for the world itself. Mussolini stated it when explaining the importance and fundamentals of Fascism, considered as an idea, doctrine, and universal fulfillment. "Italian in its particular institutions but universal in its spirit, because the spirit is universal by its very nature."

When Mussolini, with divine reason—it should not be forgotten that the great man is one chosen by the divinity—rather than human.[157]

He passed away in Galapagar, Madrid, on April 25, 2001.

The Tragic Fate of the Spanish Fascists

José Antonio Primo de Rivera, lawyer, membership card number 2 of Falange Española de las JONS, first triumvir and later national leader, after a mock trial in the Provincial Prison of Alicante, would be assassinated at dawn on November 20th, 1936, at the age of 33, in the closed courtyard of the now abandoned penitentiary. In the place where he fell, holding a crucifix in his hands, struck down by the twelve bullets fired through his heart, a thick cross of wooden planks was erected for many years, a symbol of the martyrdom of gods and heroes. His tomb can be found today at the foot of the main altar of the Valley of the Fallen in Madrid.

Ramiro Ledesma Ramos, philosopher, membership card number 1 of Falange Española de las JONS, founder of the JONS, triumvir of the Falange, and first president of its political board, was arrested in Madrid on August 1st, 1936, by the militiamen of the Fifth Regiment, and was assassinated, shot at point-blank range, in front of the Ventas Prison in Madrid on the 29th of the same month, without trial or defense, at the age of 31, during a *saca* of political prisoners that the reds were carrying out.[158] Among these *sacados* was Ramiro de Maeztu, who was "taken for a walk"—murdered—in the small town of Aravaca, on the outskirts of the capital. In its cemetery there is a common grave, where the name of the great patriot born in Vitoria is inscribed under a granite cross, together with hundreds of other murdered people that rest in that graveyard of martyrs.

Julio Ruiz de Alda, military aviator, membership card number 3 of F.E.,

[157] Ibid., 36.

[158] The *saca* is the illegal removal of a prisoner, the *sacado*, from prison for execution.

national triumvir, last president of the political board of the JONS, and hero of the *Plus Ultra*, was arrested on March 14th, due to the Popular Front government's cronyism. He was imprisoned in Madrid's Cárcel Modelo and charged with illegal association. He was assassinated, at the age of 39, on August 22nd, when the criminal red militias broke into the prison enclosure and took the eighteen patriots whose names were on their ominous list, headed by that of Julio Ruiz de Alda himself, to unload, with impunity, their shots on them in the basement.

Onésimo Redondo Ortega—lawyer, caudillo of Castilla, founder and main triumvir of the JONS of Valladolid, membership card number 6 of Falange Española de las JONS—was arrested on March 19th, 1936, in Valladolid, and was first taken to the prison of that city only to be transferred later, on June 25th, together with a group of comrades, to the prison of Avila, from which they were released in the early morning hours of July 19th. He was killed in an ambush, at the age of thirty-one, under the gunfire of members of the F.A.I. on July 24th, in the small village of Labajos, as he was again on his way to Alto de los Leones de Castilla, where a page of glory in the history of Spain was being written by the brave squads of Valladolid. His mausoleum is in the cemetery of Valladolid.

Fernando Primo de Rivera—doctor, brother of José Antonio, and temporary national leader of the Falange during its clandestine existence in 1936—was assassinated in Madrid on August 22nd, 1936, in the Cárcel Modelo, in the same circumstances and on the same day as Ruiz de Alda and Dr. Albiñana.

Rafael Sánchez Mazas, membership card number 4 of F.E. de las JONS, was arrested and imprisoned during the National Liberation Crusade. He miraculously escaped the firing squad of the red militias in Catalonia. He is buried in the Almudena cemetery in Madrid.

Colonel Emilio Rodríguez Tarduchy, membership card number 8 of F.E. de las JONS, survived the National Liberation Crusade, taking refuge in an embassy in Madrid for three long years. During the war, on the same day, three of his four sons were killed when they left the shelter and went to their home at 3 Calle Marqués de Cubas, in search of some of their mother's personal belongings, where they were surprised by bloodthirsty red militiamen, who killed them on the spot. Colonel Tarduchy passed away in Madrid on August 29th, 1964, and his body is buried, together with those of his three murdered sons, in the Almudena Cemetery in Madrid.

Ernesto Giménez Caballero, membership card number 5 of the Falange, and Ángel Alcázar de Velasco, Palma de Plata, live to tell the tale.

6.

F.E., An Unequivocally Fascist Newspaper

The idea of founding a movement and immediately launching a newspaper can be dated to May 2nd, 1933, when José Antonio wrote a vibrant, energetic, and youthful manifesto against the falsely patriotic and deceiving bandwagon of the Spanish right wing and against the twisted and criminal left wing in denial. At the bottom of these manifestos, widely distributed in the streets of Madrid, one could find the initials "F.E." The idea behind these initials was the work of Colonel Tarduchy, and their meaning—Fascismo Español—was an expression of the unifying and totalitarian ambition of the new movement.

A series of meetings were held in José Antonio's professional office, attended by Ruiz de Alda, Giménez Caballero, Alvar González, José María Alfaro, Sánchez Mazas, and Peiró—the latter being the editor of *La Nación*. Everyone present excitedly voiced their thoughts and viewpoints regarding the newspaper in an atmosphere of enthusiasm. The most heated debate centered on its title. José Antonio, Alfaro, and García Valdecasas were in favor, from the very first moment, of *F.E.*, to be used as it was in those leaflets of May 2nd.

If the weekly *F.E.* were to keep the old and authentic meaning—Fascismo Español—it could have turned out that the national tension of the emerging movement would have been lost in a counterproductive attempt at imitation. It was Julio Ruiz de Alda who came up with the solution: it was necessary to look for a term beginning with the letter 'E.' Felipe Ximénez de Sandoval explains the name *F.E.* as follows:

The name chosen by José Antonio is clear and magnificent. It suggests what the Fatherland, battered by old and new skepticisms, most urgently requires: F.E. The interpretation of the two capitalized initials separated by a period, on the other hand, results in explosions of dread or anger at the two halves of Spain, incapable of a whole national feeling. The 'E' stands for 'Español,' there is no doubt. The 'F' has to stand for *Fascio* or Fascism.[159]

Only one month had passed since the meeting at the Teatro de la Comedia, when on November 30th, 1933, José Antonio, in his own handwriting, wrote a request to the governmental authority for the necessary permission, which was presented at the Registry of the Civil Government on December 2nd, to publish "as owner and director" a new political weekly whose name would be *F.E.*:

Your Excellency:

José Antonio Primo de Rivera y Sáenz de Heredia, of legal age, single, lawyer, resident of Chamartín de la Rosa (Madrid) and domiciled at 43 Carretera del Hipódromo, as stated in the personal certificate which he exhibits, falling under the tax bracket 1-, class 2-, number 142,386, issued in Chamartín on the sixth of last November, being in full use of his civil and political rights, respectfully expounds to your Excellency, that he intends to publish, as owner and director thereof, a weekly magazine of literature, news, and political doctrine entitled *F.E.*, which will be printed in the workshops of El Financiero at 11 Calle Ibiza, whose tax registration receipt is attached, and will have its editorial office at 10 Avenida de Eduardo Dato.

Accordingly, he begs your Excellency to accept the preceding statement as valid for all legal purposes.

Madrid, November 30th, 1933.
José Antonio Primo de Rivera[160]

F.E., the Falange's weekly magazine, was launched on December 7th, 1933, and its development was marked by a series of vicissitudes that required audacious diligence and a massive amount of effort and tenacity to overcome. The U.G.T. trade union declared a boycott and instructed all the affiliates of the Casa del Pueblo who belonged to the publishing section to refuse to compose and publish *F.E.* because they considered it a

---

[159] Ximénez de Sandoval, *José Antonio*, 136.

[160] José Antonio Primo de Rivera, *Escritos y Discursos. Obras Completas 1922–1936)* [*Writing and Speeches. Complete Works 1922–1936*] Vol I. (Madrid: Instituto de Estudios Políticos, 1976), 226.

"Fascist weekly." In the face of this opposition, on Tuesday, December 5th, at four o'clock in the afternoon, the editors of *F.E.* locked themselves in the workshops of El Financiero at 11 Calle Ibiza, not to write but to compose the pages on the linotype machines. The photoengravings were being made in the offices of the newspaper *La Nación*. Two hours later, the first page was ready with the new label, *F.E.*, thickly drawn and framed with a rectangular black border. The headline, in its presentation, was identical in background and form, albeit slightly more vertical, to the logo of the Movimiento Español Sindicalista–Fascismo Español, which had been used in pamphlets and flyers distributed throughout Spain prior to the birth of the Falange. At ten o'clock at night, in this race against time, the first five copies, which, by legal prescription and for preliminary censorship, had to be taken two hours in advance to the building of the civil government, had already left the press. That early morning of the 6th, under the deluge that raged in Madrid and with no taverns open in the capital because of the waiters' strike, those heralds of the new hope spent the night under the doorway of a building near the official center, which opened at five in the morning. The civil servant informed the soaked editors that he could not complete the process because, as it was a new publication, it had to be supervised personally by the governor.

José María Alfaro was in charge of drawing the layout of the weekly and of finding a draftsman to do the headlines and the small titles of the sections. This illustrator was the architect Víctor D'Ors, a friend of those gathered and a participant in their political concerns. The drawing of the small titles was based on some decrees of Carlos III that were on the table in José Antonio's office, who suggested the idea of placing the head of the newspaper in a vertical layout, beginning with the title of the weekly on the first page.

All the information concerning international politics published in *F.E.* and the commentary it sparked tended to reinforce the positions of Fascism and the existing Fascist regimes in Italy and Germany, effectively turning the Falangist newspaper into a propaganda outlet for the foreign policy measures adopted by the Duce and the Führer. As a historian of the weekly writes: "Such is the function of the articles on international politics in *F.E.*: to reinforce the propaganda in favor of the Fascist ideology. The overwhelming presence of Italy, covered with praise, and the sympathy shown for Germany and Japan are parallel to the systematic contempt for the democracies."[161]

Regarding the contents of the weekly, the American historian Stanley G. Payne makes a pertinent observation: "All doctrine presented in *F.E.* was completely parallel to or similar to that of Italian Fascism, and there was no criticism whatsoever of any aspect of the latter's policies or ideology."[162]

---

[161] Jean Michel Desvíos, *Le contenu de FE hebdomaire de la Phalange decembre 1933–juillet 1934* [*The Content of FE Weekly of the Falange December 1933–July 1934*], Etudes Hispaniques et Hispano-Americaines (Rennes), XIV (1 trim. 1979, 91–125). The quoted text is found on 122.

[162] Payne, *Fascism in Spain, 1923-1977*, 96.

Jean Michel Desvíos, who has studied the weekly in depth and published several works on the Falangist press, concludes:

> From Fascist theories, the Falange retained the essentials: the use of violence, the abolition of the democratic regime and its replacement by corporatism, the return to the imperial myth, and the establishment of a totalitarian state. To these, it added ideas tailored to the Spanish situation: the preponderance of Castile and the rural regions, the use—to the extreme—of the ideas of the "Generation of '98," the defense of Catholicism, and the leading role of young intellectuals among whom it has taken root. Despite a few differences, it is thus sufficiently in line with the ideological line that has triumphed in Italy and Germany.[163]

When everything was ready for the publication and distribution of the magazine, at six o'clock on the morning of Thursday, December 7th, the telephone rang at José Antonio's home. They were calling him at home from the printing house to inform him, all of a sudden, that the issue, which had not yet seen the light of day, had been denounced by the public prosecutor for the insertion of two unauthorized articles, "Julito en la Unión de Derechas" [Julito in the Union of the Right] and "Victoria sin alas" ["Victory Without Wings"], the latter written by José Antonio himself—although curiously, this article had already appeared on January 11th, 1934, in the weekly *Decimos*, published in Cáceres, without any censorship issues. The police showed up at the printing facilities to collect the twenty thousand copies of the print run that were ready for distribution and sale. José Antonio took a swift decision. He ordered the cancellation of the two articles and left hastily for the printing house. At five minutes past eleven, once again, and with the two articles silenced by the censor's grip removed, another five revised copies were presented to the civil government, with no further justifications for the seizure. They allowed the two required hours to pass, and then, precisely timed at five minutes after one in the afternoon, the Falangist boys went outside in celebration to announce their public appearance with copies under their arms. The cries of "*F.E.* is out! *F.E.* is out!" could be heard in the vicinity of the Puerta del Sol in Madrid, the main forum of the town. A group of communists, always on the lookout, caused some incidents. Manuel Gordejuela, who was walking with José Antonio, was hit in the head with a blunt weapon. Another Falangist was injured while protecting the sale of the paper on the street. The strength of the response deterred any hesitation. Not a single copy of the newspaper was burned or damaged.

---

[163] Desvíos, *Le contenu de FE hebdomaire de la Phalange decembre 1933–juillet 1934*, 113–114.

The following day—Friday—a second edition was distributed in the neighborhood of Cuatro Caminos. The newspaper embarked on a bitter and glorious journey from that day, December 7th, 1933, until July 19th, 1934, when, after fifteen memorable issues, its publication was definitively discontinued.

F.E., the Printed Exaltation of Fascism

Since its very first issue, the weekly magazine of the Falange, *F.E.*, has stood as the leading mouthpiece of the innovative and revolutionary ideas of Fascism. In the heading of the front page, over the title itself, a warning was placed that had already been pointed out in a September leaflet of the MES, titled "Consignas de depuración fascista" ["Instructions for Fascist Purification"]. It stated, as we have already seen, that:

> The initial success attained has sparked an appetite for speculation on the word *Fascism* among many elements that are completely unrelated to us. Let us all be on the lookout for these impostors! . . . Therefore, only those who have been approved by this organization should be regarded as legitimate Fascist organizations, and only that which has been approved by our commanders should be propagated as good Fascist doctrine. Additionally, we must exert every effort to prevent the masses who are inclined to join us from becoming confused by self-serving pseudo-fascisms.

In that statement, José Antonio claimed to represent the purest and most authentic Fascism. The weekly *F.E.* often opened its editions with similar advice: "Beware of impersonations! Beware of falsifications! Our movement is, above all, spirit and agility. Beware of the office Fascists, mere corporatists, without grace and without temper!"

It should be noted that *F.E.*, according to Sánchez Mazas in the editorial "Consignas," is already mentioned as "the only publication of our movement authorized by the command." This statement is critical because it validates the true doctrine pursued by the political movement, as presented and developed in the weekly *F.E.*

Next to the headline, a necessary digression by Rafael Sánchez Mazas made in a recurring and introductory section entitled "Guiones" justified the bringing of Fascism to Spain in the following terms:

> The most ignorant of those who, referring to us, speak of "foreign models," is the one who, calling himself a traditionalist and a Catholic daily communicant, fell into the most obtuse racism when claiming this.

From the very first page, "hierarchy and discipline" were already mentioned in bold letters in the form of adages. This was to be expected: *Gerarchia* was the name of an

Italian publication founded and directed by Mussolini, another doctrinal magazine of Fascism.

On the third page, Julio Ruiz de Alda explains himself in these words:

> We have succeeded in fostering a pre-Fascist environment in Spain thanks to the mistakes and conduct of the previous rulers. The rally at the Comedia embodied this atmosphere. And now we are organizing the elements that have answered our call.

On the following page there appeared a recurring section of the weekly, titled "Noticiero de España," which defined the position of the publication regarding recent political events, pointing out the solutions provided by the new ideology of the Falange. Here one could read:

> We do not like the term *right wing*. Right wings, left wings—innocent words that indicate the existence of a latent civil war. We are absolutely opposed to this type of dialectic. We believe in everything that is totalitarian, and only in what is totalitarian. We believe that the only political experience that fits in Spain is that of a totalitarian government that organizes in a superior unity interests, men, differences, ideas . . . . The only logical solution to the workers' problem is to be found in Fascism. Without the creation of the totalitarian state—that is, of the Fatherland that acts—there is no possible and decent way to overcome class interests. Democracy taints the issue. Socialism blackmails people with it. Only Fascism gives to everyone his due, in accordance with higher and eternal demands: those of the state as an active component of the Fatherland.
>
> We do not oppose mixed courts. We want to rework and complete them, giving their organization real meaning. We intend to achieve this by putting ourselves at the forefront of the only effort seen in history to solve the workers' problem. We relate to the effort of Italy, which on this matter, as on many others, has an undisputed primacy.

On the same page, in the lower right corner, the conclusion of Giménez Caballero's book *La Nueva Catolicidad* is reproduced, being described as "an excellent guide to Fascism in Europe and in Spain," and it is reported that, having sold out its first edition, a second edition is soon to be published. The colophon of the book is worded as follows:

> Spain—before the new Fascist Europe that shows its serene and radiant face, before the new Catholicity—raises its arm of acceptance to combat! The spirit of Spain was only fully realized in history when it

incarnated this same sign that today dawns on the horizon: under a Germanic Caesar and for the God of Rome.

The *IX Puntos Iniciales* [*Nine Initial Points*] of Falange Española, written by José Antonio, which are a synthesis of the ideas set forth in his founding speech at the Teatro de la Comedia, are inserted on pages six and seven of this first issue. They constitute the first programmatic text for the movement. Spain is defined as a unit of destiny in all things universal, and the "new state, by and for everyone, [is] totalitarian." This speech discusses, in relation to the individual, the foundations of authority, hierarchy, and order. The programmatic document closes with this statement: "Those who speak to the workers, for instance, of a Fascist tyranny, are lying; everything that is *haz* or Falange is union, courageous and fraternal cooperation, love. Falange Española, inflamed by one love, firm in one faith, will know how to conquer Spain on behalf of Spain with the spirit of a militia."

Page 8 of the weekly *F.E.* was devoted, in its entirety, to a special section that bore the title "Vida fascista" ["Fascist Life"], which was doctrinal, apologetic, and informative. According to Stanley G. Payne,

> *F.E.* did make clear the political and ideological character of the movement, acknowledging its debt to Italian Fascism, running a regular column on "Fascist Life" that dealt with Italy and other countries, and also reporting on "the movement," as Fascist and proto-Fascist groups were referred to, in various countries. Of all references to foreign lands, 40 percent of the space went to Italy, with entire speeches of Mussolini reprinted. France came second with approximately 15 percent, and Nazi Germany a poor third with 10 percent.

An article by Ernesto Giménez Caballero with the title "Año XI Octubre" ["October of Year 11"] stands out because, among other milestones, it commemorated the month in which "on the 28th, the March on Rome took place, and the era of Fascism began." There one reads:

> Italian Fascism has just commemorated its eleventh October, the eleventh year of the revolution.
>
> Its greatest achievement has been to coincide the holy year with the eleventh year of the Revolution. Caesar and the God of Rome have been brought together in this eleventh year: The *Mostra della Rivoluzione fascista* [Exhibition of the Fascist Revolution], on the one hand, and on the other, the blessing of the pope delivered from the Chair of Peter.
>
> These have been the two fundamental events of this eleventh year. The Holy Father has blessed Mussolini, a providential hero who has brought God's peace and glory to Rome, with his benediction. And Mussolini saw

in the Church a great source for the spiritual resurrection of Rome, an attraction for the faithful and romantic world that was scattered throughout the globe. Rome—with its domed soul, its maternal lap—successfully brought once again into history the meaning of this eleventh and holy year: the great politics of Fascism and the eternal ecumenical Catholicism. That is to say: "a new human Catholicity."

I already presented in my book *Genio de España* (1932) the evangelical formula that Fascism entailed in the face of history: "Caesar and God." To Caesar, what was Caesar's, and to God, what was God's (an evangelical and Fascist formula that has been masterfully unraveled by our prodigious lecturer García Sanchiz of late).

These two fundamental events of the eleventh year—the sanctity of the year and the greatness of the Mussolini regime—had a magnificent culmination: the Duce's speech, which announced the definitive establishment of the corporative system over the parliamentary one, the total and definitive dissolution of the parliament in Italy.

This speech by the Duce was one of the most transcendent and profound ever uttered.

With that speech, the Fascist revolution had reached, in its eleventh year, one of its most exciting, original, and sincere peaks.

There are still people who do not understand that Fascism was and is a complete and far-reaching revolution, and therefore of slow and methodical development. These are the people who confuse it with one of the phases of revolution: *terror*.

It would be good to set straight these confused spirits by reminding them of Mussolini's own words:

"Nobody can deny that this is what the profound revolution entails. The replacement of men, the transformation and correction of institutions, the renewal of spirits, the moral climate of the people, the works and the laws.

"The fact that a revolution is at work is demonstrated by the fact that the struggle for or against Fascism is being fought in all the countries of the world.

"So much interest would not have been aroused in the world if Fascism were an ephemeral phenomenon with no tomorrow; that it is a revolution is demonstrated by the fact that Fascism has faced the problem of the modern state in terms of its characteristics and functions. This creation of a new state, which is authoritarian (but not absolutist), hierarchical, and organic—that is, open to the people of all classes, categories, and interests—is the great revolutionary innovation of Fascism, and a lesson perhaps for the whole modern world that oscillates between the authority of the state and the prerogative of the individual: between the state and the anti-state.

"The Fascist revolution, like any other revolution, has also had its dramatic course, but this is not enough to set it apart from the other revolutions. Terror is not the revolution, but only a necessary instrument in a certain phase of the revolution.

"No Fascist should delude himself into believing that the work is finished or is about to be completed. It needs to be said that we will never have a year of rest. But this is advantageous because it helps to awaken and hone all of our skills. I confirm that rest is not permitted. Let us consider this necessity the greatest reward for all of our hard work."

Its eleventh October has been for Fascism a reward for its glorious toil. A new call has been issued to march no longer on Rome, but from Rome to the rest of the world.

In the weekly *F.E.*, a great deal of news on Italy and Germany was reported, concerning the domestic and foreign policies of both states and also their cultural novelties, such as the appearance in Italy of two new magazines, one of them titled *Roma Universa*, published by the Committees of Action for the Universality of Rome, and the other *Occidente*, both with the same ambition of being a point of reference for literature throughout the world. Due to the fact that news from Italy represented most of the content of the section in this first issue, the portion of news and information about National Socialist Germany was introduced with these words: "In our next issue, we will give Germany the coverage that its Fascism deserves, and the recognition required by the greatness of this nation that is undergoing its rebirth, and the dignity of Hitler, its leader." From the Netherlands, good news was given of the existence of a "Fascist movement of remarkable size, of which we will give an account in due time. Its leader is a young son of the people, J. A. Bears."

The ninth page of the weekly is devoted to a section titled "Lecturas propias" ["Readings of Our Own"], which collects articles by Falangist writers or from the Spanish Fascist milieu published elsewhere. In particular, in these first readings, we find an article by José Antonio, "¿Euzkadi libre?" which was initially published in the newspaper *La Nación*, and the article "Castilla en pie" by Eugenio Montes, extracted from *Acción Española*, which began with a suggestive verse: "El primero de Agosto, / cuando madura el grano, / se ha puesto en pie Castilla, / con un haz en la mano." ["The first of August, / when the grain ripens, / Castile has stood up, / with a sheaf in its hands"]. It was a hymn to Castile that has set the standard for the world. Pure, upright, and vertical, like the white poplars of Arlanza. Linear and heroic Castile, homeland of the righteous, of the right and the Right, sum and substance of normality itself. Rule and order, civility, and law are demanded by this agrarian multitude, this peasant humanity that has now flourished, purely ripe, in the season of grain; in August, a Fascist and fecund month.

The third article included in this section of *F.E.* was written by José María Alfaro and was taken from the newspaper *Informaciones*. It is titled "Voz de la Tierra y razón de la sangre" ["Voice of the Earth and Reason of the Blood"] and reads as follows:

The deed has been sealed with blood. With blood—with red blood—which is how history is written. And furthermore, with popular blood, yet barely differentiated from the soil, to which it has returned to merge—to blend in —its clots with its clods. Popular blood of Spain, shed in an autumn that resembles an overflowing Spanish spring!

The fact has been loudly reported with brutal simplicity by the press. As a rally of socialists was passing by, returning from a sad and pompous civil burial—I have never been able to find out what the "civil" cult of the dead consists of!—two young people shouted: "Long live the *fascio!*" The result was bloodshed—here where there has been so much talk of bloodless revolutions! One of them died almost instantly after being shot twice; the other, wounded, was also arrested.

And now, on the commentary. The deceased was twenty-eight years old, from Valladolid, and worked as a streetcar driver.

Death, therefore, took him while he was still in his sleep, in the middle of the dream of life. His blood, still young, has not been afraid to jump out of his body to become pure and correct blood. In his conscience slumbered the certainty of the efficacy of his scream, made into a living propaganda message, sewn to the earth by the lead of the two bullets that riposted the clear protest of his throat.

He raised his voice in protest. The man from Valladolid, a streetcar driver, was protesting on behalf of the land: of his Castilian land, which found a reason to be anointed once again with the captaincy of Spain, when on its soil the cards of betrayal were being repeatedly dealt.

And his voice was the voice of the people. Therefore, it was the voice of God, of the God of Spain, who promised new heavens from the steppingstone of Castile. It was the voice of the soil as well. The man from Valladolid was filled with good sense. In his mind danced the misfortunes of Spain. For some time now, everything was whirling in unreasonable winds of dissolution; everything was a game of destruction and treachery. The crushing machines erected on the Spanish soil were working relentlessly. The man from Valladolid, who had carried along with the waves of the Cantabrian Sea—the sea of Castile—saw his land being crucified. And he screamed, he screamed as much as his throat would allow him, with a cry in which he wanted to synthesize the whole world of his protests and all the thirst of his affirmations.

This was a man of the people. He was by trade a streetcar driver. The sense in him was blind and firm: the sense of an old plough that ploughs the land, or of a gale that devastates it. His spontaneous reaction sings the sincerity of his voice. Perhaps he did not know clearly, with the lucidity of a political theorist, everything that was in his cry. But inside him, in that pure inner self that led him to face death with the joy of its affirmation, hope was firmly planted. For his cry was a hopeful cry. A new voice of the people, who wanted to be satiated with the reasons of blood and soil. After all, these are the most powerful sentiments in history.

And this man from Valladolid, the voice of the people, was writing the history of Spain. In his attitude one could discern eternal forces. He did not know about subtleness, and that is why his voice became a shout in the street. His blood would give him resonance. He represented the new and ancient challenge of the popular and eternal Spain against the dominant oligarchies, which were dressed in the shady clothing of a devastating and sad internationalism.

There were also certainly, in this man of Castile—of Spain as a whole—reasons for joy. And that is why he fell happily, victim of the anonymous oligarchic hand, which, ignorant, did not realize that with his gunshot he was pouring out the eternal reason of blood, which sang the reason of the soil.

On this same ninth page there is inserted a review of two books, one by Professor Vicente Gay of the University of Valladolid: *Qué es el socialismo, qué es el marxismo, qué es el fascismo* [*What Socialism Is, What Marxism Is, What Fascism Is*]. The review is signed with the initial "C." The reviewer praised the professor's academic prowess, describing him as "an illustrious economist and writer of good letters." His commentary ended with this statement:

Gay's book, like many others in which the two triumphant Fascist revolutions are described or commented on, holds for the Spaniards, above the usefulness of the remembrance of the discovery in either case, the importance of bringing to the forefront the parallelism between the problems of Italy and pre-Fascist Germany, and this Spain of today, which in its continuous and obstinate political turmoil searches in trembling eagerness for salvation in a tomorrow already loaded with prospects of fortune and risk.

The second reviewed book is *Seis meses con los nazis: Una revolución nacional* [*Six Months with the Nazis: A National Revolution*], by César González Ruano; it was published by Editorial La Nación, released that same year, and subsidized by Fascists. The literary critic wrote:

In the greatest spring of Germany, César González Ruano hastened to fill himself with Gothic winds. The swastika rose in triumph against the orientalism of the hammer and sickle and the dissolving shooting of the Iron Front. *Seis meses con los nazis (una revolución nacional)* is the title of the collection of his experiences as a Spaniard on German soil during those frenetic days that followed the seizure of power by the National Socialists. Versailles retreated toward the dark horizon, and Geneva played tug-of-war over a lost card. Hitler, holding high the plan for Germany—just like his outstretched arm—was securing the frontiers of the Reich with a cross. Rome, watchful, proclaimed the good news. The Spaniard, in a collapsing Spain, gnashed his teeth, and his fists clenched as if they were the cry of Spain. Thus, César González Ruano, whose pen depicted the plans of Hitler's Germany, also suffused them with Spanish connotations and with references to our own land.

Seis meses con los nazis not only describes Hitler's first years in power but also provides a brief history of the German revolution by examining the situation of the National Socialist movement. It is thus a complete picture that González Ruano's pen brings to life with his Spanish character. In this writer, who possesses so many different virtues, swift understanding is perhaps among his best qualities.

I would like to end this very brief note in the same way that, some years ago, I concluded a sonnet that appeared on the cover of a book of verse by César González Ruano: "*Y el marcial arreo florecido en las Cruces de tu emblema*" ["And the martial adornment flourished in the crosses of your emblem"].

In the weekly, on page ten, the following books are recommended:

- *Qué es el socialismo, qué es el marxismo, qué es el fascismo,* by Vicente Gay.
- *Seis meses con los nazis: Una revolución nacional,* by César González Ruano.
- *El Fascismo: Sus orígenes, organización, doctrina, lucha y triunfo de Mussolini en Italia* [*Fascism: Its Origins, Organization, Doctrine, Struggle, and the Triumph of Mussolini in Italy*], by N. Cebreiros.
- *La Nueva catolicidad,* by Ernesto Giménez Caballero.

On page ten there also appears an interesting article by Víctor D'Ors Pérez-Peix entitled "Crónicas de Italia" ["Columns from Italy"]. It begins as follows:

Communism declared: May everyone get an equal share.
    Fascism solemnly announced: May everyone have what they deserve.
    Communism insisted that everyone be equal.

And Fascism expanded on the idea that everyone should be able to develop all of their talents.

And this clear and geometric justice of Fascism, centered on man and his possibilities, defeated the so-called justice of the East, which was a kind of new *lex talionis*, based on a bad algebra of class struggle, which attempted to reduce to equality the wealthy, fertile, unavoidable inequalities of the world.

Then the artists, like any other citizens, could ask themselves: "Why is it necessary to serve the state?" And they answer themselves: "Because the Fascist state is the Fascist law, and the Fascist law is the justice we feel." As a result, all artists, great and small, contribute to the creation of this *primavera di bellezza* [spring of beauty] that the Fascist hymn sings to us.

The section dedicated to the world of labor appeared on page eleven with the headline "Economía y Trabajo" ["Economy and Work"]. It featured two enlightening articles, two genuine pieces of the feeling and thinking by José Antonio and the Falange, which we reproduce here because of their significant eloquence:

AGAINST THE ONE AND THE OTHER

There are three internationals in the world: the communist one, which desires the destruction of Europe under an oriental and barbaric avalanche of massive proportions (Moscow); the liberal-democratic one, which aspires to the predominance of the purely capitalist powers (Geneva); and the Fascist one, which seeks the triumph of justice in the world by uniting capital and labor in a harmonious and creative peace (Rome).

The communist one goes against the freedom of the worker with its tyrannical laws since everything is absorbed by the state, which becomes the most intransigent employer.

The liberal-democratic one, by resolutely supporting capitalism, can bring little benefit to the working class.

Fascism unites capital and labor in brotherhood, valuing both the worker and the employer equally.

Fascism is neither of the right nor of the left, since, by bringing together capital and labor, it is a national movement without any politics whatsoever. There is room for the right and the left as collaborators for social welfare, far from the destructive international socialist methods.

F.E. does not want to imitate any foreign movement. It seeks to extract Fascism's universal values, apply them to the vibrant Spanish reality, and make it react in accordance with its own spirit. That is why it is against capitalism *and* against socialism, against liberal democracy *and* against the Soviet, against the one *and* the other.

The second article on labor and social issues, published on the same page, is entitled "Fascism and the Workers," and reads as follows:

> Those who have an interest in not letting the workers know the truth want to portray Fascism as the enemy of the working class. The deception will last only as long as it takes for the workers to know what Fascism is.
>
> Fascism is the overcoming of the two tyrannies that loom over the working class: the liberal and the socialist.
>
> On paper, liberal capitalism gave the worker all the freedoms he could imagine; it did not force him to accept working conditions other than those he freely desired. But, since the capitalist was wealthy and the worker was impoverished, in the end, it was always the worker who was forced to submit. The liberal states watched, undaunted, the extension of terrible working hours and the contraction of starvation wages.
>
> Socialism stood up for justice against the liberal capitalist economy. But against the tyranny of the capitalists, it advocated no other solution than the tyranny of the workers: the dictatorship of the proletariat after the triumph of the class struggle.
>
> Capitalism and socialism are two monstrous solutions: the triumph of one class over another class and the tyranny of the victor over the vanquished.
>
> Only Fascism achieves the right solution. The Fascist state does not belong to the powerful class nor to the proletarian class; it belongs to everybody. That is why it protects, with determination, the interests of all. It does not give the worker what is just as a spoil of victory nor as a humiliating gift: it gives it to him because it is just, without bargaining, all at once.
>
> This is how, in Italy and in Germany, labor has been elevated to the highest civil dignity. There is work for everyone, and everyone works. There are no lavish parasites. The labor unions are directly part of the architecture of the state, without the need for intermediary political parties, which only serve to place on the shoulders of the workers a few happy wire-pullers.
>
> In our next issues, we will closely follow the characteristics of workers' lives in the Fascist countries so that everyone may get to know them.

The last page, the closing page of the weekly, contained a long article signed under the pseudonym of "El Gran Inquisidor" ["The Grand Inquisitor"]—Ernesto Gimémez Caballero—titled "Autos de F.E." and with the subtitle "Antifascistas en España: Don José Ortega y Gasset" [Antifascists in Spain: Don José Ortega y Gasset], which began as follows: "Fascism's opponents are divided into these three groups: socialist communism, Masonic liberal democracy, and Catholic populism." Among the thoughtful digressions in his text, he stated: "Our Fascism—like the rest of the European fascisms—needed and still needs the liberal enemy. If it did not exist, it would have to be invented, as Voltaire said of God. Our Fascism needed and still needs a liberal enemy in Spain as strong and talented as an Italian Croce."

The Second Issue of *F.E.* Is Finally Out

On January 11th, 1934, at eight o'clock in the evening, near Madrid's Puerta del Sol, José Antonio was among the group of vendors shouting that the second issue of the Falangist weekly would be published. Incidents and clashes occurred. A large group of leftists attempted to assault the young Falangists who were selling the newspaper. An angry mob surrounded some other young Falangists. José Antonio was forced to draw a pistol to fend off the assailants. Scenes of violence followed one after the other and were repeated on Calle de Alcalá, at the intersection with Calle de Sevilla, in front of the Alcázar theater. There, Francisco de Paula Sampol Cortés, a twenty-two-year-old student and mechanic at Telefónica, was shot at point-blank range from behind for having bought a copy from a street vendor. In the neighborhood of Cuatro Caminos, eight Falangists were also arrested, among them the eighteen-year-old José María Ríos, who was seriously wounded. He was treated at the Casa de Socorro de Chamberí. Identical scenes occurred throughout Spain. On January 15th, on the occasion of the sale of the weekly, assaults took place in Toledo. On the 16th, in Murcia, the socialists set fire to several boxes of *F.E.* In Zaragoza, on the 17th, a group of ten people, taking advantage of the night's darkness, assaulted on Calle Santa Clara in Zamora a Falangist who was selling the weekly, Ángel Noguera Peláez, seriously injuring him.

On page 3, there is an article by Javier Díaz in which Mr. Gil Robles' position regarding Fascism is criticized with the following arguments:

> Mr. Gil Robles claims that he does not believe in the Fascists or that they can achieve anything in Spain; this is exactly the same belief that the Fascists hold about the so-called democrats, with the difference that we have history to back our opinions up, while they have only the wish for theirs to be true. But then Mr. Gil Robles adds an exception: "Unless things remain as they are."
>
> One must agree, Mr. Gil Robles, that if you fill your democratic ideology with exceptions, many of us will end up sharing your opinions, but even with all the exceptions in the world, we will never be able to believe in the incompatibility of Catholicism and Fascism, since you seem to have tacitly set these doctrines against each other in your talk with the journalist of *El Heraldo*. Nor can anyone believe in the exoticism of Fascism, which, regardless of its name, is a political phenomenon that has occurred almost simultaneously in several nations. In the same way, for a

similar reason, we accepted the idea of the constitution a little more than a century ago, and likewise, there is no exoticism in it, because similar causes produce identical effects, with the exception of the idiosyncrasies of each country. Nor can anyone who is not naïve believe that within democracy we can enjoy strong governments for long enough without the most heinous ambitions showing themselves shamelessly. Here, *here* is the key to something very important that in politics constitutes the epicenter of all earthquakes and, if we do not opportunely remedy it, will inevitably lead us to chaos. And it is that, of all the ideas that involve sacrifice, the idea of renouncing so many things that, until the present, have been considered rightful, is, undoubtedly, most painful to our human satisfaction.

But Fascism is this, among other things: sacrifice, and, if not annulment of our political personality, at least renunciation, as I have said, to certain satisfactions of the ego. With this comes as a reward the enjoyment of living in a vigorous and wisely governed fatherland, always infinitely better governed than by parties and their political clients, phony political pretenders who have not infrequently made sterile the best judgment, integrity, and talent of distinguished men.

On page 4, occupying a quarter of the page, we find the recommendation of *El Fascismo*, a book by N. Cebreiros. In the following page, there is an eloquent doctrinal article, probably written by José Antonio due to the disposition and form, the syntax and style, the clarity and concision. Under it, there is a drawing in which an allegorical arrow collides and shatters against a hammer and sickle:

FASCISM AGAINST MARXISM
Necessity has created the reality of Fascism, as opposed to the dissolving, manic, and suicidal Marxist ideology.

Marxism advocates the inhuman class struggle, the source of hatred and injustice, criminal backlashes, and destructive exclusivisms. Fascism upholds the doctrine of concord and mutual aid among all social classes and the harmony of all the organs of production in order to achieve greater equity in distribution.

Marxism aspires to and has as its immediate goal the dictatorship of the proletariat; the tyranny, hence, of one class over all the others, perpetuating the odious thesis of victors and vanquished. Fascism advocates the formation of a corporatist state in which, free from political intermediaries, or parasites of any kind, all the classes of a nation, by means of syndicates and unionization, have a share in the governance of the state.

Marxism enslaves the majority for the exclusive benefit of a small faction. Fascism, on the contrary, brings equal benefits to all social classes.

Marxism is materialistic and atheistic. Fascism is faith and spirit.

Marxism, by destroying the foundations of the institution of the family, the fundamental unit of the national principle, attempts to annihilate the concept of the fatherland. Fascism protects the development of the family by cooperating in the exaltation of the fatherland.

Marxism is hatred, blood, destruction, and regression. Fascism is mutual understanding, progress, and well-being.

Marxism is the denial of tradition and of the history of peoples, as if the repeated experiences of previous generations were useless baggage. Fascism, by gathering all the teachings of the past and adapting them to the needs of the present, serves as a bridge to the salvation of civilization and culture.

The materialistic conceptions of Marxism nullify all that is noblest in the human spirit, leaving man powerless to address his spiritual problems. Fascism, on the other hand, fosters the highest and most generous mental temper by reconciling the social problem with a poetic view of history and life.

Marxism is disorder, anarchy, and disintegration for the benefit of a few. Fascism is order, unity, and authority for the common good of all social classes.

Marxism persecutes religion. Fascism adopts the evangelical principle: give to God what is God's and to Caesar what is Caesar's.

It could have been said louder, but not clearer.

In the section "Noticiero del mundo," when writing about "Roma, la Paz, y Ginebra" ["Rome, Peace, and Geneva"], the position taken by the weekly is unequivocal: "The raised arm of Benito Mussolini, extricating itself from the devious tactics of Geneva, will point the only clear path toward peace."

Page 5 was dedicated in its entirety to "Vida Fascista" ["Fascist Life"], with an interesting piece entitled "Germany: Nazis and Jews," in which, among other things, we find the following:

In this magazine we will write—accurately and extensively—about the position that a Fascist Spain will have to take regarding the Jewish question. Now is not the time to flesh out our ideas in their entirety, but it is necessary to point out the following: For Spain, the Jewish question is not and has never been and never will be a problem of race, but one of faith . . . . There are only two people in the world that consider the race, the *ius sanguinis*, a vital political principle: the Aryans and the Jews. These are two people who root their historical meaning in the blood. They practice endogamy. And they confer a religious and spiritual value to the somatic ties.

This is one of the reasons—perhaps the most profound—for the hostility between Germans and Jews. This hostility is not unique to the Hitlerian system. In fact, it has an ancestral, thousand-year-old origin . . . .

Therefore, the accusations made by the Jews against the Hitlerites may have some foundation. But the Hitlerites themselves also harbor their own accusations against the Jews.

The Jews—a well-organized international race—have waged the fiercest worldwide propaganda campaign against Hitler's Fascism. They have relied on people like the Yankees and the English, where they count up to millions of co-religionists and where they can rekindle in the natives resentment against Germany, reminding them of the Great War and the enemy against whom they fought in that war. But the country that has done the most to protect and develop the Jewish campaign against Germany has been France.

In France, in the words of the famous lawyer Henry Torres, the Jews "united themselves in a single impressive sheaf."

The Jews—the great creators of social democracy, socialism, and communism —accuse Hitler of restoring anti-Semitism, which was "the classic amusement of autocrats and the disease of enslaved peoples."

But the Germans, for their part, do not hesitate to accuse, clearly and categorically, the Jews in Germany of enslaving the country from 1918 until the present day. The Germans offer much evidence, and some of it is incontrovertible.

The Revolution of November 1918 was sparked by the Jew Salomon Kosmanowsky, who, under the name of Kurt Eisner, seized power in Bavaria.

In the garden of the Luitpold gymnasium in Munich, several members of the racialist Thule society were shot. The leaders of that revolt were all Jews: Levin, Leviné, Toller, Landauer, Toller, and Mühsam.

When Hitler triumphed, it was said in the *Volkischer Beobachter* that the Jews hurried to spread the most perfidious slanders.[164]

The Jew Hasenclever wrote in his drama *The Son* that the family is "a medieval sore." And Ehrenstein called the Sisters of Charity "God's sows."

In Hamburg—while most of the German population was living badly and with no work—the top jobs and professions were mostly occupied by Jews.

Among the doctors, they made up 30 percent. Lawyers, 43 percent. Among judges and magistrates, 60 percent. Members of the Bundestag, 50 percent.

The lists that were seized from the communists—Jews for the most part—contained strict death warrants for the German population: "Shoot them on the market square. The citizens must witness the execution."

Jews told of Hitlerites raping Hebrew girls, murdering detainees, and

---

164 [Translator: The *Völkischer Beobachter* (*Völkisch Observer*) was the official newspaper of the NSDAP.]

desecrating graves during the National Socialist seizure of power. But nothing is less true, claim the Nazis. With the exception of some exemplary and bloodless punishments through ridicule, there had never been more order and peace in Germany than during those days. And as indisputable proof, they quote the statement of a Frenchman, the editor of *Le Petit Journal*: "Life in Berlin and in the provinces has never been so peaceful and normal as it was precisely in the days of the national uprising."

The Nazi–Jewish quarrel will be a long-lasting one because it is an old one. France knows it. And, today, it protects Judaism more vehemently than ever. Thus, it secures for itself a powerful and fearsome ally.

Adolf Hitler appears today in history with the eternal lot of the Aryan hero, of the Teutonic knight, of the mythical Siegfried, fighting alone against many enemies, and perhaps falling one day to the betrayal of a Hagen.[165]

It is beautiful to see this new specimen of a medieval knight, of Nibelung, cleaving with his axe the waves of ghostly creatures surrounding him!

Regarding Italy, these are some of the answers from the interview the Duce gave to Henry Massis on youth and life, together with a curious anecdote about Mussolini:

One day, Mussolini was visiting some construction sites, surrounded by workers, high-ranking officials, and a few foreign diplomats.

One of these diplomats, very well dressed and well mannered, called the Duce's attention as he passed on a scaffolding plank, as if warning him of the danger.

Mussolini promptly turned and, smiling, asked him:

"Has Your Excellency been a bricklayer?"

"Oh, no!" replied the diplomat.

"Well, I have been, and I know where you should put your feet on the construction site."

In this article is outlined a "definition which has become fundamental in the corporative system and which is attributed to its great organizer, Giuseppe Bottai: 'The syndicate is the indestructible cell of the corporation.'"

In the "Fascist Life" section, when referring to Brazil, the following is said with evident satisfaction:

In the next issues, we will be covering Fascist panoramas around world.

---

165 Translator: Hagen is a figure in Germanic mythology who is found in many stories. Among his roles, he is the slayer of Siegfried.

Today we report the news that Fascism is taking root in all continents and countries, however distant these countries may be from Rome. Thus, for example, in Brazil . . . a young and ambitious party has emerged with the Fascist emblem . . . as its insignia: the Integralist Party. It has already participated in elections and developed its ideology through a struggle of faith and effort. Let us wish it great fortune and fearlessness.

Page 10 was completely dedicated to Giménez Caballero's serial article on "Spain and Rome," which was intended to be divided into ten chapters. It was a hymn to Rome and the mutual and reciprocal influence, both political and cultural, that the two nations on the shores of the Mediterranean had exchanged for millennia. To know Rome, according to Ernesto Giménez Caballero, was like "the awakening" of his "deepest Spanish instinct. An instinct for which I wanted to seek today a firm foundation, a spiritual ancestry, a perfect tradition: a lineage." Right after he got to know Rome, the Rome of the Caesars and of Mussolini, the capital of the empire and of Fascism, it immediately "became everything" to him. Giménez Caballero "found in Rome the scent of a mother" and confessed that "this impression felt about Rome and in front of Rome was decisive for my life. It was a case of love."

On page 11, devoted to "Readings of Our Own," there is an article initially published in the magazine *Blanco y Negro* by the writer Andrés Revesz with the suggestive title "Italia se transforma en Estado Corporativo" ["Italy Transforms into a Corporate State"], where, among other panegyrics, he writes:

The Duce has told the author of these lines that the thinker who exerted the greatest influence on him was Georges Sorel, the great theorist of syndicalism and opponent of socialism and parliamentary democracy. On other occasions, he affirmed that he was an "old syndicalist." Despite fighting within the socialist party, Mussolini was always an enemy of parliamentary corruption and a supporter of direct action, a method advocated by the syndicalists. Nevertheless, between them and Mussolini, there was always the important difference that syndicalism is "anarchic" in the Greek sense of the word (that is, it does not recognize central power), while Mussolini places the state above all private interests, even those of the syndicates and corporations. The state must be freed from various material concerns (Mussolini is anti-statist in a certain qualified sense), but must reserve for itself the supreme right to supervise, control, and coordinate the activity of all entities. The capitalism of today, supercapitalism—as the Duce calls it—would, without the intervention of the state, lead to state capitalism, which is nothing but the opposite of state socialism. The state must not allow its prerogatives to be usurped.

Fascism can thus be characterized as "nationalism plus syndicalism." However, while old syndicalism wants to perpetuate class struggle, Fascism suppresses it . . . . It is often believed that Fascism is hostile to workers' organizations, but in reality, the truth is just the opposite. The syndicates are the foundation of the Fascist organization.

The lengthy article, from which we have transcribed some basic ideas, concludes with this statement: "The corporate system is the disciplined economy, and, therefore, it is also controlled, because one cannot think of discipline without control. Corporatism overcomes socialism and liberalism and creates a new synthesis."

On the same page, there is a review of N. Cebreiros' *El Fascismo*, which is presented as follows:

The world's growing interest in Fascism's gradual triumph has brought back to relevance in today's news those heroic days that marked its arrival in Italy. Benito Mussolini's strong and resolute figure grows larger every day: to rescue a people from subjugation and humiliation and to propel it once again toward the conquest of history while laying the foundations of a new social and economic organization, which is the titanic enterprise of a genius.

The attempts to conceal the Fascist phenomenon have been of no avail. Its development over perhaps the most difficult years in the history of the West has been its most compelling argument. Against all odds, Mussolini has continued to work unabatedly on the reconstruction of Italy, which, until his rise to power, had been suffering under the suicidal weapons of Marxism.

In his book, N. Cebreiros presents an account of the first phases of the Italian Fascist movement. A brief study of the Italian situation places the reader before the scenario that served as a stage for the revolution of the Blackshirts. The incidents that occurred during the early struggles, with their sequence of deaths, the guidelines of the movement, and the ideology of the men who were preparing for the construction of a new state, are clearly exposed in the pages of this book.

In a report, the weekly *F.E.* informs the readers of a similar publication, another weekly, entitled *Decimos*, of which it is stated that:

Under this name is published in Cáceres a weekly faithful to the ideas and discipline of Falange Española. It is written by a group of young and enthusiastic men with clear heads and firm tempers. The issue, dated January 4th, which we have before us, contains an announcement of the provincial Falange, some quotes by Mussolini, accurately chosen, and several vibrant works of their own. It also includes our "Initial Points."

We send our warmest greetings to the comrades of Cáceres and to their newspaper.

The Denounced Third Issue of *F.E.*

The release of the third issue of *F.E.* was scheduled for January 18th. Needless to say, there was great anticipation. In the early hours of the morning, huddles of people swarmed restlessly on Calle de Alcalá and the sidewalks of Puerta del Sol. A young man, in front of those baleful faces, cheered loudly for Fascism. The reaction of the fanatics was not long in coming; they insulted him, knocked him down, hit him, and attempted to lynch him, leaving him lying there with serious injuries all over his body. The Assault Corps took up positions and charged against the aggressors to try to rescue the boy. José Antonio was the first to shout, announcing the sale, thus prompting the reaction of a knife-wielding socialist who tried to stab him.

The prosecutor denounced the issue in its entirety. When it was seized by the police, the issue had only been on sale for two hours. José Antonio appeared in court, where he was notified of the resolution of the Public Prosecutor's Office. Two days later, in Cáceres, a series of aggressions against the Falangists who were trying to sell *F.E.* in the old town of the city took place.

The copies of the issue were not to be wasted. On the front page, emphatically, in the "Guiones" column, it is stated categorically that "*La vida es milicia. La Falange es milicia*" ["Life is struggle. Falange is struggle"]. The editorial is harsh, clear, blunt, and, without ambiguity, under the slogan *Libertad y Unidad* [Freedom and Unity], the following is stated:

They believe that authority, hierarchy, order, and discipline are the enemies of freedom, whereas they are freedom itself. They are the supreme example of freedom and only among sovereignly free men have they existed and can they exist. That which we have proposed as an urgent objective, as a first and indispensable goal, in the face of all this rhetoric of slaves and eunuchs, is precisely freedom. We are the only Spanish political movement that has proposed with absolute mental and practical rigor *the freedom of Spain* as the first indispensable condition to give freedom to the Spanish people. Such rhetoric of slaves and eunuchs, which turns against us, invoking liberalism, democracy, the rights of man, and so forth, is the muddy, feverish, pallid rhetoric typical of all the countries influenced by the great powers and the great internationals. Nowhere does this rhetoric flourish with greater inflation and melodrama than in the miscegenated countries, where the blood of the Sambos or the Miskitos prevails to an alarming degree over the white and civilizing minorities. The question of freedom must be taken seriously, with the conscience of free men. Everything else is but the delusion and megalomania of the impotent and the degenerate, who speak of "love." This is the problem. As long as we do not have the freedom of Spain, facing the sun, facing the world, pure and whole— something that for almost two centuries *we have not had*—any desire for freedom *within* Spain will be no more than the freedom of a prisoner allowed to do whatever he likes in his bare cell.

The presence of the expression "facing the sun" in this paragraph represents a curious anecdote, as there was no suspicion that, two years later, those same words would be the first letters of the first stanza of the official anthem of the Falange.

On the front page, occupying a whole column, all in capital letters, well highlighted and clearly visible, we find the following:

ITALY POLISHES ITS FASCIST ARCHITECTURE WITH THE IMPLEMENTATION OF THE CORPORATE REGIME.

MUSSOLINI HAS DELIVERED A SPEECH BEFORE THE ITALIAN SENATE ON THE SUBJECT OF CORPORATIONS. THE LAW OF CORPORATIONS, ACCORDING TO THE DUCE, IS NO LONGER JUST THE RESULT OF A DOCTRINE, BUT THE RESULT OF TWELVE YEARS OF EXPERIENCE. THERE ARE NO ECONOMIC EVENTS WITHOUT REPERCUSSIONS THAT EXTEND BEYOND THE INDIVIDUALITY THAT PRODUCES THEM. THE CAPITALIST ECONOMY IS OF OUR TIMES; IT DID NOT EXIST BEFORE. IT GREW UNTIL IT EXCEEDED THE FAMILY SPHERE AND HAD TO RESORT TO THE FORMATION OF JOINT-STOCK COMPANIES AND THE AID OF THE BANKS. TODAY, THE STATE MUST INTERVENE. BUT IT IS NOT PLEASING TO DO SO IN THE COMMUNIST SENSE, WHICH BUREAUCRATIZES THE ECONOMIC LIFE OF THE NATION, NOR BY MEANS OF FINANCIAL MANEUVERS. IT MUST BE DONE THROUGH A CORPORATIVE ECONOMY THAT RESPECTS THE INDIVIDUAL'S INITIATIVE, WHILE THE STATE BRINGS ORDER TO THE ECONOMY. IT IS IN THE INTEREST OF THE TOTALITY OF THE PEOPLE THAT THE ECONOMY BE GUIDED IN ALL OF ITS ASPECTS, AND THAT IS THE AIM OF THE LAW. THEN THE CORPORATIONS WOULD BE CONSTITUTED, AND LASTLY WOULD COME THE POLITICAL REFORM, WHICH WOULD DECIDE THE DESTINY OF THE CHAMBER OF DEPUTIES. "WE WILL PROCEED CALMLY," SAID THE DUCE, "BECAUSE, JUST LIKE THE FASCIST REVOLUTION, WE STILL HAVE BEFORE US THE WHOLE CENTURY."

WHEN WE HAVE THE COMPLETE TEXT OF MUSSOLINI'S SPEECH IN OUR HANDS, WE WILL RETURN TO IT IN THE NEXT ISSUE AND GIVE IT THE ATTENTION IT DESERVES.

On the second page is reproduced the invitation to the youth of the world, sent out by

Germany on the occasion of the official announcement of the Olympic Games to be held in 1936 in Berlin, the capital of the Third Reich.

On the third page is an advertisement and recommendation: "Read *The Making of the Corporate State: A Study of Fascist Development* by the Englishman H. E. Goad, translated and prefaced by the Marquis de la Eliseda." The Marquis de la Eliseda, translator and author of the book's preface, was a Falangist congressman and personal friend of José Antonio, who, after the legislative elections of 1933, from their seats shared the electoral representation of the new political movement.

On page 5, there is an article signed by Víctor D'Ors Pérez-Peix with the resounding title "Fascismo es elevación" ["Fascism Is Elevation"], which, for its importance and conciseness, we reproduce in its opening paragraphs:

> The best ideal with which the romantic, individually, burned itself, the work of constant self-improvement on which a Goethe or a Goya toiled, the desire for continued perfection, which could only be realized by some powerful genius, will become collective will.
>
> Pouring itself into Christian love, filled with Catholic universality, and built on clear and eternal things such as family, township, profession, and sport—clear and eternal as bread and water, the moon and the meadow—Spanish Falangism carries the impulse to raise humanity to higher places.
>
> Why shouldn't Spain conquer the universal will in favor of this new message of elevation? Fraternally, in a firm and generous way, our Falangism imposes on itself a moral elevation analogous to that pursued materially and culturally by the population.
>
> In the contemporary world, American civilization represents a great crusade in favor of material progress. Good. Their telephones and gramophones are today our daily bread. The Germanic countries transmitted to everyone their determination to improve man culturally and physically. The progress made has been great. Now it is our turn. And Spain returns to what belongs to it: moral and spiritual improvement, which is necessary. Because it seems that this well-groomed golf player, who travels through countries at high speeds, and this stockjobber who makes phone orders from his bathroom, and all these villages where there is not a single illiterate person, commit sins equivalent to those of inferior races.
>
> It is necessary to undertake this great work of elevation that we impose on ourselves, a total education of the individual, which encompasses all the potential improvements of the human being, an education that must prevail in the Spanish Falangist movement.

The brilliant article "Hábito y Estilo" ["Habit and Style"], which appeared in the middle pages, reads:

We have to prefigure the state, the nation, the Fatherland. We have to participate in the rebuilding of a new Europe by prevailing and not languishing. We have to return to Spain its essence, its way of being, its great style. One is nothing more than what one has been, or one is nothing at all. Therefore, our entire movement must be the way of being, the style of the coming Spain, the perfect, legitimate, unmistakable homogeneous evolution of the great Spain. We embody the reform of Spain, and Cisneros —the first Fascist in history—is our captain general.

The section "Fascist Life" filled the entire eighth page with two major international mentions, the first one to France and neo-socialism, of which it is said that "it is simply the effort to adapt the current French spirit, which is democratic and bourgeois, to the Fascist current." And to the question "Is neo-socialism strictly a French Fascist movement?" the following digression is made in response:

Yes, to a large extent. Yet it is still very undefined and vague in other respects. This is how it is recognized, for example, by the Italian Fascists. Giorgio Granata, in a recent commentary published in the Roman magazine *Critica Fascista* [*Fascist Critique*], notices, however, something fundamental in this movement: "What we can admit today about this movement and its great implication is this: that the leaders of neo-socialism have finally understood that Fascism is not something reactionary, as the democratic chatter put into play has led us to believe until now. Just the contrary: only through the corporative state can true democracy be achieved.

The second of the international topics dealt with concerns about Turkey and Mustafa Kemal Atatürk.

Giménez Caballero continues to unravel the whole history of the strong ties between Spain and Rome. In antiquity, "Roman fertility populated Spain. Spain married Rome. And thus was achieved unity, meaning, soul, name, succession: Hispania." He then gives an overview of the great contributions of both:

From the Roman Cordoba will rise up in the ancient world two great Caesars (Trajan and Hadrian), the two Senecas, and Lucan the poet. Of the five emperors that Spain gave to Rome—Galba, Trajan, Hadrian, Maximus, and Theodosius—two were from Cordoba, and they were the greatest and most famous.

The section "Lecturas propias," on this occasion, borrows its articles from the Italian Fascist magazine *Ottobre*, in which Francois Coty writes in the article "Soldados desconocidos" ["Unknown Soldiers"] the following:

In the Italian Army, there was a completely unknown soldier who fought the war with a knapsack on his back, was wounded, and experienced all the horrors of the battle. His name was Benito Mussolini.

In the German Army, there was a completely unknown soldier who went to war with a knapsack on his back, was wounded, and witnessed the trials and the ugliness of battle. His name was Adolf Hitler.

They were both men of the people. Through their own sufferings, they weighed the sufferings of the people.

Thus, the Italian people and the German people have entrusted them with the duty of upholding the rights of millions of other unknown soldiers.

The Turbulent Life of the Fourth Issue of *F.E.*

The fourth issue of the weekly *F.E.* was also censured and seized. It was published on Thursday, January 25th, 1934. The police worked diligently to try to prevent it from being put up for sale. Selling the newspaper of the Falange on the street was a deadly challenge. The next day, in Seville, the police confiscated from Falangist students the package of copies they were trying to sell.

However, the most tragic event occurred on Saturday, January 20th, when Vicente Pérez Rodríguez was assassinated on Calle del Clavel in Madrid. He was the sales representative of the weekly *F.E.* and was also in charge of the distribution and sale of *La Nación*. The most horrendous crimes were being committed in order to try to silence the newspaper.

In the fourth issue, the Fascist message of the weekly grew more radical. The Republican government, which cynically boasted formal liberties, used an iron fist to try to prevent the spread of the new and noble European Fascist ideas, which the Falange, with its deep Spanish identity, made its own.

The editorial addressed the subject of "Estado e Historia" ["State and History"]. It clarified and defined the topic, explaining:

The strong virile modesty of the individual and of locality can only be achieved at the service of a great collective pride that would open onto universal horizons and that ought to be enough to place each one in his place in the face of the great enterprise. Hence, the national will to rule imposes itself, not as an irresistible ambition, but as the indispensable and converging objective to order and unify the parts of a whole. The national order must not be static, but dynamic, geared toward a supreme driving force, toward a supreme cause that justifies the unitary, *totalitarian*, and authoritarian function.

The "Guiones" on the front page speak for themselves. Regarding the countryside, it is written:

There is a rural culture and society that we must promote and revalue. The gist of that great familiar, religious, hereditary, and hierarchical sense, in which the civilized order of Europe had its roots, has been corrupted in the cities and remains in the countryside, even though it originated from the *cives*. Almost all of European political agrarianism understood the countryside through a sociological criterion of predominantly utilitarian and specialist ethics, shrinking and cooling that great national and lyrical sense of the countryside. It is the countryside that restores to the nations their poetic understanding of history and their great innocence as a baptism for the new beginning on the great path. Both fresh and very ancient, the countryside has given back to Italy and Germany their great virtues.

In the article "Comodidad y crítica" ["Comfort and Criticism"] it is remarked:

It is very comfortable to be at home in slippers or in any other conservative, Hispanicist, and elegiac attitude and to demand daily from a movement started twenty weeks ago, with its branches constantly suspended and its publications denounced, the same efficiency as the fully mature Italian Fascism on the eve of the March on Rome.

In the sports section "Aire libre," the report is about the Olympic Stadium prepared for 1936:

By the decision of Chancellor Hitler, taken on December 14th, 1933, the Olympic Games to be held in Berlin in 1936 will be provided with an impressive technical facility. The sports facilities already available in the German capital will be expanded to magnificent proportions.

A plan of the Olympic Village and a detailed description of each of its areas were included.

On the third page, there was an extensive article signed by the writer Samuel Ros, titled "Carta a un condiscípulo" ["Letter to a Fellow Student"]. It was a public reply to a fellow university student in which, among other things, he said:

I see that I have lost your admiration and, what is worse, your esteem and that of other fellow students with whom you communicate: "We always read what you wrote with special attention and esteemed you deeply, but now we can no longer, because you have become a Fascist." This is what you told me. What I could never believe is that you, by the simple circumstance that you believe me to be a Fascist, or by the real fact that I am one (I humbly confess that I do not know), can go from loving me and liking my writings to just the opposie. I do not deny that this first classification encapsulates a certain dose of justice, but not enough to satisfy those who must seek the *exactness of justice*. For this reason, I will not mind the derogatory Fascist label given to me by a communist, but I will mind it if it comes from you and others like you. After all, are you really sure, dear fellow student, that you are not as Fascist as I am? I cannot believe that your youth should bleed out in a comfortable intermediate position, in that languid liberal zone that, while promising to any citizen the highest judgeship of the nation, also allows any citizen to starve if luck, in the daily striving, does not allow him to reach the necessary ration to survive.

Now I will tell you that you know that I am a Fascist, because you are accustomed to see all those who do not know what they are put themselves under the cloak and label of whatever party, so that others may know what they are. This only gives those who are eager to get to the very limit of truth a vague idea of the reality of each man.

You see, even after getting in trouble for saying what I think, I still don't know what I am. What I am, the rest of you must tell me, but tell me well, without fear of words, because in the end, none of these words are enough to protect those whose destiny in life is to be more than a vote in elections and a number in the conscription rolls.

It is likely that I am more than a Fascist, but I don't know. Just as it is quite possible that I will not become one. Do you remember how similar we were when we collaborated on those notes on Roman law?

I will always think highly of you, and of all our colleagues—of all men who are sons of God.

In the "Noticiero del mundo," the topic is the revolutionary attempt in Portugal, and the opinion of the weekly is that:

In Oliveira Salazar, the Portuguese people saw the man who, in the midst of the storms of our time, has undertaken the only effective way to rescue them from these storms. The battered Portuguese economy has found in Oliveira Salazar its restorer, who, piercing through the most immediate setbacks, is headed toward a successful continuation. Once the revolutionary attempt was victorious, the position of the Portuguese government was strengthened. The certainty of Oliveira Salazar's steps, well flanked by public support, remains the only way to integrate the people in their all-encompassing mission.

In an article entitled "Para el mañana" ["For the Future"], the Italian film industry is discussed, and it is recounted that:

In 1924, Mussolini, aware of the effectiveness of cinematographic propaganda, transformed the Syndicate of Cinematographic Instruction into a corporation called L'Unione Cinematografica Educativa (LUCE). This company's shares were then purchased by various official or national entities, raising its capital to two and a half million pounds.

In 1925, LUCE became a state institution . . . . Mussolini knew how to place at the head of LUCE the right man; he needed someone with a clear intelligence and an energetic power of execution, a man who could reform, but within the most severe administration and with maximum efficiency. That man was the Marquis Giacomo Paulucci de' Calboli Barone. When Mussolini came to power he had already entrusted him with the position of head of his private cabinet. From 1927 to 1932, he was the secretary of the League of Nations . . . . In the industrial films, the great work of reconstruction carried out by Fascism is portrayed. The historical-geographical and technical-military films are also noteworthy . . . . The magnificent film *Black Shirt* was also made, which was a cinematographic synthesis of the Italian resurgence from the war to the present, a demonstration of the great work of the Fascist revolution.

This is how propaganda that elevates and invigorates the national spirit and exalts and gives prestige to the nation internationally should be made. By imitating their guidelines, making mandatory the projection of the national propaganda film in all cinemas, forming itinerant cinematography teams, and forcing the great national financial companies to pay for shares of this work of patriotism and culture, we will succeed in giving prestige to Spain, too, and finally create a national cinematography.

Ernesto Giménez Caballero, in the third chapter of the series "Spain and Rome," dedicates more than two full pages to "Séneca o los fundamentos estoicos del Fascismo" ["Seneca, or, the Stoic Foundations of Fascism"], in which he writes that:

this essay on Seneca attempts to substantiate the Fascist doctrine from a philosophical and Spanish point of view. So too, it seeks to establish for Spain a deep, intimate, and original tradition of a movement that today is called "Fascist," but that for us was as old as our Christian Senecanism.

The essay is extensive, profound, and academic. Giménez Caballero concludes with the following suggestions:

One of the essential characteristics of Fascism is its antidemocracy, which is, likewise, that of Senecanism. *"Argumentum pessimi turba est,"* said

Seneca in *De vita beata II*.[166] Then Petrarch, influenced by Seneca, expressed it in such a way that it reached our *Celestina* in the fifteenth century: "Nothing is further from the truth than public opinion."[167] And Erasmus completed Seneca's maxim by saying: "The truth is that popular judgment is not and has never been a very reliable or valid rule by which man should be governed."

This is what Mussolini would say later, with other words: "Fascism rejects the idea that numbers can govern human societies, due to the simple fact that they are large numbers." A genuine characteristic—perhaps the purest—of Fascism is that of considering life as a struggle.

"Fascism conceived of life as a struggle," declared Mussolini. "War is the life of man on earth," stated Seneca. "To us Fascists, life is a constant and endless struggle which we embrace with great bravery." Senecan thought in its purest essence. "The very first thing I would advise is to remember once and for all that the entire life of mortals is nothing but a perpetual war," a great interpreter of Seneca wrote during the Renaissance. The man, the Fascist—states Mussolini—will have to "acquire for himself that life truly worthy of him." "A joyful life is one that is worthy of its nature." "Everyone is the craftsman of his own life," said Seneca. "Making one's entire life one's own masterpiece," Mussolini would later say. The practical, ethical character of life that had been observed in Seneca's philosophy is what appears to be the structure of Fascism: "This positive conception of life is obviously an ethical one." "Life, therefore, as conceived by the Fascist, is serious, austere, and religious; all its manifestations are poised in a world sustained by moral forces and subject to spiritual responsibilities. The Fascist disdains the 'comfortable' life." "The core of Fascist philosophy: we are against the comfortable life." Essential Senecanism: essence of the *vita beata*, of the Christian knight, which the Renaissance would translate into the concept of the virtuous man, always on guard in the face of events, toughened up against all deceitful comforts. "I appreciate most highly the fruits of toil, those that rely on fatigue and are based on action, constantly struggling against fate." "Overcome habit," Seneca advises Lucilius. And also, "It is necessary to accustom the spirit by means of continuous, relentless exercises."

Fascism's vision of man, understood as a being that is able to reach the highest heights of the will through heroic exercises, is, fundamentally, that of Seneca. Whereas Seneca wrote "the wise man," "the strong man," today it is necessary to write the "Duce," the "Führer," the "hero." Seneca was,

---

[166] [Translator: This Senecan expression means that the crowd is the worst exponent of truth.]

[167] [Translator: the *Tragicomedy of Calisto and Melibea* (Spanish: *Tragicomedia de Calisto y Melibea*), known in Spain as *La Celestina*, is a medieval novel published in 1499.]

long before Nietzsche, the great craftsman of the will to power.

The force of adversity does not move the heart of the valiant man; he is steadfast in his frame of mind. For he is mightier than all things that befall him from the outside. I do not say that he does not feel them, but I say that he overcomes them, says our Cartagena in 1551.

This was a concept that was carried forth by Seneca, Petrarch, Leon Battista Alberti, Machiavelli, Montaigne, and would reach, through Nietzsche, Mussolini. "Love hardships! Live dangerously!" the Duce often repeated.

Thus wrote Seneca in *De Providentia*, highlighting the heroism of Phaeton: "What you think frightens me is what enlivens me most, and thus it pleases me to be where even the sun is afraid. For it behooves the lowly man to seek safety. Virtue aims upward." This is Seneca: Against what is safe! Against the comfortable life!

This concept of the *ardito*, of the hero, of the wise Senecanist, entailed in the Rome of the first century the same concept of natural aristocracy, of natural royalty, that Fascism would bring to today's world.

"Who is, then, the nobleman? The one whom nature has made for virtue." "I do not judge a man for being different from the crowd because of the position and prestige he possesses, but rather for the heart that I see he holds." And then our Vives would add: "True and firm nobility is born from virtue."[168]

This Senecan thesis is the foundation of "the new Fascist hierarchy." Seneca thus unveils his hero, his duce: "Such a man will be balanced and full of order, bringing together with his natural majesty, a sense of piety in every one of his actions."

Nowadays, Fascism does not use the word "virtue" to denote what Seneca did. But it uses another word so analogously that its recurrence in all Fascist speeches and doctrines makes it equivalent: *fatica* [toil]. When the Duce uses the term *fatica* he is referring to exactly the same idea that virtue represented for Seneca. It is the effort, work, courage, and tension of living that the strong man needs to overcome the hard and difficult thing that is life. "*Non est delicata res vivere*" [To live is not a delicate thing].

I must not forget that this study of mine can only deal in some detail with a subject such as this, which here is encapsulated in a more general one. But to conclude this note on Senecanism and Fascism I will transcribe the remarks of Benito Mussolini: "If Fascism were not a faith, how would it give stoicism and courage to its members?"

"I do not care" (*me ne frego*): this proud motto of the fighting squads

---

168 [Translator: Juan Luis Vives was a Spanish Renaissance humanist.]

scrawled by a wounded man on his bandages is not only an act of philosophic Stoicism, but it also sums up a doctrine which is not merely political. It is evidence of a fighting spirit which accepts all risks. It signifies a new style of Italian life.

Fascism, like Senecanism, the *"puro stile di vita"* ["pure way of life"], is in its essence the eternal style of Rome. It is the conception that, after Seneca, would later be referred to as *Christian* and, today, as *Fascist*. That is, the acceptance of life as struggle. In contrast to the East, where life is absolute deprivation, and to the West, where life, according to Faust, is "action," Rome conceives it through the minds of its most brilliant sons (Seneca, St. Ignatius, Mussolini) as struggle, as virtue, as faith, as toil. For some reason, someone takes pains in considering Fascism as a new doctrine for Spain, while it is an old wisdom that has yielded its best fruits to it. It is the old secret, today more and more new, that the great Cordovan Lucius Annaeus Seneca whispered to Rome, in the first years of the era of Christ.

The following page of *F.E.* was completely dedicated to the transcription of Mussolini's speech to the Italian Senate. It is a dense page. The full speech that was inserted in the issue was composed of five blocks: the chrism of the Great Council, the capitalist economy, the dynasties of industrialists, the intervention of the state, and the indefatigable people. In it, the Duce explained the doctrine and the deeds of Fascism. It had already been announced on the cover of the third issue of the weekly, "when we have the full text of Mussolini's speech in our hands, we will return to it in the next issue and give it the attention it deserves." The Duce's fervent, resounding, and clarifying speech is reproduced in its entirety, in a literal, genuine, and authentic way, as the founder of Fascism undoubtedly deserved. Also published was a letter, hitherto suppressed, from Fernando Primo de Rivera.

There are many manipulations that we can detect in the successive editions of the misnamed *Complete Works* of José Antonio Primo de Rivera. His responses had either been transcribed incorrectly, not as they appeared in the original version published by the press of the time, or, on other occasions, terms that were more accommodating to the situation of the subsequent period had been substituted. For instance, in a report included in the newspaper *Luz* published in Madrid and dated January 27th, 1934, also excerpted by *La Nación*, and which in the *Complete Works* appears as "Declaraciones del Jefe de Falange, Don José Antonio Primo de Rivera" ["Declarations of the Leader of the Falange José Antonio Primo de Rivera"], was published originally as "Declaraciones del Jefe del Fascio Don José Antonio Primo de Rivera" ["Declarations of the Leader of the Fasces José Antonio Primo de Rivera"]. As can be seen, the word *fascio*, which appeared in the newspaper, was intentionally concealed in favor of the word "Falange"; this is how history is rewritten. As for the content of the interview, not once did the word

"Falange" appear in the newspaper, but always the term "Fascism"; but, likewise, the thought police sweetened this term by transforming it into "Falange." Thus, for example, when he begins his statements to the reporter, his words are as follows: "What happened in San Carlos between students of antagonistic political beliefs—Fascists and FUE—is the culmination and conclusion." In his *Complete Works*, this appears differently: "What happened in San Carlos—Falangists and FUE—is the culmination."

In that same edition of the newspaper *Luz*, corresponding to January 27th, 1934, a reporter of the newspaper published an interview with the brother of José Antonio, Fernando Primo de Rivera, a student at the faculty of medicine, in relation to the report presented by a student of the FUE who claimed to have spotted him at the faculty on the day of the assault on the premises of the FUE in the San Carlos Hospital. He denied his participation in the events because he had arrived at San Carlos "after the events." The interview ended with the following statement by Fernando:

> "I have heard that the one who led the assailing group is an amateur Greco-Roman wrestler who is tall, strong, and rough. His name is known. Do you know him?"
>
> "I do not associate with wrestlers. There is no chance of that. I tell you one thing: I don't know that wrestler nor any Fascist."

Fernando Primo de Rivera, upon reading his published reply, hurried to urgently send a letter of correction, dated January 28th, 1934—published on the front page of the following day's edition—to the editor of the Republican newspaper *Luz*, a brief but clarifying and unequivocal letter. This letter has not been quoted subsequently by historians, although its content definitely gives a different outlook on the matter. It reads as follows:

Mr. Director of *Luz*

Dear Sir:

In the conversation that an editor of your respectable newspaper had with me, which is inserted in the issue of the 27th, there appears at the end a paragraph that does not express fairly what I meant.

It is true that I do not know any Greco-Roman wrestlers, but on the other hand, I know many Fascists, and I consider them among my best friends, since all of them have magnificent qualities that make me value their friendship as an honor.

You will understand, Mr. Director, that if I had not made this clarification, it would appear that I was trying to deny my friendship with these people and my complete identification with their ideas out of cowardice.

I would be very grateful if you would publish this letter.

Yours faithfully,
Fernando Primo de Rivera

José Antonio, during the parliamentary session that was held on February 1st, 1934, in which he spoke to the deputies with elegance and refinement, told them, as is recorded in the parliamentary journal of the Cortes:

> Fascism is a European inquietude, a new way of conceiving everything: history, the state, the arrival of the proletariat into public life; a new way of conceiving all the phenomena of our time and interpreting them with their own meaning. Fascism has already triumphed in several countries, and in some, as in Germany, it has prevailed in the most irreproachably democratic way.

Before the Cortes, José Antonio, in that same session, also admitted that the appearance of the Falange was associated "with the phenomenon of Fascism, which is taking place in Spain as in all of Europe."

The Fifth Issue of *F.E.*, Through Blood and Gunpowder

That Thursday, the first day of February, the fifth issue was published. Hatred was unleashed against the dissemination of Fascist doctrine. A powerful bomb exploded at 11 Calle Ibiza, the building where the weekly was printed. Five employees were injured by the strong blast and were treated at the Casa de Socorro. The socialists had already announced the terrorist attack, threatening with insistence to blow up the workshops where "the Fascist publication was being produced." Due to the fierceness and seriousness of the threat, the socialists' intentions had been reported to the general directorate of security, which sent a couple of civil guards to the place for the surveillance and protection of the building and its furnishings. The civil guard conducted patrols in the vicinity of the enormous complex. Taking advantage of the fact that the pair of guards was turning a corner of the building, the terrorists threw the device through a window. The explosion was tremendous and deafening.

Puerta del Sol was once again the scene of violent incidents when the boys of the Falange were selling *F.E.*, as was the case with the release of the previous editions. In the midst of the turmoil, police forces intervened with violent charges in an attempt to separate the victims from the rage of the leftists. The violent brawl resulted in arrests and injuries once more. The following day, clashes over the sale of *F.E.* took place in

Valladolid. Four days later, the Malaga newspaper vendors' association held an assembly in which it was decided to take repressive measures against those who sold "Fascist" publications. On February 7th, in Gijón, on Calle Corrida, the Falangist Fernando Cienfuegos was seriously injured while trying to sell the weekly.

One could read on the main page of the fifth issue a serene analysis concerning "Nuestros enemigos" ["Our Enemies"]:

> There are two major antifascist factions. The first group is those who claim that Fascism exists and poses a huge threat, and that all of the state's security forces and police must mobilize against it; it is the union of all the left-wing parties and newspapers, with their inflated fuss; it is the mobilization of professional delinquents, and so on. This first group, which is the most uncouth, crude, and elementary, is necessary in some ways to ventilate the struggle between Spain and anti-Spain, which will, of course, last until one of the two sides wins. The second group is more subtle and moderate. Their strategy is to claim that Fascism does not exist, that it is a new intellectual product, a kid-glove Fascism, a foreign imitation, and so on and so forth.
>
> While the press of the first group engages in a loud and exaggerated outcry, the press of the second group engages in a pious silence, no less loud and disproportionate (there are silences that are also very loud and exaggerated). Bringing these two groups together will be one of our most entertaining and exemplary missions in national life. The first group provides the most emphatic emotional confirmation of Fascism's existence. However, the second group determines and demonstrates the existence of Fascism in terms of its historical rationale. Almost always, the things that are said not to exist with suspicious reiteration do in fact exist. It could be said that those who, for centuries, have affirmed that God does not exist are the most palpable proof or counter-proof of the existence of God. Even the one who claimed that Spain had ceased to be Catholic immediately promoted the evidence of Catholicism in Spain. As a rule of thumb, it can be asserted that only those things that are said tenaciously not to exist undoubtedly exist. It does not occur to anyone to say that there is no Brahmanism in Spain. Because, of course, there is not. And it is said that there is no Fascism, *precisely because there is.*

On the third page, an anonymous article, attributed to José Antonio, lashes out against Gil Robles because he had affirmed that his political formation aspired to a "corporative organization" but "nothing of Fascism; we are not Fascist!" The writer responds to these affirmations of the leader of the *derechona*[169] with the following clarifications:

---

[169] [Translator: Literally, "the big right wing."]

As the audiences listening to Mr. Gil Robles are not usually very demanding in dialectical matters, they applaud with more or less heat those words, and then they disperse with more or less order, convinced that their leader is not a Fascist, that Fascism is rather a bad thing, that it deifies the state and is incompatible with religion, and that, in short, the convenient choice is to be antifascist and, at the same time, a supporter of the corporative state, of social reforms, and of all the other things that Mr. Gil Robles enumerates.

There are, however, dissatisfied people who ask themselves questions such as the following: *If Fascism is the sum of a few things, all of which, one by one, Mr. Gil Robles likes, why does he dislike Fascism?*

As we do not want anyone to be trapped in a mental labyrinth, we will try to clarify what Mr. Gil Robles likes about Fascism and why he is not a Fascist and does not seem to be on the way to becoming one . . . . Now it is Fascism's turn. In the face of materialistic barbarism—capitalism on one side, socialism on the other—which threatens to destroy the world's whole spiritual unity, a warm and joyful movement is rising up, returning back to the living core of each population in search of its own intimate unity. This movement seeks to end discord by elevating the rules governing the common cause above individual interests. No class struggle: the interest of the workers is, in its entirety, the interest of the collectivity; it is necessary to give the workers, at once, everything they need to enjoy a decent life without waiting for them to earn it by threatening and blackmailing. No political parties: the destiny of a people imposes a common duty incompatible with the existence of factions. This is how the new world movement known as Fascism works. To achieve the spiritual unity that it seeks, Fascism employs a variety of tools, one of which is the corporative organization, which suppresses political parties and the entire organization that relies on them. But note well, the instruments are never the essence, but rather that which is at the service of the essence. To assume that the instruments are the essence is to get the wrong end of the stick.

Well, this mistake defines the attitude of the popular parties toward Fascism. Just as they have invented a canned sociology to mislead the people, they now want to invent a cold-cut Fascism, too. Something that appropriates all the techniques of Fascism but without capturing its emotion. A cold organization, but structured in corporations, institutes, and who knows what else, maybe even mock militias. Something that is, with respect to Fascism, what canned sociology is with respect to socialism. But it will be futile: that did not stop the proletariat's push forward, and it will not stop the impetus of any eternal and young people who are determined to find themselves. The most it could accomplish is to deceive a few people, not to encourage caution in others. But it has already been seen a thousand times how the cautious are usually the clumsiest and how the inner core of history, like God, repels the lukewarm.

In the section "Noticiero de España" ["News from Spain"], it was reported how the FUE was attempting to resemble a political club and how the FUE's Association of Students of Medicine decided in its governing board on April 10th, 1933, to declare itself antifascist, approving the following agreements:

First: to declare the Association antifascist.
    Second: not to admit, within the Association, those individuals who profess Fascist ideas.

F.E. chimed in: "Hey, what's the matter? It is not those who are politically active who are being expelled, but those who hold Fascist views. The FUE establishes the tribunal of the inquisition to investigate the thoughts of its members."

To the lie suggested by the FUE that "the Fascists have introduced the use of firearms in student affairs," the reply is: "The Fascists? On January 18th, our comrade Manuel Baselga was shot in the back in Zaragoza. It was the FUE who tried to assassinate him, with the help of a hired gunman. Baselga suffered serious injuries."

The branch of the Falange in Madrid remained closed. A minister threatened to outlaw "Fascists" in response to the FUE incidents at the University.

This time, in the section "Fascist Life," the topic was Austria and "the difficult and rough program, planned by Chancellor Dollfuss . . . . This Dollfusian program is apparently clear: 'anti-parliamentarianism,' 'anti-liberalism,' 'anti-capitalism,' and 'anti-Marxism.' A comprehensive political and economic nationalism built on the foundations of a corporatist state." Regarding the development of Fascist activity in Belgium, there is mention of the National Party, founded by Jean Nyssen in collaboration with Paul Hornaest, president of the War Volunteers. From Chile, there was news of the appearance of certain *camisas pardas* [Brownshirts] during a patriotic rally at the Providencia Theater in Santiago de Chile. "The movement is still restricted and limited to the intellectual and student class and has a nationalist program achievable through corporatism." The tendency in South America toward a political and spiritual reordering was celebrated with joy. Italy is mentioned in an agricultural publication article titled "Para el mañana. El Estado propagandista: un ejemplo" ["For the Future. The Propagandist State: An Example"].

In a prominent spot, next to the heading of the "Fascist Life" section, is a premonitory note anticipating the revolution of Asturias that would break out in October serving as a warning and a voice of alarm:

To make up for their lack of essential virtues and moral courage, certain factions—better called gangs than parties—are stockpiling weapons with the full knowledge of all Spain. These are the same ones who talk the most about the Fascist threat; those who benefit from the impunity granted by the political stupidity of some and the cynical complicity of others. They are the ones who, in Spain's impoverished and fearful world, keep public alarm alive as a form of credit for their next chance to suckle at the government's teat—not to seize control of the state. These weapons, bought to sustain a mediocre and criminal permanent revolution, will one day serve for a petty revolution. This petty revolution will once again place the rifles of the assaulted authority back into their hands, to stab in the back those who preach when they aren't already latched onto the udders of the ideal cow-state, hidden at the end of the demagogic labyrinth.

Weapons in the hands of the merchants of the revolution, of the professionals of disorder—a few assassinations in the near future, or, if the calculations are different, a shot in the back. Anything could happen.

In this fifth issue of *F.E.*, the fourth part of "Spain and Rome" is published, discussing "Romance andaluz y humorismo aragonés" ["Andalusian Romance and Aragonese Comedy"].

In "Readings of Our Own," on the tenth page of the weekly, there was an article by Pier Maria Bardi with a more than suggestive title "Duce, a noi!" It began with these words: "My Duce, you, riding on a white horse—with your panache in the wind—placed yourself at the head of the people, advancing without stopping, and today you still are keeping on." We have before us a poetic portrait, in the style of an ode, dedicated to the new *condottiero* of the Italian revolution. It concludes with "Keep marching on: A Roman arch awaits, raised just for you."

On page eleven, the section "Economy and Work" is dedicated to "Política terrera" ["Politics of the Soil"], which begins with the following words:

> National Socialism evolved in cities but did not take root in Germany's landscape. It was necessary for the present minister of agriculture of the Third Reich to bring the propaganda of the new ideas to the countryside and procure for Hitler's program the agricultural character that it lacked at first, so that the great peasant masses would join the movement and allow the Führer, in successive and glorious stages, to achieve victory.
>
> Fascism, in the beginning, was not a doctrine preached on farms but in workshops. It was born in Milan, Italy's industrial powerhouse, and one of its most powerful stimuli was the factory crisis caused by the subordination of socialist organizations.
>
> It was after the first period of Fascism that Mussolini turned his gaze to the countryside and realized that, even in a country as densely populated and heavily industrialized as Italy, the salvation of the economy had to be sought in the cultivation of the ancestral land.

The article describes the agrarian achievements of Italian Fascism and National Socialism. It describes the "battle for grain" undertaken by Italy as the triumph of wheat. The article includes whole paragraphs of the Duce's speeches on rurality, which is described as "a formidable program of Fascist government, a manly and salvific program that advocates the policy of the countryside over that of the populous city. Because there, in the village, is the rich, inexhaustible stream of humanity, of births, the wide reservoir of serene, persistent, and healthy work, the storehouse of civic, domestic, and religious virtues." The article depicts a somber picture of the situation of the countryside in Spain and concludes its long and detailed account by bluntly declaring: "All of this must come to an end. Spain must pursue the agricultural path paved by Mussolini and Hitler. And from now on, *F.E.* commits itself to showing this path to those who ignore it." With this definite resolution, the weekly assumed a political commitment with its supporters and readers: a brotherly, consanguineous bond with the twin revolutions that had come before it in history and served as a template, a direction, and a compass to follow.

The last page ends with an intense article titled "Los mártires inocentes" ["The Innocent Martyrs"]:

> In the anecdotal books of the Italian Fascist movement, in the propaganda and printed history of German National Socialism, the figures of innocent martyrs concerned us both in their martyrdom and their innocence. Throughout these readings, they summarized the climate that was ripe for all the excesses of the pre-Fascist world—the dawn of a new age in the course of human movement, which finds in communism its eruption, returning to regressive forms, and in Fascism its Renaissance, which in Spain also represents its Counter-Reformation.
>
> The advance of these rigid tendencies towards the conquest of the state by the state itself and the grandeur of those propositions inherent in the national spirit, in its aspiration for empire, did not stop in either Italy or Germany at the criminal roadblocks placed in their path. It is futile, and the use of unchecked violence, without lofty goals, causes each new victim to fall just a few steps beyond the shadow of their own corpse. These innocent martyrs of their own martyrdom serve as milestones along the path to triumph, marking the proximity of the end of an itinerary which, due to historical biology—whether we like it or not—leads to the inevitable victory over the efforts of the regressive revolution. This victory will come at the expense of those who, amid ruins, raise the low and feeble towers of the supplementary, which grows at the cost of what is essential and feeds off the funerals of what is essential.
>
> Among us, in Spain and in all things Spanish, it could not have happened any other way. In the pre-Fascist dawn of the only possible salvation for our nation, amidst catastrophe, the first innocent martyrs have

fallen. They have fallen without even being chosen to uphold the ghost of terror, which is beginning to lose its shroud.

Fascist victims of the red terror? No, at least not all of them. They are victims of the mediocre terror of a revolution that is always on the verge—laughable if it were not beginning to turn dramatic—precisely and solely because of these cases, in which the need to maintain the criminal prestige of the ghost has led to pointing a pistol at the victims, who, once the 'spectacle' has taken place, are less able to endanger the criminal institutions, vaguely disguised in political costumes.

One day, a young man who was reading our weekly paper is killed. Another day, a true man of the people falls—a worker who, after proving his efforts in several trades, was a sales inspector for *La Nación*. Something worse than savagery, the premeditated convenience of creating victims, shrouds Spanish life in shame and inexorably accuses authorities who seem incapable of maintaining even the bare minimum of order in the streets. There, an equal and opposite violence will inevitably arise, if only out of a logical sense of self-defense, because when authority fails, only terror can suppress terror. The faith in the triumph of our ideals can only be strengthened by each of these attacks, which remind us that the only bastion capable of resisting the wave of administered barbarism is a swift takeover of the mechanisms of power under our control in Spanish life.

These innocent martyrs, along with an entire society terrified and subject to the whims of a party—or gangs—create the need for urgent action that the Spanish Falange keenly feels in its conscience, as a procession of people calling for intervention against the national gangrene, which has been uselessly treated in parliament with half-measures. And these victims, who are not always from our ranks, bring into sharp relief the necessity of resorting to the ultimate measures against organizations weakened by their natural discredit, organizations that are rejected by the Spanish proletariat, over whom the dawn of a new day is already rising, filling their understanding and their hearts with light.

Amid epitaphs for innocent martyrs, our flags advance, battered by the winds of the best omens.

This masterful article bound, even in blood, the protomartyrs of the Fascist revolutions of Italy and Germany with the martyrs of the Spanish Fascist revolution of the Falange. It was more than unity; it was identity. The blood shed in Fascism's rise to power, the innocent martyrs, were sacrificed in common. The Falange, in this article, felt as its own the coming of what in reality was nothing else than a continental revolution, a European revolution.

F.E. and the Dialectic of Lead

The release of *F.E.* on February 8th would have satisfied once again the eagerness for barbarism. On the same day, the police conducted an extensive search of the JONS branch in Calle de los Caños. The following day, a medical student, Matías Montero y Rodríguez de Trujillo, was shot and killed near his home as he returned from participating in the sale of the weekly. The date of Matías Montero's death would be commemorated as the day the student fell for the revolution. In him were embodied all the university martyrs who fell victim to hatred. The murderer, Francisco Tello Tortajada, affiliated with the socialist youth organization, shot him in the back, treacherously, on Calle Juan Álvarez Mendizábal.

Matías Montero fell mortally wounded, carrying as a badge, at the moment of his assassination, an article that was soaked with his own blood, shot out from his body by the criminal bullets.

> He was among the best. He accepted our movement with the fervor of those who had waited too long to find faith. Once found, he embraced it with zeal, courage, and joy.
>
> He was also among the greatest at what he did. Serving as a guide to the students, he set an example for them on the job and in civic life. His own calling and the eternal calling of Spain filled his spirit.
>
> On February 9th, he was, with others, defending the sale of our newspaper. A hired gunman followed him, and when he was alone, as he approached his house, he shot him three times in the back. Then he finished him off on the ground with one more shot.

That same day, in the Plaza de Santa Barbara in Madrid, communists and socialists, armed with batons and clubs, tried to intimidate the sellers of *F.E.*, who defended themselves with slaps and punches. In Gijón, the same scene occurred, resulting in four people being wounded in the scuffle. The following day, Falangist Fernando Cienfuegos, still convalescent and with his head bandaged, was stabbed, causing him serious injuries.

The following year, in the first days of 1935, José Antonio had lunch with Francisco Bravo at the Hotel Nacional. After the meal, their conversation continued, and José Antonio shared this confidence with him, with a serene outlook on the events of the previous year:

> Mussolini is right when he says that violence must be chivalrous, effective, and not exceed the necessary limit. In those first weeks, we had to demonstrate to the people that we were not a hired gang, prone to eliminating our adversaries by shooting them. I spoke at the Comedia regarding the dialectic of fists and pistols, not thinking of the street

ambushes where our best boys of the first hour fell, but of the conquest of the state and the defense of the Fatherland. But when the streets of Madrid turned red with the blood of those young men, or rather boys, who went out to sell *F.E.*, defenseless and courageous, I understood that we would have no other choice but to defend ourselves at all costs.[170]

The third page of the issue contained a drawing in bold lines. A worker, with a pickaxe in his left hand and a Mussolini-like profile, salutes with his arm raised, strong and muscular, the horizon where, among seven arrows in a solar semicircle, two eschatological initials stand out: "F.E." It was the greeting to the sun, to the dawn, to the sunrise. It was the Fascist, proletarian, and bare-chested salute of an unyielding figure, the Duce, who greeted the birth of the Spanish Falange.

A photograph on the fourth page powerfully attracted the attention of the reader. A large banner, as if it were a Flemish tapestry, with an inscription in huge letters and the following caption: "F.E. *VIVA EL FASCIO.*" The monumental tapestry hung from the upper cornice of the Casa del Pueblo building on Calle del Clavel in Madrid.

Next to the photograph was an advertisement for a book by H. E. Goad: *The Making of the Corporate State*. There is likewise an article titled "Genioteca de España" in which it is written:

> The truth is that just as it falls to Fascism to create an art, an architecture of a new style, so too will one of our tasks (on the day when it falls to us, inevitably and biologically, to rule the winds of all things Spanish with love and discipline) be to establish a control—both tender and severe—over the elderly, who are inclined toward careless, boundless opinions. These are the famous men who, in the winter of their lives, jeopardize their hard-earned reputations for a few coins of attention disguised as courteous flattery.

The central pages provided a detailed account of the political meeting held on February 4th in the Gran Teatro of Cáceres, during which the host, Alfonso Bardají, introduced the speakers, who were then joined by Rafael Sánchez Mazas and Julio Ruiz de Alda, who openly addressed the people of Extremadura:

> We are revolutionaries; and we are revolutionaries because we want to transform Spain. Nothing of previous revolutions; the revolution is yet to be made, and either the proletarians, poisoned by the revanchist propaganda, will make it, or we will have to carry it out ourselves because the Spanish youth is entirely revolutionary, whether it leans toward communism or toward the other side: Fascism.

---

[170] Bravo, *José Antonio, el hombre, el jefe, el camarada*, 45.

The event was concluded by José Antonio, who, when mentioning socialism in his speech, expressed the following thought:

> They thought that those starving workers were their brothers, but . . . if the first socialists were gentlemen, almost poets, socialism took on a horrifying darkness when the figure of that Jew Karl Marx appeared, and it became so dark because he considered religion, the fatherland, and every sentiment, including love, to be false, believing in nothing but economic factors. Thus, he pitted capitalism against the proletariat in a fratricidal struggle. So Karl Marx takes his position, contemplating this tremendous drama and deducing his fatal laws.

With regard to liberalism, he remarks:

> Liberalism has lost faith in ideas; everything is equal in its view, and then Europe, in desperation, when it believes its last moments have arrived, embraces faith; it realizes that in the heart there is love, there is fraternity, there is union.

He then illustrates the way of the Falange with these words:

> There is a way to save Spain and achieve the triumph of all parties; that is, to achieve Spanish unity, which cannot be achieved either with words or with speeches in the Cortes.
>
> Italy is smaller than Spain and has a larger population than our fatherland; it was in a state of total destruction and unfathomable neglect. Well, with enthusiasm, energy, and faith, the Italians have succeeded in making it glorious and strong, carrying to the farthest corners of the world their triumphs and their glories, and they have achieved this because they are all united there under a strong and firm hand, which is worth more than any parliamentary resolution; a hand that holds the sheaf of wheat: the sheaf that represents union and the wheat that was extracted from the marshes, which were unproductive but today are cultivated. That is what we need; but when we hear that we are imitators, we will answer that it is not true, because imitating is not the same as looking back on ourselves, as they did, because when we look back on ourselves, we find ourselves; because Spain knew how to be strong, sober, austere, and knew how to sacrifice itself for what is spiritual, knowing how to be heroic above all things and how to have its own people die when it was necessary. Spain did not have any factions until it lost its strength. How do you picture socialist radicals during Philip II's reign? [Great laughter.] And without factions and political

parties it fought gloriously, having as its stage the whole surface of the earth and as its enemy nothing less than Satan.

In this issue, the section "Fascist Life" was dedicated to Italy, bringing together quotes from the main Italian Fascist ideologists on the topic of the press, which, according to Starace, secretary of the National Fascist Party, should have as its mission, according to the Grand Council, the following points: a) dissemination of the Fascist doctrine; b) cultural activity; c) preparation of young people. The commentary finished with a phrase from Spengler:

Italy, as long as Mussolini lives, is a great power; may it perhaps find in the Mediterranean the great foundations to become an authentic world power. For this task, the press is a wonderful tool. Newspapers and magazines— under this idea—will find a great way to develop.

News and comments are also given with regards to Germany and Ireland, mentioning O'Duffy: "In Ireland, the supporters of General O'Duffy are constituting a force that must be taken seriously." The words of the general are quoted from a conference with journalists in which he specified the political viewpoint of his party: "I aim to create in Ireland a corporatist state based on the Italian Fascist model." Regarding North America, the situation of the individual and his helplessness is discussed. A quarter of the page is filled with a reproduction of the propaganda poster of the Mostra della Rivoluzione fascista [Fascist Revolutionary Exhibition] headed by a bust of Mussolini, his first political office, and a collage of the main achievements of the Fascist regime.

On the ninth page, and in a large part of the tenth, one finds the speech that José Antonio delivered on February 1st in the Cortes, under the title: "F.E., la FUE y la Universidad" ["F.E., the FUE, and the University"], from which we extract the following paragraphs:

On April 10th, 1933 (that is, before any Fascist movement had publicly manifested itself), the Board of Directors of the Medical Students' Professional Association, which was affiliated with the FUE, solemnly proclaimed its antifascist stance. In accordance with that agreement, made on April 10, 1933, the Board of Directors of the Medical Students' Professional Association convened a General Meeting for January 13th of this year, and on the agenda were these two points: First, the Antifascist Declaration of the Association. Second, the refusal to admit into the Association those individuals who profess Fascist ideas. This antiliberal declaration—antiliberal even if it seems otherwise—goes so far as to exclude from the Professional Association of Students not only those who actively engage in Fascist activities, but anyone who merely holds Fascist ideas. In other words, the FUE, reviving the methods of the Inquisition, but in a more subtle form, is now investigating not what the students do outside, but what they think, in case that displeases the leadership of the FUE.

One day, this clash between the FUE, which had officially, dogmatically, and canonically declared itself antifascist, and a handful of students interested in this European movement called "Fascism," became more serious. And do the government and the chamber know how it was resolved the first time? By attempting to assassinate the student Baselga, from Zaragoza, who was labeled a Fascist by the FUE.

Indeed, an assassin from the FUE followed Baselga in Zaragoza. The assassin was part of a group of FUE students, and someone told him, "Shoot now." And in fact, the assassin followed the student and, as Baselga was about to enter a café, shot him four times, two bullets piercing a lung, leaving him on the verge of death . . . . But moreover—and this is the criticism I would cautiously direct at the Government—facing the phenomenon of Fascism, the government, and especially the subordinate authorities, are acting in a most peculiar way. To the Director General of Security, Fascism is some kind of secret organization that must be closely watched, to the point where the Director General of Security says it is his "nightmare." Well, this idea of Fascism—and I apologize to the Director General of Security—is a completely coarse one. Fascism may be understood this way, as a band of thugs, by some local councilman from a remote part of Spain. But Fascism is a European unrest, a new way of conceiving everything: history, the state, the entry of the proletariat into public life; a new way of understanding all the phenomena of our time and interpreting them with its own sense. Fascism has already triumphed in several countries, and in some, like Germany, it has triumphed by the most unimpeachably democratic means. ("By murdering," a socialist deputy mutters. Murmurs follow, and the president calls for order.) Murdering, says His Excellency, but the fact is that it secured over 90 percent of the votes. I don't hold votes in very high regard, but that's the way it is.

Faced with these facts, this universal unrest of Fascism, for the Director General of Security to say "We have Fascism under close watch" is like saying "We have Euclidean geometry under close watch," or "We are closely watching the materialist interpretation of history." (Mr. Menéndez: "That, they are watching.") It's a perfectly absurd attitude. I would completely understand if the Director General of Security were to repress violent acts by Fascism or any other movement, but I cannot understand why the Director General of Security feels it is his duty to monitor the spread of an idea.

The Director General of Security has found an admirable assistant in the Press Prosecutor. Every issue of that magazine called *F.E.*—which Mr. Hernández Zancajo, with his good taste, reads (laughter)—and which he must have seen is a perfectly respectable literary magazine; every one of those issues, I say, ends up in the hands of the Press Prosecutor and rouses his wrath . . . . I don't believe the government will resort to the FUE's argument, that we are an antiliberal association. But I don't think the government—at least not without injustice—can say that we are a violent association either, because here, faced with these vague accusations of violence, Fascist hordes, our assassins, and our gunmen, I invite Mr. Hernández Zancajo to name a single case, with names and surnames. Meanwhile, I tell the chamber that we have had one man murdered in Daimiel, another in Zalamea, another in Villanueva de la Reina, and another in Madrid, and the recent case of the unfortunate foreman of the newspaper *F.E.* And all of them had names and surnames, and it is known that they were killed by gunmen who either belonged to the Socialist Youth or were closely inspired by them. These are the facts.

In this issue, Giménez Caballero's series "Spain and Rome" discussed "Foro y campo" ["The Forum and the Countryside"], and, as always, it ran for a full page.

In the eighth issue of *JONS*, which corresponded to January 1934 (pages 40–43), was inserted the announcement of "a forthcoming meeting of the National Council of the JONS," in which the first point on the agenda was the position of the members "regarding the Fascist group F.E."

On February 13th, José Antonio signed a document together with Ramiro Ledesma, triumvir of the JONS, which contained the "approved rules of the agreement between the JONS and F.E." It consisted of seven brief points. A collaboration agreement between the two most active Fascist entities in Spain:

> First point: creation of the political movement Falange Española de las Juntas de Ofensiva Nacional Sindicalista [Spanish Falange of the Councils of the National Syndicalist Offensive]. It is founded by F.E. and the JONS merged together.
>
> Second point: it is considered essential that the new movement insists on forging a political personality that does not lend itself to being confused with right-wing groups.
>
> Third point: merger of the hierarchies of F.E. and the JONS. Recusal in the leadership of the new movement of comrades over the age of forty-five.
>
> Fourth point: National Syndicalist affirmation in the sense of revolutionary direct action.
>
> Fifth point: the new movement must be preferably coordinated by the current hierarchies of the JONS of Galicia, Valladolid, and Bilbao in

immediate agreement with the current organizations of the Spanish Falange in Barcelona, Valencia, Granada, Badajoz, and their respective areas.

Sixth point: the emblem of the new movement must be the arrows and the yoke of the JONS and their current flag: red and black.

Seventh point: elaboration of a concrete National Syndicalist program where the fundamental principles of our movement are defended and justified: unity, direct action, anti-Marxism, and a revolutionary approach that ensures the redemption of the working population, peasants, and small industrialists.

Madrid, February 13th, 1934.

Ramiro Ledesma Ramos publicly and solemnly declared himself to be a Fascist, and with this statement he begins his book *¿Fascismo en España?*: "Regarding the thing that the people out there call Fascism: the author has been, from the very beginning, one of the most fervent supporters of that design."[171] According to the revolutionary from Zamora, the identity of both organizations could not be achieved without the evolution of José Antonio "more and more every day toward a revolutionary interpretation of Fascism, which facilitated the agreement with the JONS."[172] The biographer of José Antonio, Carlos de Arce, explains that Ledesma and his small minority movement followed the example of Mussolini and Italian Fascism, along with some similarities to the National Socialism that Hitler was introducing in Germany.

The fusion was possible because, as we have already pointed out, and as Ramiro Ledesma writes, "Primo de Rivera, since the immediate post-dictatorial times of his ultra-right propaganda of the Monarchist Union in 1930–1931, evolved more and more every day toward a revolutionary interpretation of Fascism, which facilitated the agreement with the JONS." [173] The agreement was reached by the National Council of the JONS during a secret meeting held on February 11th and 12th in an attic of the Gran Vía in Madrid, where the Ercilla brothers, from Valladolid, were lodging. According to the official announcement, one of the topics to be discussed was the future relationship with the Falange organization, which they considered a "Fascist group."

As stated in the article "El espíritu y la decisión jonsista" ["The Spirit and Decision of the JONS"]:

The constitution of the JONS as a "political action group" was the

---

[171] Ledesma Ramos, *¿Fascismo en España?*, 39.

[172] Ibid., 149.

[173] Ibid., 149.

consequence of an ideological movement that had materialized earlier in *La Conquista del Estado*, the first Fascist newspaper published in Spain, whose first issue appeared on March 14th, 1931, boldly challenging the coming social democratic revolution.

On February 15th, the governmental authority banned the publication of the weekly *F.E.* for the second time. Meanwhile, the Supreme Court petition to proceed against the deputy José Antonio Primo de Rivera was approved in the Cortes on February 20th. This was due to two articles in the first issue of the Falangist weekly that were condemned: "Julito y la unión de derechas" and "La victoria sin alas."

F.E., Organ Of Falange Española de las JONS

Finally, on Thursday, February 22nd, the seventh issue of *F.E.* was released, once the suspension was lifted. At eleven o'clock that night, near the newspaper's headquarters in Plaza del Callao, a confrontation took place between socialists and Falangists, between those willing to use violence to silence this organ of opinion and those determined to proclaim the good news in Spain's streets and squares. The intervening authorities arrested Falangist students Fernando Reyes Gonzalez and Vicente Gaceo del Pino, who were bravely fighting back. They were charged with unlawful possession of weapons, and their case was heard in the Emergency Court on March 8th. Defended by José Antonio, both were found not guilty after it was established through expert testimony that the weapons they were carrying were unusable. Another student was brutally lynched, receiving violent blows all over his body. The following day, and for the same reasons, four Falangists were arrested in Murcia. On the 24th, violent events occurred again on Calle Florida in Madrid, where three Falangists were wounded while selling the weekly. The socialist youth, taking advantage of their numerical superiority, brutally unleashed their rage and anger once more. In Barcelona, on the 26th, the workers, stirred up by leftist organizations, went out in protest to prevent the sale of the weekly.

The seventh issue featured on its cover the new symbol of the union: the yoke and arrows, straight and geometrical. As the Italian journalist Nello Enriquez writes in his work *La Spagna Risorge*, "for the Falangists, the arrows and the yoke have the same symbolic meaning as our *fascio littorio*: in them is symbolized a whole program of unity and collaboration."[174] This issue can be rightly said to be a memorable copy. The following note was written in the final section:

Everyone is aware of the innumerable obstacles that our publication faces

---

[174] Nello Enriquez, *La Spagna Risorge*, 97.

along its path. Another unavoidable impediment prevented *F.E.* from appearing last Thursday.

There has been no shortage of waffling commentators who have deemed *F.E.* definitively defunct. We are sorry to spoil such a sweet illusion. But as our readers will see, not only does *F.E.* exist, it also offers you this extraordinary issue with four additional pages.

Allow this new proof to serve as a proclamation of our standards of conduct. On the one hand, we are incited to commit violence in accordance with the expectations of the commentators; on the other hand, we are threatened, and painful gaps are opened in our ranks. But our people remain steadfast, which is the best sign of fortitude.

This is how we understand our mission: in the face of defeatism and in the face of murder, the unshakable slogan does not waver: to carry on.

The editorial was dedicated to F.E. and JONS: "Since last week, F.E. and the JONS have formed a single organization with a single board of command, with a perfect fusion in all the national and local levels of the hierarchy and an endearing fraternity among all affiliates."

In the section "Aire Libre," a sports anecdote is featured:

A sportsman was asked a few days ago:
   "And after the Fascists triumph, what will you do with the Cortes?"
   The sportsman had a variety of options for his response. He could have announced that a ping-pong stadium or an indoor tennis court would be built there, for example. But he is a generous man, and instead he remarked:
   "There, we will install the National Museum of Wax Figures."

It is worth mentioning the article "La verdad y la muerte" ["Truth and Death"], in which a militant of the Falange, days before his death, tells a comrade:

One day, we witnessed the overwhelming growth of European nationalist movements, which also demonstrated the lucid truth of action and self-sacrifice based on constructive postulates rather than destructive fantasies. On that day, many of us consciously turned our gaze toward the dawn, which signaled the arrival of a glorious day of sunshine . . . . Synthesis of Spanish virtue, nectar of the eternal youth of a country that refuses to die in the mercenary hands of Metics and Mozarabs, Jews and Freemasons, international pacifists who work for Amsterdam; instead, with a proud gesture so many times repeated, it wants to flourish luxuriantly in the perennial spring of its history, with the eternally renewed vitality of its youth.

In "Fascist Life" the topics discussed was "La juventud en la Rusia Soviética" ["Youth in Soviet Russia"], in which it is reported that "these days, Italian education specialists studying the new youth are paying close attention to a recent book by the German author Klaus Mehner, entitled *Youth in Soviet Russia*. A truly interesting book." The commentary concludes: "Fortunately, the Fascist revolution knows how to confront this subversion of intellectual and spiritual values with a strong and opposing ideal, this typically oriental subversion of the Russians." In the section "Mosaico Noticioso" ["News Mosaic"], it is reported that,

> One year since the founding of Littoria by Mussolini, the Duce has inaugurated new projects rewarding the settlers of the Pontine marshes. In his speech to the people, the Duce announced that in a year's time the province of Littoria would be inaugurated, "the greatest thing realized so far by the Fascist regime in Italy," and that "in Switzerland, the Fascist Federation of the Canton of Ticino has begun to publish its newspaper *The Swiss Fascist*.[175] Its program is against Marxism and Freemasonry, advocating a true democracy based on love for the people and the common good."

Among other articles, the following news item stood out:

> Attention, worker! Loebe, former head of German socialism, has said the following: "An easy thing for me to do, since I have lost the confidence I once had in the efficacy and success of my idea. For a long time, I faithfully served it; today, I cannot serve it because I do not believe it to be beneficial. We must surrender to the evidence: the hour of socialism has passed. Socialism has fulfilled its mission, and its historic time has definitively come to an end. All of its possibilities have now been exhausted, not only in Germany, but throughout Europe. I agree with Hitler in believing that a new political system has come into the world. I am already aware that I risk being labeled a traitor and subjected to anathemas and insults from former friends. But I cannot lie. I have seen for myself that this new regime is doing things that we were not able to do; I have become convinced that the National Socialist idea must last and prevail. I am a spiritual follower of the policy led by Hitler."

---

[175] [Translator: The city that today is known as Latina was founded as Littoria in June 1932 by the Fascist government, when settlers coming from the north of Italy worked to drain the swamp that had occupied its area since antiquity. It was inaugurated by Mussolini in December of the same year. The etymology of the old name of the city comes from *fascio littorio*.]

Awaken, worker! Listen to the voices of unwavering belief!

On the seventh page of this issue, for the first time, a short overview of Falange Española was narrated, noting that "Sánchez Mazas had been the first to speak in Spain about Italian Fascism." In this brief historical synthesis of the life of the movement, there is a summary of the rally at the Comedia on October 29th, 1933. It is pointed out that, although the history of the Spanish Falange is not long,

> It is already ennobled with the names of five martyrs. All of them were either militants in our ranks or were killed—always cowardly, treacherously —for proclaiming their faith in our spirit. Their names were: José Ruiz de la Hermosa, Juan Grau, Tomás Polo Gallego, Francisco de Paula Sampol Cortés, and Matías Montero y Rodríguez de Trujillo. For their honor and example, their names live on in us. Their sacrifice will grant us, from God, new gifts of perseverance. When speaking of victims, we cannot fail to remember Don Vicente Pérez Rodríguez, agent of sales for *F.E.* He did not militate in the Falange; but perhaps those who assassinated him chose him to frighten our fellow travelers.

This short history of the Spanish Falange ended with the section "Nueva Vida" ["New Life"]:

> On February 13th, the official union between the JONS and Falange Española was signed. The two twin movements could not remain separated. The barriers to unification would have been insurmountable for old-style parties where the petty and personal prevail, but not for us, for we have our sights set on achieving our goal.
>
> Consequently, JONS and Falange Española are no longer separate entities. There is only one movement now, which is called Falange Española de las Juntas de Ofensiva Nacional Sindicalista. Now comes the great phase. Soon, better days will come for Spain.

Page twelve included a long article by Viscount Rothermere on "Fascism in England," which José Antonio's newspaper presented in the following way:

> We publish below an article by the great press tycoon Viscount Rothermere, in which he urges the English to adapt their political constitution to the needs of the times. The old political parties are in agony in England, as they are elsewhere . . . . It is not surprising, then, that the parades of the Blackshirts excite men and women in England who are tired of the party system, liberalism, and their inaction. They see a strong and vigorous organization that is modern and, most importantly, young. It is not in the hands of the timid dodderers who dominate all the organs of English public

life. The motto of the Blackshirts is "action," rather than "drift," and, as Goethe said, *doing* is the most important of human activities. *Hurrah for the Blackshirts!*

The article begins by stating:

Because Fascism comes from Italy, shortsighted people in this country think they show a sturdy national spirit by deriding it. If their ancestors had been equally stupid, Britain would have had no banking system, no Roman law, nor even any football, since all of these are of Italian invention.

The socialists especially, who jeer at the principles and uniform of the Blackshirts as being of foreign origin, forget that the founder and high priest of their own creed was the German Jew Karl Marx.

Though the name and form of Fascism originated in Italy, that movement is not now peculiar to any nation. It stands in every country for the party of youth. It represents the effort of the younger generation to put new life into out-of-date political systems. That alone is enough to make it a factor of immense value in our national affairs.[176]

This was followed by an explanation of the spirit and doctrine of the Blackshirts, their symbols, and their demonstrations.

The article "Política terrera," which discussed the agricultural problem, emphasized:

To the faint-hearted timid spirits who cling to routine, the undertaking will seem impossible. What has already been achieved in Italy and Germany by Fascism and National Socialism has shown, with unexpected speed, the opposite; from now on, no one will doubt that the greatness of a country is not to be measured by culture, luxury, and the advancement of its capital, but by the better distribution of wealth, the degree of general welfare, and the gradual progress shown by all its towns, even the smallest, since those who live in them are as much citizens as the other inhabitants of the nation.

Ernesto Giménez Caballero also published a new chapter, the sixth of his essay "España y Roma," this time focusing on "Orbe y pueblo" ["World and People"]:

We are going to cover this first stage—the ancient stage—of Spain's spiritual ties with Rome.

---

[176] [Translator: "Hurrah for the Blackshirts," Harold Harmsworth 1st Viscount Rothermere, from the *Daily Mail* of January 1934.]

We have seen, studied, and digested the indices of Roman history: That which notable ancient Spaniards bestowed on the city of the Tiber.

Andalusia and Aragon were the most generous in providing exemplary souls.

Seneca, the philosopher, was the great founder of an entire school of Roman philosophy. Lucan, from Cordoba, was the creator of Caesarean poetry. Martial, the humorist, was the creator of a whole literary genre: the epigram. Quintilian was the restorer of eloquence. And Columella originated the love for the land. Mela saw the vision of the world. In addition, other minor figures, such as Seneca the rhetorician, Gaius Rufus the poet, Marcus Porcius Latron, the stoic Decianus, and the orator Valerius Licinius, contributed to other great achievements.

Together with these men of spirit, the five men of action were Trajan, Hadrian, Galba, Maximus, and Theodosius.

Is that all? Did Spain contribute only these individuals to the greater glory of Rome? The obscure, anonymous people, of whom there are no signatures or names left, made their own contribution. The Spanish people knew how to erase their indigenous and barbarian cults to elevate their hearts to the Roman divinities: to the state, to the goddess Rome, to the Pantheon, and to the most authentic Roman spirit. There we find—in the provincial archaeological museums of Spain—the remains of those religious devotions to the Victoria Augusta, to the Pax Perpetua, to the Libertas, and to the Bonus Eventus.

In the historical memory that goes back to the medieval corporations and perhaps, today, to the corporate unions, there are the names of the Confraternities, of the Herculanos of Tortosa, of the Adoradores de Diana of Sagunto, and of the Lares Públicos of Caperea.

But above all, what remains as a striking reminder of the Spanish popular offering to Rome is the Testaccio hill next to the Tiber, on the outskirts of Rome. There, the amphorae that came from Spain to Rome have been gradually collected—from Ecija, from Cordoba, from Seville, from Cádiz, from Malaga. In those amphorae came wine, oil, wheat, and minerals from Spain. All of our country's outpourings: our olive groves, vineyards, wheat fields, and mines.

Spain nourished ancient Rome with its bread and soul, as only a mother could do.

That is why Seneca, Lucan, and Martial referred to her as *mater*.

In the section "Lecturas propias," the weekly *F.E.* covered two topics: several excerpts from Benito Mussolini's book *Vita di Sandro e di Arnaldo* [*Life of Sandro and Arnaldo*], and an article from the newspaper *Informaciones*, whose author was Giménez Caballero, with the title "Se buscan cuadrillas" ["Cuadrillas Wanted"], in which he comments on the murder of Mario Sonzini, a Fascist of the early days, "who was thrown into a smelting furnace," as well as that of the Fascist student Maramotti, "who wrote to his mother: 'Mother, perhaps I'm going to die. Do not cry. Be proud of your son. Long live Italy! Long live Fascism!'" He also wrote of Matías Montero, of whom he remarks:

> The blood of the Spanish student Matías Montero Rodríguez—that blood that the boys pointed at on the sidewalk, running down the stream of Calle Mendizábal—is no longer blood; it is the myth of youth, transubstantiation, the crimson light of dawn.
>
> The death of the student Matías Montero does not need to be avenged by a cuadrilla of good professional matadors, as the bullfighting audience would demand in a spectacular bullfight, beginning at four o'clock in the afternoon.
>
> The painful, deep, silent stupor of the best Spain before that death is today the most beautiful revenge. May Spain weep with virile tears. The finest preparation for combat has always resided in heroes.

The last page, which concludes the edition, contains a posthumous article by Matías Montero entitled "Las Flechas de Isabel y Femando" ["The Arrows of Isabel and Fernando"], which ends with this exhortation: "We await, future comrades, with our arm outstretched, the symbol and defense of the *Pax Romana*."

The Eighth Issue of *F.E.* Reclaims An "Authentic Fascism"

The fusion of the Spanish Falange and the JONS strengthened the movement. A large public rally was announced in Valladolid, the stronghold of Onésimo Redondo and his Castilian squadrons. Three days before the event, the eighth issue of the weekly was published. For the second time on the front cover, right above the title page, the new political movement's emblem of the yoked arrows was proudly displayed.

The editorial *Por el absurdo* [By Absurdity] tackled this dilemma: "In Spain, as in all Europe, we have only two forces in charge of deciding: a destructive, disorderly, and shapeless revolution and a constructive, orderly, and reforming revolution, which is ours."

The first of the "Guiones," the one that opens the series, is titled "Anatema." In it, it is written that:

> The pope has never condemned Fascism in Italy. He has referred to Mussolini as the "man given to Italy by Divine Providence." He has assigned chaplains to each legion of the Blackshirts. He has celebrated the

social and religious benefits of Fascist legislation, from the return of the crucifix in schools to the moral elevation of Italy in all aspects of life. But Fascism has been condemned as anti-Catholic in *El Heraldo* by the young gentleman Gil Robles, who was nervous precisely after the unanimous emotion aroused by the Christian honors paid to one of our dead. The gentleman Gil Robles must understand that the anathemas of Holy Mother Church can never come from below or from such a low position.

Between *El Heraldo* and the *Acta Apostolicae Sedis*, there is more or less the same distance as between the anathema of Mr. Gil Robles and the anathema of the Vicar of Christ.

Another broadside of the weekly *F.E.* against the leader of the *derechona*, elaborating on Gil Robles' statements in the newspaper *El Heraldo* wherein he accused Fascism of being anti-Catholic, was to be found in the energetic response of José Antonio's article "El señorito Gil Robles está nervioso" ["The Young Gentleman Gil Robles is Nervous"]. In it, he reclaimed for the Falange the essence of Fascism and sharply criticized the substitute that Gil Robles was opportunistically and shamelessly seeking to push to the electoral masses. We emphasize the following points in this clairvoyant article, among others:

First, he sought to frighten devout women by claiming that Fascism was anti-Catholic. This caused some uproar. The advocate of that idea, however, was ridiculed when he was reminded that no less than the pope—an authority superior to that of Mr. Gil Robles in the entire Catholic world, except in the offices of Acción Popular—had signed the famous pact with Mussolini and ennobled the Fascist organizations with the presence of Catholic chaplains. Thus, the anti-Catholicism argument was somewhat flattened. However, Mr. Gil Robles, out of habit, blurts it out once again in the interview with *El Heraldo* that the lines of this article comment upon. We imagine that the delicate religious consciences of *El Heraldo* readers shuddered with scrupulosity upon learning that Fascism is anti-Catholic.

But it was obvious to Mr. Gil Robles that a stronger dish was required for the *Heraldo*, and so it was served. He said he did not believe in Fascism. "At least the type of Fascism they want to present to us now as Fascism. Fascism, in Spain or anywhere else, cannot be represented by the gentlemen; they will not achieve success in any way."

The gentlemen! Has no one informed Mr. Gil Robles about our meeting in Carpio de Tajo last Sunday? He would have seen a crowd of gentlemen there! If all these ordinary people, authentic and tenacious, who hardly applaud, ended up acclaiming us with their arms raised, it was after demanding very clear and sincere things from us about the eternal Spain—which nobody ever talks to them about—and about social justice. The gentlemen in denim shirts and corduroys believe in us because they know we are going there, wearing ties and all, to become part of their destinies in a common patriotic enterprise, and not to ask for their votes in elections or to collect data on their anguish in order to include them in cold statistics manufactured by research institutes.

The common people have a clear-sighted instinct. That is why they believe in us and respect us. On the other hand, they reserve their antifascist hatred—as Mr. Gil Robles can see how things are—for the supporters of Acción Popular. Does Mr. Gil Robles not read *La Lucha, La Tierra*, and other similar publications? Well, if he read all these publications, he would notice that under each truculent antifascist headline there appears a reference to the actions of Acción Popular; almost never to ours.

We are respected because we are authentic. We paved a good path for Spain, and we are steadfastly following it, with the sacrifice and danger symbolized by our five martyrs. On the other hand, Mr. Gil Robles regards Fascism as a fad, and, while he attacks it in *El Debate* and in *El Heraldo*, he launches, to take advantage of the fad, an imitation of Fascism, the JAP, which is attempting to win over the fervor of the youth with certain vague invocations to the great Spain and to the corporative state.

But to no avail: such a cold Fascism, without authentic spiritual warmth, cannot nourish anyone. No one trades the hot meal, with its true flavor, for the same dish that spent the whole night in the pantry. Thus, while twenty-seven boys of the JAP turn out when they are summoned to defend the machines of *El Debate*, we mobilize several thousand, in spite of all the dangers, as soon as we announce our intention to hold a rally. And the fact is that, for the honor of mankind, men risk their lives following spiritual impulses, but they have not yet fallen into the frozen monstrosity of facing death to preserve the integrity of a few typesetting machines.

Calm down, Gil Robles. We understand that you have plenty of reasons to be in a bad mood: the crisis has been delayed; people are getting impatient; the JAP has not been able to replace us . . . . All of this is unpleasant. But you have to control your nerves. Or, at least, do not let your bad mood show. Remember that some will have a place in history and others will never have it, but in any case, places in history are not won by jostling.

On the "Noticiero del Mundo" page, there were stories about France and the magistrate prince, the announcement that "Sandino, the romantic leader, has died," and also news about Austria.

The first meeting of the new organization, Falange Española de las JONS, was held in the lands of Toledo, in Carpió de Tajo, in a rustic and wheaten setting. The speakers were José María Alfaro, Emilio Alvargonzález, Julio Ruiz de Alda—who addressed the audience and "pointed out to them that, in their role as workers, the only way to follow is to form trade unions that, in a totalitarian state, are, unlike the political parties, the ones that intervene in the governance of the country"—and José Antonio Primo de Rivera. The triumvir, Ramiro Ledesma, also attended the event along with the speakers that day. The event's conclusion was described in the report as follows: "The conclusion of Carpió de Tajo was crowned by the enthusiasm of the entire town. Along the streets, the Roman greetings symbolized the depth reached by our words."

In the section "Economía y trabajo" ["Economy and Work"], a large portion of the page is dedicated to a rigorous analysis and critique of the liberal economy and the alternative to its ravages. A comparison is made between liberal and Fascist economics, with the conclusion:

The Fascist-directed economy, as it is being developed in Italy and Germany, besides giving splendid results, allows the Fascist state to control all the economic activities of the nation, not allowing illicit business to be carried out due to the selfishness or speculation of a mass of capitalists, who, in addition to harming the nation's economy, oppress and coerce the worker. Furthermore, it directs and leads those activities that directly benefit the people. It creates industry for items that were previously taxed from abroad and intensifies agricultural production to meet the country's needs while also generating the derivative industries that provide so many benefits.

This past year was the first time in the Fascist era that Italy did not need to import foreign wheat, and when we consider that its territory is nearly half the size of Spain and its population density exceeds forty-two million inhabitants, we can see that the victory was truly magnificent.

How can this be accomplished? By having thousands of patriots, wisely led and paid, who began with an ardor never seen before the drying and cultivation of the Pontine Marshes: an immense patch of land near Rome that is twenty-eight miles long and six to eleven miles wide, and has an area of 460 square miles, which for centuries had turned into a swampy plain that provided Rome with malaria, causing illness to spread during the months of spring and summer. Despite numerous attempts dating back to the reign of Appius Claudius (312 B.C.) and continuing to the present day, no ruler, ancient or modern, has ever managed to restore these lands.

Work was carried out with enthusiasm, knowing that the effort was for the advancement of Italy and for the advancement of the Fatherland that the Fascist regime wanted to achieve as the supreme aspiration of its existence, and it succeeded! The first town was born: Littoria. The evocative name recalled the Roman lictors, who carried the bundle of sticks with the axe coming out of the center, a symbol of strength and justice. And it was the Duce who, instead of giving a pompous and pretentious speech lasting several hours, like the typical politicians, picked up the pitchfork and began to lift the bales of wheat with the peasants, a supreme expression of gratitude for the work. And there arose plants for the production of tractors, ploughs, and other agricultural machinery so necessary to further develop this wealth. And thirty thousand families moved into the new peasant settlement to work with faith and enthusiasm for the future of that new town.

But the greatest display of Fascist content in this issue is on pages ten and eleven of the newspaper, which are entirely devoted to a reproduction of a speech by Mussolini addressed to the National Council of Corporations. These are two four-column pages, each one of them densely written, with subsections and segmented spaces containing the main ideas and statements that characterized the Duce's speech. A summary of the Falangist speeches and rallies was also included. Mussolini's speech is featured in its entirety.

On the last page, there was the usual section on parliamentary views and a highlighted note, in a larger typeface, placed in the upper center with the heading "La Guardia de Europa" ["The Guard of Europe"], where it is written:

Chancellor Hitler's attention has been drawn to our civil guard while searching for the best police force in Europe for the most delicate mission. The Spanish government determined that the request to have civil guards guard the Saar referendum could not be granted. So be it. However, just the fact that our civil guard has been invited to act as guard of Europe must have sent a shiver of pride under the tricorns and appears to have filled Spain once again—since when last time?—with a certain imperial air of the best days.

The March 4th Rally in Valladolid

On the 4th of March, in the Teatro Calderón of Valladolid, the sacred unity of the new political movement was sealed with an impressive rally attended by Martínez de Bedoya, Gutiérrez Palma, Ruiz de Alda, Onesimo Redondo, Ledesma Ramos, and Primo de Rivera. And it was precisely in Castile, in those faithful lands of the Spanish heartland, that Valladolid, once again, put faith in the yoke and arrows.

José Antonio once again launched into the wind of the Castilian plateau, "absolute earth, absolute sky," an unforgettable and transcendental speech, an oratorical piece befitting the level demanded by the situation. We highlight from his speech the enlightening paragraph he devoted to Fascism:

They tell us that we are imitators. Onésimo Redondo has already responded to this. They tell us that we are imitators because our movement, which aims at a return to the true essence of Spain, has already occurred in other places. Italy and Germany have turned inward toward themselves in a gesture of desperation toward the myths with which they tried to sterilize them, but because Italy and Germany have done so and have found themselves entirely, shall we say that Spain is imitating them by searching within itself? These countries have returned to their own authenticity, and, in doing so, the authenticity that we will also find will be our own; it will not be that of Germany or Italy, and therefore, in reproducing what the Italians or the Germans have done, we will be more Spanish than we have ever been.

To comrade Onésimo Redondo, I would say this: Do not be too concerned because they tell us that we are imitating. If we managed to destroy this idea, they would already be inventing new slanders against us. The sources of malice are limitless. Allow them to claim that we imitate the Italian Fascists. After all, beneath the local characteristics of Fascism, as in all movements throughout history, there are certain constants that are the patrimony of every human spirit and are universal. So it was, for example, with the Renaissance; so it was, if you will, with the hendecasyllable: they brought us the hendecasyllable from Italy, but soon after bringing us the hendecasyllable from Italy, Garcilaso and Fray Luis sang the fields of Spain, the Castilian hendecasyllable, and Fernando de Herrera extolled the lord of the sea plains, who gave Spain the victory at Lepanto.

The following is how the news, which was later reproduced on the last page of the weekly *F.E.*, was reported by the newspaper *Luz*:

Fascist rally in Valladolid. A success. It's pointless to insist on denying this. For what purpose? Are we making any progress by deceiving ourselves? Let us stop fooling ourselves and start calling things by their proper names. Fascist rally in Valladolid. A few thousand attendees; almost all of them in their youth. One speaker, Onésimo Redondo, a young student, launched a Fascist curse on political agrarianism: "Castilian farmers," he said, looking energetically at a group of countrymen, "I do not call you agrarians because that word disgusts me." The crowd's enthusiasm shook the theater. Next came Ruiz de Alda, then Ledesma Ramos, and finally Primo de Rivera. At the conclusion of the meeting: a concert of pistols, as befits a Fascist party. Four people were seriously injured, while six others were treated for minor injuries.

After the success of the meeting at the Teatro Calderón, Gumersindo Montes Agudo wrote in his work *Vieja Guardia*: "*Luz* was calling loudly for the union of the Republicans to crush the newborn organization. It claimed: 'There is only one way to stop this movement in its tracks, and that is to ensure that there is no other Falange in Spain but that of the Republicans.' It also provided its own interpretation of the event, calling it a Fascist rally."[177]

Following the violence unleashed by the antifascists at the end of the event at the Teatro Calderón, upon the speakers' return to the capital, José Antonio made a decision that quickly became popular among Falangist militants and was reminiscent of Fascism. From that day on, Falangists would refer to one another with the *tuteo*, thus adopting a resolution of communication and courtesy that had previously been adopted by Mussolini in Italy, when he spread the use of the *voi*—second person plural—used colloquially in place of the more formal *lei*—third person singular—which would become for us Spaniards *usted*.

Ramiro Ledesma commented in his book *¿Fascismo en España?* that "Marxist elements became aware, because of the events of Valladolid, that the Fascist organization was preparing to accept armed struggle in the streets."[178]

The Heroic Distribution of the Ninth Issue of *F.E.*

On Thursday, March 8th, *F.E.* met once again with its readers. The tensions escalated in Don Benito (Badajoz), where on March 7th, Eduardo Ezquer was attacked and, despite being the victim, was imprisoned for seventeen days. In Zaragoza, on the Paseo de la Independencia, young people who attempted to announce the sale of *F.E.* were chased down by a mob of socialists. The following afternoon in Madrid, the sale of the newspaper sparked a tumultuous fight in Calle de Fuencarral, leaving six people injured; one of them, Angel Montesinos, a salesclerk, was left in critical condition and died the next day. At the Glorieta de Bilbao, the sellers who had gathered there were assaulted with truncheons by the socialists. And on top of all this, the Falange Center was closed off once more.

F.E. began its editorial entitled "Valladolid" with these words:

> Just seventeen weeks have passed between the rally of the Comedia and the rally of Valladolid. This means that no opposing force or weakness on our part was sufficient to prevent the planned steps from being carried out with perfect regularity.
>
> The second goal, which was established from here, had to begin to be realized, and Valladolid is already the great sign of its national fulfillment.

---

[177] Gumersindo Montes Agudo, *Vieja Guardia*, 46.

[178] Ledesma Ramos, *¿Fascismo en España?*, 160.

In these seventeen weeks, our people have known how to endure prison, wounds, persecutions, death, and, what is even worse, the crafty maneuvers of the Pharisees. But in these seventeen weeks, the enemy has suffered infinitely more, and above all, Spain has gained infinitely more.

In the March 6th edition of *Luz*, on the front page, there is a short interview with José Antonio, which to date has not been included in his complete works and which, as it has never been published among the writings of José Antonio, we transcribe in its entirety:

Following the bloody events of the Fascist rally in Valladolid, Primo de Rivera claims that nonviolence is an admirable virtue but not the most important one.

This morning, one of our journalists asked Mr. Primo de Rivera:

Luz Interviewer: "How can it be possible that you declare yourself an enemy of violence and that you disavow Alcalá Galiano for that tirade to the Spanish Falange, but at the end of every rally you take part in the Red Cross shows up?"

José Antonio: "First and foremost, you must recognize that we are always the ones who are attacked, and that when we respond, it is in the exercise of a legitimate defense against our aggressors. This in the first place."

L.I.: "And in the second place?"

J.A.: "That the virtue of nonviolence appears to me to be very interesting, but not at the top of the hierarchy of virtues. That is why it is permissible to violate this virtue under the impulse of a higher virtue."

L.I.: "Will you intervene in the Cortes to defend Albiñana's immunity?"

J.A.: "No. I am on the sidelines of that lawsuit because, on the one hand, no political discipline binds me to Mr. Albiñana since we belong to different parties, and on the other hand, I am an opponent of parliamentarism, so the issue of privileges and prerogatives of the deputies does not concern me."

L.I.: "So, the statesman doctor already knows; he cannot count on Primo de Rivera this time."

On the third page of *F.E.*, two very ironic comments are made on the journalistic treatment given to the Valladolid meeting by the most emblematic newspapers of the left, *El Socialista*, and of the *derechona*, *El Debate*, in both cases described as "deceitful." It is reported that the organ of the left devoted half a page to the Valladolid meeting, commenting that:

It is clear that the half page could replace very well any melodramatic feuilleton. Everything one could imagine is not much compared to what, according to *El Socialista*, happened in Valladolid. To begin with, it should be known that the Valladolid socialists managed to prevent (thus far) the Fascist attempt. Which attempt? That of celebrating the rally? *No*: the rally vanishes in the information given by *El Socialista*, to the point of leaving doubt as to whether it was indeed held or not. Our intention was, apparently, to carry out a Hitlerian putsch in Valladolid. And it was the socialists who bravely prevented this from happening. We suppose that a battle between besiegers and the people of Valladolid would take place on the outskirts of the city. Since the attempt was foiled, it is clear that we were not in Valladolid.

Nonetheless, in addition to the wounded we had among ourselves (many fewer than those suffered by the socialist provocateurs we met at the end of the act), more than ten Fascists were treated in the Hotel de Francia, according to the press organ. More than ten, but how many? Eleven? Fifteen hundred? *El Socialista*, with discretion, remains silent about it. In relation to what was published by *El Debate*, it was said that the Tuesday issue of *El Debate* "cooked up" for the act of Valladolid the most pharisaic version that has ever been told about us by the Spanish press.

On that same page there was included an article, strikingly titled "Final de El Poder. El Saber. El Amor" ["The End of Power, Knowledge, Love"], in which is written:

When these moral values converged in Rome, Rome obtained the power of Caesar, the knowledge of Seneca, and the love of Octavian. Then came imperial Rome, which dominated the world. Then it regained them with the power of the Crusades, the knowledge of Gregory VII, and the love of St. Francis of Assisi, and so came the pontifical Rome of universal catholicity. Today it has found them again; it is the Rome of Mussolini, undefeated and august.

The article ended by stating:

The combined and integral application of the trilogy of moral values is the maximum ambition of the Fascist state, which we aspire to raise from the unpatriotic rubble formed by pedantic members of cultural associations, conscienceless Masons, and penniless Jews, in sad collusion with the shameful Mozarabs, who, lacking the courage to take up arms and fight like men on the cliffs and on the plains, prefer to argue like busybodies in their criminal national playground while they tear our Spain to pieces, which waits anxiously like a virginal bride for the beloved, who will come to bring her out of her shadows, in an infinite impulse of power, knowledge, and love, thus bringing her back to her glorious destiny for centuries and centuries to come. Amen.

On the page dedicated to "Fascist Life," there is, firstly, a commentary on "El Hombre Nuevo" ["The New Man"], which begins as follows:

> It is interesting to read the thesis on the National Socialist revolution and the new man that is emerging from it, maintained by the professor of the University of Leipzig, Mr. Hans Freyer.
> According to Mr. Freyer, revolutions are never—in their deepest sense —a disorganization of society or a change in political institutions, but, on the contrary, they are laboratories for historical fermentations that originate and give birth to "a new man."

The second of the subjects addressed is that of the "Moral de Milicia" ["Morality of Struggle"]: "The Reichsminister and chief of the SA, Ernst Röhm, recently gave a remarkable speech in Berlin, from which we extract some of its central concepts on the morality of struggle that Fascism entails." This was then followed by an extensive literary review of Röhm's lecture, in which he spoke of Hitler and Mussolini as examples and role models.

Regarding England, it is reported that "W. E. D. Allen, in his article 'The Fascist Idea in England,' which appeared in the last January issue of *The American Review*, exalts Fascism 'as one of the most accurate creations of human thought.' . . . Allen also wrote beautiful praises to the Italian Duce, 'synthesis of the man of action and of the serene philosopher,' hailing him as the creator of the greatest and most fruitful political and social movement of our time."

There are also some declarations by De Jouvenel, the former French ambassador in Rome, in support of the Fascist revolution. In the world news section, the subjects are Dollfuss, the Habsburgs, Mussolini, and pacifism.

The page dedicated to "Economía y Trabajo" discusses corporatism in an extensive article. Here are some of its contents in a very summarized and abridged form:

> Corporativism, or corporatism, is the latest political-philosophical experiment in Europe . . . . Thanks to the corporative state, the deflation that preceded the fall in world prices did not trigger a violent crisis in Italy because it was possible to readjust prices and the cost of production via the corporative mechanism . . . . In some way, we would want to copy the Italian corporate organization in Spain. Specifically, the essential characteristic of the Fascist movement is the search for each country's most intimate and traditional essences, adapting them to the needs and

configurations of modern times and their own circumstances.

However, as in Italy, the corporate state that we will establish will be that spirit of national optimism that is achieved by developing a new conception of life and a new relationship with the state. What is needed is a concept of function, common reliance, and solidarity in the production and distribution of economic and spiritual goods. Under this new conception, all producers and consumers will have to consider themselves in a certain way as public employees. At the same time, producers and consumers will be part of Spain's administrative organization. This duality of powers instills in them the idea that they are part of the state and that their interests are identical with those of the fatherland.

It is not possible to summarize in a few words what a corporative state is. It is not enough to say that corporatism is an economic political system based on professional, familiar, or municipal representation, rather than on a soulless geographic representation. Nor will it be enough to say that corporatism is an industrial system whereby the interests of different economic groups are coordinated within a social system that subordinates individual or class interests to the interests of the fatherland.

The corporative state presupposes a new political-philosophical conception, a new will for economic cooperation, and a new conception of one's own responsibility. "One for all, and all for one," that is its motto.

F.E. Comes Back to Life for Its Tenth Issue

From March 8th until Thursday, April 12th, *F.E.* would not be published again. A new interruption—the third in its brief existence—was imposed on the Falange. An honest and simple note bitterly and helplessly informs its readers about the unjust suspension that, for more than a month, silenced the newspaper's interventions:

F.E. has been suspended once more. We will not discuss the injustice of this. It is our rule, as we have often stated, not to open the pretentious faucet of lamentation.

Nothing will discourage us or lead us astray from our path.

The note was a confirmation and further validation of the doctrines disseminated by the newspaper. The path was hard, hostile, rough, and full of traps and dangers, but the will, as a sign of tenacity and victory, to move forward and advance along the same path taken was a definite and firm resolution.

Only forty-eight hours had passed since José Antonio's car had been the target of a criminal attack in which four gunmen stationed on a street corner threw a bomb as it passed along Calle Vicente Blasco Ibáez (Altamirano) on April 10th. José

Antonio was on his way back from the Cárcel Modelo, where he had just represented the private prosecution against the alleged murderer of the young Falangist Jesús Hernández.

After a month of forced silence, the reappearance of *F.E.* in mid-April came with renewed vigor. "Las Lechuzas y la Pascua" ["The Owls and Easter"] was the title of its editorial, which made reference to the publication's suspension and mentioned "the Pharisee owls with crooked necks." It is stated that:

> The two months preceding the suspension had been splendid for the Falange, as will be the months ahead. With restricted space in our offices and with thin wallets, without a single newspaper, and with three or four fliers, we had managed to enlist thousands of Spaniards. Our diffusion—as we have previously stated—has been of a religious nature. It has been carried out with poverty and spirit, with sleeplessness and blood, rather than with money, crutches, and deceptions. The rally in Valladolid initiated a series of impressive demonstrations throughout Spain, because Valladolid itself was impressive, with its thousands of students and farmers.

In an article entitled "Picaresca y Dieguismo," part of the series "Fantasmoteca de España," the grand master of Spanish Freemasonry, of the 33rd degree, Diego Martinez Barrios, is chastised because "his figure, in the national underworld, winks in the other direction. He simply obeys a complex of obedience to the Masonic brotherhood and to the ambition of the best radical political style," and he is characterized as "the visible figure of the anti-Spanish bloc."

An article about "The phantom of war and peace under the fasces" in the weekly's international news section claims that:

> Serenely, the axe of the lictorial bundle is cutting the mooring ropes of hindrance. The Duce is well aware of the tight spot in Europe's shoe. This is why he is overcoming one and the other. Retracing lost paths is rarely the best solution. Mussolini sets sail with the *Pax Romana* at his heels. And now he's declared that "Europe will almost certainly not witness war in the next ten years." His words have been like a balm poured over the wounds that the Geneva clamor wants to divert attention away from for the sake of its own affairs. From Versailles to the present, everything has been a weaving and unweaving of intransigence. Except for Mussolini, no one has thought of anything as obvious as the fact that one cannot pull the rope too hard. And he has made the decision to loosen those constraints that were overly tight by putting thought into action.

In an interesting essay on "Nationalisms," a topic that was popular all over Europe, we find:

The populations who have not resigned themselves to die under this avalanche have turned their eyes toward their own intrinsic nationalisms; they wanted to create, for the time being, some watertight compartments, true oases of peace, from where they could stop the total collapse and begin the work of reconstruction. Italy is today the Covadonga of the reconquest of Europe by the universal spirit of the Church.[179]

The Church has never been, and cannot be, in opposition to these constructive nationalisms. Good proof of this is not only the Lateran Treaty between the Vatican and Mussolini, but also the fact that one of the first actions of the National Socialist regime was the establishment of a conciliation agreement with the Roman Catholic Church. Currently, superficial observers like to point out a discrepancy between the racial theories prevalent in Germany and the spirit of the Church, centered on the writings of Rosenberg and the responses of Cardinal Faulhaber. It is true that there is a racial sentiment, a superior idea, congenial to all Germans, which serves as a supreme binding force in the work of national reconstruction, but even if it may seem otherwise, this guiding ideal can never, in its luxuriant flourishing, be opposed to Catholic doctrines, but rather just the contrary. And the unmistakable proof of this is that, whenever a glaring error occurs along that path, the number of people leaving the national Protestant churches rises automatically, and they join the ranks of the faithful of St. Peter. Recently, there has been talk of a group of seven hundred Protestant pastors traveling to Rome to join the true faith.

When nationalists have as their supreme purpose the fundamental revaluation of the virtues of a people, they can only lead them toward the truth, forcing them to abandon all the ballast of errors that have gradually led them to the decadence they are currently suffering and from which they wish to be freed. For this reason, and because of our profound conviction that all the evils that are now coming to pass stem from the theories of the Reformation, we believe that the nationalist movements must be of great benefit to the Church, to Europe, and to the whole of humanity by awakening it to its own destiny, infinitely more elevated than the stagnation in which it has been submerged.

In a forthcoming article, we will discuss the Spanish national sentiment, which is eminently Catholic, and the possible relations of the various nationalisms among themselves, which, far from leading to fears of warlike or economic conflicts, lead to mutual understanding and comprehension, which will ensure in the future the beneficial coexistence of men, differentiated by their peculiarities but united in a common

---

[179] [Translator: the Battle of Covadonga, in 722, was the first Christian victory in the Iberian Peninsula over the Moors. It is often considered to be the start of the Reconquista.]

aspiration for Christian improvement, which will culminate in the maximum expansion of Catholicism.

The "Economy and Work" page is once again dedicated to promoting corporatism as a model and example of Spanish Fascism:

The economic aspect of the Fascist movement entails and embodies the corporatist organization of the state. However, the corporative state, or corporatism, is an economic system that cannot coexist with a liberal political state.

The effective, complete, and advantageous guidance of an organized economy cannot be achieved if the state operates on a large mass of inorganically dispersed individuals. Corporatism requires that the social forces that give rise to the state be organized and conform to a structure whose internal law is the principle of hierarchical coordination.

The corporatist state is founded on the principle of interconnected political and economic interests, a syndical hierarchy that is parallel to the political hierarchy.

As a result, there is no point in attempting to implement a corporative economic organization without also constructing an anti-democratic and anti-liberal hierarchical political framework. It is also necessary for the state's highest authorities to inspire faith and zeal .... That spirit of a common undertaking that exists today between the Italians and the Fascist state amazes and astonishes all those who contemplate the current pulse of life in modern Italy.

Thus, separating the economic from the spiritual and political spheres is impossible when implementing a corporative economic organization. Trying to construct corporatist models for Spain without completely upending and altering the whole organization of the state would be like trying to compare the music of a piano with that of a gramophone record. The corporatist state comes later. The first step is to instill a sense of defense, sacrifice, patriotism, and loyalty to Spain's imperial cause. Only then will the human melodies produce the harmony of all the contributing elements of Spanish production.

The corporative state is a vibrant and ardent body, not a shapeless collection of statistics and machines .... The corporative unit, so to speak, is today the trade union, and the corporative organization must be built around it.

Trade unionization is both rational and humane .... We have aligned our definition of an organized economic society's general outline with the principles and language of the Italian corporative state. This is because Italy has found a modern solution to these trade unionist concerns. Our corporatism will have to be a reflection of their corporatism, which, on the other hand, will have its own features and will present distinctly Spanish characteristics.

Another chapter, the sixth in Giménez Caballero's series "Spain and Rome," is published in this issue, this time on "La primera cristiandad" ["The First Christianity"], in which, after narrating the story of the patronal foundations and martyrology of Spain, he concludes that "this was the heroic page of the first Spanish fasces for the faith, the first Spaniards to fall as a result of their Catholic longing for a new and resurrected Rome: The Rome of the first Christianity."

José Antonio, as the director of *F.E.*, knew very well that in order to popularize Fascism in Spain he had to resort to the original sources, of which nobody could doubt the authenticity. The dissemination of Fascist ideas in Spain was the first and ultimate purpose of the weekly. After the mandatory closure, the most extensive part of this tenth issue is offered and dedicated to Mussolini, publishing the entire "Speech of Mussolini in the Second Quinquennial Assembly of the Regime" on two of its pages. It is an important and extensive speech, in which the Duce deals with the cardinal points of the Fascist ideology: the aspects of Fascism, party and corporation, the Rome of the modern day, peasant life, international relations, military power, the demographic problem, the expansion of Fascist Italy, the creed of the Blackshirt, and the epigraph under the lictorial symbol. The content of the speech was a complete program of politics and action. That is why José Antonio reproduced the entire speech in *F.E.* without annotations, additions, or comments. The best way to teach a doctrine is through the original words of the teacher.

The speech was accompanied by a photograph of the Duce with the following caption: "The people of Rome, in front of Palazzo Venezia, acclaim Mussolini."

On April 14th, forty-eight hours after the tenth issue of *F.E.* appeared on the streets, the police went to the Falange Center for the umpteenth time, conducted a thorough search, closed the premises, and arrested several Falangists.

The Eleventh Issue of *F.E.*: Recourse to the Parable

The eleventh issue, dated Thursday, April 19th, was the last one published at the editorial and administrative offices on Calle Eduardo Dato.

The editorial "Tránsito" ["Transit"] recounts the story of a legend, a parable that is relevant to Spain. It is the parable of the Kavir:

This Kavir is an enormous desert, or rather, an enormous lake of mud, situated to the north of Persia. The heat and dryness of the air cause a white crust of salt to form on the mud of the Kavir for many days of the year. So the Kavir appears to be a magnificent landscape: safe, candid, firm, and icy.

The caravans venture across it. The slightest rain or humidity of the night melts the salt crust. The caravans then begin to hasten their passage and drop their luggage in order to avoid sinking due to their weight. The travelers then get off their camels. Finally, they take off their shoes and clothes and run in a terrifying "run for their lives." Many drown. Certain rightists in Spain are attempting to carry out the same experiment, motivated by their greed for profit. But if Spain goes that route, it will sink in the mud with all its baggage. The German Center and the Italian Popular Party have met the same fate as the caravans of the Kavir.

Over the liberal-democratic mud and in close complicity with it, they managed to form a crust of candid and new appearances that seemed solid, and in the meantime, they started to set up their caravans. They prepared such deceptive and lucid caravansaries as that poor "bluff" of the Escorial. But they ended up being disgracefully disbanded. Don Sturzo—the most similar to those here—has thrown all his ideological baggage into the democratic and anti-nationalized mud already thoroughly stirred in the last great antifascist offensive. He sank into the mud with the lodges, with the radicals, with a portion of local banks placed at his service, with hundreds of academics, while the bricklayer Benito Mussolini rebuilt out of living rock, *facing the sun*, facing the world, the Italian fatherland.

Let ours be a great ancient and popular history of a gentleman who was able to save himself from swamps and precipices in order to reach the high peaks of the Fatherland and have his natural dominion all around, across the entire width of the horizon.

But it is not enough for the knight, the leader, to be the sole survivor. It is necessary that he save an entire people and that an entire people arm themselves as knights alongside him and place themselves at the high service and dominion of the Fatherland. It is necessary that in one phalanx, in this Falange of ours, set in motion, we save the poor deluded ones from the swamp and the poor furious ones from the precipice. It is necessary that we save the entire youth of Spain from the deceptions and dangers directed against the Fatherland. We will have to load ourselves with parables against the evil, furious, or crafty beasts that symbolize today anger or hypocrisy and wage war against the high destiny of the Fatherland. When the struggle and the path are protracted and arduous, so much greater are the victory and the destination. Raise your heads high, young men of Spain, to be worthy of being called yourselves "youth," in a straight march, with clarity and courage, against hypocrites and wrathful men.

¡Arriba España!

It is a curious coincidence that, in the editorial, allusion is made to Mussolini, who is said to be rebuilding on living rock, *cara al sol* [facing the sun]. It was the second time that, in the newspaper *F.E.*, the expression *cara al sol* was used, the opening verse and rhythm of the hymn which, in December of the following year, would begin the triumphal march of "amor y de guerra" ["Love and War"], the song of hope of those young people called upon to join the revolution.

The second installment of "Nationalisms" was published, an article in which the editorial staff of *F.E.* takes a doctrinal stance toward a common Fascism:

> For this reason, Italy, the origin and most outstanding exponent of this theory, was aware that in its most recent national unity, it could only encounter the foggy sorrows of a democratic doctrine that had ruined it; so it turned its eyes, in a majestic leap, to the she-wolf that nurtured an empire that dominated the entire known world, civilizing it and giving it a law, a peace, which even today is known by the name of *Lex et Pax Romana*. On that foundation, built with the marble of the Forum, with the red stones of the blood of the martyrs of the Colosseum, and with the triumphal arches of Trajan and Titus, the building of the new Fascist state was begun, putting in musical harmony the ardor, the effort, and the indomitable intelligence of the Blackshirts, mourning for the lost fatherland, mourning for those who fell before seeing the blossoming of the reconquering spring of the fatherland.
>
> Germany, aware of its own lack of stature as a historical entity, has sought the common denominator of all Germans in the deeds of the Aryan race, in the songs of Odin, in the legend of the Nibelungs, and in the ride of the Valkyries, who descended on the world to pick up the fallen warrior and carry him to savor the mead of Valhalla. For this reason, and in natural opposition to the Semitic race—a plague and pestilence that plunders the country where it falls—it has based its nationalism on the virtues of the Aryan race, as the historical expression of the diverse tribes that constituted the fundamental core of the population of those regions, which are demarcated as if by the fingers of God in a Byzantine blessing, by the Rhine and by the Elbe.
>
> Every Spanish nationalist idea must necessarily point to the marvelous dawn that pierced the English darkness, creating national unity, discovering a new world, and giving the impulse of glory that would bring our troops from Italy to Flanders; our men from Oran to the Pacific; our culture from creating international law with Father Francisco de Vitoria to the intellectual militia of Ignatius of Loyola, which propagated faith in the most remote regions, but also the Spanish spirit and the universal sense of Catholicism. The supreme synthesis of that historical moment, which cast so much light on the future, is the sheaf and yoke; it is Cardinal Jiménez de Cisneros . . . . Those who oppose modern Fascist nationalisms ignore the

fact that these are the rational and definitive solutions to economic problems, based on the authority of the state, which plans and directs individual efforts rather than leaving them in the disorganized liberal, and thus free-market, state. Later, when the private economies of each nation subjected to this rescuing regime have been firmly rebuilt as a result of the various national Fascist efforts, it will be much easier, through partial agreements, to reach international agreements to regulate production and consumption. Thus, contrary to what opposing economists claim, free markets will not be destroyed, but there will be orderly regulation that will provide assurance to the world, possibly denying them the moments of disorderly rises and cyclical and periodic crises at the cost of constant work.

These will be, to put it briefly, the material and spiritual benefits that our strategy will unavoidably bring. They are well worth our intellectual effort and the generous sacrifice of our love, with all the joy of one who ploughs a new furrow through untouched land.

In the section "Fascist Life" this time the article examines "El Francismo" ["The French Movement"]: "The republican, leftist, and democratic France, which wanted nothing to do with authoritarian and Fascist regimes, is allowing and favoring the propagation of these doctrines." It provides a summary of Fascist parties in France:

We complained on more than one occasion of the Iberian tendency to split groups, which makes it so that any day a gathering of friends can get together and come forward with the pretension of being a political party. This dispersion, which is the most anti-totalitarian and antifascist phenomenon against which our phalanxes fought, is also distinctive of contemporary French Fascism. We are not quite sure if we are giving the complete list of the Fascist parties in France, but we will offer the main ones:

1. Solidarité Française;
2. Croix-de-Feu;
3. Le Socialisme National;
4. Action Française;
5. Néo-socialisme and
6. Mouvement Franciste.

According to Coston and his friends, the Jews are the cause of all the ills of France:

In this regard, the publications of *La libre Parole* are excellent for reading and studying the subject.

In one of them is discussed "The French Cinema in the Hands of the Jews." Another dealt with "The Undesirable Jews." Another covers "Jewish Finance." Yet another was on "The Jews in France." Another was on "The Role of the Jews in the Coming War." And another "Disrespectful Considerations on the Judeo-Masonic Republic."

And also in this newspaper, the anti-Jewish headlines are alarming and violent: "Jewry Seeks War!" "Gold, Mud, Blood!"

At the time of the February riot, this paper published a sinister sketch on a full page with the heading: "The Jew (Occult Leader of Freemasonry) Says to the Police: Shoot; Kill Those French Pigs!"[180]

Coston's magazine and newspaper carry great anger and nerve. It is an authentic Fascist pamphlet, full of violence, rage, ardor, youthful insolence, and enthusiasm.

Its photographs, drawings, reports, headlines, literary content, advertisements, and snippets all correspond to a tone that Mr. Bucard, who is calmer and more reflective, clearly lacks.

We hope that the Francism of our young friend Coston will find fortune and a bright future. He is generous and likable. But we also hope that our national party and this small party will establish in France a deep, serious, and sacred union.

A new and temporary section was introduced in the weekly under the title "Falanges Universitarias" ["University Phalanxes"]. In a brief introductory note, we find: "The Sindicato Universitario Español (S.U.E.) [Spanish University Union] intends to launch soon a newspaper of its own. As the preliminary phase draws to a close, *F.E.* provides a page that will be filled in by the Sindicato students themselves."

The page begins with a one-page piece titled "Spain, University, Corporation," with "three initial points by which the university phalanxes, organ of the Spanish University Union, are born." Note that in the beginning the university organization of the Falange was the SUE and not SEU.[181]

During those times, José Antonio also gave interviews to the media, such as one with Irene Polo, in Catalan, for *L'Opinió*, published in Barcelona on April 26th, 1934, on page 5. This interview was reproduced in the appendix of the

---

[180] [Translator: This refers to the crisis of February 6th, 1934, also known as the Veteran's Riot. This was an anti-parliamentarist street demonstration in Paris organized by multiple far-right groups, culminating in a riot on the Place de la Concorde, near the building used for the French National Assembly. The police shot and killed seventeen demonstrators, nine of whom were in far-right organizations.]

[181] [Translator: The Sindicato Español Universitario (Spanish University Union; SEU) was a corporatist students' union in Spain, created in the 1930s during the Second Spanish Republic, by the Falange Española.]

book *En busca de José Antonio* by Ian Gibson, with the disclaimer that these words are not included in the misnamed *Complete Works* of the first Jefe of the Falange. When asked by the journalist, "Well, what do you think is the future of Fascism in Spain?" José Antonio answered:

José Antonio: "The current movement in Spain is not, strictly speaking, Fascism. In reality, it happens to coincide with the era of fascisms. Fascism is a universal constant that, in each country, comes with its own characteristics and name. Here, it is a synthesis of national and social factors, which is the only way to find a complete solution to the situation. Wouldn't any other solution be partial and thus ineffective? If the solution is purely social, it would be Marxist. If it is just a national solution, it would not last. In this regard, I would like Catalans to read the 'Essay on Nationalism' that I published in the magazine *JONS.*"

Irene Polo: "And do you think this new political model will triumph in Spain?"

J.A.: "Oh! ... Anyone who embarks on an endeavor does so because they have faith in its triumph."

I.P.: "It seems that the atmosphere in Spain is not very favorable."

J.A.: "No ... But it's not that there's a completely adverse environment. The fact is that there is confusion. People believe Fascism to be something that it is not. They have a false, clueless idea, which I want to clarify; we'll do everything we can to correct and clarify it."

I.P.: "How must Spanish Fascism be?"

J.A.: "It must not be right-wing."

I.P.: "Ah?"

J.A.: "No. I'm not right-wing, as people believe. Absolutely! So much so that if I had to choose between reactionary and current revolutionary work in Spain, I would undoubtedly side with the trade unionists. At least trade unionists have a pulse."

The Weekly Magazine Changes Its Headquarters

The twelfth issue of *F.E.*, released on Thursday, April 26th, had a variation on its front cover. Its editorial office was moved to 16 Calle Marqués del Riscal, a villa on the corner of Avenida de la Castellana, where all of the services of F.E. de las JONS would be centralized.

The editorial is entitled "Fundación" ["Foundation"] and is expressly addressed to the whole Brotherhood of the Falange. In the article, it is stated that:

A policy of unity of destiny and a policy of mission, which are the same thing, are only known as empire. Get now well into your heads, into your chests, and into your guts, which enable you to be Spanish and virile, this inflexible rule: "*A policy of mission is not achieved without a policy of foundation.*" The Caesarean, Catholic (or a mixture of Caesarean and Catholic) foundation is the genius of Spain as a policy of mission and as the key to the unity of destiny.

In the sports section "Aire Libre," the page propagandizes Fascist Italy:

> The organization of the World Cup by Italy is remarkable. The state plans on crowds of people from all over the world arriving in its territory. It wishes to present itself to the general public.
>
> It wants its enthusiasm, its progress, and its patriotic fervor to be witnessed; it wants people to contemplate its stadiums and its lively and strong youth .... Italy will offer us, on the occasion of the soccer world championship, its faith in itself. It will demonstrate what is done and what can be done in a country when there is a head in front and a heart that draws all the hearts of the fatherland.

The page on "Economy and Work" is once again devoted to the study and theoretical development of corporatism, a series now in its third installment, and, in the most significant paragraphs, we read:

> The very essence of Fascism is cooperation within a hierarchy of disciplined labor.
>
> In England, the most characteristic symbol of power is its square and compasses; in Italy, the most relevant symbol today is the corporation; and its most transcendent law is its Charter of Labor.

Giménez Caballero takes up more than a page with his ninth chapter of "Spain and Rome," which is about "La Cristianidad española" ["Spanish Christianity"].

On the page devoted to "Fascist Life," there is news of the Swiss Fascist movement, which reports: "In Lausanne last January occurred the first national congress of Swiss Fascism .... The Swiss movement is already spread throughout the country and has a militant newspaper, *The Swiss Fascist*, published in French, German, and Italian." It also included information on Poland and its new constitution, and it briefly focused on Italy to praise the corporative initiatives in the Magistracy and the phenomenal welfare work of the National Fascist Party.

The Swan Song

Under the pretext that Spain was in a state of emergency, the weekly was closed down once more. The suspension lasted from April 26th—the twelfth issue—until the appearance of the thirteenth issue on Thursday, July 5th. The publication explained the censorship to its readers with the following statement, written in capital letters:

UNDER THE STATE OF EMERGENCY.
OVERCOMING THE DIFFICULTIES OF THE STATE OF EMERGENY DURING THESE TWO MONTHS OF SUSPENSION OF *F.E.*, FALANGE ESPAÑOLA DE LAS JONS HAS NOT STOPPED ITS WORK OF PROPAGANDA. FUENSALIDA, LUANCO, AND BURRIANA HAVE HEARD OUR VOICE OF SPANISH RESURGENCE.
DESPITE THE FORCED SEMI-SILENCE, SUSPENSION OF OUR NEWSPAPERS, AND UNJUST CLOSURE OF OUR CENTERS, INCLUDING THE HARDWORKING AND ADMIRABLE BRANCH OF SEVILLE, OUR ENTHUSIASM HAS REMAINED ALIVE.

The front page of the weekly was redesigned. The headline was shifted to the right margin. At the start of the text, the symbolic arrows evolved into the logo. The format and size were changed. Rather than using a double, hollow stroke, they appeared with a single black stroke.

With thick letters, the alarm was raised with the words "España, a la deriva" ["Spain, Adrift"], which, after an overview of the national scenario—"the right wingers in slumber, the government perplexed, Marxism on the horizon"—called out distressingly:

This is the panorama of our Spain today: weak right wingers, a vacillating government, and anti-Spanish forces marching on what is left. Marxism, separatism: Anti-Spain, in short.

But it shall not pass! Against all the indifferences, against all the neglect, against all the dangers, in life and in death, the firm National Syndicalist squadrons will sweep through Spain from end to end, multiplying their alarm bells, and they will not give peace to the assailants nor to the traitors.

On page two, the section on "Fascist Life" can be found.

The "News from around the World" section was dedicated to the "Tempestad sobre Alemania" ["Storm over Germany"], in which it is written:

Brimming with poetry and a mystique that was perhaps too direct, National Socialism, which took on the enormous task of reconstructing Germany on its brown shoulders, had to go stumbling over obstacles which the haste of the conquest of power neglected to remove at the appropriate time . . . .

Hitler, true to himself, to his avowed vocation and to the imperatives of national action, had to rein in the potentially dissolving agitation of the German people. His arm was straightly raised unyieldingly and inexorably in the face of the conspiracy, dark in its night of plots. The insurgent militias were surrounded by blood and gunpowder, and their leaders fell as a toll for their betrayal. On the other hand, the need to moralize, to clean up the undesirable burden left over from the days of haste, completed the task of reducing the insurgents.

On a double page, another cry of national anguish: "Cataluña camino de la insurrección" ["Catalonia on the Way to Insurrection"], the culmination of separatism.

The twelfth issue of *F.E.* also devoted two full pages to the reproduction of José Antonio Primo de Rivera's speech in the Cortes on June 6th, in defense of his father, Miguel Primo de Rivera:

In the world today, a series of systems that have reached conceptual maturity are being implemented. In 1923, no doctrine had been fully developed capable of replacing the then-existing bourgeois liberal-democratic doctrine of the states. If you consider that that general of 1923 followed Mussolini for no more than eleven months, you will be astonished that he had to deduce all the conceptual bases of a system during that time while that same system has taken ten or twelve years to produce the bibliography with which it is now illustrated.

There are two initiatives that deserve to be mentioned: The call for young female students to join the National Executive Board of the Spanish University Union, as well as the invitation to participate in La Barraca, the university theater, the "theater of the students: a young project that brings the ancient flavor of our classic theater to towns and villages . . . . The SEU calls you to join its ranks; you and La Barraca. It calls you, as a member of the youth, and La Barraca as a pedagogical mission to be conducted only by those who yearn for a new fatherland; those who work for the coming of an empire; not by those who navigate the murky and muddy waters of Jewish Marxism."

On July 7th, on the occasion of the publication of *F.E.*, two people were wounded:

Santos Aranda Fernández, a valiant and magnificent comrade, and Cecilio Cumplido Manzanedo, were attacked. The latter was not a militant yet because of his young age, but he was reading *F.E.* and this brought him his baptism of fire before the definitive enrollment. Santos Aranda was shot in the shoulder and endured the pain with a cheerful spirit. Cecilio Cumplido was wounded several times with a penknife. They are both well now and fitter than they were before being injured.

On Tuesday, the 10th, the police once again searched and seized the registered office, at 16 Marqués de Riscal, which housed the editorial and administrative offices of the weekly *F.E.* and Falange Española de las JONS, the SEU, the Bolsa de Trabajo, the parliamentary office of the deputies Francisco Moreno Herrera and José Antonio, as well as the editorial office of the magazine *JONS*; all had their headquarters there. They arrested the sixty-seven Falangists who were present in the building, accusing them of secret meetings, and forced them into their vehicles. José Antonio and his seatmate, the marquis of Eliseda, Francisco Moreno, were also arrested, despite their status as members of the Cortes. The premises were closed and locked.

The board of command issued a note:

The board of command of Falange Española de las JONS must state the following:

First: At its headquarters in Calle Marqués de Riscal, no meeting was being held yesterday, neither public nor covert. This is proven by the fact that the duty judge has only verified the presence in the headquarters of about forty people distributed among the parliamentary office, the Bolsa de Trabajo, the administrations of the magazines *F.E.* and *JONS*, the garage, the janitor's office, the garden, and so forth. Forty people in a place where all these services operate, with their teams of employees, is not enough to move the entire directorate of security.

Second: The police search in which the impressive arsenal described in the newspapers is said to have been found was carried out by the agents without the presence of any witness—as the law would require—and, for the most part, those who were on the premises and could supervise the search had already been transferred to the directorate of security.

This is the truth. Well, now, if this simulation of a terrifying discovery is meant to divert public opinion away from more serious issues or to console Mr. Salazar Alonso for the lack of other successes, the Falange Española de las JONS has nothing to say about it.

Madrid, July 11th, 1934.

The Penultimate Issue of *F.E.*

Breaking the silence, *F.E.*, weakened in content—but not in its substance—with fewer pages, reached its readers on Thursday, July 12th with its fourteenth issue. Its first two pages are dedicated to the transcription of the report of the police assault on the headquarters of the Falange. Slogans are provided to instill courage in the face of hard times. Its contents are, straightforwardly, a sort of rallying cry.

On the third page, two articles were published with contrasting titles: "La España que hace: Los muertos" ["The Spain That Does: The Dead"] and "La España que deshace: Los vivos" ["The Spain That Undoes: The Living"]. The latter is a serious reflection on separatism in Spain and the impact in this respect of the First World War, and of it is this written testimony:

> When Mussolini intervened and united Italy under Fascism, Spain was divided into two halves: the Italophile and the Germanophile—Joselito or Belmonte?—united by their shared morality of swindlers.[182]
>
> This is because the war had been without remedy, the union, our sacred union. War with some or war with others, but in the end, war. Germany and Italy both ended up the same way: fiercely united.
>
> In the field camp, the rich and the poor could meet, united by the same toil and facing the same dangers, and, in the hospital, decorated by the same shrapnel. And the same death brought them together in the village cemeteries.
>
> Once the war was over, the national revolution and Hitler's success were simple. Coming from the same trenches, the Croix-de-Feu is now on its way to save France.

On page 4, another article returns to the main topic: "Separatismos internacionales" ["International Separatisms"]:

> Precisely in these days, constructive nationalisms have been discussed extensively and quite authoritatively as a logical antithesis and effective antidote to the separatisms that plague us. There was also no lack of considerations on the possible theories against these regenerative movements, on the assumption that they are in conflict with Catholic universality, although the Church as such has provided no statements on the matter and, on the contrary, has signed beneficial agreements with the two most outstanding exponents of the new order: Italy and Germany.

In the section "Readings of Our Own," there is reproduced a literary and political review previously published in *El Adelanto* by Ernesto Giménez Caballero on the book *Spagna cattolica e rivoluzionaria* [*Revolutionary and Catholic Spain*] by the Italian author Niccolo Cunneo, from which we extract the following paragraphs:

> It is true that before Fascism, there were already writers in Italy who were concerned with international issues. But they approached the subject as if

---

[182] [Translator: Joselito and Belmonte were two rival bullfighters, among the best.]

they had an inferiority complex, looking at cultures other than their own with a certain provincialism. But now it is different. Now, the Italian writer is able to look at the world from a firm and systematic point of view. And in this resides the secret to his current growing desire for interest.

As far as Spain is concerned, it is enough to recall some of the most recent and notorious efforts of Italian comprehension. Pascazio's excellent book on the *Revolution in Spain* is still fresh, and Piccoli's book on the *Twilight of the Myths* is not far from the former.

We will not go over slightly earlier testimonies, like those of Marinetti, Monelli, Ciarlantini, Fraccaroli, and Angioletti, and the press coverage of men like Cullino or Tomaselli.

We must also remember the systematic and valuable contributions of outstanding Hispanists: among others, Croce, Farinelli, Sanvisenti, Ezio Levi, Mele Savi, and Boiselli. Thanks to them, Spain is gradually resuming its profound spiritual contact with Italy. However, there is still a long way to go for the understanding and knowledge of both peoples to be perfect, productive, and fruitful.

Niccolo Cunneo's book on Spain of the present day is a purely ideological book. An "intellectual" book. In this lies its main peculiarity. Perhaps it is its greatest merit. Perhaps it is also its weakness.

On the page devoted to the Falanges Universitarias, a posthumous article by Matías Montero on "Universidad e imperio" ["University and Empire"] holds the place of honor, concluding with the following lines: "Our march in search of the eternal will be protected by the maternal embrace of a flag: austere and universal, Catholic and imperial; the flag that Spaniards defended throughout the world when the word dwelt among us and we had faith in our fate: the sacred flag of eternal Rome."

Issue Number 15: The Final Copy

The fifteenth—and last—issue of *F.E.*, which is dated July 19th, 1934, is the final one of this early foundational period. This issue comes with a smaller number of pages. It nevertheless possesses the same fervor and passion as the preceding ones. There was no farewell, only suffocation, persecution, and heinous government strangulation. It had been nearly eight months of valiant, one-of-a-kind struggle, cultural dialectic, and Spanish affirmation. Seizures and accusations had occurred on a regular basis since the publication of the first issue. The organization of the newspaper was problematic, and for the majority of the time it was in circulation, the editorial and administrative offices were sealed and closed; the press was hit by terrorist attacks and bombs thrown at the workshops, and the distribution was marked by young and martyred blood—

too much blood. The distribution manager himself was murdered; many salesmen were assaulted, almost stoned to death, mortally wounded, or suffered concussions. The readers were beset with words, violence, or the lead of murderous socialist gunmen.

On the second page appears an article with a rallying cry, "Who Are Our Own?" in which an appeal to struggle is voiced:

We know that our objectives are to be achieved and obtained, they are to be conquered, and that is why our voice is a call to fight, a call to action. We will reveal a path for hopeless Spaniards to follow, as well as a task for all those who are currently unjustly neglected and helpless . . . . It is necessary to state and reiterate that we support and long for a national revolution. We will not be satisfied unless it triumphs completely. And our revolutionary motivation stems from the fact that, through our presence, we bring into Spain ideas and desires that are diametrically opposed to what exists today.

Next to the article is a paragraph, perhaps—due to its style—written by Ramiro Ledesma:

We are nationalists because we want the greatness of Spain. We are syndicalists because we demand state unionization. We are revolutionaries because our movement is lively, with eternal aspirations, and it is driven by the irresistible force of our youth.

On the sixth page was inserted an article by Ernesto Giménez Caballero, which had already been published almost a year earlier, on August 3rd, 1933, in the newspaper *Informaciones*, with the title "Un complot no puede ser fascista" ["A Plot Cannot Be Fascist"]. It is published because:

Again, there are rumors of a planned coup involving Falange Española de las JONS

A plot cannot be Fascist for the simple reason that *plot* and *Fascism* are antithetical terms. There is no greater political monstrosity than to pair these two concepts.

Plot is a word that has a very concrete historical significance: it is the secret movement, generally of a few, against a system of government. The main characteristic of the plot is, therefore, secrecy.

In this sense—*complot*—its meaning is brought closer to that of conspiracy: something prepared quietly, taking in the breath— *cumspirare*—if possible, while being cloaked in ample shrouds, up to the eyes.

If possible, it is done while concealing a pistol or rifle beneath those cloaks, and far from the romantic light of any lamp.

Is this Fascism? The characteristic of Fascism is precisely the opposite: the open air, the public square, direct action, bare chests, and not hiding from anything or anyone.

In this last issue is reproduced the foreword, written by José Antonio Primo de Rivera, for the Spanish translation of Mussolini's book *Il Fascismo* (Madrid, 1934). The title is concise, lapidary, Caesarean: "Mussolini."

The last page was a lament and a reflection: "España, he ahí lo prohibido" ["Spain, Behold the Forbidden"], an article in which we read:

The Church is the unsurpassable model of the uselessness of all those methods against the symbol of a faith. Ah, so foolish . . . . Without a press, without money, without branches, the marvelous and tenacious dissemination of our idea throughout Spain in a few months has been a model of religiously successful diffusion, with poverty and heroism, with martyrs and enlightened people, not by dint of money, pharisaism, and bureaucracy.

The Weekly *F.E.* and the Jewish Question

In the second issue, an article entitled "Alemania: Nazis y Judíos" ["Germany: Nazis and Jews"] is published that points out that the anti-Semitism of German Fascism is a peculiar and differentiating characteristic with respect to Italian Fascism and to "other fascisms that are in the making, like the Spanish one." According to the article, in Spain, "the Jewish problem is not and never has been a problem of race, but an issue of faith."

Considering the Jewish problem to be an "issue of faith" does not imply that José Antonio and Falange Española were unaware of the Jewish threat that loomed over Spain behind the capitalist, stateless, and financial apparatuses, or grafted into the structures of international communism.

In the fourth issue of *F.E.*, in an extensive article that discusses the alternative between Berlin and Moscow, Waldo Balbuena writes:

The blame for the evils that afflict humanity does not lie in capital, as the Marxists claim. The capitalists who misuse capital are to blame. The solution lies, then, in subduing these capitalists either with their collaboration or by force, so that at all times their capital may serve a social purpose. No longer should a capitalist be the one who freely disposes of his capital for unspeakable purposes. Capital must be respected and protected, but it must be subjected to the principles of a convenient national function, which the capitalist will not be able to avoid under any circumstances. We must persecute the Jew who practices usury and profits from the hunger of the people, but we must respect the man of good faith who works with his person and his money for the advancement of the fatherland.

José Antonio Primo de Rivera delivered a significant speech in Cáceres in which, when commenting on socialism, he stated with emphasis:

Socialism took on a horrifying darkness when the figure of that Jew Karl Marx appeared, and it became so dark because he considered religion, the fatherland, and every sentiment, including love, to be false, believing in nothing but economic factors, and thus, he pitted capitalism against the proletariat in a fratricidal struggle. Thus Karl Marx takes his position, contemplating this tremendous drama and deducing his fatal laws.

José Antonio emphasized the Jewish origins of Marxism in several of his other speeches. In the grandiose rally of March 4th, 1934, at the Teatro Calderón of Valladolid, when dealing with the issue of class struggle, he clarified:

Many streets have already been named after Karl Marx in many towns in Spain, but Karl Marx was a German Jew who, from his office, observed with terrible passivity the most dramatic events of his time. He was a German Jew who, before the English factories in Manchester, while he formulated ruthless laws on the accumulation of capital and relentless laws on production and the interests of employers and workers, wrote letters to his friend Friedrich Engels, telling him that the workers were plebs and scoundrels, with whom he should be concerned only insofar as they served to validate his doctrines.

In the seventh issue, an unsigned article on "La verdad y la muerte" ["Truth and Death"] contained the following: "Synthesis of Spanish virtue, nectar of the eternal youth of a country that refuses to die in the mercenary hands of Metics and Mozarabs, Jews and Freemasons."

The Jews are mentioned in the same issue as one of the "races that have until now lived parasitically and covertly in our country."

Another allusion to the subject can be found in the ninth issue, in the article "Final de El poder, El saber, El Amor" ["The End of Power, Knowledge, and Love"], with the following text:

The combined and integral application of the trilogy of moral values is the maximum ambition of the Fascist state, which we aspire to rise from the unpatriotic rubble formed by pedantic members of cultural associations, conscienceless Masons and penniless Jews.

When in the eleventh issue a full page is reserved for the analysis of the French Fascist movement, when commenting on the position of its leaders, it is said that "Coston's Francism is fundamentally—in the style of Germany—anti-Semitic . . . . According to Coston and his friends the Jews are the cause of all the ills of France." This does not prevent the article from concluding with the following wish from his Spanish Falangist comrades: "We hope that the Francism of our young friend Coston will find fortune and a bright future."

In that same issue, Giménez Caballero, speaking of the poet Prudentius, transposes him in time and says: "His polemic soul—in opposition to the liberals and Bolsheviks of the time, Priscillianists, Aryans, and Jews—vibrates like a rapturous bell, whose sound of struggle and combat is heard by St. Isidore, Dante, and Milton. It is heard by every militant soul of the European Middle Ages."

The issue is completed with a direct allusion to the dissolving ferment of Judaism, which can be found in the article on "Nationalisms," where, in reference to Germany, it is stated as follows:

> "For this reason, and in natural opposition to the Semitic race, a plague and pestilence that plunders the country where it falls—it has based its nationalism on the virtues of the Aryan race, as the historical expression of the diverse tribes that constituted the fundamental core of the population of those regions, which are demarcated as if by the fingers of God in a Byzantine blessing, by the Rhine and by the Elbe."

It is a fact that the Jewish problem was not the central theme of early Falangist rhetoric, but it is also true that its ideologues were ignorant of the precise nature of the Jews and the deceptions they had devised whenever the chance presented itself.[183] Consider today's behavior by Jewish Zionists in Israel toward the Palestinians, a subjugated and humiliated people being mercilessly and perfidiously massacred under the scandalously complicit eyes of a West that tears its clothes over barbarities and injustices of far less significance and importance.

---

[183] To delve deeper into the Jewish question in the early Spanish fascism, the reading of *Delenda est Israel* (Madrid: Ed. Barbarroja, 2001) is essential.

7.

Foreword to Benito

On April 15th, 1934, the first edition of Benito Mussolini's book *El Fascismo, su doctrina, fundamentos y normas legislativas en el orden sindical corporativo, económico y político* [*Fascism, Its Doctrine, Foundations, and Legislative Norms in the Corporate, Economic, and Political Syndicalist Order*] was distributed in Spain by the Madrid bookstore San Martín, which was located at 6 Puerta del Sol. It featured a prologue by José Antonio Primo de Rivera and an epilogue by Julio Ruiz de Alda, two of the triumvirs of Falange Española de las JONS.

Four days before the book's presentation, journalist César González Ruano published an interview with José Antonio in the newspaper *ABC*, which was conducted at Julio Ruiz de Alda's home, with Rafael Sánchez Mazas also present—" the official trinity of a faith," as the reporter and great friend of both described them. José Mara Alfaro from Burgos and two interns from José Antonio's law firm, Cuerda and Sarrión, were also present at Julio's house. The journalist describes José Antonio as being "in a situation that only an Iberian Fascist leader can understand as difficult." The interview addressed the criminal attack that José Antonio and his assistants experienced on April 10th while returning from a trial held in the Cárcel Modelo courtroom in Madrid. The refined and perceptive journalist, a friend of the interviewee, did not waste the atmosphere of an interview and began the conversation with the following reflection:

> As I pass through a double row of outstretched arms—palms bearing a will promising an empire—I think that perhaps the interview is the literary

subgenre that is most at odds with what I understand to be the Fascist style. And this is due to the interview's element of rhetorical realism and poverty, as it is usually nothing more than the sad result of necessity placed at the service of vanity.

The interview took place only two hours after the events that could have cost the interviewee and his companions their lives, and he acknowledges the difficulty, not of the questions, but of the answers: "The situation of this young leader is an anthology of hardships. Should he be cautious and cryptic, it will be said of him: 'This man already thinks he is Mussolini.'"

On February 11th, the magazine *Blanco y Negro*, belonging to the same publishing house as *ABC*, also featured an interview by journalist L. Méndez Domínguez, who, when describing the intimate atmosphere of José Antonio's office, noted:

> Primo de Rivera pauses for a moment. He glances over the fireplace: there is a portrait of his father; another one, of Mussolini, dedicated to him.
>
> "Well, Mr. José Antonio, what is your attitude toward the present moment?"
>
> "My position is the one I expressed in my speech at the Comedia on October 29th, 1933: To devote my energy to that totalitarian, national, and social state, which may be considered an instrument of the total destiny of Spain on a universal level, not according to the strongest class or party."

Mussolini's book was published in Spain by two centurions of the highest level of Spanish Fascism: José Antonio Primo de Rivera and Julio Ruiz de Alda. The Spanish edition was made by V.P.S. and had the author's direct approval.

The work is dedicated "To His Excellency the Ambassador of Italy in Spain, Most Illustrious Gentleman Raffaele Guariglia, a true and excellent diplomatic representative, in whom the highest rank of the most exquisite diplomacy is bound up with that of intellect and personal nobility."[184]

The translator gives a preliminary warning in the preface to José Antonio's foreword, justifying the opportunity of the work "to make known to the Spanish-speaking public the explanation of the Fascist doctrine, written by the Duce himself for the *Enciclopedia Italiana*," with the disclaimer that "the translator has not wanted to alter, in many cases, the austere, categorical, and direct concepts with which the Duce expounds his convictions and ideology in order to give it the authenticity and style that characterize the diction of Mussolini, limiting himself, therefore, in the

---

[184] Benito Mussolini, *El Fascismo* (Madrid: Librería de San Martín, 1934), "Dedicatoria."

translation, to the most faithful expression of the true Fascist doctrine."[185]

The fact that José Antonio wrote the foreword to Mussolini's book can be considered a matter of genetics. In 1924, his father, Miguel Primo de Rivera, also wrote the foreword to Homem Christo's book *Mussolini arenga a la raza latina* [*Mussolini Rallies the Latin Race*].

In his prologue, Captain General Miguel Primo de Rivera writes:

The figure of Benito Mussolini, well known in Italy since his early days, was revealed to Europe when Fascism elevated him to its command and leadership, and especially when, after the arrival of the legions in Rome, he was invested by the king and the people alike with the powers of head of state.

The army and the navy, being acutely aware of the fact that these institutions cannot serve in an environment of indiscipline and disorder, decidedly supported Mussolini, and they have not regretted it because the great man has known how to reconcile in his democratic spirit the indispensable prestige of power with the progress of culture and life that Italy longed for and deserved after the efforts and sacrifices of the Great War.

Regarding myself, I had admired this master of energy and patriotism before I met him, and when I got off the train in Rome with the king and queen of Spain, his eyes and mine sought and greeted each other before we could even shake hands. Following that, I had the opportunity to speak with him several times, each time receiving confirmation of the elevation of his thought and the sympathy that this man, in love with the qualities of the Latin race, feels for Spain. Our farewell in Rome was no longer a handshake but the connection of arms and the union of chests. Mussolini is a person who magnetizes with his manner and the clarity of his intellect, which fosters friendship.

Italy and Spain have pursued, in recent times, similar paths in their governments. The people, the king, and the military have united against professional politicians who, in a false and conventional environment, had lost the energy and qualities that, even in those who personally had them, found no way or time to be applied because the strength and value of men were not in them but in the number of votes they had—that is, in the number of electoral districts they had at their disposal, thanks to the despotic organization, which can only be sustained by the constant partiality in favor of those who maintain it, thus prostituting the principles of justice and equity, which are precisely the fundamental ones in any

---

[185] Ibid., "Advertencia" ["Disclaimer"], 9–10.

honest democracy.

When Italy and Spain, people of fine, intelligent, and vigorous race, will have purified their politics, much can be expected from their performance in the world, and they will be important factors of rebirth.

No one can deny Benito Mussolini's first place in this endeavor. To him, I send my warmest greetings in these lines.

Miguel Primo de Rivera.[186]

The front page of the book, where José Antonio's father writes his foreword to Mussolini, is evocative. In the center, reminiscent of a spinal column, is the lictorial fasces, the symbol of the new and eternal Italy. At the top is a portrait of the Duce adorned with a labarum eagle. At the bottom, one finds a black and white photograph of Captain General Primo de Rivera, and above it, an attentive lion.

Ten years later, his son, José Antonio, with the same admiration and respect that his father had for Mussolini, would sign the foreword of the first book of Fascist doctrine written by the Duce himself to be published in Spain, which Falange Española would be responsible for promoting, propagating, and disseminating. In this case, the cover of the book was printed in two colors, green and red, which stood out against the white background—thus the three colors that make up the Italian national flag. In red were the names of the author, the Duce Benito Mussolini, and those of José Antonio and Julio Ruiz de Alda, who acted as the apses of the work, as firm and stable human caryatids, as the literary honor guards to a text embraced by the three of them. In green, and in more marked letters, was the title of the work: *El Fascismo*. In red, again, were the names of the paladins of the national revolution. The color green represents hope, the watchword of the great European and universal dream.

José Antonio's introduction reads as follows:

Man is the system: this is one of the profound human truths which Fascism has brought to light again. The entire nineteenth century was spent devising mechanisms of good government. One might just as well seek to discover a machine for thinking or for loving. No machine has ever managed to produce anything authentic, eternal, and exacting such as government; it has always been necessary in the long run to turn to what has, from the beginning of time, been the only apparatus capable of governing men, namely man himself. That is to say: the leader, the hero.

The opponents of Fascism mistake this truth and use it as an aggressive debating point. "Yes," they admit. "Italy has derived benefit from Fascism,

---

[186] Homem Christo, *Mussolini arenga a la raza latina* [*Mussolini Rallies the Latin Race*], Foreword by Captain General Primo de Rivera (Madrid: Imprenta Latina, 1924).

but what happens when Mussolini dies?" They think that they are thus dealing the system a crushing blow, as though any system could possibly be guaranteed to exist for ever. It is very likely that momentary unease will befall Italy when Mussolini dies, but it will only last a moment; in due course, with more or less travail, the system will bring forth a new leader. And this leader will in turn embody the system for many years. And he (the duce, the guide) will keep faith with his people in man-to-man communion, that basic, human, and eternal way of communicating that has left its mark on all the paths of history.

I have seen Mussolini from up close, one afternoon in October 1933, at the Palazzo Venezia in Rome. That meeting did more to make me understand Italian Fascism than reading a great many books.

It was half past six in the evening. There was not the slightest bustle in the Palazzo Venezia. At the entrance there were two militiamen and a placid doorman. It seemed easier to get into the palace where Mussolini works than to gain access to any provincial government building in Spain. As soon as I had shown the doorman the notification of my appointment, I was taken up wide and silent stairs to the reception of Mussolini's office. Three or four minutes later the door opened. Mussolini works in a huge drawing room, all marble, with hardly any furniture in it. There he was, behind his desk in the far corner opposite the door. One saw him from a distance, alone in the vastness of the room. With a Roman salute and a candid smile, he asked me to approach. I walked toward him for I don't know how long. And once we were both seated the Duce began his conversation with me.

I had seen him before, years ago, at a formal audience, when I was received together with a number of students from Madrid University. Besides, like everyone in the world, I knew him from photographs, which almost invariably depict him in a military pose, saluting or haranguing. But the Duce of the Palazzo Venezia was quite different, with strands of silver in his hair, with a subtle air of weariness, with his civilian clothes neat and yet casual. He was not the leader of the public speeches, but a man of wonderful serenity. He spoke slowly, with every syllable pronounced distinctly. He had to give some instructions on the telephone and he did so as calmly as can be, his voice anything but authoritarian. At times, when something I said surprised him, he would throw back his head and open his eyes exceedingly wide, so that his dark pupils would for a second be surrounded by white. At other times he would smile calmly. The way he listened was remarkable.

We talked for about half an hour. Then he accompanied me to the door, across the enormous room. He is not very tall; he no longer has, supposing he ever had it, the upright stance of a militia chief; in fact, his back is beginning to be slightly bent. When the two of us reached the door, he said to me with paternal calm, without the slightest emphasis: "I wish you the very best, for yourself and for Spain."

Then he returned to his desk, slowly, to resume his work in silence. It was seven o'clock in the evening. With the day's labor done, Rome was streaming through the streets in the warm evening air. The Corso was alive with movement and chatter, like our Calle Alcalá at about the same time of day. People were going into cafés and cinemas. It seemed as though only the Duce was still at work by the light of his lamp, in a corner of a huge empty room, watching over Italy, to whose breathing he listened from there as to that of a small daughter.

What kind of a government apparatus, what system of weights and scales, councils and assemblies, can possibly replace that image of the hero become father, watching beside a perpetually glimmering lamp over the toil and slumber of his people?

José Antonio Primo de Rivera.[187]

Benito Mussolini gave him a large photograph of himself with a dedication written in his large, bold handwriting, with highlighted vertical ink lines. José Antonio regarded Mussolini, as we have just read in his prologue, as the "image of the hero become father." It was that signed portrait, the souvenir of the meeting prior to the formation of Falange Española, which José Antonio always kept with him in a privileged place throughout his political career, placed next to an oil painting of his father in his own office, where he spent his most reflective hours and where he welcomed everyone with his generous hospitality. José Antonio's legacy of loyalty to his father and his recognition and admiration for the Duce were absolute and definitive. There are numerous testimonies of the remarkable display of that famous photograph with Mussolini's handwritten dedication from all periods of the political life of the leader of the Falange. He kept it as a treasure and was proud to have it nearby and in view.

The epilogue of the book *El Fascismo*, written by Julio Ruiz de Alda, takes a stance and clarifies the meaning of Fascism:

There is a legend that says that Fascism is only a regime of oppression and tyranny whose aim is to preserve privileges for the wealthy, and the means which it employs to achieve this end is violence.

Nothing could be further from the truth, as will be noticed by those who have read this book, in which the doctrines are expounded by their very founder in his peculiar style of great decider. He is clear, concrete, and

---

[187] Translation from *José Antonio Primo de Rivera: Selected Writings*, trans. Hugh Thomas (London: Cape, 1972).

concise, having put them into practice. After ten years, his principles have made Italy a strong, optimistic, and joyful nation, confident of itself, fully identified with its state, instead of the chaotic and pessimistic nation that it was only twelve years ago.

Fascism, in its early stages, is, above all, faith—faith in the nation, faith in ourselves—and this integral, complete, and absolute faith is what heightens in men their qualities of sacrifice and heroism. For this faith we fight, we work, and, what is more sacred and important, we die. In short, the masses and men triumph over themselves, and it is our responsibility to instill in our people this desire for self-actualization, this will to be and to create, by considering not only oneself but also the community: Spain.

The nineteenth century has left us with its materialistic view of life, which has already degenerated into a selfish and individualistic view, to which Fascism opposes an anti-positivist, but nevertheless positive, view.

Socialism and revolutionary syndicalism had real reasons to exist, and Fascism recognizes these reasons, adopts them, and incorporates them into its state through corporations. Only by recognizing and imposing its reasons will there be a solution to the class struggle that divides and kills a nation.

In place of the state without faith in itself, inefficient and useless, such as the present one, it puts forth the living state, which gives to the people, conscious of their moral unity, a will, a superior idea; only this state will be able to incorporate in a willful way the common destinies of Catalonia and the Basque country, which being the richest and most pampered regions of Spain, have fabricated a separatist ideal, finding in the Spanish state nothing more than an amorphous and demoralized entity that fulfilled no other purpose beyond scraping by; this, as Mussolini says, can only result in death.

Fascism does not believe in eternal formulas of salvation, because it knows, as history shows, that life is a continuous process being and becoming; it is realistic and is satisfied with solving the problems that arise; and what it believes in, and educates the people for it, is that the essential thing is the way of being, the sense of living, and, therefore, it says that life is struggle and has a serious, austere, and religious sense; it despises the comfortable life.

Fascism is truly serious and profound; one may not agree with it, but one must acknowledge its human desire toward improvement and its generous spirit.

Julio Ruiz de Alda.[188]

---

188 Mussolini, *El Fascismo*, 277–279.

8.

José Antonio Visits Adolf Hitler

On November 2nd, 1933, Falange Española began its march. Neither the rally at the Comedia of October 29th nor the development of the newly formed organization went unnoticed by the German National Socialist diplomats in Spain. The German ambassador in Madrid, Count Welczeck, an old acquaintance and friend of José Antonio, with whom he shared pleasant evenings at the ambassador's home and hunting trips in the La Torrecilla reserve, sent, on December 15th of that same year, the dispatch 4756/33 with the label "Faschismus in Spanien" ["Fascism in Spain"] to the Minister of Foreign Affairs of the Third Reich. In this missive, he gave an account of the global situation of the Fascist parties and movements that were operating in Spain at the end of 1933, the year that saw Hitler's rise to power.

The report first mentioned the Legionnaires of Albiana, then the JONS led by Ramiro Ledesma Ramos, and finally the emerging movement led by José Antonio, which was described in the following terms:

> The roots of nascent Spanish Fascism can be traced back to the time of Primo de Rivera. Presently, there are three parallel groups . . . . The result of the elections, with the clear victory of the right wing parties, allows us to hope that the new government will leave more room for action and freedom for the still-developing young Fascist movements to thrive . . . . The Fascist movement is here in its initial stage. It currently lacks responsible and confident leadership, which is necessary for a promising development. It requires a charismatic personality who not only has excellent organizational

skills and is free of prejudices, but who is also a solid, popular type who can stand up like a prophet and persuade the masses and win them over. In the absence of an authentic leader of such character, a national uprising will not be possible, even if Fascism is in reality the only possible salvation for Spain . . . .

The third group is under the leadership of Primo de Rivera's eldest son, and it has only been in existence for a few weeks. The young Primo is about thirty years old, a lawyer, quite clever, and a good orator. He is referred to as the "*señorito*," because he is young and elegant. He may be able to develop well; everyone admires his good qualities of character; however, as a politician, he is said to be too young and inexperienced. His father's name helps him in some regards, but it represents an obstacle for him before all those who reject dictatorship and who, in his efforts, foresee a return to his father's regime. Primo de Rivera has openly proclaimed himself a Fascist during the last elections and has declared that these elections do not interest him in any way, because parliamentarism is of little use to Spain. His supporters are primarily young aristocrats, but he is attempting to spread his movement among the armed forces, despite the fact that he is said to be primarily interested in officers. Behind him is the well-known right-wing newspaper *La Nación*, and its director Delgado Barreto, who, certainly, does not have an impeccable reputation in Madrid either.

The group has now opened an office during the elections, which has been promptly closed down by the government. It has also launched, with the support of *La Nación*, a newspaper titled *F.E.* (that is, *Falange Española*), of which only the first issue could be published, which is attached to this report.[189]

José Antonio closely followed the events in Germany after Hitler's rise to power on January 30th. After visiting Mussolini in Rome on October 19th, just before the Comedia rally, he was scheduled to make his second significant political visit to Hitler, this time with the Falange in motion and the deputy seat secured in the most recent constituency elections. He wanted to travel to Germany as soon as possible, to study firsthand its social organization and its new achievements, to establish contact with the National Socialist leadership, and to be able to meet with the very champion of the Third Reich, who had burst onto the European political scene with such force and vigor.

On January 13th, 1934, the German ambassador in Spain, Welcseck, sent an official telegram to his government, reading as follows:

---

[189] Report 4756/33, "Faschismus in Spanien," December 15th, 1933, File No. 18. Politic 29. Nationalsozialismus, Faschismus uns áhnliche Bestrebungen: márz 1920–mai 1936. Available at the political archive of the Ministry of Foreign Affairs in Bonn.

I recommend extending an invitation to the events of January 30th in Berlin and Munich to the founder and Fascist leader here, José Antonio Primo de Rivera, eldest son of the renowned deceased dictator, who is extraordinarily interested in the new Germany and, especially, in the organization of the SA and the SS I request telegraphic response.[190]

José Antonio himself had taken the initiative and expressed interest in the trip to Germany, which was immediately taken into consideration by the highest representative of the German embassy in Spain. The proposed date was chosen to coincide with the first anniversary of Hitler's rise to power. The Ministry of Foreign Affairs forwarded Ambassador Welcseck's recommendation to Herbert Scholz, the head of foreign policy of the National Socialist Party's Liaison Committee, who was organically under Hitler's lieutenant, Rudolf Hess. The Reich Ministry of Propaganda, headed by Joseph Goebbels, was also contacted to determine who should organize José Antonio's visit and the suitability of the proposed date.

On January 28th, the Falange planned to hold a rally in the Gran Teatro de Cáceres, in which Alfonso Bardají Buitrago—provincial head of the Falange in Cáceres and owner of the weekly *Decimos*—together with Rafael Sánchez Mazas, Julio Ruiz de Alda, and José Antonio, would speak. In the event that José Antonio's trip to Germany would be confirmed, *Decimos* published on January 18th the following report: "Mr. José Antonio Primo de Rivera cannot come to Cáceres on January 28th, as we had announced, because on that date he will be in Berlin, invited by Chancellor Adolf Hitler to attend the celebrations of the anniversary of the rise to power of the racists." As José Antonio's trip to Berlin was postponed, the meeting in Cáceres was delayed to February 4th, a situation that was announced in *Decimos* on February 1st with the following advertisements: "Fighting for Spain. The Fascist rally that will be held in the Gran Teatro." In the subsequent issue, following the rally, the chronicle of the event was preceded by this headline: "The Fascist Rally of Last Sunday. The success achieved by Falange Española in Cáceres has been enormous."

On January 19th, a telegram from the German Embassy reached Madrid through the required procedure mentioned above, informing that the proposed date was not the most suitable since no relevant events were to be commemorated, and it was suggested that José Antonio's visit should be postponed for a more suitable occasion. Not knowing about this telegram, José Antonio was unaware the following day that news of his intention to visit Germany in the coming days was passed on to German press correspondents, reaching the *Volkischer Beobachter*, which was the official National Socialist Party press organ, and the newspaper *Deutsche Allgemeine Zeitung*.

---

[190] Telegram No. 3 of January 13th, 1934, in file No. 18. Available at the political archive of the Ministry of Foreign Affairs in Bonn.

José Antonio's intention and desire to travel to the capital of the Reich did not go unnoticed by the Spanish press. On January 20th, on the front page of the Republican newspaper *Heraldo de Madrid*, with great emphasis, in the section on the political scene, the following piece of news and its corresponding commentary appeared with great headlines: "El viaje de Primo de Rivera a Berlín" ["Primo de Rivera's Trip to Berlin"], with the following information:

The breaking news was missing. A newspaper has provided us with it.

According to this information, one of the Spanish Fascist organizations . . . has secretly sent to the group leaders, or better said, to the heads of the centuria, some secret instructions that could give us the sensation that we are sitting over an active volcano if there were the slightest hint that, indeed, this may be something that goes beyond the boundaries of fantasy and enters into those of reality.

We do not really think that things are moving as quickly as our colleague believes. In our opinion, we are still in the early stages of Fascist propaganda, and these orders to the centuria chiefs implying the completed establishment of the Fascist organization, or falangist organization, as we believe it is or will be called, are an assumption.

Nevertheless, there is still much to be done. This is demonstrated by Gil Robles' hilarious and eloquent "tug of war" with the Lerroux government, which, as we have noted, serves no other purpose than to buy time. Proof of this is that very trip announced by Primo de Rivera to Germany, to which *El Socialista* adds a generous commentary that seems to us, for the moment, more interesting than those secret instructions to the heads of the centuria, and which we are going to reproduce:

"This trip is being negotiated for some time now by the correspondent of *El Debate* in Germany, Eugenio Montes, who has supplied the Nazis with detailed news of the personal and moral characteristics of the aspiring caudillos of Spanish Fascism. The most intriguing of these reports concern Dr. Albiñana and Giménez Caballero. The person who has observed them could sustain these statements: 'Albiñana: demented character without any possible rooting in the Spanish people,' and 'Giménez Caballero: writer fond of getting into everything with volubility and absence of responsibility.' The report only favors Primo de Rivera. In his visit to Berlin, Primo de Rivera will be received by Goebbels and, most notably, by Rosenberg, who is in charge of instructing him on the activities that Fascism should conduct in Spain. We will wait for this news to be confirmed."

And so will we. This is very interesting.

Immediately, the German ambassador contacted José Antonio to inform him of the inconvenience, which he understood to be justified. Then, on January 21st, a new telegram from Welcseck to his superiors stated, "Given the circumstances, Primo de Rivera has postponed the trip." The German ambassador had insisted that José Antonio "would be pleased if he could be offered the opportunity to contact important leaders of the party and be received by the chancellor, his lieutenant, the prime minister of Prussia, and the minister of propaganda, and learn more about the organization of the party, the SA and the SS, especially in Berlin and Munich."[191]

On January 29th, in a new report sent from Madrid, the German ambassador justified the invitation of José Antonio to Germany by stating that "Primo already sees today in our Führer his teacher and is making an effort to translate the ideological foundations of National Socialism for the Spanish situation and conditions."

The second date for the trip, deemed as the most suitable, was Hitler's birthday, April 20th, considering that the NSDAP had planned parades and rallies on that date. The matter was looked into by the Ministries of Propaganda and Foreign Affairs, and it was considered that the best occasion would be the celebration on the first of May. It was also decided that the invitation would be mediated by Ludwig von Winterfeldt, who previously served as the German airline Lufthansa's delegate in Madrid. Unfortunately, José Antonio had an unavoidable engagement on the 29th in Madrid, so he would not arrive in Germany until the evening of May 1st, thus missing the demonstrations and the events of Labor Day so celebrated by the National Socialist regime. This was reported by the German ambassador on the 24th via telegram, and it was thought in Berlin that the late arrival and consequent absence from the commemorative rallies would undermine the purpose of the invitation. They tried to confirm and adapt the schedule of the trip and its planned program with the exchange of various telegrams and communications, and finally José Antonio was able to cancel his commitments in Madrid and, by train, on April 28, he set out for Berlin, with a stopover in Paris, where he had the opportunity to meet with the great Spanish artist Ana de Pombo, who was waiting for him on the platform. Remembering that day, she had memories of feeling terribly cold when she saw José Antonio get off the train carriage "without a coat and hat. He was on his way to Germany, where he would meet Hitler."[192] In Paris, he went to the German embassy to pick up his train ticket to Cologne and Berlin, a prudent precaution to avoid arousing suspicion or drawing the attention of Spanish authorities. On April 30th, he reached, with no delays, the German capital.

His guide during the trip was Arnold von Engelbrechten, member of the

---

[191] Quoted in Angel Viñas, *La Alemania Nazi y el 18 de Julio* (Alianza Universidad), 124.

[192] Ximénez de Sandoval, *José Antonio*, 198.

NSDAP and general secretary of the Deutscher Auslands-Club, which had among its duties the reception and organization of trips in collaboration with the Ministry of Propaganda. He had spent a considerable amount of time in Spain, first serving as a combatant from 1916 to 1918 during World War I, and then professionally working in German cinematography as the director of the company Odeon S.A., which had its headquarters in Barcelona, where he had lived since 1922. This earned him a certain friendship with José Antonio's father, General Primo de Rivera, for whom he had felt great regard and personal respect. He was a true National Socialist gentleman, cultured and affable, who understood very well the psychology of the Spanish people, and he politely attended to José Antonio and his companions throughout the tour. A photograph of the trip is still preserved, in which José Antonio poses with the Baron von Engelbrechten in Sanssouci, Potsdam.

It was von Engelbrechten who introduced José Antonio to the Führer on April 30th, in a long interview, according to his own written testimony. This contrasts with José Antonio's brief statement in the summary of the proceedings initiated by the Special Court of Alicante on November 10th, 1936, in which, when asked about the trip to meet Hitler, the court records:

> If, notwithstanding what he has stated about his involvement in the preparation of the insurrectionary movement in Spain, he negotiated with the foreign nations, Germany and Italy, or paid visits of pure courtesy to Messrs. Mussolini and Hitler, he replies that, in the years 1933 and 1934, he was received by Messrs. Mussolini and Hitler during brief visits, and that it never occurred to the declarant to fall into the tactlessness of proposing to those foreign personalities proposals of Spanish insurgency in the long term, not concealing the fact that he had been in Italy several times, the most recent at the beginning of the summer of 1935.[193]

The dismissive response is fully justified by the extremely serious circumstances and allegations under which the interrogation was conducted.

The news of José Antonio's stay in Germany, despite the discretion with which it was arranged, led the German ambassador in Spain to send, on April 26th, on the eve of the departure of the Spanish guest, a confidential telegram in which the German authorities were instructed that "it was necessary that the press should keep quiet about the visit."[194] In spite of the secrecy on the German side, the commitment to silence was broken by the Spanish journalist Antonio Bermúdez Cañete, correspondent in Berlin of the right-wing Catholic newspaper *El Debate* ran by Mr. Angel Herrera Oria, who surely crossed paths with the leader of the Falange during his trip to Berlin.

---

[193] Primo de Rivera, *Escritos y Discursos, Obras Completas 1922–1936*, vol. II, 1035.

[194] Telegram No. 36 dated May 2nd from Welczeck, in file 18. Available at the political archive of the Ministry of Foreign Affairs in Bonn.

Bermúdez Cañete, who disclosed the news to the Spanish public, had been one of the signatories of the Political Manifesto of *La Conquista del Estado* [*The Conquest of the State*] in February 1931, and Roberto Lanzas—that is, Ramiro Ledesma Ramos—spoke of him as follows:

> Bermúdez Cañete was in charge of the economic and financial section of the newspaper. He was the only unofficial Catholic contributor to *La Conquista del Estado*. He was sometimes seen as hesitant and reserved, until one day in the editorial office he discovered that Mr. Angel Herrera, his mentor and teacher, had described them all as inveterate Hegelians, state idolaters, and a slew of other heresies. He often complained to Ledesma about the spirit of the newspaper, but the director, who knew him well, did not bother much to reassure him, entrusting this function to the administration's typist, who did a marvelous job just by being punctual in the delivery of the twenty-five monthly *duros* that Cañete received.[195]

José Antonio's trip to Germany helped him study the organizational criteria of the National Socialist Party, as recounted by German historian Schulz-Wilmersdorf in his book *Spanien: Politiker und Generale* [*Spain: Politicians and Generals*]. This is confirmed by Felipe Ximénez de Sandoval in his biography of José Antonio:

> José Antonio undertakes a trip to Germany. He wants to learn through his own eyes and astute ears what the Nazi experiment, so distorted by the hostile press and propaganda, truly is. The new Germany has not yet taken the first loud strides of its awakening—which would astound the world—but is working feverishly and silently to set in motion its secular energy. The National Socialist phenomenon—still in its beginnings—attracts José Antonio's curiosity even before the newsreels broadcast around the world the spectacularism of its Nuremberg Congresses . . . . José Antonio became interested in the experiment of the Third Reich long before our War of Liberation brought Germany's sympathies for our cause to the attention of Spain; long before the Falange established comradeship with the Brownshirts who had preceded us in the street fights against Marxism.
>
> The intuitive genius of José Antonio did not give in to curiosity only when the desire or the need to know grew irresistible. His thirst for knowledge drove him to look into the original sources of great things. For this reason, after having theoretically convinced himself of the National Socialist ideology through careful readings of Hitler's *Mein Kampf*, Rosenberg's *The Myth of the Twentieth Century*, and its Nietzschean

---

[195] Ledesma Ramos, ¿*Fascismo en España?*, 79–80.

antecedents, he decided to go and see how all that theory of profound Germanism, of essential German romanticism called National Socialism, was put into practice.

As he is still only a young deputy, and the movement he leads has not crossed borders, nor has it given him any popularity, he expects from the trip the richest fruits, which are those obtained by direct observation on the field, with the company of good German and Spanish comrades who are familiar with the environment.[196]

The contacts established with the authorities of the National Socialist Party (including Alfred Rosenberg himself, the movement's ideologist, with whom he discussed the possibility of translating and publishing his books in Spain) also contributed to increasing the exchange of propaganda material, which, from that moment on, began to be more widely distributed, although not sent to the press office or the headquarters of the Falange, to avoid complications during the repeated police searches and periodic closures to which they were often subjected.

Alfred Rosenberg himself, in his book *Grossdeutschland: Traum und Tragödie* [*Greater Germany: Dream and Tragedy*], provides the following firsthand testimony:

During his visit to Germany, the founder of the Falange, José Antonio Primo de Rivera, came to see me, evidently to get a personal impression of a person attacked by ecclesiastical circles like myself. I immediately pointed out to him, so that there would be no misunderstandings, that, although we were also fighting against communism like him, we were not thinking of recommending any German way of thinking to him. Spain possesses its very own ancient traditions, and if it strove for new and proper ways of living for our times, it would probably combine these with its own traditions. As far as I am personally concerned, I refused to have my work, which is only intended for Germany, translated into Spanish. I think my visitor understood me at once, and we bid each other farewell without this misunderstanding that so often occurs.[197]

José Antonio was also accompanied during his visit by the writer and journalist Eugenio Montes, columnist for the newspaper *ABC* in Berlin, a fluent German speaker who guided him,

through the cafés of the Kurfürstendam, the Pergamon, and Kaiser Wilhelm

---

[196] Ximénez de Sandoval, *José Antonio*, 217.

[197] Alfred Rosenberg, *Grossdeutschland. Traum und Tragödie*, 2nd ed. (Munich: Selbstverlag H. Härtle, 1970]

museums, across the Unten der Linden, which still has linden trees, through the Tiergarten, with swans and squirrels, and through the Wansee, already crowded with the white sails of the sloops and the red bathing suits of swimming girls. With them were sometimes González Ruano and other journalists and students of medicine, law, architecture, engineering, philosophy, or music. He gained insightful knowledge about National Socialism and various aspects of the German character from Eugenio. José Antonio understands—José Antonio's comprehension was divided into love and criticism—and selects from the new political-social system of Germany what he can take advantage of for the Spanish youth in search of a new ideal of discipline and faith in the Fatherland.[198]

During his tour of Germany, he did not miss the chance he was given and visited the famous University of Heidelberg, which left a great impression on him due to its outstanding cultural output and academic excellence. Upon his return, José Antonio made clear his admiration for the German university when comparing it with the "dry and sad" university classrooms of Spain.

José Antonio resided with his friends and companions at the Pensión Latina in Berlin, where Spanish university students and intellectuals used to lodge, including his friend and writer Eugenio Montes and the journalist César González Ruano, who were pursuing higher studies in Germany, as well as González Ruano, who went to Berlin to study the new awakening of Germany, later writing a famous book entitled *Seis meses con los nazis*, which was financially supported by the German embassy and widely publicized and announced in *F.E.* Left in the guest book of the Pensión Latina in Berlin is this record and testimony in his own handwriting:

> Remembering—thankful for this hospitality—the Spain that may not exist physically, but the one that is as eternal as mathematical truth and that will be projected again in history.

Mrs. Elsa Paege, an active militant of the National Socialist Party and correspondent of José Antonio, had her residence in Germany. On the occasion of his visit, she ran multiple errands and made numerous arrangements in order to obtain economic aid and financing for the Spanish Falange, which she estimated at half a million marks. Mrs. Paege held strong connections with the National Socialist Party's upper echelons, maintaining a close friendship with Edith Faupel, the wife of the future German ambassador to the Salamanca government during the National Liberation Crusade. Elsa spoke fluent Spanish, and her contacts with the Spanish mainland dated back to the dictatorship of Primo de Rivera and General Martínez Anido,

---

[198] Ximénez de Sandoval, *José Antonio*, 197.

when she held the office of the Ministry of the Interior. Once informed of José Antonio's visit, she headed for the Wilhelmstrasse, showing up with "the utmost discretion." Mrs. Paege moved easily behind the scenes of politics and her contacts with certain circles of the Falange would endure for many years.

Some years later, José Antonio's sister, Pilar Primo de Rivera, together with Javier Conde, who acted as a translator, and Blanca Tetuán, also visited Hitler in Berlin, to whom she donated a steel sword from Toledo—symbolizing with her gesture the recognition of the bearer of the sword in Europe—a replica of the weapon carried by one of the greatest and most distinguished protagonists of Spanish history.

After José Antonio's visit, during 1934, she continued to manage financial aid, openly requesting the aid to the head of the Service in Spain and Portugal of the Wilhelmstrasse Kurt von Kamphoevener—later Minister Counselor in Madrid— who reported the request to Deputy Secretary of State Gerhard Kópke, in a letter dated November 12th of that same year, commenting that German aid to Spain should be consolidated as events evolved toward Fascist approaches and not through what was considered, by the Ministry of Foreign Affairs and the Ministry of Propaganda, as "tips" to like-minded political groups, which could cloud the official relations between both governments if such aid, which would not solve anything, were to come to the knowledge of the Spanish Republicans,

José Antonio, in Spain, was accompanied by one of his most enthusiastic collaborators from the early days of the Spanish Syndicalist Movement: José Sainz de Nothnagel, whose father was from Montañes and whose mother was German. Pepe Sainz, despite being born in the small Cantabrian village of Meruelo, had a Germanic upbringing. He lived in New York from ages five to fifteen, after which he moved to Berlin to live with his maternal grandparents, witnessing the awakening of the new National Socialist Germany. On his return to Spain, he settled in Toledo with the role of delegate of the National Tourist Board. He proudly wore the swastika on his lapel, and upon learning of the existence of the MES, led by José Antonio, he enthusiastically embraced it. He attended, at the head of a group of young comrades from Toledo, the rally on October 29th at the Comedia. José Antonio immediately appointed him provincial triumvir and, later, provincial head of Toledo, national councilor, and member of the command board, in possession of membership card number 191 of the *iniciadores*, a term used to designate the first two hundred membership cards of the Falangist organization.

9.

What Chances Do You Believe Fascism Has in Spain?

This direct and clear question, the only one on a questionnaire provided to different personalities of the time such as Alejandro Lerroux, Francisco Largo Caballero, José A. Balboti, Andrés Nin, and so forth, was also posed to José Antonio by the prolific writer Alfonso Martínez Carrasco, who wanted to gather various opinions in order to put the finishing touch to a study, the first of its kind to be carried out at that time in Spain, published in the middle of 1934, on *Fascismo en España* [*Fascism in Spain*], which was distributed exclusively by the Sociedad General Española de Librería. The answers were collected for the editorial illustration of the book.

Martínez Carrasco's book was based on the premise that:

Fascism is possible in Spain, without any difficulty for the spirit of the people, now dead because of the misery that has invaded us, sunk in the disorder which Spain has entered since the Republic, and a little tired out by the universalist current.

Having said that, we believe that Fascism adapts to people's psychological conditions better than other political formulas of our time (something Marxism cannot do due to its universalist and materialist inflexibility, as well as its programmatic phlegmatism). Aside from its reactionary character, which is universal, Fascism differs in each country; it can be so diverse because its ideological nature allows it to be so.

Concerning the nationalist aspect, Fascism seeks to be and can be, for better or worse, the historical national resurrection of the peoples through the use of the most outstanding spiritual qualities of each nation in which it develops. The national aspect of Italian Fascism differs from that of German Fascism, and each is appropriate for and adapted to the circumstances of the respective peoples. The symbol of German Fascism can be, more accurately, Bismarck, but now with a toothbrush moustache and all, while the Italian is Caesar—with a black shirt. In Spain it would be Isabel the Catholic.

One of the best qualities of Fascism that makes it easy for it to rule nations is, precisely, that it understands historical, national, and racial qualities, and can mold itself to them. Who can doubt that the Spaniard will be inflamed by a program that promises him the "sacred union of Spain"?[199]

The author provides a review and a political and sociological analysis of the prelude to Fascism in Spain and the social factors that led to its development until its definitive consolidation on October 29th at the Comedia.

In the journey through the path of Spanish Fascism, in such an early period—1934—he begins his work by saying: "To talk about Fascism in Spain is still as if we were talking about the seed that has not had time to sprout, that fertilizes without having reached its full life *cara al sol* [*facing the sun*]."

The reason Martínez Carrasco wrote this work was because he had realized that Fascism had gone from being an idea to becoming a reality, and because a sociological look at the environment of non-professional beggars, of creatures shivering in the arms of hunger, with six hundred thousand workers condemned to forced unemployment in Spain at that time, presented the same sad and painful aspect that pre-Fascist Italy and Germany faced in 1921 and 1932.

He believed that the Republic hastened Fascism because of the prevailing disorder, which paved the way for this ideology. Among the precursors of Spanish Fascism he cited, in the first place, the dictatorship as the most distant predecessor, arguing that just as the origins of Italian Fascism were in the deeds of D'Annunzio when he took Fiume, the origins of Spanish Fascism were to be found in the dictatorship of Miguel Primo de Rivera. In the same way that the precursors of the Mussolinian Blackshirts had been the Arditi, the precursors of the Spanish Falange were to be found, first in the early Patriotic Union and in the Somatenes, and later in the Legionnaires of Albiñana.

He then goes on to remark that the dictatorship brought Spain back to itself, taking it out of the deadly state into which the old politicians had plunged it, into

---

[199] Alfonso Martínez Carrasco, *Fascismo en España*, with the opinions, among others polled, of José Antonio Primo de Rivera. (Madrid: Ed. Júpiter, 1934), 19.

the arms of theocracy and old nepotistic politics. Spain regained its vitality; it felt again a kind of patriotic love toward itself, to inflame the people and to keep its distance from the stale politickers. It was a symptom of Fascism, which the dictator and his general staff promoted through the Italian example:

> The Patriotic Union was nothing but a kind of bourgeois and good-natured "Fascism," a peaceful Fascism, because before it there was no enemy that would have made violence necessary. The Somatenes were a patriotic national guard of a Fascist type, and if the hunting shotguns with which the dictator armed them never started shooting, as did the weapons that Mussolini provided to his squads, it was for that very reason that the Patriotic Union—U.P. (Unión Patriótica)—did not become a militia organization: because there was no enemy.[200]

The dictatorship disseminated on Spanish soil the first seeds of Fascism, with the resurgence of patriotism that reached its peak with the end of the war in Morocco—the restoration of peace—and with the new winds of security and socio-economic benefits, with its policies of stability and employment that were later continued with the foundation of the Patriotic Union Party, which, although it had curtailed some freedoms, had almost eradicated hunger.

According to Martínez Carrasco, the Dictatorship not only made Fascism manifest itself for the first time in Spain but also allowed it to spread in various sectors of the population, and in his contribution to Fascism, Primo de Rivera even donated a son, who would be its future leader.

After the dictatorship, the Legionnaires of Albiñana represented a clear and defined manifestation of Fascism, although it was only a limited and reduced group of minimal presence, whose forces were absorbed in part by the Spanish Falange.

Among the causes for the acceleration of Fascism in Spain, the author cites in the study the burning of convents, allowed by the Republic in May 1931, a month after its establishment; the Catalan Statute, which marked the beginning of the dismemberment of Spain; and the dark and sinister policy of Azaña with his position in favor of the Catalan Statute, his attacks on Catholics, his anti-militarism, and his Masonic policy toward the university and the market.

In José Antonio, whom he considers "the head of Spanish Fascism," he found two major flaws for such a responsibility: not being a man of the common people and being too overly polite and lyrical.

Concerning the characteristics of Spanish Fascism, he considered them to be its marked Catholicism, its historical point of reference in the Spain of the Catholic monarchs, and its general lack of concern with too many racial distinctions.

---

[200] Ibid., 30.

10.

Fascist Confessions of José Antonio

Francisco Bravo came from the old JONS. He was later issued national card number 129 of Falange Española's *iniciadores*, and card number 1 in Salamanca, recognizing him as the pioneer there. He was the representative of those "*gallos de marzo*" [March roosters] in Salamanca, where he worked as a journalist for the Catholic newspaper *La Gaceta Regional*. His participation was decisive, together with Ernesto Giménez Caballero, in the union of the JONS with Falange Española, which,

> was made possible, in part, because we managed to convince several friends of Ledesma who had been helping him in his work but who recognized the urgent need to achieve the unification of the two Fascist groups that had arisen in Spain. Several comrades helped me with this task, in particular Giménez Caballero. Since the early days of the Spanish Falange, I always advised Ledesma to make a pact with José Antonio, whom I also regarded with suspicion because of his origin, fearing that he was not the leader capable of arousing, guiding, and channeling the Spanish Fascist movement, for which the forerunners had already prepared the appearance.[201]

---

[201] Bravo, *José Antonio, el hombre, el jefe, el camarada*, 64.

It was Ledesma Ramos himself who, at the end of the rally in Valladolid on March 4th, introduced José Antonio to Francisco Bravo, who, upon meeting him, declared: "I already know about you and your journalistic work. I count you as one of us. We'll see if we can get the Falange in Salamanca organized soon so that we can put on an even better rally than this one."[202]

In the afternoon, José Antonio, Ledesma, Julio Ruiz de Alda, and Francisco Bravo met at the Francia Hotel in Valladolid, where they entrusted the latter with the duty of organizing and leading the movement in that city and its province.

José Antonio, in a long interview granted to the newspaper *Ahora* on February 16th, 1934, stated the position of the Falange in relation to Fascism. Because of their didactic clarity and conceptual illumination, Francisco Bravo reproduced the statements of the national leader in his *Historia de Falange Española de las JONS*, published in 1940.[203] The interview comes to an end with the following questions and responses:

Ahora Interviewer: "There is a quite widespread belief that Fascism will not be able to take root in Spain. How would you counter this argument?"

José Antonio: "Against those who talk about the possibility of Fascism in our country, with the same faith that I am inclined to hold in the racial vitality and immortality of Spain, I believe that not only is it possible but necessary, so that the Fatherland can be saved. Spain has carried out wonderful works of discipline. What is happening is that this necessity is reaching us after a century of decadence. At this moment, our virtues of discipline and organization are perhaps much weakened, but no one can tell us that we will not be able to find the means to reawaken them. Fascism is a universal attitude of turning toward oneself. We are told that we are imitating Italy. We do imitate Italy in seeking our most profound *raison d'être* in our own inner core. However, this approach, imitated if you will, although eternal, yields the most authentic results. Italy has found Italy. We, by turning inward, will find Spain."

A.I.: "Fascism is essentially nationalist. In what is the nationalism that you seek to inspire rooted?"

J.A.: The Fatherland is a mission. If we confine the concept of the fatherland to a territorial or ethnic concern, we risk succumbing to unfruitful particularisms or regionalisms. The Fatherland has to be a mission. There are no more continents to be conquered, it is true, and there can be no more dreams of conquest. But the international democratic idea that the League of Nations offered us is already falling apart. The world

---

[202] Ibid., 67.

[203] Bravo, *Historia de Falange*, 31–36.

must again be governed by three or four racial entities. Spain can be one of these. It is located in a strategic geographical location and has a spiritual dimension that could make it a contender for one of these leading roles. And that is what we can stand up for: Not being a mediocre country; for one is either an immense country that fulfills a universal mission or a degraded and meaningless people. The ambition to be a leading country in the world must be rekindled in Spain."

A.I.: "Not all citizens are capable of grasping the great nationalist ideals. What could lead the ordinary man to Fascism?"

J.A.: "The social ideal remains the motivating factor for those unable to achieve the great national ideal. Undoubtedly the movement's most immediate objective is social justice; it is an elevation of the way of life. Fascism aspires to national greatness, but one of the steps toward this greatness is the material improvement of the people. The social is an interesting aspiration even for elementary minds, but, nevertheless, the national is attainable to many more people than is believed. Each Spanish socialist carries within him a nationalist."[204]

The use of the term *Fascist* to define rallies, ideas or even the Falangists themselves was not rare. *Decimos* referred directly to Falange rallies as "Fascist acts," and even on May 31st, 1934, an article appeared in that weekly, authored by the Falangist Sánchez Marín, with the title "¿Por qué soy fascista?" ["Why Am I a Fascist?"], in which he argues:

The fierce spirit of Fascism subjugates us; its vibrant heart of patriotic beauty attracts us; and its pure soul of fortunate realities echoes in us with the joyful resonance of the glorious resurgence of a new golden century for our history.

Fascism, as opposed to the prose that destroys, understands how to elevate the sublime that José Antonio Primo de Rivera described as poetry "that promises."

On Sunday, June 24th, 1934, Francisco Bravo met again with José Antonio in his office at 8 Calle Alcalá Galiano. Comrade Gil Remírez, an industrialist and father of a large family who had accompanied him all the way from Salamanca, also attended the meeting. The presence of a guard at the law office's door, as a precaution against potential attacks, attracted their attention. Serious suspicions were aroused when multiple people were spotted that same day hovering and lurking around the building.

Bravo describes the welcoming atmosphere of the room as follows:

---

[204] Francisco Bravo Martínez: *Historia de Falange Española de las J.O.N.S.* (Madrid: Ediciones FE, 1940), 35–36.

His office was ordinary, that of a working lawyer. There was a large portrait of his father; another one dedicated to him, of Mussolini. Books on the shelves; a couple of comfortable armchairs. Through one of the windows—the office was on the ground floor—a bomb could have easily been thrown.[205]

After exchanging greetings and formalities, they took their seats. They still addressed each other with formal pronouns, with the *usted*, which they would replace only later on.

José Antonio began by expressing his regret that "some elements that were [with him] in the Spanish Falange are deserting, frightened of the propositions of National Syndicalism and of the aims of the national revolution that our generation should carry out."

Bravo's response was prompt:

I am pleased to see that you identify so much with those of us who have recognized long ago that Fascism represents the nationalization of the disenfranchised's desire for social justice while also exalting patriotic values.[206]

José Antonio continued:

I appreciate your frankness. I know that you wrote in *JONS* that April 14th was the first Fascist event in Spain. I agree. Concerning the governmental system, we consider the issue to be surpassed and resolved. It is not of interest to us. The different examples of Italy and Germany prove it. The monarchy in Spain fell on its own due to its lack of vitality.[207]

In an atmosphere of greater complicity, while looking at the portrait of his father hanging on the wall, he concluded the sentence by stating, "As for me personally, there are certainly not many reasons that urge me to work toward a restoration."

After that, the discussion moved on to other topics. They discussed religion and education in schools, and, at one point in the conversation, Bravo commented, asking him a question at the same time:

"I see that you have already paid a visit to the Duce. Is he interested in the affairs of Spain?"

"Very much," replied José Antonio. "I first met him in 1929, when I traveled to Italy with my father. I have recently returned to Rome a few more

---

205 Bravo, *José Antonio, el hombre, el jefe, el camarada*, 68.

206 Ibid., 69.

207 Ibid.

times. He is extremely interested in the unfolding events in our country. He despises the moronic experiment of Marxist democratic liberalism that some are attempting to perpetrate in our country. And he trusts that the youth will bolster our movement, and that, after the failure of this experiment, we will achieve victory."

We then spoke of Germany, Hitler, and National Socialism. José Antonio shared my belief that social work could be done there that would go even deeper than it did in Italy. And he said that in a few years, the German people's discipline, courage, and faith would take their country to the forefront of the Western powers.[208]

The most diverse topics were discussed in the intimacy of that June Sunday. They spoke of the difficulties of the struggle, the obstacles erected by the government, and how detrimental it would be to return to being clandestine, because it would effectively eliminate the ability to reach the masses through propaganda. The Falange was not a group of conspirators but a Fascist-inspired movement that was "youthful, political, and mystical, in need of light and fresh air to develop."

The conversation drifted toward more internal issues. They commented on the low number of Falangist militants in Salamanca, since it was Gil Robles' stronghold. On that occasion, Francisco Bravo, who was also a friend of Miguel de Unamuno, told José Antonio that, while Unamuno was sometimes critical of Fascist ideas, it was painful for him also to see Spain fall victim to separatism. He told him how Miguel's eldest son, who was an architect and lived in Palencia, was a "very close friend and does not hide his sympathy for Fascism." They both acknowledged that José Ortega y Gasset "had a lot in common with us," and that his children and those of Dr. Marañón were active in the Falange.

Three hours of conversation flew by in the blink of an eye.

On February 10th, 1935, just a few months after this endearing conversation between José Antonio and the provincial chief, Francisco Bravo, the first meeting of the movement in that province was held in Salamanca. After a meeting of José Antonio, Sánchez Mazas, and Bravo with Miguel de Unamuno, who received them in a cold office in his house in Calle Bordadores, where he wrote his works, he accompanied them through the streets to the event wearing a black beret with a short brim. They occupied a special place on a balcony and, later, Miguel de Unamuno shared dinner with the boys of the Falange in the Gran Hotel, near Plaza Mayor.

Another anecdote of José Antonio's life is what was once said amongst an intimate circle of friends—José Manuel Aizpurúa, Francisco Bravo, and the National Leader of the Falange himself—which is also narrated by Bravo; it occurred on "a cloudy afternoon in August 1935," in Fuenterrabía.

---

[208] Ibid., 71.

Bravo asked the leader if he had read Georges Roux's book *La leçon de César* [*The Lesson of Caesar*], to which he replied affirmatively:

José Antonio possessed the modesty of great souls when alluding to their psychology, as few others do. Only someone like me, incorruptible, incapable of being bribed, who shouted at him the truth about the risks that flattery can cause to the powerful, could afford such audacity. José Antonio smiled ironically, facing the sea, rejecting my words, and I remember what he said:

"Julius Caesar is possibly the greatest man in the history of the West. Over time, he has become our mentor. What Mussolini is carrying out is exactly what he had already attempted. He was a great revolutionary, the prophet of a new classical and imperial age. We shall see if we are capable of producing a soul as magnanimous and a temper as steadfast as his."[209]

José Antonio monopolized Fascist leadership in Spain. The atomization of Fascist groups and circles was in contrast with the sense of unity these movements inspired. Already in the early phase of the Spanish Syndicalist Movement, he had proclaimed it in the last leaflet launched by the organization a few days before the celebration of the rally at Comedia. There he warned about the emerging and competing fascisms, claiming that only one, his, was the genuine and authentic one, the one that represented the men and ideas of the MES. On June 18th, 1934, he insisted again and gave the same advice in a letter he sent to Benigno Pousa Candedo, from Rivadavia, in response to the request he had made to send him a dedicated photograph for a group called Juventud Fascista [Fascist Youth], which he had founded in his town. The fragmentation and divisions did not fit in with the unitary spirit of Falange; for that reason, José Antonio wrote to him, saying:

Dear Sir:

If you belong to the Falange Española de las JONS, you can only be subject to its discipline, not that of any other group that may have been formed under a different name.

Therefore, I am sorry I cannot send you the photograph you requested for your Juventud Fascista, because sending such a photograph might appear to be an act of approval.

With best regards,
Yours affectionately.[210]

---

[209] Ibid., 168.

[210] Miguel Primo de Rivera y Urquijo, *Papeles postumos de José Antonio* (Madrid: Plaza & Janés, 1996), 106.

He made it clear that fragmentation into small groups and small cells of the same orientation was counterproductive, and that if there was already a Spanish Falange representing those feelings, creating acronyms or groups not subject to the movement's discipline made no sense, because the so-called and unknown Fascist Youth already belonged to the Falange's collective nature.

11.

José Antonio, Founding Member of the GAUR

Fascism was a national and revolutionary idea. A doctrine. A conception. A spirit. A solution. A universal attainment.

The reach of Fascism, the inner gaze, the look into the depths of the respective peoples, all served a redemptive purpose. Its implementation was unique to each population and could not be transferred, but its formula could be universalized. Fascism was the solution to the two antithetical worlds, equally wicked and detrimental for society: capitalism and communism. A new, realistic, and attainable hope was to be provided by Fascism, which aimed to end the antiquated and corrupt nature of traditional politics.

As early as 1930, Mussolini, the most authoritative and authentic voice on the subject, directed Fascism toward its universal dimension. When gazing from the famous balcony of Palazzo Venezia, the place of inspiration and testimony of his resounding harangues, toward the foot of the Altar of the Fatherland, where the inextinguishable flame of the vivifying fire is kept, he said with a brief sentence of profound meaning to the federal governors that "as an idea, doctrine, and attainment," Fascism is universal.

Asvero Gravelli, a Blackshirt of the early days and liberator of Fiume with D'Annunzio in 1919, leader of the Fascist youth, together with Michele Bianchi, Secretary of the Quadrumviro and founder of the magazines *Antieuropa* (1928) and *Ottobre* (1932), is one of the pioneers who considered Fascism not just limited to

Italy as an idea, but rather a doctrine for the restoration of a new and ancient civilization: Fascism as a reality emanating from the deep history of the peoples and at the same time as a creative revolution. In his book *Verso l'Internazionale fascista* [*Toward the Fascist International*] (1932), in his role as journalist, enthusiastic propagandist, and disseminator of "universal Fascism," he remarked:

> Fascism must provide European Fascist elements with a model of revolutionary tactics for establishing movements similar to those in our country in more mature countries, because Fascism is no longer an Italian phenomenon.[211]

His theses advocated carrying over the spirit of the Fascist revolution across Europe. During the Second World War, he served as commander in the Italian Waffen SS. Later, he was appointed head of propaganda for this group in Italy. As one of the Fascist veterans, he received the Duce in Germany when he was liberated by Skorzeny in 1943, and he remained at his side throughout the entire period of the Italian Social Republic.

In 1932, Guglielmo Marconi, the brilliant inventor and president of the Italian Academy in Rome, appealed to young European thinkers and intellectuals to gather for a congress on the Tiber River. The event, organized by the Section of Moral and Historical Sciences of the Royal Academy of Italy, was held at the Villa Farnesina near the Septimine Gate and Mount Janiculum from November 14th to 22nd, 1932, and its purpose was to discuss the unitary and imperial sense of Europe in depth. The call was made to steer toward a new direction in the course of history: ideas should come first, followed by action and the politics related to those ideas.

According to what was written in the announcement, it was expected that, from the debates and conferences among Europe's most restless and vibrant intellectuals, "a new order, a plan of new life in the world" would emerge from the clash of their opinions and inspirations. Europe was called to discuss Europe, the crisis it was suffering, and its possible and necessary renaissance.

Communist Russia and capitalist America, Bolshevism and mammonism, were two versions of the same cancerous disease: materialism. The Volta Congress sought solutions to the crisis caused by the stranglehold of these two realms.

Among the participants in the Volta Congress were Ernesto Giménez Caballero, who responded quickly to the call from Rome, as did Rafael García Morente and Sánchez Albornoz from Spain. Notable among the French participants was Pierre Gaxote, and from Germany, the figures of Werner Sombart, Alfred Rosenberg, Hjalmar Schacht, and Hermann Goering stood out.

Thus, the congress gave rise to the dream of a juridical, economic, political, and

---

[211] Gravelli, *Verso l'Internazionale fascista* (Rome: Nuova Europa, 1932), 225.

spiritual unity of Europe, along with another dream: that of peace, which could come neither from the Judaic designs prevailing in Geneva and New York, nor from gregarious and exploitative communism, but rather from the *Pax Romana*—from the hand of a "providential" and "God-sent" man. This man was Benito Mussolini, who recognized, as Giménez Caballero pointed out, that the secret of Rome was in "casting its light over the whole world with generous ecumenism."[212]

Fascism represented contemporaneity and actualism. The antidote to the European crisis was a revitalizing doctrine. Mussolini proclaimed it loud and clear: "The twentieth century will be the century of Fascism . . . because there is no salvation either for individuals or for peoples outside of our principles."

Italy began organizing the Italians scattered across the globe in the Foreign Fasces. It established and inaugurated a number of *case del Fascio* that would serve as refuges and safeguards for culture and civilization in the most important and influential cities. Several Italian press agencies were set up abroad, and, as of June 1933, the CAUR, the Committees of Action for the Universality of Rome, were activated.

The CAUR were promoted and financed by the Duce himself. The Committees' headquarters were located at 54 Via Gregoriana in Rome, and were presided over by an old dean of Fascism: Eugenio Coselschi, a veteran fighter in the Great War and one of the early organizers of Fascist militias. During the Fiume government of 1919–1920, he was Gabriele D'Annunzio's private secretary and a National Fascist Party deputy. In March 1935, the Roman headquarters relocated to 32 Via delle Botteghe Oscure in Palazzo Caetani, where more space was available for its operations.

The first and only president of the CAUR from their founding until their dissolution in 1943 was Eugenio Coselschi, the president of the Italian Federation of ex-combatants, parliamentary deputy, and close friend of Benito Mussolini.

The CAUR were constituted as "an organization of propaganda and culture with the mission of asserting that character of universality that embodies the essence of Mussolini's thought," as stated in the first article of its founding statutes. The Duce was considered, in the founding charter of the CAUR, "the creator and modeler of a new universal truth."

The Committees comprised personalities from the fields of culture and science, diplomacy and politics, the intelligentsia, and the military, united under the common guiding principle of the universality of Fascism and with their sights turned toward the horizon.

The aims of the Committees, within the larger Press and Propaganda Office of the Italian State, were fundamentally centered on the dissemination of books, pamphlets published in various languages, magazines, printed material, filmography, essays, news,

---

212 Giménez Caballero, *La Nueva Catolicidad*, 119.

music, and songs, relying on two chief organs of expression. The first was *Roma Universa*, which was renamed *L'Idea di Roma* [*The Idea of Rome*] in 1938; the magazine of the organization and something with which Giménez Caballero collaborated, it was oriented toward foreign countries and directed to the intellectual class. Its first issue appeared in October 1933, nearly four months after the Committees were established, and it ran continuously until 1943. There was also an internal weekly bulletin, *Il Notiziario Settimanale d' Informazione dei CAUR*, a folio-sized serial, in the form of an informative newsletter consisting of six to eight sheets, without signatures or names on the news that was gathered, addressed exclusively to the members of the Committees, and translated into different languages—including Spanish. In it was published news and commentary on the various national Fascist groups and movements scattered throughout the world. Its first issue was printed in the spring of 1934.

The Committees observed two commemorative dates: March 15th, the anniversary of Julius Caesar's death, and April 21st, the anniversary of the founding of Rome.

Within the administrative scheme of the Italian State, the CAUR was initially dependent on the Ministry of Foreign Affairs, whose chair was held by Mussolini. Subsequently, in 1934, they were placed under the administration of the Press and Propaganda Office. Dr. Guido Baroni, the head of this office, played an important role, coordinating the Italian Committees and maintaining a regular correspondence with the Committees abroad, as well as actively participating in the organization of the international events and meetings held under the patronage of the CAUR. Mussolini's son-in-law, Count Galeazzo Ciano, was the Undersecretary of State for Press and Propaganda from 1935. Later, in 1936, he would become Minister of Foreign Affairs, with the diplomat Dino Alfieri thus taking charge of the Ministry of Press and Propaganda and, consequently, of the CAUR.

In other countries, the Committees would be very selective in their membership, attempting to bring in relevant personalities from the cultural environment who shared the spirit and thinking of the new Fascist order on an individual basis. These selected groups would form National Committees in each country, led by a local president. An inspector sent from Rome would be in charge of coordinating the efforts and activities of the various Committees that arose abroad to promote the "universality of Rome," and they would ultimately be governed by a general council made up of all the Committees, which would make its decisions collectively and by consensus. The *ispettore* of the CAUR for Spain, Portugal, Sweden, and Norway was Dr. Ferruccio G. Cabalzar. Also, since the Italian nationals were not integrated into the Committees of the other countries, a trustworthy person of Italian nationality, resident in the respective country, was designated to serve as a contact person between the National Committees and the Roman headquarters. This liaison officer in Spain was journalist Cesare A. Gullino, correspondent of the Agenzia Stefani and the newspaper *Corriere della Sera*. This restriction on the participation of Italians in the National Committees was intended to avoid the imputation of partisanship, which could be argued by enemies of Italy and its political system.

The CAUR abided by the rule of non-interference in the internal affairs of the countries where its Committees operated and gave special value and significance to the national traditions of each people.

The formation of the CAUR in Spain began early. The first and most influential contact in Rome was Ernesto Giménez Caballero, who attended the Convegno Volta in Rome in November 1932. Ernesto Giménez Caballero had been publishing literary and political works in full harmony with the Fascist doctrine, and, as he himself writes in his work published in 1933 under the title *La Nueva Catolicidad*:

I have personally met Mussolini on three separate occasions. The first time was at the Parliament, in Rome. The second, at Palazzo Venezia. The third, at a dinner in a grand hotel.

The first time—in Parliament—he appeared to me as if he were Julius Caesar. He was almost motionless in his presidential chair. As if he were made of marble. Not a single gesture. Nor a movement. Not even a twitch. That man was his own statue. He listened to the presentation of an entire financial project. He quickly skimmed through a document about Africa that had been handed to him. He attended a vote. At the end of the session, he came out upright, firm, and serene, with that peculiar majesty of his gait that is best seen in movie newsreels: a confident, Herculean, sure-footed gait. Full of elasticity and boldness at the same time. The gait of a natural king. A lion's gait.

The second time I saw Mussolini, we were face to face. It had been some time since I expressed to my illustrious friend Giuseppe Bottai my desire to behold the Duce in conversation. Late one night, I received a telegram from his private secretary, Chiavolini, summoning me for the following day at five o'clock in the afternoon to Palazzo Venezia. When Mussolini offered me a Savonarola-style armchair in front of an armchair of the same style, the one right over the other side of the table, I found myself sitting steady, illuminated, and silent. Mussolini began by throwing a question at me in Spanish: "*¿Qué pasa en España?*" ["What is going on in Spain?"] I assumed—and later gained the certainty—that he knew it much better than I did, so I answered him in a simple and concise way . . . . The entire Caesarean, marmoreal, privileged impression that he had given me in the Chamber had vanished to make way for the *popolano* [man of the people]; something very real, vital, healthy, and tangible. Mussolini laughed and smiled, with a type of laugh that we Spaniards describe as *campechana*, to allude to his peasant, earthy, and simple origins. Mussolini's voice, which in speeches and during dangers and ceremonies is low and deep like the roar of a kettledrum, turns melodious, soft, and tender in close conversation. That voice belonged to a man of flesh and blood, a human comrade, almost a companion. The distance eased, and one felt as if they were in the most comfortable of conversational worlds.

I realized the secret to this man's incredible power to captivate people's hearts and wills. Or as he says: bending the souls. There is an enormous secret to being what he is. It consists in giving to the common man—the other men—the impression of equality while at the same time establishing an unapproachable hierarchy. Trust and respect. Closeness and infinitude. The two levers capable of moving entire legions of wills. Thus, the characteristics of the "hero" were made clear to me: being nearly a man; being nearly a god.

When, after three years, I met him again at a dinner that he offered to the members of the Volta Congress, Mussolini recognized me almost immediately. He told me about the success I had achieved with my book *Genio de España*, which he had read, and about the chapters that had most impressed him.[213]

Spain was a country with which Fascism showed particular affinities and sympathies since the beginning, since the time of the Military Directory presided over by Miguel Primo de Rivera, due to the similarity of language, character, culture, mutual affection, and the proximity within the landscape of the Mediterranean. Spain has been bound since ancient times to Rome by language, law, and religion: the plough and the sword.

In the official press publications of the Falange, such as *Decimos*, this connection was openly expressed. In the issue published on February 1st, 1934, the provincial chief wrote an article for the front page with the title "Día 4 de febrero" ["February 4th"]—the date on which the meeting was scheduled to take place in the Gran Teatro of the city with the intervention of José Antonio, Ruiz de Alda, and Sánchez Mazas, the leading triumvirate of Falange Española—in which it is stated:

> Falange Española is a Fascist movement. Our fanatical nationalism does not render us ignorant, nor does it prevent us from properly appreciating the universalist spirit contained in the doctrines elaborated in Italy over the last fourteen years by the creative genius of Benito Mussolini. This does not mean that we are, nor could we just be, a mere copy. Every political movement has some intrinsic characteristics and some others that are accidental: we accept the fundamental norms and fit them into our tradition in order to obtain a Spanish nationalist doctrine. Thus, Italian Fascism seeks its roots in the tradition of the Roman Empire; German

---

[213] Ibid., 132–137.

racism, in the alleged supremacy of the Aryan race; and Falange Española will have to find it in Catholicity and in the cult of the ideal, which throughout our historical trials and tribulations have always been the two most outstanding virtues of our race.

The meticulous Falangist historian Rafael Ibáñez Hernández, in light of this and other similar texts that he has found and collected for his doctoral thesis, was forced, in the face of the evidence, to correct and amend a statement of José Antonio himself, made in an article he wrote while in prison during 1936 for the newspaper *Informaciones*, against Miguel Maura, noting that "with these texts, José Antonio Primo de Rivera's claim that the Falangist movement 'has never been called Fascist either in the forgotten paragraph of the least important official document or in the most humble propaganda leaflet' is disproved."[214]

While José Antonio was in Germany, in May 1934, an interview with him was published in the important Italian Fascist newspaper *Ottobre*—which has not yet been included in his complete works. In the interview, which was conducted on May 1st, he declares himself very close to Italian Fascism, to *romanitá* [Romaness] and *cattolicitá* [Catholicity].

In May 1934, the Inspector of the CAUR arrived in Spain from Portugal. It was Dr. Guido Ferruccio Cabalzar, who was received by the Italian ambassador in Madrid, Raffaele Guariglia, informing him with a report on the active Fascist groups and the present political, economic, and social situation of the country. Both agreed on the best candidate to represent the Spanish Committee of the CAUR, and they landed on Ernesto Giménez Caballero, who proudly and honorably accepted such a proposal. Giménez Caballero was already a member of the newly formed Falange Española de las JONS when his nomination became effective. An official account was written about the joint agreement to elect Ernesto Giménez Caballero "representative of the Committee with the task of keeping in contact with Rome both for the formation and for the functioning of the Committee itself," describing him as "one hundred percent Fascist, very loyal to Italy and to the Duce."[215]

Ambassador Guariglia wrote a report on the trip of the inspector of the Committees, Dr. Cabalzar, synthesized it into the following points:

1. Cultural character of the Spanish Committee, "organized so that not only the purely Fascist elements of Spain could join but also the intellectual sympathizers who wish to keep themselves on the fringes of

---

[214] Rafael Ibáñez Hernández, *La prensa del Movimiento Nacionalsindicalista durante la Segunda República*. Work of research. Unpublished (UNED: Departamento de Historia Contemporánea, 1997), 311, note 172.

[215] Guariglia, *Appunto sulla missione Cabalzar in Spagna* (A.G.S. Minculpop, June 26th, 1934), 423.

political struggle";

2. "Bringing into the Committee the heads of Spanish Fascist organizations, but as individuals";

3. "Instructing Mr. Gullino to ensure that contacts between Giménez Caballero and Rome are maintained."

Cesare A. Gullino was a journalist, a trusted man of the Italian Fascist authorities, a correspondent in Spain for the *Corriere della Sera* through the official news agency Agenzia Stefani, and a public official of the Press and Propaganda Service.

One of the first interviews arranged by Dr. Cabalzar was with José Antonio Primo de Rivera. Giménez Caballero and the Italian ambassador Guariglia acted as intermediaries and advisors in arranging the meeting. José Antonio had visited the Duce in October 1933, and Mussolini's work *Il Fascismo*, which he had personally written the foreword to, had just been published—with the ink still fresh—in Spain.

The Fascist regime in Italy valued José Antonio. He was regarded very positively because of his heritage, his personality, his character, his manners, his intelligence, his presence, his public speaking, his gallantry, and his thinking, all of which were fully in tune with Fascist ideas. It was only three months after Falange Española and the JONS merged. In the new movement, José Antonio was a Triumvir, together with Ramiro Ledesma and Ruiz de Alda.

The meeting happened quickly after the interview was requested. Dr. Cabalzar visited José Antonio at the small palace on Calle Marqués del Riscal, next to Paseo de la Castellana, the headquarters of Falange Española de las JONS The meeting was marked by great cordiality and camaraderie. The inspector of the CAUR was pleasantly impressed by his interlocutor. The report of the visit to José Antonio, written by Dr. Cabalzar, could not be more eloquent:

> He received me with the utmost courtesy, immediately returning to me the CAUR application form with his signature on it, expressing his gratitude for the delivery of the badge and membership card of the Committees.

It was going to be a source of pride for him, Cabalzar continues, to be "among the most active members of our Madrid Committee."[216]

Two noteworthy points stand out from the report: José Antonio's immediate decision to join the Committees and his prominent role of protagonism in them.

---

[216] Reproduced in the book by Professor Ismael Saz Campos, *Mussolini contra la II República* (Valencia: IVEI Ediciones Alfons el Magnánim, 1986), 128.

The inspector of the CAUR concluded his report with an annotation on José Antonio's personality which was of concern in the Fascist environment of the time:

It is true that he is associated with the aristocratic environment due to the social class to which he and his friends belong. He is being called a snob. Indeed, he is surrounded by many young snobbish gentlemen, but he is aware of the situation and is concerned at all times and on all occasions to demonstrate that this old conception of class division should be replaced by a common ideal capable of reaching the hearts of all.[217]

He came to the conclusion that José Antonio was a "young man endowed with all the qualities required to lead a movement in these times of political and social struggle." Likewise, the movement he led represented something positive, "bearing a sincere and passionate attitude full of courage," whose growth was hindered by the "paradoxical character of the Spanish people."[218]

During the interview, José Antonio provided him with statistics and information about the Spanish Fascist movement, estimating the number of registered members at fifty thousand across thirty-two provinces. José Antonio also took advantage of the visit of the official Italian representative of the CAUR to introduce him to Ramiro Ledesma Ramos, who was holding an office under the title of National Triumvir, in that same building, which was the editorial office of his magazine *JONS*; so, when he introduced him to his comrade in the triumvirate, besides extolling his personality as a pioneer of the cause, he did so in his role as the director of the aforementioned publication.

It became clear after that meeting that Primo de Rivera was the most exemplary representative of Spanish Fascism. From the moment of his investiture as a founding member of the CAUR in Madrid, José Antonio began to receive a wealth of information and documentation, as well as a large amount of Fascist propaganda material sent from the Roman headquarters of the Committees, the monthly magazine, the weekly newsletter—where constant allusions were made to his person and to the development of the Falangist movement—and the offprints of the Duce's speeches, edited and published by the Committees.

Dr. Cabalzar, upon his return, wrote an article entitled "Fascismo di Spagna" ["Fascism of Spain"], which was published in the magazine *Roma Universa* (1934), reporting his impressions of the recent visit and his warm and cordial meeting with José Antonio. In it we read:

---

[217] June 6th, 1934, quoted by Erik Norling in the article "Falange y C.A.U.R.: Un intento de penetración ideológica del fascismo en España (1933–1936)." From the magazine *Aportes*, no. 39 (1999), 25.

[218] Ibid.

The members of the Falange Española, who are constantly restricted from carrying weapons and uniforms by the constant state of emergency in force throughout the Republic, are distinguished by a blue armband on which the red emblem of the Fascists of Spain is displayed: a fasces with five arrows bound together by the yoke.

F.E.—Falange Española. The initials match those of the word *fe* [faith] and are not less fortunate than the choice of the emblem . . . . In under one year of life, Fascismo Español already has its glorious fallen and a few hundred wounded. An important result has been obtained recently with the merging of the two movements that fought for the same revolutionary Fascist ideals: Falange Española, founded by José Antonio Primo de Rivera, son of the dictator, and the Juntas de Ofensiva Nacional Sindicalista, created by Ramiro Ledesma Ramos. Essentially, they were two very similar movements—at a certain moment, the two leaders met and demonstrated the wisdom to understand that they complemented each other perfectly. Today only one solid Spanish Fascism exists: F.E. de las JONS, led by a triumvirate formed by Primo de Rivera, Ledesma Ramos, and Ruiz de Alda.

"What we are currently most interested in," the triumvirs told me, "is propagandizing the masses. We will overcome all obstacles methodically and successfully. We want to explain to the Spanish masses, who have been misled for years by all the false shepherds, the true program of true Fascism—a complete revolution . . . . The great Spanish press, the so-called 'free press,' is completely associated with the conspiracy of silence surrounding Spanish Fascism and would rather give space and voice to shady movements of dubious Fascist orthodoxy instead of publishing the successes of authentic Fascism."

Although one could level various criticisms at the Fascism of the Falange Española de las JONS, one cannot argue that it does not trace the same path of Mussolini. These Latins, these Mediterraneans, have felt that Fascism is something unique and irreplaceable. Their proudly proclaimed Mussolinian and Roman heritage is thus considered the greatest demonstration of the nobility of Spanish Fascism. Primo de Rivera and Ruiz de Alda have recently edited the Spanish version of Benito Mussolini's *Dottrina del Fascismo* [*Doctrine of Fascism*] in order to provide their compatriots with an authentic and perfect text of the doctrine in the name of which they fight, and thus avoid any uncertainty on the subject.

The Spanish comrades are, therefore, comrades in the truest sense of the word. And they are the best and most worthy sons of their fatherland.

Spanish Fascism, which bears the sign of Rome and was born from the example of Mussolini, is entirely Spanish. This perfect dual allegiance to the doctrine of Fascism and to the Iberian peculiarities and necessities attests to a rapidly attained maturity.[219]

Another of the young Falangists who readily joined the CAUR with enthusiasm was the writer Ángel Alcázar de Velasco, first Palma de Plata of the Falange in Madrid, awarded to him by José Antonio for his heroic participation during the Asturian Revolution in October of that same year.

Because of José Antonio's outstanding impression, response, and enthusiastic and lively involvement in the CAUR project, President Coselschi himself contemplated visiting the Iberian Peninsula, specifically Madrid and Lisbon, in the fall of that same year to personally observe the Fascist atmosphere in these two capital cities. If this intention did not materialize, it was due to the recommendation of the *chargé d'affaires* of the Italian Embassy in Madrid, Geisser Celesia, who did not consider the opportunity of such a trip because of the revolutionary situation in Asturias and the separatist problems with Catalonia, for which reason the president desisted. In August, however, during a conversation with Cesare Gullino, he expressed that nothing would have pleased him more than to go on such a trip.

On September 2nd, 1934, in an official publication of the CAUR, *Le Franciste* [*The Francist*], which was edited in Paris and was also the press organ of the movement of the same name led by Bucard, an active member of the Committees in France, there was published an interview that Claude Planson had conducted with Julio Ruiz de Alda, leading member of the Falange, with the following headline: "Le Fascisme espagnol: Une interview avec Ruiz de Alda" ["Spanish Fascism: An Interview with Ruiz de Alda"].

In September 1934, the Falangist member of the Cortes Francisco Moreno, Marquis de la Eliseda, a close collaborator of José Antonio and for some time an economic supporter of the Spanish Fascist movement, traveled, commissioned by the Falange and sent at the request of José Antonio, to Italy for a visit to the birthplace of Fascism, a tour that was reported in the CAUR's weekly news bulletins. Francisco Moreno wrote in 1935 a book entitled *Fascismo, Catolicismo, Monarquía* [*Fascism, Catholicism, Monarchy*], in which one finds the following: "What I want to explore the most in Fascism is its philosophical foundations and to demonstrate, more than the Fascist doctrine, the universal principles that Fascism embodies." The Marquis de la Eliseda, in the midst of the Spanish war, published in Santander a book with an unequivocal title: *El sentido fascista del Movimiento Nacional* [*The Fascist Sense of the National Movement*], in which, when referring to the Duce, he refers to him as a "political genius." Regarding Fascism, he states:

---

[219] Ibid.

Fascism is a complex phenomenon; it is not a regime, nor a system of government; it is a movement of salvation, which seeks the truth . . . . It remains as a permanent, universal value of Fascism, for the glory of Mussolini and of Italy, to have given strength and shape to the counterrevolutionary attempts of political philosophers by dressing with a new and attractive appearance the eternal principles of Christian and Western civilization: principles of hierarchy, unity, the idea of duty, corporatism, and spirituality.[220]

Francisco Herrera, later on, would claim:

Our national movement is undoubtedly the translation of the Fascist phenomenon which, because it is being produced in Spain, will be the most positive and progressive Fascism of all—because one can be perfectly Fascist without being afraid of feeling like an importer of foreign ideas as long as one taps into Spanish essences.[221]

In September 1934, the weekly internal bulletin of the Committees declared with satisfaction in an article that, unequivocally, the Falangist leader Primo de Rivera had opted for Italian Fascism rather than the consanguineous model of German National Socialism:

"Falange Española, led by Primo de Rivera, does not disregard, making some clarifying statements about Germanic Nazism, that the origins and purposes of Spanish Fascism, even though differing by nationality from Italian Fascism, are inspired by it,"[222] and, as evidence of the pursuit of the Italian model, the statements of José Antonio to the Madrid newspaper *La Epoca* are partially reproduced:

The *jefe* of Spanish Fascism has declared not only that Hitlerism is not Fascism but that it is its counterpart. As far as Spain is concerned, he has state . . . and expressed his faith in the success of Falange Española, which is faithfully inspired by the example and the ideas of Italian Fascism.[223]

This distinction between Italian Fascism and German National Socialism had

---

[220] F.G. Cabalzar, "Fascismo di Spagna," in *Roma Universa*, 1934.

[221] Marqués de la Eliseda, *El sentido fascista del Movimiento Nacional* (Santander, 1939), 24 and 27.

[222] Ibid., 30–31.

[223] "Fascismo e razzismo in un giudizio spagniuolo," in *C.A.U.R.—Notiziario Settimanale*, no. 10 (September 16th, 1934), 3.

already been pointed out by José Antonio in some of his public speeches. In an interview published in the Barcelonian newspaper *La Rambla* and later included in the Madrid newspaper *Luz* on August 14th, 1934, he stated: "Hitlerism is the final consequence of democracy, a turbulent expression of German romanticism; whereas Mussolini represents classicism, with its hierarchies, its consequences, and, above all, reason."

In the speech he delivered in Santander, in the Athenaeum of the city, on August 14th, he describes Italian Fascism as "the safeguard of Western principles," while "the German movement is of a romantic type."

After the first visit of the CAUR inspector, news about Spain and the Falange began to appear in the organization's internal weekly bulletin and even in the monthly magazine *Roma Universa*, which, it must be said, was impeccably and luxuriously edited.

In the September–October 1934 issue of *Roma Universa*, there appeared an article by Giménez Caballero on José Antonio, with the following title: "Fascismo Español: José Antonio Primo de Rivera." It was not an original article written specifically for the publication of the CAUR, but the Italian translation of the additional chapter to the second edition of his book *La Nueva Catolicidad*, in which Gecé states that José Antonio "could very well be in a Fascist future in Spain something like Augustus, the young Octavian, was in Rome."

In the autumn issues of the *Bulletin* of the CAUR, Falange Española and its leader José Antonio are always presented, whenever their names are mentioned, as the official Spanish representative of Fascist concerns, not sparing any words in emphasizing the Fascist character of their movement. In the issue dated October 16th, 1934, a literal quotation from José Antonio is reproduced as follows:

Falange Española, led by Primo de Rivera, does not disregard, following German Nazism, the task of clarifying that its origins and its aims are different, since the Spanish Fascist movement's source of inspiration is in Italian Fascism . . . . The head of Spanish Fascism . . . expressed his faith in the success of Falange Española, which is faithfully inspired by the example and the ideas of Italian Fascism.

The CAUR *Bulletin* reported in November on the formation of the Central Obrera Nacional Sindicalista (C.O.N.S.) [National Syndicalist Workers' Union] by Falangist leaders, and in the issue corresponding to November 25th, some paragraphs of a speech delivered by José Antonio "before a great mass of Spanish Fascists" are quoted. In December, once again, among the news contained in the *Bulletin*, Falange Española was mentioned as the only party capable of bringing Spain out of the chaotic state in which the nation was languishing.

The weekly *Bulletin* published on November 18th the following proclamation of the Spanish Falange sent by José Antonio:

Spanish people: enough with the Cortes and obscure politics, enough with the left and right, enough with capitalist selfishness and proletarian indiscipline! It is time for Spain, united, strong, and resolute, to take the helm of its great fate. This is what F.E. aspires to and works to inspire everyone to accomplish. Students, farmers, workers, and young people in body and spirit, reject the appeals launched on one side by hatred and on the other by selfishness and rally around our flag, which is the liberating flag of the National Syndicalist revolution.

Regarding the weekly *F.E.*, one could read in another article entitled "La Falange Española de las J.O.N.S" published in that same issue of *Roma Universa*: "It actively disseminates the principles and activities of young Spanish Fascism."

In the month of December, on the 16th and 17th, the first International Congress of the CAUR was held at the Carlton Hotel in the Swiss city of Montreux, with the attendance of numerous representatives of the European Fascist movements associated with the Committees. The initiative for the convocation and celebration of this meeting came from the reunion that took place in April in the Helvetic city of Evian, where it was agreed to convoke a "congress of chiefs, leaders, and representatives of movements of Fascist, corporatist, and nationalist character" that would be in charge of the organization of the several Committees, which would cover the travel and accommodation expenses of the attending participants, representatives of the most active European Fascist parties.

The Montreux meeting debates resulted in the formation of two new entities within the CAUR structure: The Entente of Universal Fascism or the Montreux Fascist International, and the Coordination Commission for the Entente of Universal Fascism, which would serve as the organizational hub of the Montreux Front, linked to the proposed "Fascist International." It would operate as a permanent secretariat, based in Rome, of the annual General Assembly of Fascist and European Corporative Movements.

The Entente that resulted from the Congress, although it did not organically depend on the respective National Committees directly, assumed the important mission of spreading the ideals of Romanity around the world.

Due to the dangerous and repressive political situation in Spain, no representative of Spanish Fascism could attend the Montreux meeting. The two highest representatives of the CAUR in Spain were expected to participate. Giménez Caballero's name even appeared in the papers of the material distributed at the Congress, as he had confirmed his presence, although this error was corrected in the weekly *Bulletin*, published after the meeting, where it is stated: "Mr. Ernesto Giménez Caballero, delegate of Falange Española, headed by José Antonio Primo de Rivera, unable to intervene, has sent his support and approval to the work of the Congress."[224]

The Italian organizers and their European comrades considered the absence of the two Spanish representatives as a merely accidental and circumstantial matter, so that "at the beginning of the session, President Coselschi apologized on behalf of Primo de Rivera, leader of the Spanish Falange, who, at the time of his departure, had been restrained due to force majeure."[225]

The antifascist press in Spain lashed out at the Falange on the occasion of the Montreux Congress, accusing them of blatant emulation of Italian Fascism. This note was published in several newspapers on December 19th:

> The news that José Antonio Primo de Rivera, head of Falange Española de las JONS, was preparing to attend a certain international Fascist congress, which is being held in Montreux, is totally false. The head of the Falange was asked to attend, but he firmly refused the invitation because he understood that the genuine national character of the movement he leads rejects even the pretense of international leadership.
>
> On the other hand, Falange Española de las JONS is not a Fascist movement, though it shares some universal values with Fascism. However, it is developing its own unique characteristics and will find its most fruitful opportunities along that path.

The apparent separation of the Falange from the project of the CAUR was more an *official* position than an actual one, which was comprehended by all those present and also by the Italian leaders, who were very well aware of the difficult Spanish situation and the repression to which the Falange was subjected because of its avowed Fascism.

Ramiro Ledesma recognized that the reasons for not intervening in the Montreux Congress were due "solely to reasons of internal tactics." The same explanation was provided by José Antonio when attending, in September 1935, the reunion of the commission of the CAUR The decision not to attend the Montreux Congress, in which Giménez Caballero was supposed to participate in representation of the Spanish Falange, was intentional. José Antonio and Ramiro, after examining the Spanish political scenario, decided not to attend for purely strategic reasons, never for ideological disagreements, as Ramiro Ledesma has left in a written testimony.

Professors Saz Campos and the German Manfred Böcker believe, according to the text of the lecture he gave at the German Conference of Romance Philology held in Jena in 1997, that "the fact that Primo de Rivera did not attend the

---

[224] *C.A.U.R.—Notiziario Settimanale*, no. 24 (December 23rd, 1934).

[225] La Salle's report on the Montreux Congress, in *Le Franciste*, January 1935.

Montreux Congress was not the result of an ideological evolution but a process of tactical maturity."

On November 17th, 1934, the police closed, for the umpteenth time in Madrid, the premises of Falange Española and arrested a Falangist. The headquarters of the Falange in Seville, one of the most active territorial sections, were still closed in November. On December 15th, the head office of the Falange in Bilbao was searched. The fallen of the Falange, in 1934, had reached the bloody death toll of twelve martyrs for the cause. The survival of the movement in that state of suffocation was nothing short of miraculous.

In the early days, the members of the JONS, the Falangists, and all the other "Fascists" in Spain were all jointly called "Fascists." But the contradiction of a "national" movement using a foreign label was so evident that the definition of "Fascist" was discarded and the Spanish terms *Jonsista*, *nacionalsindicalista*, or *Falangista* were adopted within the country, with the name "Fascists" being reserved for the Italians and "Nazis" for the Germans. The desire of the Spanish Fascists to nationalize the word that distinguished them was felt previously by the German Fascists, who called themselves "Nazis." However, all the Falangists were convinced that they were Fascists. Ledesma Ramos did not share this peculiar interpretation of the word "Fascist," however.

The anniversary of the March on Rome in 1934 did not go without notice among the Spanish founding members of the CAUR, Giménez Caballero and José Antonio Primo de Rivera. Together, they wrote and sent to Rome the following telegram addressed to the Italian head of state: "On the thirteenth anniversary of the March on Rome, the Spanish Committee of the CAUR extends its arm to the Duce of the new universal Rome."[226]

The text of the telegram was reproduced on page seven of the November 18th, 1934 edition of the CAUR *Bulletin*.

On January 3rd, 1935, when José Antonio was in Paris, he sent an intimate and private letter to Carmen Werner. In it, after describing to her the Parisian environments he explored during his visit, he confessed to her that the city on the Seine produced melancholy in him, reproaching himself with the following words: "And the bad thing is that a Fascist should not feel melancholy because of that."[227] That is, José Antonio termed himself a Fascist even in his most reserved, intimate, and personal correspondence with a woman like Carmen, his confidant.

On January 30th, 1935, the first meeting of the Coordination Commission, born from the Montreux Congress to establish the Secretariat of International Fascism, was held in Paris. The first members of the Commission were: Frits

---

[226] *C.A.U.R. Notiziario settimanale*, 19 (November 18th, 1934), 7. It should be noted that the telegram contains an error in the chronology of the anniversary, which was actually the twelfth.

[227] Primo de Rivera y Urquijo, *Papeles postumos de José Antonio*, 109.

Clausen (Denmark), Marcel Bucard (France), George Mercouris (Greece), Arthur Fonjallaz (Switzerland), Quisling (Norway), O'Duffy (Ireland), and Thomas Damsgaard Schmidt (Denmark). The choice of Paris as the location for this first meeting of the CAUR Commission was a sign of gratitude to the fidelity of Bucard, the leader of Francism. The gathering was held under the presidency of Coselschi, and Baroni assumed the role of secretary.

On March 30th, the Commission of the CAUR reunited again at the Carlton Hotel in Amsterdam to continue its consolidation work. The Dutch city was selected in order to promote the activities of the leader, Mussert.

On the occasion of this second meeting of the CAUR Commission, held in Holland, Ramiro Ledesma Ramos sent a letter requesting to be part of the CAUR as the representative and most genuine exponent of Spanish Fascism, after the split that had taken place in the Falange, following his disagreement with Primo de Rivera. Ramiro Ledesma, founder of the JONS and national triumvir of the Falange until the National Council of October 1934, when it was decided to dissolve the triumviral system and adopt the single command that fell to José Antonio, did not want, under any circumstances, to be excluded from the Entente of Universal Fascism. At the meeting of the Coordinating Commission of Amsterdam, during the preparatory session of March 29th, the President of the CAUR, Coselschi, submitted the approval of the leader of the JONS to the consideration of the attendees, as reported in the records of the assembly:

> Before we begin our debate on the president's communications, I have the pleasure of announcing to you that two movements have registered to join the Montreux Front and the Spanish JONS movement, which is beginning to develop in Spain and that is sending its approval to the deliberations voted in Montreux. The leader of the latter—of the JONS—states: "I am aware of the activities of the CAUR as I have been briefed on the resolutions taken in Montreux by the representatives of Fascist organizations. I am glad to inform you that I am submitting the approval of the JONS and also my personal approval to the Front of Montreux, and that I am at your disposal to defend and disseminate the common ideal. I assure you of the full sympathy of the JONS movement, which, for reasons of internal politics alone, could not be present at Montreux.[228]

The assembly decided to postpone the integration of Ledesma Ramos since the only valid interlocutor of the CAUR in Spain was still José Antonio and his Falange, which enjoyed the confidence and support of European Fascism for its political work and was backed by General Coselschi, the President of the CAUR. At the

---

[228] *Minutes of the Amsterdam Meetings* (March 29th, 1935), reproduced by Gisella Longo.

closing of the Amsterdam conference, it was even suggested that, in order to support the Fascist leadership of José Antonio in Spain, the next sitting of the Commission could take place in the month of August in Spain, but this initiative was later abandoned due to the civil war and the repression of the government.

After the first meeting of the new Commission, held in Paris on January 30th, 1935, the inspector of the CAUR, Dr. Guido Ferruccio Cabalzar, traveled again to Madrid on February 19th, 1935. His stay in Madrid lasted ten days, after which he returned to Rome on March 1st, according to the report of the Italian diplomat Celesia, sent to the undersecretary of state for press and propaganda, Count Ciano, on March 2nd, 1935. The previous Italian ambassador to Spain, Guariglia, was replaced by Orazio Pedrazzi in the autumn of 1934, and Celesia was tasked on this occasion with assisting the CAUR Inspector.

The first person to meet the Inspector of the CAUR during his visit was José Antonio, who confirmed and approved the project of the Committees, as mentioned in the notebook of Celesia, who led the interview with José Antonio in the place of honor.[229] The Inspector of the CAUR also came into contact, on this occasion, with Lerroux's radical minister, Mr. Salazar Alonso; with the head of Renovación Española, Mr. Antonio Goicoechea; with the director of the newspaper *Informaciones*—very close to Fascism in its editorial position—Juan Pujol; with Ernesto Giménez Caballero, and with Dr. Gregorio Marañón. Inspector Cabalzar was advised by the Madrid Committee that the next president of the Madrid Committee should be a highly esteemed and distinguished intellectual, of great importance and prestige, such as Don Jacinto Benavente, winner of the Nobel Prize for Literature, who gladly took on the role. Giménez Caballero would become, from then on, the new secretary general of the Madrid Committee, serving in more of an administrative than a representative position.

The inspector of the CAUR, Dr. Cabalzar, took advantage of his trip to extend a personal invitation, on behalf of the Fascist organization, to José Antonio to make an official visit to Fascist Italy, which was arranged for the first week of May 1935, with evident satisfaction on the part of José Antonio, who accepted and thanked him immediately and heartily for the courtesy.

José Antonio sailed for Italy, as agreed with Cabalzar, from the port of Barcelona on May 4th, 1935, reaching Italy from the port of Genoa, where he was received by Eugenio Coselschi, the President of the CAUR himself, who expressed with this act the sympathy of the Fascist hierarchs for the head of Spanish Fascism, with whom he held "top secret meetings," the topics of which were not disclosed until the famous meeting of Gredos on July 16th, 1935, in which José Antonio reported to the Command Board of the Spanish Falange what had been discussed. Count Galeazzo Ciano was also promptly informed of the plan for the Falangist

---

[229] [Translator: I believe the author refers to José Antonio's office.]

leader's official visit as a guest of the Regime, both by José Antonio and by Eugenio Coselschi, during his meeting with the Undersecretary of State for Press and Propaganda on April 16th, two weeks before the national leader of the Falange would set foot on Italian soil. The visit was of the highest importance and would conclude with a meeting with the Duce, who had granted his consent.

During José Antonio's official trip to Fascist Italy as a guest of the CAUR, he had the opportunity to engage in an in-depth meeting with Count Ciano, whom he informed of his plans to solve the critical Spanish political situation by means of an act of force, rebellion, and armed insurrection, which would be undertaken by the militias of the Falange. He would later present this project in the middle of the following month at the conspiratorial summit of the Parador Nacional de Gredos, held on July 15th and 16th, when he summoned the Command Board of the Falange in complete secrecy and confidentiality to inform them of the plan of an armed uprising. Ciano, Mussolini's son-in-law, assured him that beginning the following month, he would make fifty thousand lire available to him at the Italian Embassy in Paris to cover certain expenses.

Through meetings and interviews arranged by Coselschi, José Antonio made contact with individuals at the highest levels of the Italian regime. Even the press covered his visit, with some interviews, such as the one published in the newspaper *Il Lavoro Fascista* [*The Fascist Work*] in its May 25th issue, when he had already returned to Spain. José Antonio reiterates in the interview with the aforementioned newspaper that his mission is fully aligned with that of the CAUR and that he can see himself reflected in the mirror of Italian Fascism:

> We look to Italian Fascism as the most outstanding historical fact of our times, from which we intend to draw principles and political approaches that will suit our country, which is otherwise very similar to Italy. Fascism has laid the universal foundation for all political movements of our time. The core idea of Fascism, which is the unity of the people under a totalitarian state, is identical to that of Falange Española. Our allegiance to the Committees for the Universality of Rome is the proof of our beliefs.[230]

Throughout the official visit, he was accompanied by his comrades—and close friends—Eugenio Montes and Rafael Sánchez Mazas, with whom he took pleasure in an unforgettable stroll through the Eternal City. On May 10th, he returned to Madrid after a series of memorable days filled with hospitality, affection, artistic experiences, and camaraderie.

On August 8th, 1935, the first Falange headquarters outside of the country were established. Of course, the opening took place in Milan, the cradle of the combat fasces, the birthplace of the new doctrine. José Antonio appointed Arturo

---

[230] José Antonio's statements on his trip to Italy that later appeared in the newspaper *Il Lavoro fascista*, May 25th, 1935, quoted by Ismael Saz Campos, *Mussiolini contra*, 138.

Cuartero as head of the Falange in Italy. Cuartero belonged to the Italian Fasces since 1919, the year in which he enlisted in the Oberdan squadron. The Italian Fasces, the party in which Cuartero was active, granted approval for his double membership in the Italian branch. Agustín de Foxá dates the effective foundation of the headquarters of the Spanish Falange in Milan to December 14th, 1935, and even states that "Milan has the honor of being, as a city, the first home of the Servicio Exterior [Foreign Service]."

Arturo Cuartero was assisted by Juan Ordinas at the head of the local secretariat in Rome, since the Milan headquarters became the headquarters for Italy. Arturo Cuartero, the Falange Chief for Italy, in a letter to the Roman Falangist Secretary Juan Ordinas, dated April 1st, 1937, informs him:

> I have put the date of December 14th, 1935, which was the date of the inauguration of the JONS in Milan, since our Chief José Antonio Primo de Rivera signed the membership cards at that time and later he was imprisoned, etc. From that date onwards, he did not sign any more membership cards.[231]

On January 16th, 1936, the newspaper *Arriba*, in the section on the news about the movement, published the following article:

> Last December, the constitution of the aforementioned JONS took place in Milan at the hands of a group of Spaniards living in Italy.
>
> After a few remarks by the leader, Arturo Cuartero, the Command Board was elected, consisting of Enrique Moreno, secretary and administrative delegate; Juan de Ponte, head of Propaganda and Organization; Carmelo Abadías, head of the Front Line; and María Molano, head of the women's section.
>
> Great enthusiasm reigned, and the event ended with shouts.

Francisco Blanco writes in *El Rastro de la Historia*: "Since 1935, the Italian framework has been gradually built. Other groups had joined the initial Milanese group, broadening the geographical and human sphere of the Italian Falange. Thus the Roman Falange was founded in December 1936 and, in October 1937, that of Genoa." Groups of Italian sympathizers were also formed, which merged with the Falangists, among whom was the secretary of the CAUR Dr. Emanuele Gnecco, who joined the ranks of the group of sympathizers to the Falange in Italy.

Cuartero enlisted in the National Army at the outbreak of the Spanish War, with Bibiano de Guzmán temporarily taking over his leadership role. When, on

---

[231] Francisco Blanco, "El servicio Exterior de la Falange Española de las J.O.N.S. Qué se hizo de la Organización exterior de la primitiva Falange," in *Rastro de la Historia*, 2.

March 9th, 1940, the diplomat and poet Agustín de Foxá, a close friend of José Antonio since the early days of Spanish Fascism, took over the Italian leadership, he declared: "Faithful of Latin culture, we therefore consider the Duce's collaborators distant *camisas viejas* [old shirts] belonging to the great community of the open hand."

In 1941, Ángel María Pascual, a Falangist writer, assumed the position of head of the Italian Falange and replaced the Falangist headquarters in Milan and Turin with new and larger spaces. In 1943, Ángel María was replaced by the general secretary of the Spanish Falange, Raimundo Fernández Cuesta, upon taking over his former position as Spanish ambassador in Italy. Among the most noteworthy militants of the Falange in Italy was Vicente de Cadenas Vicent.

The third of the meetings of the Coordination Commission for the Entente of Universal Fascism of the CAUR was once again arranged and held in the Swiss city of Montreux, this time at the Palace Hotel, on September 11th and 12th, 1935. José Antonio, who received the invitation from Rome in August, attended —with discretion—this meeting. He went there not to be noticed as a prominent element in the meeting, which could pose an unnecessary personal and political risk to him given the dire situation in Spain, but to maintain close and reserved contacts with his European Fascist comrades from all nations, as well as the heads of the CAUR who attended the event. His presence at the hotel where the meeting took place was militant rather than ceremonial. There, he had the opportunity to learn firsthand about the Fascist International's plans for the future and discuss them in personal meetings with Coselschi and the other delegates present. Given the critical state of Spanish politics, it was decided not to publicize his presence in the CAUR's internal *Bulletin*, which published the topics discussed by José Antonio with the other leaders. The weekly newsletter of the CAUR, which appeared the week that followed this meeting, limited itself to the following statement:

> The Honorable Primo de Rivera, Head of the Spanish Falange and Member of Parliament, finding himself in Geneva, has declared that the Spanish Falange, in spite of being in good friendly relations with the CAUR, has not attended the work of the Commission to prevent its enemies from spreading malicious interpretations.

Despite his attendance behind the scenes at the CAUR Commission, José Antonio had no qualms about appearing among those summoned or traveling to Montreux to attend the Commission's work, albeit with the precautions mentioned above.

During the work sessions, the leader of the Falange made a brief public intervention lasting slightly more than fifteen minutes to greet those present. As per the agreement with CAUR President Coselschi, he entered the meeting room where the sessions were held at approximately ten in the morning on September

11th. Coselschi unexpectedly interrupted the session and, in a dramatic fashion, gave José Antonio the floor with these exact words, which are documented in the minutes:

> Allow me to interrupt this presentation to greet the representative of the Falange Española, Primo de Rivera, who fights bravely against communism in his fatherland.
>
> Falange Española carries a halo of martyrdom and glory because it fights almost every day on the streets of Spain. The youth of the country have shed their blood to defend the ideal that unites us all.
>
> I am sure to express the sentiments of all of you by saluting, in the person of Primo de Rivera, the young Spain, and I ask you to keep a minute of silence in memory of the many fallen of the Spanish Falange and also to all the fallen of all the movements that are represented here today.[232]

José Antonio stood upright, observing a respectful and profound silence with the rest of his European Fascist comrades, their throats knotted in memory of the blood shed for the common struggle. After the tribute of honor to the fallen Falangists, President Coselschi continued the presentation of the head of the Falange:

> Primo de Rivera has been long observing our organization with sympathy, and if he is not an official member of it, it is only for internal political reasons, which he himself will explain to you. By the time we have formed the United Front, which will be the conclusion of our proceedings, Primo de Rivera will have, I believe, prepared the public opinion of his country to let it know that he felt the necessity of not being absent from a meeting such as this.
>
> I think that Spain's feelings on this matter—and if I am mistaken, let Primo de Rivera be the one to tell me—arise from its aversion to getting entangled in international affairs.
>
> The Spaniard possesses an individualism that pushes him to reject any international organization; but you will see from the conclusions of the Comintern Congress that when it comes to building a united front, even the extreme right wing socialist (radical socialist) parties are seen to reach out to unleash the world revolution that would be the end of European civilization. I therefore believe that to unite is not to engage in internationalism, but to respond with the union of pure and healthy forces to the union of the forces that want to unleash the bloodthirsty revolution.[233]

---

[232] Minutes of the meetings of the Commission for the Entente of Universal Fascism in Montreux, September 11th, 1935.

[233] Antonio Gibello, *José Antonio ese desconocido*, 193–194.

After the words of introduction and welcome by the President of the CAUR, José Antonio took the opportunity to address his European comrades in French with the following speech:

I sincerely appreciate your warm welcome, not to me, but to the Spanish Falange, which fights every day in my country's blood-stained streets. I feel truly moved by your reception and I sincerely extend to you the greetings of the Falange Española and myself. For the time being, I am forced to refrain from engaging in the activities of your Commission. The chairman has already informed you of the reasons behind this. However, Spain is not yet prepared to join, through my mediation, a movement which is not of international, but supranational, universal character. And this is not only due to the Spanish people's overly individualistic nature, but also because the internationals have caused so much suffering in Spain. We are under the control of at least three internationals: a Masonic one, a socialist one, a capitalist one, and perhaps some other powers of an extra-national character that interfere in Spanish affairs. If we appeared before Spanish opinion as part of another movement without a slow, thorough, and laborious preparation, the Spanish public conscience, and even the democratic conscience, would revolt. For this reason, in light of these supranational works, souls must be appropriately prepared.

Often, leaders find themselves forced to rein in their own parties. If I were to compromise my position as leader, I would probably do so against the will of the majority of my party. Now, you all are aware that Falange Española, whether for its glory or its misfortune, has already had thirty-four dead (we fight every day; Barone was telling me a moment ago that the French newspapers reported an encounter in which we were fortunate to prevail, but in which there were dead and wounded), and this creates stronger ties for me than mere duty or vanity and binds me to my position as leader . . . . I do not consider myself authorized to contradict the blood of our martyrs, because I am bound to it. Nevertheless, I believe that we must acknowledge, in the face of communist and internationalist threats, the right and duty of civilized peoples to civilize those who have fallen behind.

I believe that it is the duty of all of us to prepare the public opinion in our various countries before embarking on any collective action. I promise you all that I will do everything in my power to reawaken a national conscience.

I must now leave this meeting for the reasons I have stated and also because I have several duties to attend to. However, I hope to be able to attend your meetings in the near future.[234]

---

[234] Ibid., 194.

The attendance of José Antonio in Montreux was communicated in the report sent to the Ministry of Foreign Affairs on November 14th by the Consul General of Spain in Switzerland, Joan Teixidor, also informing about the Reunion of the Central Committee of Universal Fascism and confirming that the head of the Falange had given his agreement and support to the work of the Commission: "Mr. Primo de Rivera has been, according to the information I have received, in Montreux for some days, but he has abstained from taking an active part in the meeting."[235]

The purpose of José Antonio's appearance at the Montreux meeting of the CAUR Commission was, above all, to testify, to expressly state that he was standing alongside his European comrades. And, secondly, it was to maintain discreet and fruitful exchanges with those attending the meeting outside the spotlight of the formal sessions.

On the same day that José Antonio spoke in Montreux—September 11th, 1935—the General Secretariat of Falange Española, representing the unanimous feeling of F.E. de las JONS and in the absence of its national leader, issued a note to the press condemning the attack of September 8th in Renedo, during which a bomb was thrown at a Republican Left meeting, with the authorities fixing the responsibility for the attack on Falangists José Albo Fernández and Jesús Roca Salvador, nineteen and seventeen years old, respectively, who were wounded. Following the incident, that same day, the minister of the interior ordered the closing of the Falange branches in Santander. The note issued by the Falange—in the absence of the national leader—assured that "the leadership of the Falange in the province of Santander is completely extraneous to the aforementioned event, in which neither directly nor indirectly they have played a part."[236] On September 13th, all the branches of Falange Española in the capital of Spain were closed down. Therefore, José Antonio had to return hastily.

On September 19th, upon his return from his trip to Montreux, José Antonio wrote a very harsh article against the anti-Italian policy of British and Spanish diplomacy, which was never published due to the government-imposed suspension of the newspaper *Arriba*. On October 2nd, José Antonio would deliver an unrestrained speech in the Cortes demanding Spanish neutrality in the Abyssinian conflict, which was the position most likely to benefit Italian interests.

The Madrid Committee of the CAUR continued to be operative, and, in the spring of 1936, on April 27th, its secretary Ernesto Giménez Caballero, who was still free, sent a telegram testifying his loyalty to the Duce and promising to "fight fervently from the midst of this tragic Spain against the enemies of Fascist civilization."

---

[235] Quoted in Ismael Saz Campos, *Mussolini contra*, 137 n.

[236] Francisco de Asís de la Vega Gonzalo, *Aniquilar la Falange (cronología persecutoria del Nacionalsindicalismo)* (Ovideo: Tarfe Artes Gráficas, 1999), 131.

12.

Fascist Programs

The Falange's *Norma Programática*, the party's official political program, is briefly and concisely summarized in the *Twenty-Seven Points* that represent the core of its ideology and goals. It was drafted after the First National Council, held in Madrid on October 6th and 7th. It was necessary to express, clearly and unequivocally, the doctrinal principles, the essential foundations of the Falangist ideology.

It was José Antonio who took responsibility for the last revision and approval of the final text, which was perfected in November 1934. Until then, the only outlet for schematic thought and ideological structuring had been the initial points published in the issues of *F.E.*, by the pen of José Antonio, that would later be published in a small pamphlet widely distributed among the Falangist groups, branches, and squads all over Spain. It was a compendium containing essentially the main points discussed by Primo de Rivera at the rally held at the Comedia, presented in clear prose and with profound depth of meaning.

The *Twenty-Seven Points* constituted the movement's official program. They consist of six thematic blocks or sections: a) Nation. Unity. Empire; b) State. Individual. Freedom; c) Economy. Work. Class Struggle; d) Land; e) National Education. Religion; and f) National Revolution.

Each of these major sections is further elaborated in firm, rigorous, and expressive articles. The program of the Falange is, simultaneously, a statement of its principles and an exhaustive list of solutions to the problems and threats that loom over Spain.

The style of solemn declaration of the *Norma Programática* recalls by association of ideas the twenty-five points of the National Socialist German Workers' Party (NSDAP) program, formulated in Munich on February 24th, 1920, and that of the National Fascist Party (PNF), conceived at the Congress of Rome held between November 7th and 9th, 1921. The program of the Falange shares some similarities in its identity with both of these programs, which largely concur.

They are the essential, indisputable, almost dogmatic points on which the action and mission of the movement was based and motivated; they represent the highest order, the fundamental norm, the point of reference.

In his book *La Spagna Risorge*, the Italian writer Nello Enriquez commented on the Falangist doctrinal synthesis as follows:

> It contains a collection of "initial points" or doctrinal principles based on Mussolinian and Hitlerian principles, molded, clearly, to Spanish life. In Italy, Spanish Fascists are highly appreciated; their movement and the human quality of their militants are regarded very positively. They also long for the redemption of the Fatherland, the reestablishment of the eternal and fundamental values of the Spanish nation. We Italians have praised the worth of this movement, and we have done so because it was born from our own roots.[237]

The influence of Fascist doctrine is evident. We are going to compare the content of the *Twenty-Seven Points* of the Falangist doctrine with those of their analogous Fascist and National Socialist movements that influenced José Antonio. For this purpose, we will refer to Roger Bourderon's essay *Le fascisme, idéologie et pratiques* [*Fascism, Ideology and Practice*],[238] which studies and analyzes monographically the similar position and meaning of these three Fascist movements that shared principles while, obviously, preserving national specificities.

The starting point, which is where the programs fully coincide, is the "revalorization of the nation and the state." The concept of nation as an eternal reality occupies the first place in the respective programs. In the case of the National Fascist Party, it is the "supreme synthesis" of the material and spiritual values of the race, and in that of the Falange, it is the "supreme reality" to which any individual or societal interest must inevitably bow. In the program of the NSDAP, the nation embodies the national eternity, grounded in the community of blood, representing the value of permanence. The meaning of nation is a community of people interested by identical endogenous and exogenous concerns.

Within their individual goals, all three programs present an imperial vocation. According to the Italian concept, Italy serves as the "bastion of Latin civilization in

---

[237] Enriquez, *La Spagna risorge*, 91.

[238] Roger Bourderon, *Le Fascisme, idéologie et pratiques (essai d'analyse comparée)* (Paris: Editions Sociales, 1979).

the Mediterranean that supports and sustains its expansion." Germany aspires, as is stated in the program of the National Socialist Party, to the reunification of the German community under the aegis of the Third Reich, of the Greater Germany. In the program of the Falangist party, the "will to empire" is voiced, by which it must recover its lost glory and wealth through the sea routes until it reaches the leadership of the Hispanic community of nations: "With respect to the countries of Latin America, we favor the unification of culture, economic interests, and power. Spain proclaims its inherent role as the spiritual axis of the Hispanic world as a title of pre-eminence in universal endeavors."[239]

Professor Santiago Montero Díaz, founder of the JONS, once concluded one of his lectures by stating:

> In 1933, in 1935, National Syndicalism called for the universal destinies of Spain. I would like to cite only illustrious voices. José Antonio Primo de Rivera used to say that in the empire, populations accomplish themselves. Spain, power of an empire, specified Ramiro Ledesma. At that time, National Syndicalism was yearning for power in order to transmute—by a neat dialectic—national politics into imperial politics.[240]

The state is yet another connection point between the three programs. The state serves as a tool to help the country realize its fundamental potential. The state is considered by the Italian Fascists the "juridical embodiment" of the nation; the only state they envision is the "national" one that overcomes private interests. The NSDAP identifies the state with the racial state, serving as the zealous guardian of the national interest. According to the definition of the Falange, the "state will be a totalitarian instrument at the service of national wholeness." In either case, the state will require strength and political centralism. It is noteworthy that all three movements use the term "totalitarian" to refer to their respective states. The state must undertake the realization of the national purpose. The state is not an end, but rather a tool. The state must be, above all, a spiritual and ethical force. In Mussolini's words, the "will of the people," "the immanent conscience of the nation"; in José Antonio's words, "the servant of the conscience of unity" with "moral duties"; in Hitler's words, the state must be founded on "moral virtues," embodied in the people as an expression of the "unanimous will" or of the "philosophical idea."[241] Fascism is not concerned with the structure of the state.

---

[239] [Translator: translation from Justin Crumbaugh, *Spanish Fascist Writing* (University of Toronto Press, Toronto, 2021).]

[240] Santiago Montero Díaz:,"Idea del Imperio," lecture delivered at the conference organized by the Headquarters of the Escuela de Formación y Capacitación de Vieja Guardia de Madrid in July 1943, 31.

[241] Bourderon, *Le Fascisme, idéologie et pratiques*.

Regarding the army, which is another key element of the three programs, the National Fascist Party states that the army's mission will be to guard and secure the new borders, clearly advocating for the militarization of the country. The National Socialist Party's aspiration was instead to build a true national army that would take over from the mercenary army imposed after the Treaty of Versailles. The Falange's armed forces on the ground, at sea, and in the air must be as capable and numerous as necessary to guarantee Spain's complete independence and the world order that befits it. We will restore to the army of the ground, sea, and air all the public dignity that it deserves, and, in its image, we will ensure that a military sense of life informs Spanish existence.

The Fascist movements are organized hierarchically in vertical structures, developing their own militia formations: the Squadre d'Azione [Action Squads] in the National Fascist Party; the SA and SS in the NSDAP; squads, phalanxes, and centuria which represent the front and second line in the Falange Española. José Antonio, in a letter addressed to his cousin Sancho Dávila on August 15th, 1935, praised with fond satisfaction "the perfect style of this militia, of which I consider myself increasingly proud and more and more overwhelmed to command."

The three Fascist programs that we are comparing agree on the issue of the regeneration of political life, limiting parliamentary prerogatives in the case of the National Fascist Party, and condemning parliamentary corruptness in the case of the NSDAP. In this regard, the Falange's rule is the most prompt in stating: "The system of political parties will be implacably abolished along with all its consequences: inorganic suffrage, representation by fighting groups, and the same old parliaments." The three Fascist movements believe that the electoral system is inadequate because truth lies in its own raison d'être rather than in the pronouncements of statistics. Democracy is the most corrupt of all systems, because of the constant infighting among the parties that devour each other and compete for votes at the polls.

The three doctrinal frameworks are very sensitive to social and economic issues, expressing their positions on:

> Private property: Both the National Fascist Party and Falange Española recognize it openly, as long as it fulfills the triple individual, familiar, and social purpose, opposing any exploitation that may result from a lack of fulfilling this role. The NSDAP, through the economist G. Feder, the ideological mind behind the text, acknowledges its existence as a principle, albeit one that is supervised by the state. The three programs oppose monopolistic capitalism because they believe it to be abusive and overpowering, posing a serious threat to real social interests.

> Agrarian revolution: Characterized as a fair and equitable redistribution of land. This is in order to consolidate family ownership and emphasize the social role of real estate.

Corporations: All three programs share the same goal of strengthening or developing channels of professional or labor participation, irrespective of the participants' social circumstances or economic status. The corporation would serve as the intermediary between employers and employees, managers and workers, and business owners, bolstering national unity and encouraging class cooperation rather than class conflict., thus developing national production through the corporatist principle. Every individual is a productive element, whether he is a worker, employer, artist, or professional.

Class struggle: The source of social conflicts and clashes, it is rejected as a programmatic ideological principle in the three programs because any class interest is subordinated to the national interest and the common good, with all producers constituting an organic and solidaristic entity within the corporation, thereby eliminating all Cainite social tensions, fights, confrontations, and antagonisms. Within the National Socialist Party, mention is made of the joint management of corporate profits. According to the Falange program, conflict would be eliminated if Spain were conceived economically as "one gigantic workers' union of producers. We will organize Spanish society corporatively through a system of vertical unions, based on branches of production, at the service of national economic wholeness." In Italy it is the corporative regime, or within Germany the racial community.

Improvement of the living conditions of the people: This is essential for the state to ensure the existence of its people, which is a higher and inescapable commitment.

Labor as a human right and as a national duty: This is unavoidable. "All able-bodied Spaniards—as written in the Falangist program—have the duty to work. The National Syndicalist state will not grant the slightest consideration to those who do not fulfill any function and aspire to live like guests at the expense of others' efforts." The three Fascist dogmas emphasize the value of work, the dignity of work, and the nobility of work. Labor is given a material value based on its practical importance in social life, as well as an ideal value, namely, dignity. In all three cases, the moral significance of work is recognized; thus, its protection from the abuses of any unscrupulous exploiter comes first.

The rejection of the strike: The strike, by disrupting production, damages the legitimate interests of the workers.

Education: The three Fascist programs seek to transform the school into a furnace for tempering and forging souls capable of leading the nation along paths to glory, fostering the national spirit, and turning educational institutions into an outlet for social promotion open to all, regardless of their economic status, where they will find the path to social ascent through the personal merits of effort, sacrifice, and willpower.

The position of the Fascist movements in their relations with the Church is addressed similarly in the Falangist and National Socialist programs, which defend the principle of the independence of the state and the autonomy of the churches, without mutual or reciprocal interference in their respective tasks, without this being incompatible with the Falange adopting a Christian conception of the world and incorporating into its ideology the Catholic spirit in the work of national reconstruction, or with the NSDAP advocating a "positive Christianity." The program of the National Fascist Party does not mention the religious question, although Mussolini, in his public interventions, always upheld the "Catholic mission of Rome." As Santiago Montero Díaz reminds us in his lecture on Mussolini:

> Above all, Mussolini gave the Italians a national mystique, a new political morality. The Fascist conception of life was founded on a firm religious basis. Man was subordinated to higher and transcendent purposes. It was the Duce himself who brilliantly defined this religious background of his doctrine: "Fascism is a religious conception, in which man is seen in his immanent relationship with a higher law, with an objective will that transcends the particular individual and elevates him to a conscious member of a spiritual society."[242]

It must also not be forgotten that Mussolini demonstrated unrivaled respect and generosity toward the Church by signing the Lateran Treaty with the Holy See on June 7th, 1929, which resolved a very delicate issue, reinstated the freedom of the Pontiff, and opened a path to cordiality between the Church and the Italian nation.

The three Fascist movements are characterized, similarly, by the following essential themes found among their principles:[243]

- Supremacy of total and complete nationalism.
- Will to empire.
- Strength of the national state.
- Prominent role of the army.

---

[242] Santiago Montero Díaz, "Mussolini 1919–1944," lecture delivered in the auditorium of the Central University during the inauguration of the course of political orientation on March 23rd, 1944, 37.

[243] Bourderon, *Le Fascisme, idéologie et pratiques*.

- Questioning of the liberal parliamentary system.
- Desire for the renewal of political customs.
- Corporatist principle.
- Recognition of private property accompanied by criticism of the abuses it engenders.
- Preference toward small- and medium-sized companies.
- Overcoming of class struggle by means of national solidarity.
- National role of education.
- Renovation of the elite through individual effort and education and the role of the schools in this process.
- Integration of the individual into a set of naturally occurring communities of coexistence.
- Assertion of the independence of the state from the churches.

We can also synthesize, broadly speaking, the ideology defined by the common features that supplement the principles and foundations already mentioned in the respective key programmatic guidelines.

Italian Fascism, German National Socialism, and Falange Española were anti-Marxist movements, and this was a recurring argument in the speeches of José Antonio Primo de Rivera, Adolf Hitler, and Benito Mussolini: in their propaganda, in their writings, in their conferences, in their declarations, and in their rhetoric. All three declared themselves to be actively and militantly anti-Marxist. Their struggle against Marxism is relentless and knows no ideological mercy. Marxism is harmful, and its stance is perverse due to its materialistic and reductionist idea of man, which pursues class struggle and strips the individual of his national sentiment through the loss of community identity, for the sake of an internationalism that undermines the foundations of national coexistence. They consider Marxism a destructive doctrine that destabilizes and dismantles social order due to its contradictions with the natural order.

The three movements are committed to a politics of action and accomplishments rather than wishful thinking. "Our politics is the deed," affirms Mussolini, and the philosopher Giovanni Gentile adds that the "real theory is always practical, a way of life." Deeds and not words, facts and not reasoning. Less liberal verbiage.

Nationalism as a way of rediscovering one's own identity—the innards and marrow of the national community. Falangism, Fascism, and National Socialism long for the historical glories of their respective peoples, which are a point of reference for greatness and dignity. Mussolini turned his eyes to Rome, which with the plow, the sword, law, culture, and faith brought the Roman Empire to life. Hitler longed for the times of the Holy Roman Empire and of Teutonic honor. José Antonio yearned for the Spanish Golden Age, when the captain ship of Spain sailed to the New World with a sense of mission and civilization, heroically. The three fascisms strive in the search for their own authentic roots, the journey back to the wellsprings of national purity.

They are revolutionary because they want to overturn the decadent and dissolving sign of contemporary times. As for Spain, which was downtrodden and weakened by a triple division between men, lands, and classes, as well as a serious process of deterioration and decomposition of traditional values, José Antonio proposed to the Spanish people that their nationalism should be based on the *unity of destiny*, which is their historical legacy. Germany, divided and humiliated after the Treaty of Versailles, and Italy, plunged into decadence and demoralization, required the revolutionary impulse of Fascist revolution.

José Antonio saw in the individual the guardian and bearer of eternal values. Mussolini and Hitler exalted his creative activity—the overcoming of the individual through art. However, if there is a deep respect for human dignity, man finds natural channels for participation, where he shares interests and responsibilities and is integrated in natural environments of coexistence within the inherent inequality of the species, which gives rise to the principle of selection and social justice based on his merit.

The three movements firmly believe in the principles of authority and hierarchy, responsibility, and leadership. The supreme leader would be the *caudillo*, the *Duce*, the *Führer*, the guide, referring in this sense to the words of José Antonio when he says: "So that a people does not sink into torpor, so that it does not decompose, the mass must follow its leaders as if they were prophets."

The Falange's *Norma Programática* begins with the concept of Spain as "supreme reality and unity of destiny," which is opposed to any separatist uprising. Luys Santa Marina reminds us that the concept of fatherland as a universal unity of destiny "was enunciated, almost with identical words, by Valera, referring to Portugal and Spain,"[244] when he wrote in his prologue to the *Odas, epistolas y tragedias* of Menéndez Pelayo, "beyond all the political differences that separates us, there is an identical civilization, unity, and mission of destiny in both nations, which constitute a single people."[245] The powerful idea of the *fascio* is unity, the lictorial rods tightly tied in a single bundle, and thus the postulates of the Falangist political architecture emanate from the sacred and immaterial unity of the fatherland. The higher reality of Spain is hindered by the toil required for aggrandizement, for reaching the aspiration of the Empire as an indomitable will of "historical plenitude," for becoming the spiritual heart of the Hispanic community of nations. The starting triptych "nation, unity, empire" will be guaranteed by the armed militia, the national army, whose military honor shall be projected onto the Spanish existence, which is intended to be imbued with a military sense.

The second of the defining and definitive sections of the program is also tripartite in its formulation: "State. Individual. Freedom." Regarding the state and its structure, the text states the following:

Our state will be a totalitarian instrument at the service of national

---

[244] Luys Santa Marina, *Hacia José Antonio*, (Barcelona: Editorial AHR., 1958), 66 and note 53 on 229.

[245] Ibid., 57.

wholeness. All Spaniards will participate in it through their familial, municipal, and labor-union functions. The system of political parties will be implacably abolished along with all its consequences: inorganic suffrage, representation by fighting groups, and the same old parliaments.

The distinctive notes are, therefore, the conception of a "totalitarian instrument" to achieve the unity of lands and men of the fatherland, with a system of participation based on the natural units of human coexistence—family, municipality, trade union —where there is no place for partisan liberalism. The conception of the state and its very structure are archetypically Fascist. There are no ideological deviations nor dissonances among the resolute proposals of Fascist doctrine.

Three conditions are listed, which are the eternal and intangible values of man: dignity, integrity, and freedom—restricted only in the case of acts directed against the union, strength, and freedom of the homeland—which can only be protected within the framework of a strong and free nation.

Concerning "Economy. Work. Class Struggle," there is a commitment to support Spain's economy through trade unions: "We will organize Spanish society corporatively through a system of vertical unions, based on branches of production, at the service of national economic wholeness." The tone could be heightened, but not the clarity. The solution had already taken shape in theory and practice in National Socialist Germany.

Both the capitalist system and Marxism are expressly rejected. The idea bound to overcome both systems was Fascism, which, just as the Falange, was incompatible with class struggle "inasmuch as all those who cooperate in production constitute in it [the state] an organic totality." Alfonso Lazo wrote that Falange Española presented itself—precisely because it was Fascist—as revolutionary, anti-capitalist, and anti-bourgeois.[246] It should be noted that, when the color of the blue nankeen shirt was chosen to represent the Falange, it was due to the fact that it was a "proletarian" color. The Falange had continuously alluded to a "social revolution" since its founding.

Obviously and accordingly, the Falange's political program recognized private property that is geared toward social purposes and states that it is committed to protecting it "against the abuses of big financial capital, of speculators and pessimists." Everyone knew in the past, and knows today, who is behind financial capital: the soulless moneylenders without a fatherland, the accursed race; those who hide behind the invisible chains of interest, profitability, profit, and speculation without any consideration or remorse. The trend toward nationalizing banks was supported by the ambition to see them replaced by a corporation and raise finance to the level of an important public service.

---

[246] Alfonso Lazo, *La Iglesia, la Falange y el Fascismo* (Sevilla: Universidad de Sevilla, 1995), 29.

Work was recognized as both a right and a duty of everyone without exception.

The paragraph related to the land dealt with the life of the countryside in a rural Spain yearning for an authentic agrarian revolution, proposing solutions for the improvement of the sector and giving guidelines for rural organization.

National education, through disciplining instruction, aimed to achieve a "strong and united" national spirit, to feel the joy and pride of the fatherland, with all boys being required to receive the necessary pre-military instruction to form a great national and popular army.

Intelligence must not be compromised for any reason. Intellectuals would be able to pursue any degree, regardless of their economic or social status.

In terms of religion, the Falange's position explicitly acknowledged the dominant Catholic spirit in Spanish society, as well as the separation of church and state in their respective powers and functions.

The Falange, just like the other Fascist movements, sought the "new order"— that is to say, in the "new order" and for its implementation, the national revolution would be carried out without external help, with purity, and without any deviations or pacts with other political forces. We must remember that Fascism advocated for the establishment of a new order that, after saving Italy, would have had to deal with the salvation of Europe as a whole.

The twenty-seven-point overview is a concise summary of Fascism's fundamentals in their most genuine, authentic, and original form. There is not a single point that contradicts or deviates from them. Both form and substance were adapted uniformly to the Fascist revolution in progress, adopting a universal and ecumenical perspective. And the Falange added its own righteous principles to the collective heritage.

Geisser Celesia, the *chargé d'affaires* of the Italian Embassy in Madrid, sent to his government, on November 29th, 1934, a report in which he gave an account of the celebration by the Falange of its first National Council and of the *Norma Programática* approved by the party, opining that the *Twenty-Seven Points* were, in all their aspects, derived either from Italian Fascism or from German National Socialism, although, as he analyzed the document, he did not hesitate to deem the invocations to the "imperial idea" to be too abstract for the popular mentality.[247]

The ceremonies and external symbols that surrounded the Falangist mystique were a transcription of those of their European counterparts at the time: red and black flags, emblems, the curtain of the fallen, squads, magazines, marches, camaraderie, shirts, belts, command badges—arrows, yokes, and stars, councilors' cordons, mass popular rallies, open-air gatherings, arms raised high,

---

[247] Geisser Celesia, TE. 3777/1919, 29-XI-34, Historical and Diplomatic Archives of the Italian Ministry of Foreign Affairs, as quoted by Ismael Saz Campos in *Mussolini contra la II República*, 123.

fraternal salutes, slogans, ritual voices, hymns and songs, exaltation of the leadership, resounding speeches, prayers for the fallen, direct action. Julio Rodríguez Puértolas asserts that "to insist on this imitative nature of Spanish Fascism would be to insist on the obvious."[248]

Professor Rodríguez Puértolas, in his essay "Literatura fascista española" ["Spanish Fascist Literature"], discussed how the blue shirt of the Falange was previously worn by the Associazione Nazionale Italiana, which was later absorbed into the National Fascist Party, from 1910 to 1923. In Spain, although with a lighter blue color, it was the uniform of the Legionnaires of Dr. Albiñana. In Portugal, the National Syndicalists of Rolão Preto also adopted blue as the color of their distinctive shirt, the same color as the shirt of the Irish supporters of General O'Duffy. Ernesto Giménez Caballero, when commenting on the blue shirt in an article published in the Sevillian newspaper *ABC* on July 30th, 1937, did not hesitate to write that:

> the blue shirt with the arm raised, Romanly, is the universal sign with which the Falange has contributed in this national and imperial resurrection of Spain . . . . Rome—Mussolini's Rome—is the source of inspiration for the party's decision to put the shirt in its proper place. In its balanced place. Just. Exact. Integrating the shirt of the body and of the corporation. Fascist . . . . And other shirts emerge in the new Fascist world that unfolds in history. And among these historical creations, the blue shirt appears in Spain. It is the shirt of the Falange.

In 1939, Juan Beneyto Pérez wrote a book published by Biblioteca Nueva in Madrid entitled *El Nuevo Estado Español* [*The New Spanish State*], which opened with an introduction by Arrigo Solmi, university professor and Italian minister of justice, establishing an analogical parallelism between the German and Italian regimes and their National Syndicalist state models, outling the degree to which they are comparable and coincidental.

Mihail Manoilesco, on page 204 of his work *El Partido Único* [*The Single Party*], published in Zaragoza in 1938, analyzed the European Fascist parties, including the Falange, asserting:

> We must emphasize the impressive ideological uniformity of all these political currents: they are against parties and the liberal regime, against political corruption, against the anti-national press, and against financial speculation. All of them support the middle class, the peasant class, and corporations. These movements are all organized militarily,

---

[248] Julio Rodríguez Puértolas, *Literatura Fascista española*, vol. I (Madrid: Ediciones Akal., 1986), 32.

inspired and made up by young people. Finally, most of them are of nationalistic and anti-Semitic character.

Luis Jordana de Pozas, in his preface to the book written by the Romanian professor Manoilesco, asserts that the Falangist movement "is inspired by Fascist and National Socialist predecessors."

13.

¡Arriba España!, A Unique Journal of Fascist Memories

Jesús Pérez de Cabo published, in 1935, the only book on the Falange to be written by a militant and printed while José Antonio was still alive, which bears as its title the motto of the Falangist movement, the rallying cry of encouragement and identification, the Fascist greeting, which prompted people to raise their arms for the Roman salute: *¡Arriba España!*

The invocation *¡Arriba España!* was the closing cry of the *Primera Proclama del Movimiento Español Sindicalista: Fascismo Español* [*First Manifesto of the Spanish Syndicalist Movement*], which concluded, with exclamation points, with a vibrant "*¡Arriba España, una, indivisible y eterna!*" ["Up with Spain, one, indivisible and eternal!"]. The word *arriba* conveys the ascending verticality, the elevation, the exaltation toward the heights, the hierarchy, the shout of strength and thrust used to impose something above the rest. It was a term that was widely used and admired since the beginnings of Fascism in Spain. *Arriba* bears within it the action of lifting, of hoisting, of reaching the highest point, and conquering the final rung in the ladder of possibilities.

José Antonio, director and owner of the first newspaper of the Falange, the weekly *F.E.*, commissioned the Spanish Fascist ideologist Rafael Sánchez Mazas to write the publication's editorials. Since his first *consigna*, which introduced the editorial section, the finishing period was always invariably preceded by this desire, this intention, this spirit, with these words: "*¡Arriba España!*" "And now, with your arm up high and forth: *¡Arriba España!*" If José Antonio was its creator, Rafael Sánchez Mazas would be its popularizer. There would be no other closing phrase. *¡Arriba España!* would forever represent the greeting and farewell, the opening and closing, the beginning and end of the Falange.

It began to be used as a farewell in letters, speeches, writings, and pamphlets. It proved to be a strong and distinguishing coinage. It would be repeated over and over again that, above so much existing vileness, it would be necessary to impose a single cry: *¡Arriba España!* Victor D'Ors himself wrote in *F.E.* that "Fascism is elevation."

In an article published in the fourth issue of *F.E.*, dated Thursday, January 25th, 1934, with great typographic quality, the headline displayed the words "*¡Arriba España!*" It was written on the occasion of an apostolic visit by José Antonio to Catalonia, and it reads:

> Falange Española is gradually developing expertise in bringing forth the best Spanish voices. Falange Española is being granted the glory of raising, wherever it treads, the rejoicing cry of the new Spain.

The novelty was brilliant. The cry of *¡Arriba España!* united, consolidated, bound together, and engaged. It represented the necessary effort. It was necessary to build the Fatherland upward, to raise it from its knees.

The masthead of the weekly *Arriba*, which began publication in 1935, was nothing more than the shortened version of those two essential words that had been popularized by the Falange.

Pérez de Cabo's book would be published in October 1935, just two years after the birth of Falange Española. It featured a very thoughtful introduction by José Antonio, written in the heat of that August in 1935, in which he narrates how:

> On a certain morning a stranger came to my house. It was Pérez de Cabo, the author of the pages that follow this foreword. With no further ado, he revealed to me that he had written a book on the Falange. It was so unusual that someone could devote himself to contemplating the phenomenon of the Falange to the point of dedicating a book to it that I borrowed the loose pages and read them in one sitting, robbing my busy schedule of precious minutes. The pages were filled with enthusiasm and not without errors. Pérez de Cabo—partly, perhaps, due to the lack of distribution of our texts, partly, perhaps (he is not by chance a Spaniard) due to the certainty that he had got everything right without the need for any text—had a somewhat distorted perception of the Falange. But those pages were written by a skilled hand. Their author was capable of far greater things. And, convinced of this, I had such long conversations with him that during the two revisions to which he subjected his book, he completely transformed it. Pérez de Cabo, contrary to what a first impression might have led one to believe, possesses a rare virtue

among us: that of being able to listen and to read. Thanks to the readings I supplied him with and to the conversations we had, there are pages of the following work that I would approve down to the commas.

That being said, there are some other passages that lack precision, and the entire work contains doctrinal gaps that could have been avoided with less hurried drafting. Nevertheless, the author felt the urgency of having his book printed and I did not believe I had the authority to repress his enthusiasm, nor, deep down, did I renounce the pleasure of seeing the Falange treated as an object of intellectual consideration, printed in compact pages. Pérez de Cabo himself will undertake new attempts with better resources; however, those of us who have spent two years in the Falange's bittersweet effort will thank him for life for having approached us with a book under his arm, like a child with a sweet bun.[249]

In the introduction, José Antonio, besides the anecdotal details of how he learned of the existence of the work and of its author, offers a detailed essay on how the decline and end of an era, of a period of history, which had begun in the eighteenth century and developed in the subsequent century, was being witnessed. To the obsolete and defunct world, he opposes the new and youthful world illuminated in that historical dawn, and, thus, he writes:

All the youth, conscious of their responsibility, strive to readjust the world. They strive on the path of action and, more importantly, on the path of thought, because action without the constant guidance of thought is pure barbarism. We, the Spanish men whose youth began among the hardships of the interwar period, could hardly escape from this universal concern. Our Spain found itself, on the one hand, as if safe from the universal crisis; on the other hand, as if distressed by a crisis of its own, as if absent from itself due to factors of estrangement that were not shared by the rest of the world.[250]

The formula that José Antonio chose in view of the collapse of that period, of the old time, of the agonizing epoch, could not be the rootless revolutionary one nor the return to the most ancient tradition, one without a future. That is why he writes:

Between these two attitudes, it crossed the minds of some of us to wonder whether it might be possible or not to achieve a synthesis of the two things:

---

[249] Pérez de Cabo, ¡Arriba España!, 10–11.

[250] Ibid., 7–8.

of revolution—not merely as a pretext to throw everything into disarray, but as a critical occasion to reshape everything with a steady hand at the service of a rule—and of tradition—not as a remedy, but as substance, not in the spirit of copying what the great ancients did, but in the spirit of guessing what they would have done in our circumstances. As a result of our inquietude, the Falange was born.[251]

The book is a brief essay that, rather than presenting a doctrine, sought to be "the revelation of spirit" of the Falangist movement, which was founded on heroism, discipline, and hierarchy. In the preface, Pérez de Cabo presented the spirit of generosity and Fascist humanism:

> We are soldiers and we must honor our oaths, but when our heroic times have passed and our banners return from the battlefield fluttering in the wind of victory, we will know how to lay a wreath of evergreens on the tomb of all those who have fallen in defense of an ideal, even on the tomb of our adversaries. They were Spaniards; they fought for Spain believing they were defending it, and they generously shed their blood for the doctrine that was erroneously presented to them as that which would have saved Spain.[252]

This description of respect and honor to the defeated enemy who perished under an ideal, however mistaken, takes us back to the old days of Velázquez's painting of the *Surrender of Breda*, in which upright spears receive the key from the defeated with a gesture of cordial kindness; in more recent times, it recalls the eternal symbol of the Valley of the Fallen, in Cuelgamuros, where the combatants of opposing fronts rest united forever and in eternity, sharing the same holy ground, the same crypt of martyrdom, and the same intense blue sky of Castile, under the broad and welcoming shadow of the greater cross that the centuries have seen rise on the stony rocks.

The first chapter of the book, "Genesis," makes clear that the Falange Española did not emerge spontaneously or by magic, "like Minerva from the head of Jupiter," but rather, it had its own causes and reasons, and naturally, it had its "precursors":

> What is regrettable, and also strange, is that causes, reasons, and excitements have met in Spain a soul so cold and a social body so insensitive that, despite being more powerful, visible, and intense than in the other peninsula of the Mediterranean, the explosion of Italian

---

[251] Ibid., 8.

[252] Ibid., 15.

revolutionary enthusiasm has been several years ahead of us . . . . The Fascist phenomenon was in the heart of Italy striving to turn patriotic eagerness into redemptive action that, as action and movement, was bound to translate into a triumphal march.[253]

He considered the Falange to be a "meditated and passionate" movement of reconquest because a lion state was needed—a strong state, a national instrument state—for that purpose:

> Primo de Rivera places, then, his powerful mind at the service of the truth and thus discovers the formula of the National Syndicalist, corporative, and totalitarian state, of the Spanish type. It is not a block from the Italian or German quarry. It is a Spanish creation . . . . Once the new Spanish nation is on its feet, and thanks to the totalitarian and syndicalist state at the service of the nation, which will be like the steel structure of the whole construction, the chariot of our destiny will advance majestically through the universe at the sound of another cry. *¡Arriba!* will become *¡Adelante!* [Forward!]
>
> *¡Arriba!* Hence, it is a cry of excitement, and of affirmation of being. The imperial cry of universal resonance will be heard by Spanish society later, when the supreme hierarchy of the totalitarian state proclaims that the time has come to fulfill the historical destiny of Spain.[254]

In this political essay on the Falangist doctrine, a serious and sensible critique is made of liberalism and inorganic democratic parliamentarism, in order to uphold National Syndicalism, which, in its own terms, undertakes the courageous enterprise of overcoming syndicalism precisely to liberate the individual—either employer or worker—from the shackles of democracy and capitalism. Placing the individual within the framework of professional unions, agreeing with this aspiration and tactic with pure syndicalism in the vertical sense, is not only about the goods produced by the unions, which are only material in nature, but also about the pride of feeling Spanish, which is a spiritual good that the totalitarian National Syndicalist state perfects.

An entire chapter of the book is dedicated to the study of "El Estado Nacionalsindicalista y El Estado totalitario" ["The National Syndicalist State and the Totalitarian State"], and it begins with the Duce's assessment:

> A juridical state cannot be the state that represents a party, but the state that represents the national collectivity, that embraces everything, that is above

---

253 Ibid., 17–18.

254 Ibid., 23–25.

everything, that legally protects everything, that, ultimately, rises with omnipotent right against whoever puts his hands on its inalienable sovereignty; a state that does not yield to the strongest; a state that is nothing like the liberal state, incapable of the minimum juridical organization and financial accomplishment; a state that is not at the mercy of all-powerful socialism; a state that does not deem the resolution of problems possible exclusively from the political point of view. Machine guns are not enough if the spirit does not prepare and fire them. The entire framework of the state collapses like an old operetta stage in the absence of a supreme awareness of the great duty of carrying out a collective mission.[255]

The author references the text of the speech delivered by José Antonio at the Círculo de la Unión Mercantil of Madrid, on April 9th of that same year, reproducing the central part of his argumentation, especially repeating his words when referring to the corporative state: "Mussolini, who has a certain idea of what the corporative state is, gave a speech during the establishment of the twenty-two corporations a few months ago, in which he said: 'This is only a starting point, but not a point of arrival.'" With this literal quotation José Antonio wanted to convey the idea that the first stone of the architecture, the bedrock, the basic foundation of the new state was precisely the corporative organization, but the ultimate purpose of the "totalitarian National Syndicalist state is not justified by its own absolute authority, but as a necessary instrument of society to guarantee freedom and to work toward individual happiness and the greatness of the Fatherland."[256]

Pérez de Cabo argues that the organization of the National Syndicalist state is not dictatorial but hierarchical, and affirms:

On this point, we agree with the ideas of Fascism, as we always do, but only when they adhere to the norms implied and imposed by nature. Mussolini has stated exactly: "There is no real and rational law without an effective and legal hierarchy. Whoever speaks of hierarchy speaks of a scale of human values. Whoever speaks of a scale of human values speaks of a scale of responsibilities and duties, rather than of liberties and rights. Whoever speaks of a scale of responsibilities and duties speaks of discipline."[257]

To validate his assertions and hypotheses, Pérez del Cabo employed quotations from the Duce, which emphasized the similarities and analogies with Italian Fascism. The Falangists were not unaware of the successes achieved in Italy. To examine the realities

---

255 Ibid., 52–53.

256 Ibid., 60.

257 Ibid., 61.

and to discover the formulas to adapt them to the Spanish nature and peculiarities, to adapt them to our character, to look for the genuine roots, was not a question of mimicry but of adaptation, while taking as a reference the evidence that the new European order demonstrated. It was a matter of embarking upon the new course, led by the flagships steered by the two political titans of the twentieth century: Benito Mussolini and Adolf Hitler.

In a chapter of *¡Arriba España!* it is stated that, after the twilight of the gods, "the revolution will only be saved by the Falange," for which history has reserved the honor of saving the human personality and of setting in motion once more the imperial destiny of Spain.[258]

That is why, when considering what attitude National Syndicalism should adopt in the face of the existing contemporary state, the answer could not be different, as he writes:

> Our attitude toward the state in force is the one advocated by Mussolini: "We will be with the state as long as it presents itself as a vigilant guardian and jealous keeper of tradition and of the national will. We will replace the state should it prove incapable of dealing with demagogy and of opposing the groups that internally undermine public solidarity. We will fight the state in case it falls into the hands of those who threaten the future of the country." "Liberalism and socialism, that is to say, economic individualism and class struggle, lead only to hunger and ruin. It is necessary to provide humane living conditions in rural Italy, reducing to a minimum the causes of the systematic destruction of the Fatherland."
>
> The corporative economy respects the principle of private property, which complements the principle of human personality and is at the same time a right and a duty. Likewise, it respects individual initiative. And, just like the Italian leader, we reject the outdated cliché of parliamentarism, of public liberties, of the government of the people by the people, which imply that the sum of individual wills shall be capable of invading specific and characteristic areas. "The individual should not be considered the supreme purpose of society," although the community's supreme purpose is the happiness of the individual alone, as Primo de Rivera frequently declared.[259]

For consistency with the principle of natural hierarchy, characteristic of National Syndicalism, Pérez de Cabo rejects the concept of "unconditional selection" of aristocratic blood, preferring appointment to ascription, and understands that selection by hereditary lineage is the opposite of selection if it is not determined by

---

[258] Ibid.

[259] Ibid., 90.

personal effort. The original aristocracy had its existence justified by the social and moral authority—*aristos*—of its creators, of the greatest, who were that because of their own efforts, of their recognized personal magnetism—*nobilis*—that is to say, notability. The false aristocrat is the heir, whose personal effort no longer has to be recognized, nor necessitates the asceticism that characterized the original position of privilege. The nobiliary title should be personal and non-transferable; its transmission and recognition to people who have no merit, nor have achieved any personal proof of relevance, would institutionalize a merit that *must* be demonstrated.

The "aristocratic legacy" signifies the loss of the natural hierarchy as well as the disrespect of the people toward the appropriators of the feats of others, of the distant ancestors, ever more distant. The nobleman and the aristocrat were no longer "oneself," but the shadow, sometimes comic, of a past, and that is tragic. Thus an archive takes shape, or rather a register, quite often filled with bums and crooks, of *señoritos*, not of lords but of parasites, of someone who earns his living from the rents and prestige extracted from others who, justly, had the legitimate pride of being at the top of the hierarchy. For that reason, the constitutional kings—who reign, though they are not required to pass any test to demonstrate that they know how to reign, and, of course, they do not govern even though they always want to "govern" with their exploits—it is enough for them to fornicate and have children to continue living off the story and the accomplishments of a first ancestor, who is lost in the night of the times and who did know how to earn the position through his renowned ability and heroism. It is better—and nobler—to be a leader than a king. The first has revealed himself to the people as such, while the other symbolizes the great farce perpetuated ad infinitum. The blood aristocracy has no need to demonstrate anything, since the title *belongs to it* regardless of its actions; it is unclear what pretense it should be based on. The greatest of heroes can father—history overflows with examples—the most miserable of wretches.

In opposition to the *aristocracy of blood*, National Syndicalism and Fascism put forward the *elites of labor and the militia*, merit and self-worth, natural selection, the authentic and genuine hierarchy, not the predetermined one. Worth and honor are not inherited; they must be earned, conquered, and recognized. Being the best does not mean being the firstborn in a lineage, but rather being the one capable of demonstrating it. Therefore:

> Being National Syndicalists does not predispose us to favor either workers or employers. National syndicalism, we repeat, is a type of state organized by trade unions, and our vertical structure allows us to serve workers and bosses alike, as well as stimulate them through the assignment of duties and orders. And we consider the person who works with his brain to be just as important as the person who works with his hands.
>
> We consider ourselves to be brothers in spirit with all those who work;

however, we do not make absurd distinctions and do not prioritize calluses, including those of the brain. We do not build altars for the new deity of manual labor. In our opinion everyone works, from the farmer to the miner, from the sailor to the artist, archaeologist, exegete, jurist, or astronomer, who observes the march of the stars. "Workers are those who contribute to humanity's economic, aesthetic, intellectual, and moral heritage."[260]

Pérez de Cabo highlights with this Mussolini quotation that the Falange recognizes no higher dignity, nobility, or aristocracy than well-done work as a social function and community service:

National syndicalism is a militant movement based on gentlemen's morals, which involve, above all, submission to norms and hierarchical categories, as well as a heroic sense of history.

The book ends with a classic quote from Virgil:

Roman, remember by your strength to rule the earth's peoples—for your arts are to be these: To pacify, to impose the rule of law, to spare the conquered, battle down the proud.[261]

It was the only monographic book, in the form of an essay, which dealt with the Falange's social, political, and economic outlook, which had strong ties to the Fascist directives of the time.

Pérez de Cabo would be executed after the war for his dissidence with the Franco regime, as he attempted to collect funds as the person in charge of the finances of the clandestine organization to which he had been appointed by Patricio González de Canales. (He worked as a high-ranking official in the Auxilio Social in Valencia.[262]) To provide funds to the Falange's secret Political Board, to which they had added the name "Auténtica" ["Authentic"], he proceeded to sell a batch of wheat on the black market, a sum of money that he intended to return when the fees of the "dissidents" would be collected. After being discovered, he was quickly sentenced to death. His dramatic elimination was a perfect example of how things went in the postwar period.

---

[260] Ibid., 98.

[261] [Translator: Quote from Virgil's *Aeneid*, trans. Robert Fitzgerald and David West (New York: Vintage Classics, 1990).]

[262] [Translator: The Auxilio Social was a Spanish humanitarian relief organization that operated during the dictatorship of Francisco Franco.]

14.

The Weekly Newspaper Arriba

The movement was in need of a written medium of expression. It was critical to establish a communication channel with militants that could serve as a point of reference for doctrine, encouragement, and promotion of activities while also making itself heard on the streets and presenting itself to public opinion. *F.E.* had ceased publication in August 1934, when the police removed its final issue from circulation.

According to Sheelagh Ellwood, in early January 1935, the Falange was offered Italian—and German—machinery to launch a newspaper in Madrid. "The Italian offer," wrote García Venero, "was equivalent to a cession without monetary compensation and did not entail any political obligation." García Venero does not reveal whether or not the offer was accepted, but what is certain is that the first issue of *Arriba* appeared on March 21st, 1935.[263]

José Antonio, faced with a Franciscan austerity, gathered a group of comrades he trusted completely and entrusted the launch of the Falange's journalistic organ to them. The invitation to the meeting reached Rafael Sánchez Mazas, poet and rhetorician, ideologist and inseparable friend of the national leader, who had already proven his worth as editorialist of *F.E.*, and who now continued to impart stylish slogans to the movement. Also included were president of the Political Board, Julio Ruiz de Alda; the secretary general of the organization, Raimundo Fernández Cuesta y Merelo, and his classmate, the diplomat Felipe Ximénez de Sandoval, who from his

---

263 Sheelagh Ellwood, *Prietas las filas (Historia de Falange Española 1933–1983)* (Barcelona: Grupo Editorial Grijalbo, 1984), 64–65.

window to the world would write on international politics; the national delegate of Press and Propaganda, architect José Manuel Aizpurúa; the head of the Central Obrera Nacional Sindicalista (C.O.N.S.) Manuel Mateo, who would be in charge of writing about syndicalist themes; Carlos Ruiz de la Fuente and Vicente Gaceo del Pino, founder of the SEU and member of the First National Council of the Spanish Falange who, together with the journalist Julio Fuertes, was going to set up the new weekly with his full personal commitment; and the very young but experienced member of the JONS, Vicente Cadenas Vicent. These last two would be in charge of the technical aspects of the publication. This was the initial core group in charge of carrying out the new journalistic project, to which Manuel Garnelo Gallego, layout designer and cartoonist, Julio Fuertes Pérez, journalist from *La Nación* and *Informaciones*, and Julio González-Hontoria, editor, later joined. The position of administrator was unanimously assigned to Mr. Mariano García; Ruiz de la Fuente was entrusted with the responsibility for the gradual distribution of the five thousand copies of the print run through the provincial headquarters and the various local branches of the JONS, of which militants would be those to shout in the streets "*Arriba*, the newspaper of the Falange has arrived!" thus dodging the regular distribution channels. Its distribution— a loud and unrestrained voice—was not without incident; generally, punches and slaps flew against any provocateurs, ensuring, with the protection of the squads, a presence in the streets and squares. Alfonso Ponce de León was responsible for designing the masthead.

José Antonio also introduced to the team a young Fascist at the time, José Antonio Giménez Arnau, who, in October 1933, had already written directly to the Duce asking for his opinion on the possibilities of success for Fascism in Spain and regarding the path that should be taken to gain power.[264] When he wrote and signed his first piece, which appeared in *Arriba*'s second issue, he was already proclaiming: "Is Mussolini a revolutionary solely because of his March on Rome? No. Mussolini achieves that glorious title by launching a revolution that speaks to people's consciences."

José Antonio Giménez Arnau graduated with a doctorate in 1933 from the Italian Regia Università of Bologna, where he resided at the Colegio de San Clemente de los Españoles, and was awarded the Vittorio Emanuele II prize for his thesis during that same winter. He met José Antonio in the summer of 1934, in San Sebastián, at the Cristina Hotel, after being introduced by his brother Ricardo, who was already acquainted with the Falange's leader:

"José Antonio, you have the winner of the Vittorio Emanuele Prize here."
    "That is important," Primo de Rivera said while shaking his hand.

---

[264] The letter dated October 1933 can be found in Rome in the Historical and Diplomatic Archives of the Ministry of Foreign Affairs, in Spanish Politics, b.5, quoted in Ismael Saz Campos: *Mussolini contra la Segunda República*, 195, footnote.

"Rather than the things we have to get involved in."

I must admit that the impression made by this man, seen from a meter away, confirms the effect that his voice had on me on October 29th, 1933. Then came the farewell, which has already   been widely disclosed by others.

"Do you wish something for Geneva?"

"If you have enough time, burn it down."[265]

Giménez Arnau had listened by radio to José Antonio's speech at the Comedia from Zaragoza in the company of some friends, ready to listen to "that *señorito* who wanted to play the Fascist, the son of Don Miguel Primo de Rivera. Once his speech was over, no one in the audience—whether convinced or not—called him *señorito* again."[266] Giménez Arnau was part of Falange Española de las JONS with number 1,435 and provincial number 985 on his membership card, which was signed by Allanegui and Ramiro Ledesma. He intervened as a speaker in the meeting of José Antonio in the *frontón* of Zaragoza on January 26th, 1936.[267] He was the founder of the newspaper *Unidad*, published in San Sebastián, and, in 1938, in the midst of the war, he was named Director General of the Press in Burgos. Because of his complete commitment to Fascism, he was appointed ambassador of Spain in Rome in 1939.

There were several names considered for the new weekly's masthead, all of which consisted of a single term. Once again, the name of *F.E.* was brought up, as well as that of *Libertad*, which was already being published under the same name in Valladolid, under the direction of Onésimo Redondo. The name *Unidad*, a word that was dear to José Antonio because of its sense of cohesion, was also suggested, and even the name *Verdad* was considered, but in view of the fact that the cry of recognition was *Arriba España* and, given that the aim was to simplify the masthead into a single word, José Antonio opted, definitively, for *Arriba*, which was a distinctive and unequivocal sign of identity, adherence, and belonging to the Falange. In addition, it spurred on, by association of ideas, the impulse to be completed with the invocation of the name of Spain, in thought or spoken word. Also, the word *arriba* evoked immediately the presence of the Blueshirts.

To obtain governmental permission, it was decided that neither the Falange nor any known member of the organization should be in charge of carrying out the necessary procedures, and that the ideal person could be, perhaps, Don José Gómez Fernández, a former assistant of General Primo de Rivera who would act as a trustee in his role as director and owner of the upcoming publication. The application for a

---

[265] J. A. Jiménez-Arnau, *Memorias de Memoria* (Barcelona: Ediciones Destino, 1978), 44.

[266] Ibid., 38.

[267] [Translator: a *frontón* is a type of court used for playing Basque pelota, a typical sport in Spain.]

literary, informative, and politically oriented magazine was submitted for administrative approval on March 5th, with the following text:

> José Gómez Fernández, of legal age, with domicile in Madrid, at 23 Calle del Molino de Viento, registered with a personal identity card of class 8ª, number 429,368, issued in Madrid on December 11th, 1934, in full exercise of his civil and political rights, has the honor to communicate to this Civil Government:
>
> That he intends to publish a weekly newspaper entitled *Arriba*, which will come out on Thursdays and will be printed at the workshop established with the name "El Financiero" at 11 Calle de Ibiza.
>
> That this newspaper, which is of a political, literary, and educational nature, is owned by the undersigned and will be published under his direction.
>
> That the editorial and administrative offices are located at 3 Cuesta de Santo Domingo on the first floor.
>
> The Civil Government is being notified of this in compliance with the current Printing Law.

At the beginning of spring 1935, the first issue of the new weekly of the Falange was published. If we consider José Antonio's letter to Francisco Bravo dated March 13th, the newspaper should have already been on the streets by March 14th:

> The paper was supposed to be published tomorrow, Thursday. However, due to last-minute difficulties, especially because of the slowness of the censorship, it will definitely come out next Thursday, unless we are suspended by the authorities. It will be titled *Arriba* because neither of the two previous titles is permitted.

Up until the fourteenth issue, the new Falange newspaper contained a booklet made up of six large pages; from June 24th, they were reduced to four.

The weekly was printed in the workshops of El Financiero. It was published every Thursday until July 4th, when the government suspended it, and it did not appear again until October 21st. More than three months of journalistic repression were imposed by the enemies of freedom of expression. The structure of the paper was divided into the following sections: editorial line, Spanish politics, *ventana al mundo* [window to the world], *central obrera* [workers' union], some articles by occasional collaborators, announcements of events, and, most importantly, the extensive reviews and detailed summaries of the speeches and events organized and promoted by the Falangist movement from one end of the country to the other—all of this, of course, decorated with the hateful "censorship visa" government stamp.

Times were hard; these were days of lead. On June 15th and 16th, 1935, José

Antonio summoned his Board of Command at the Parador Nacional de Gredos, in light of the gravity of the political and social situation, and informed them of his plans for active belligerence, requesting their support for an armed insurrection.[268]

In these circumstances, the weekly *Arriba* had already lost the euphemistic and literary grace of its predecessor *F.E.* and had become harsher, more combative, more communicative, and more discursive, sometimes using a gritty tone, hardly restraining insults.

The Ethiopian Conflict and José Antonio's Support for Fascist Italy

José Antonio regularly wrote about Spanish politics and checked galley proofs as part of his role as the weekly's actual editor, as the nominal editor only appeared for administrative purposes. The fact that he wrote about domestic politics did not mean that he ignored international issues, especially those that could affect brotherly Fascist nations, as is the case with his speech in the Cortes when the issue of possible sanctions against Italy for the annexation of Abyssinia was debated; it was a parliamentary intervention that was not immediately included in the newspaper due to government suspension. The leader of the Falange, consistent with his ideas, justified the Italian military action as follows:

> None of the open-minded individuals gathered here could have ever avoided being influenced by a multitude of sympathies; we have all been influenced, some more, some less—and I consider myself among the latter—by European culture: we have all felt the influence of French letters, of English education, of German philosophy, and of the political tradition of Italy, which is now engaged in one of the greatest experiments, a supreme experiment that no one can avoid studying seriously and to which, surely, no one is free from some form of objection . . . . So I'll dare to say that in the current Italo-Ethiopian conflict, which is currently being debated in Europe, there are only two issues at stake: a colonial issue and a British issue. Nothing more, nothing less.
>
> A colonial issue. Should we pretend to be outraged that a new colonial expedition is underway? If all the peoples of Europe have undertaken one, if colonizing is a mission, no longer a right, but a duty of civilized peoples, is anyone who aspires to universal brotherhood willing to accept the exclusion, *de facto*, of the universal brotherhood that represents barbarism? Are we to believe that by keeping underdeveloped peoples in their current state of

---

268 [Translator: The Parador Nacional de Gredos is a hotel located in Navarredonda de Gredos, Ávila.]

backwardness, we are upholding their rights within this global brotherhood? I believe it is too late for us to be scandalized by any country's colonial enterprise. Through colonization, Spain found its glory.[269]

The weekly *Arriba* clearly sided with Italy in the Ethiopian conflict, both in writing and in images. It was Felipe Ximénez de Sandoval, the person in charge of writing the section "Ventana al mundo," who expressed the position assumed by José Antonio.

Ximénez de Sandoval wrote categorically and firmly:

> If Ethiopia has been picturesquely elevated to a status it could never have had due to the democratic delirium of Geneva, the energetic will of Italy—which has strong reasons to do so—will bring down the illusion without regard for the paperwork and third-party deals of the Genevan lawyers, who conceal special interests. Because of its economic power, large population, and strong imperial vocation, Italy requires the expansion that was promised to it when it entered the war, but which was denied when it signed the peace.
>
> Mussolini recognizes this and refuses to be intimidated by the fabrication that his realist policy seeks to tear down. Italy needs an expansion in Africa because of its uncontainable vitality; it cannot be at the mercy of warlike tribes or pacifist whimpers, which cover up an unjust political inequality.

In that same international chronicle, referring to Hitler, he wrote: "Through Hitler's mouth resounded the voice of a people whose international dignity has been regained following the restoration of its national life."

Another article about Hitler followed a week later; it was an exaltation of the Führer's speech, delivered before the Reichstag on the night of May 21st. And, while he provided a thorough analysis of that oratorical piece—which he described as an "example of what should be the internal and foreign policy of a conscious people"— he also stated his desire that "we would like to be able to give the readers of *Arriba* the full version of it." However, because of space constraints, only a selection is provided.

With regard to the Ethiopian conflict, José Antonio also published photographs in *Arriba* with the caption "El estado social de Abisinia" ["The social state of Abyssinia"], in which it was possible to observe a depressing and grotesque scene of slaves in chains and mendicants plagued by leprosy, a situation from which Italy was trying to redeem the country. The following can be read in reference to the given photographic image on page 4 of the nineteenth issue of *Arriba*, dated November 14th:

---

[269] Primo de Rivera, *Obras completas*, vol. II, 753–754. Speech delivered in Parliament on October 2nd, 1935.

In the face of those who want to portray Italy as the infringer of rights of a free people, it is sufficient to present these authentic photographs of Abyssinian scenes. The Ethiopian people, whom Italy, the heir to a high European tradition, wishes to bring into civilization, find themselves in this dreadful situation.

And two weeks later—in the twenty-first issue, on page 4—this position is further reinforced by referring again to photos of human misery, with the following interpretation:

Corporal punishments; leprosy; famine; madmen treated as criminals; prisoners condemned to live in pairs surrounded by their own filth. Such is the life of the Ethiopian people whom Italy plans, according to the Freemasons and Marxists, to enslave.

Similar commentary on Fascist Italy's policies did not cease. In the face of so many outcries from the antifascist media against Italy due to its intervention in Ethiopia, the weekly *Arriba* was unequivocal about its position:

Italy abides by the norms of political doctrine because it is governed by the dignity inherited from Caesarean Rome. It follows its righteous line in Ethiopia. The laws of civilization follow the weapons, and as they arrive in Ethiopian land, roads are paved, seeds are sown, and slaves are set free. And, while guns and ploughs are gaining miles of desert for Western civilization, diplomats seek peace in chancelleries and even Geneva, where they know it will not be found.[270]

José Antonio, as a member of parliament and through his Falangist newspaper, supported Italy without any reservation, and his viewpoint coincided with Mussolini's stance on this issue, which had been raised internationally and on which the Falange and its leader aligned themselves with the Duce and Fascist Italy.

The national leader did not hesitate to write a leaflet, which he published entirely in capital letters to emphasize its contents even more, with the following message:

Our little political world is more papist than the Pope, and without any national interest to advise it, out of pure ignorance or intolerable pressures, we endorsed the sanctions against Italy, and with scruple and diligence worthy of a better cause, we rushed to apply them.

---

[270] *Arriba*, no. 18, November 7th, 1935, 2. "Ventana al Mundo".

Their approval is unjustified. The haste with which they were executed is idiotic.

Who is pushing for them? Why are we in such a hurry?

Naturally, this measure has begun to yield results. Large sectors of industry and commerce have voiced their protests because of the great damage caused to them. Their well-founded complaints will fall on deaf ears. What does it matter to our political parties if the economy suffers another loss or if we cut off our economic ties with a country with which we have a favorable trade balance?[271]

In his position as the primary author of political articles about Spain, José Antonio has authored numerous pieces in which he attacks and denounces the policies and actions of Gil Robles and his right-wing party. Already in the first issue of *Arriba*, in a long article entitled "España estancada" ["Spain at a Standstill"], he did not hesitate to use appropriate adjectives to describe the two years that had passed since the advent of the Second Republic: "At the end of 1933, we left the terrible biennium to enter the stupid biennium." In response to the confusing use of terms that the right wing of the C.E.D.A. was beginning to use, José Antonio commented:

Gil Robles continued to make promising speeches, as if he did not have three ministers in the government and the largest minority in the Cortes. The National Bloc is looking splendid. He is already bringing in new words, just for show: he speaks of unity of command, of the corporate state, and other Fascist things. Soon they will believe him! A new order brought by the far right, that is to say, by those parties privileged by the old order. Soon, the workers, the students, and all those who have long been dissatisfied with the obsolete Spanish structure will believe it![272]

He then proceeds to warn Spanish students, workers, and intellectuals not to allow themselves to be deceived, despite the terminological confusion in use, and to learn how to discern authentic Fascism from its imitators.

Since the very first issue of *Arriba*, one could already read between the lines what the wind of history was. In an article entitled "Impotentes" ["The Powerless"], an affirmation of Hispanism that could have been written today because of its raging relevance, the ending paragraph culminated as follows:

Powerless people—Many powerless people rule these different populations that have once again separated. Yes, they separated again. Catalonia does

---

[271] *Arriba*, no. 21, November 28th, 1935, 4. "El caso idiota de las sanciones a Italia" ["The Idiotic Case of the Sanctions on Italy"].

[272] *Arriba*, no. 1, March 21st, 1935, 2.

not want to be Spanish.

The Basque Country wants to be Basque. Castile, the mother, is impotent, helpless.

With the force of a yoke and a sheaf, the infertile could give birth again; the powerless would regain strength. The name of Spain will once again be a reality; the symbol will again be made flesh. Eastern winds blow; winds of resurgence. They come from the universal Rome. At their thrust, let us raise our arms and pronounce the name of Castile, our mother.[273]

From the first issue of the weekly, there were numerous references to Germany and Italy, such as in the article entitled "El gesto de Alemania y la Sociedad de las Naciones" ["The Stance of Germany and the League of Nations"], which reads:

Germany, with its honor and dignity awakened by the National Socialist horn, stands up to overthrow with one blow the insulting Treaty of Versailles, cradle, foundation, and grave of the League of Nations . . . . The German Führer and his people—who follow him faithfully with the raised arm of the will of empire and the unity of destiny—will be indifferent to any recommendations and remarks because the fate of Germany has been cast into the wind with the virile proclamation of March 16th, and the Pact seeks in the labyrinth of its constitution a solution to the conflict presented by the blow of the hand of Germania, which tears apart the shadows and throws its chains to the ground . . . . The new German generation, with their *Reichsführer* at the head, has severed its ties with the compromises of the preceding one, who lacked heroic spirit in the final hour of the war and in the time of peace. Germany will take on the consequences of its decision, an admirable display of bravery and national dignity. Patriotic men all over the world will react favorably to this deed. While the poor fools of mediocrity pull out their hair in public over the renunciation of war, the Geneva Conventions, the internationals, and the so-called rights of man, all while rubbing their hands behind closed doors over the possibilities of a new war along with its filthy business of smuggling, hoarding, clandestine weapons production, repugnant deals, high treason, and trade in honor and death, history continues. And although there is no end to merchants, there is no end to heroes either.[274]

This first issue also includes an excerpt from the speech that José Antonio gave in Valladolid, in the Teatro Calderón of Pisuerga, on March 3rd, with the title "España

---

[273] Ibid.

[274] Ibid.

y la Barbarie" ["Spain and Barbarism"], during which, referring to the corporative state, he states:

> Until now, the best attempt has been made in Italy, and there, it is nothing more than a component added to a perfect political machine. There exists a way to achieve harmony between employers and workers, something like our mixed juries, but on a larger scale: a confederation of employers and another of workers connected at the top. Today, the corporate state does not exist, nor is it known whether it is good. The Law of Corporations in Italy, as stated by Mussolini himself, is a starting point and not a point of arrival, as our politicians pretend corporatism to be.

Speaking next of the "new order," José Antonio observes that "there can be no organized economy without a strong state; and only the state that serves a unity of destiny can be strong without being tyrannical."[275]

The Fascist state is described in *Arriba* as the "defender of Western culture and civilization."[276] The guidelines are clear and have Fascist overtones:

> Revolution is necessary.
> Our revolution is that of the spirit against matter.
> Of harmony against number.
> Of quality against quantity.
> Of social bodies against purely numerical collectivities.
> Of the living nation against the Fatherland without a soul.
> It is necessary to destroy an economic system that reduces man to an abstraction, to a tool, to a static element.
> It is necessary to put an end to a regime that would insidiously drive us back to endless slavery.
> It is essential to put an end to an ideology that has no other purpose than to offer us the lowest forms of materialism.
> And in its place, it is necessary to establish a new order, based on the true foundations and essential desires of man.
> The state must have the authority and autonomy to:
>   a) Coordinate and mediate the often-opposing interests of economic and social entities (unions, regions);
>   b) Ensure a collective discipline that is both permissive and strict, with the ability to guide specific activities toward a sense of the common good;
>   c) Defend, if necessary, the rights and liberties of the individual

---

[275] Ibid., 4.

[276] *Arriba*, no. 2, March 28th, 1935, 2.

personality against abuses of authority by economic and social collectivities.[277]

The page dedicated to trade unions was under the responsibility of Manuel Mateo, the head of C.O.N.S. Curiously enough, it is in this section of the weekly *Arriba* that Fascism becomes most apparent. Beginning on July 4th, a series of articles began to be published under the generic series title "El régimen corporativo en Europa" ["The Corporatist Regime in Europe"], starting with Hitlerian corporatism, in which it is stated:

> The National Socialists believe that the interest of the community should take precedence over the interests of any particular group or class in the state. It is not the principle of capitalist profit that must be pursued, but the principle of public necessity. In the National Socialist state, there is unity of interest, as there is unity of authority.
>
> The incoherent economy of liberalism must be replaced by a corporative economy based on the sole and spontaneous cooperation of all classes. Each company will be incorporated into its specific industrial branch. Each corporation, by finding itself, will ensure, within the limits of its concerns, the execution of the economic plan established by the high economic authorities of the Reich, the correct application of which must be overseen by the state.
>
> The principle of irresponsibility of the social-democratic system will be replaced by the principle of personal and permanent responsibility of the leader, regardless of his position in the economic hierarchy . . . . Since Hitler's accession to the chancellorship, the National Socialist movement has been striving to establish the corporative state . . . . In Düsseldorf, the National Socialist Institute for Corporative Studies was founded, and in Berlin a work community was established for the formation of corporativism.[278]

The article mentioned the fundamental texts of German corporativism, the Law on the Organization of National Labor (January 20th, 1934)—the Labor Charter— and the ordinances and regulations that detailed it, also praising the two achievements reached by the German labor movement, the Labor Front and Strength Through Joy.

The article was very straightforward. The article would not continue until November 14th due to the interruption caused by the repression against freedom of

---

[277] Ibid.

[278] *Arriba*, no. 16, July 4th, 1935, 3.

expression suffered by the weekly from July 4th to October 31st. In it was discussed the application of the German corporative system undertaken in agriculture and in industry by Minister W. Darré, with excellent results: "The German economy thus presents itself as a guided economy in which initiative is subject to a form of organization that prioritizes the common good, which can only be ensured through an economic policy inspired by a new plan."

The issue of December 12th contained an analysis of "El movimiento obrero inglés y la idea corporativa" ["The English Labor Movement and the Corporatist Idea, which was continued in the following two issues. Similarly, the Falangist weekly's twenty-eighth issue focused on the American trade union system.

Giménez Caballero published his articles in *Arriba* with the same political tone that he had previously employed in *F.E.*; thus, in the fifth issue, dated April 18th, 1935, he wrote in the article "El miedo al Estado" ["Fear of the State"], with the approval of the de facto director of *Arriba*, the following:

> Mussolini is a "man of providence" sent by the God of Rome to serve Him and to bring forth the triumph of His greatest glory in the world. The state is only pantheistic when it is embodied by a Caesar who denies God's sovereignty.
>
> But talking about the "Fascist state" in Spain is even less dangerous for the Church than in Mussolini's Italy.
>
> Here, the Catholic can only be—in accordance with the historical trajectory—a Fascist. And the Fascist can only be—in accordance with the national spirit—Catholic.
>
> Isabella and Ferdinand, the inventors of the yoke of arrows, our "Fascist" unitarian kings, those who structured the first modern state of Europe, the true and full Fascist state of the fifteenth century, went down in history with the title of "Catholics."
>
> Fascism in Spain, as in Italy, is simply the updating in "new ways," in "updated modalities," of the eternal harmonizing, universal, integrating genius of Rome. Of Roman Catholicity. That is, of freedom and authority.[279]

On Monday, April 15th, 1935, the Falange secretary general, Raimundo Fernández Cuesta, gave a lecture at the branch located in Cuesta de Santo Domingo, speaking about "Economía, Trabajo y Lucha de clases" ["Economy, Labor, and Class Struggle"]. The magisterial lesson was featured in *Arriba* in the April 25th issue; in it, he criticized economic liberalism, socialism, and capitalism, pointing out:

After having discarded the previous solutions, we are left with the

---

[279] *Arriba*, no. 5, April 18th, 1935, 6.

corporative one. And, on this point, a clarification is necessary. The corporative state has not been established even in Italy. What they call a corporation in this country is really nothing more than an immense joint jury or joint committee. On one side, the Workers' Confederation; on the other side, the employers; and, at the top of the structure, the corporation. This means that today, in Italy, the premise is that capital and labor are inherently opposed terms that must be reconciled for the sake of production. In fact, what should be done is to unite the two in a supreme synthesis. This entails forming a unitary and superior concept made up of capital and labor, equally employing both as necessary components of the economic process. When this synthesis is completed, it will be possible to claim that the corporation exists.

Emilio Alvargonzález, card number sixteen of the *iniciadores*, was among the first to support José Antonio's political project as early as the start of 1933, during the days of the MES. He was a soldier and a member of Primo de Rivera's Patriotic Union. Having been affected by the Azaña Law, he remained loyal to José Antonio's cause. His loyalty was rewarded on October 29th by José Antonio, who appointed him chief of provinces, responsible for handling the correspondence and overseeing the provincial groups that were forming. He received his blood baptism at the March 4th rally in Valladolid, at the exit of the Teatro Calderón, where, while leaving the unification meeting, he was wounded in one leg by a bullet shot by socialist mobs and treated by a doctor at the Francia Hotel, where he was staying. On that occasion, José Antonio, who had an almost filial affection for him, wrote in *F.E.* a short article titled "Emilio Alvargonzález," which was published in capital letters and included the following affectionate words:

Chief of Provinces; a peaceful and special position, which he fulfills admirably.

And yet, in the Valladolid fray, he was wounded by a bullet. Emilio Alvargonzález knows that in our movement there are no sedentary positions; that is why when the Falange goes out in the provinces, he goes to the provinces with the Falange at his side, courageous as a squadron commander.

In Valladolid, they shot him in the right leg. His wound was light, fortunately. However, Emilio Alvargonzález made it seem lighter by bearing it with the smiling indifference of a good soldier, setting an example for everyone.[280]

---

[280] *F.E.*, no. 9, March 8th, 1934, 6.

He was one of the most constant and prolific writers for *Arriba*. A convinced Fascist, a militant, well acquainted with the Jewish question and its severity. In one of his many contributions, on May 9th, he wrote an article in line with his most sincere wishes and thoughts, "Para salvar a España hay que hacer milicias juveniles" ["To save Spain we must form youth militias"], in which, among other matters, he suggested:

> The tactic used to prolong and exacerbate the Great War was to incite national hatred. Its objective was to eliminate from the minds of men the most fundamental concept of humanity.
>
> Italy and Germany were two of the most notable victims. But two MEN, Mussolini and Hitler, emerged as saviors. They were prime examples of great patriots; they understood their own duty and had a clear vision of the current situation. It was essential to reinvigorate the dying spirit and have a healthy nationalist sentiment reverberate again in all its intensity. And the sure path to achieve it was to transform the spirits, so they turned to the youth, formed movements, and established civic education schools, instilling in them a strict discipline and a strong patriotic feeling. There, they were taught that work, life, and everything else had to be offered to the fatherland with determination and national joy. And in this way, the Fascists and the National Socialists not only saved Italy and Germany from a guaranteed collapse, but also elevated them to the level of global prominence that they have today.[281]

The article concludes with the following slogan in capital letters: "Spanish militias must be formed to save Spain."

In the weekly *Arriba*, due to political circumstances and to avoid government repression—always on the lookout for the contents of the weekly—Mussolini's speeches were not reproduced in their entirety, as was the customary practice of its predecessor *F.E.* This did not prevent the occasional publication of "Palabras de Mussolini" ["Words of Mussolini"], which were highlighted in the newspaper with large print letters. For instance, on the closing page of the eighth issue, we can find the following information:

> On the occasion of the Italian National Labor Day, Mussolini delivered a magnificent speech in Rome, from which we highlight these excerpts. "Distinctions are still being made between manual and intellectual labor. This distinction is purely theoretical. The day will come when the so-called intellectual workers will feel compelled to use their hands in order to touch the matter that they need to master and that provides wealth and strength. Certainly, there are still a sorry handful of intellectual circles left, who live detached from the life of the nation. However, these intellectual circles are as

---

[281] *Arriba*, no. 8, May 9th, 1935, 4.

insignificant as mud under the boots of a marching giant, and that giant is the Italian people."

"I know that a life of comfort does not await us, because very hard times are approaching that will demand the use of all the physical and moral forces of the Italian people, so that Italy may reach those ends that we have been envisioning very clearly for a long time."

In order to reach a greater affinity and comprehension with the new Germany, *Arriba* would take advantage of any event to highlight the brotherhood between both peoples, such as the case of the article published under the title "La celebración del Tricentenario de Lope de Vega en Alemania" ["The Celebration of Lope de Vega's Tricentennial in Germany"], which begins:

Together with Spain, Germany also commemorates the tricentennial of the death of the great poet of universal glory . . . . There is no doubt that the German and Spanish peoples will grow closer as the distinguished poet's works are diffused throughout Germany.[282]

Germany is even referred to, in the headlines of the weekly, as "the watchtower and sentinel of Europe": "The new National Socialist Germany is realist and visionary, like any strong population with a firm ideal."[283] In 1935, the persecution against National Syndicalism grew. In 1933, three had fallen. During 1934, the death toll reached eleven. The year 1935 did not seem to hold any better prospects and, by May, three more had been assassinated by the bullets of hatred. These continuous deaths led José Antonio to write an article in the ninth issue of *Arriba*, which came out on Thursday, May 16th, entitled "El frente rojo" ["The Red Front"], which appeared in one of the first compilations of José Antonio's writings during the war —*Bajo el tiempo difícil* [*Through Difficult Times*] (1938)—an article that would later be removed from his complete works. In it, we read:

Our own were the soul and life of Spain. Their blue shirts were a clear reflection of their disciplined, pure, and heroic days. Their cries of "Arriba España" contrasted with the wicked little screams of the homosexuals who assassinated them. And the fact is that in the ranks of the anti-Spanish bloc, there is all that is vulgar, all that is repugnant, and all that is degenerate . . . . A day will come when all Spaniards will embrace each other with sincere emotion, a day from which no more of ours will fall, there will be no more struggles, and there will be no more parties. On that

---

[282] *Arriba*, no. 13, June 13th, 135, 2.

[283] *Arriba*, no. 18, November 7th, 1935, 2.

day, you will see, comrades, how all those you now consider enemies will raise their arms in a sign of love, an expression of empire, and you will also see how the red front and the revolutionary poet, the cocky communist, and the socialist banker will return once again to their former vices, rottenness, and degeneration.

José Antonio was already envisioning Fascism's triumph in unity and order, love and camaraderie, harmony and social justice.

Arriba and the Jewish Question

The Jewish question was openly addressed by qualified writers in *Arriba*. It was José Antonio who, as a matter of fact, directed the weekly and granted the *nihil obstat* to provide guidelines and to take positions on such a critical and complex issue.

The first issue featured in the center of the fifth page a note with the emblem of the movement enclosed in a frame, calling for "Urgent Action":

> While the large banking institutions close their fiscal years with growing profits, the small industry and the modest salesman suffer for a lack of funds. The monster of big financial capitalism must be destroyed! The national economy cannot be left at the mercy of speculators and soulless individuals. It is urgent to get to the root and place credit at the service of national needs, rescuing it from the internationalist oligarchies.[284]

Commander Emilio Alvargonzález, a man of unwavering loyalty to José Antonio, signed an article in the second issue of *Arriba* entitled "¿La carrera de los armamentos o la carrera del negocio de los armamentos?" [The Arms Race or the Arms Business Race?], where he wrote:

> There is no doubt that big capitalism, which seeks to dominate the world, is involved in almost every global manufacturing industry for war equipment.
>
> All good patriots, whether German, English, French, or Italian, want peace for their countries. But those who have no fatherland, the capitalist hoarders, are not concerned with these ambitions. In a few years, they will require another war, and they will have it, consuming ships, planes, tanks, ambulances, cannons, guns, rifles, and men who will lose their lives in

---

[284] *Arriba*, no. 1, March 25th, 1935, 5.

order for them to earn their money.[285]
On the same page, Felipe Ximénez de Sandoval wrote in a paragraph about possible European alliances:

> It would not be worth the trouble of rebuilding Rome, its essence, and its high ideal of civilization only to form an alliance with Tartar barbarism and the Judaic spirit. Rome would forsake itself. It would deny the Empire's Catholic and universal nature.
>
> Because of the sense of Western Empire that characterizes their political stance, it is natural—if a war is to be logically expected—to see Italy alongside Germany.

On page four, another stab in the same direction is contained in an article on the economic crisis, in which the "abolition of big finance capitalism" is advocated, asserting: "If contemporary society wishes to preserve private property, it must employ all possible means to achieve the abolition of its greatest enemy, big finance capitalism, typically anonymous and irresponsible."

In the third issue, on the fifth page, dedicated to "National Syndicalism," it is written:

> The power of international capitalism grows stronger every day in the Spanish economy. Fleeing from the super-industrialized countries bankrupted by the crisis, it tries to invade our country, subjecting it to its political-economic tyranny. Because we are dealing with a full-fledged offensive rather than a single incident, it is critical that we sound the alarm to prevent these monsters' predatory intentions from being realized. It is in the interest of everyone to mobilize as many people as possible. It is not only the tradesmen and industrialists, but mainly the workers, who will suffer if these monsters succeed . . . . Thus, there is a necessity to organize the struggle with a broad and popular front, which includes all those who produce.
>
> We will persevere as tenaciously as the Jews, who exploit these stores. They are stepping up their campaign against small industrialists and traders. They are counting on substantial political support for this. It is possible that they will get away with it. It is possible that they will expand their business to all corners of Spain, and the blow to the struggling economy of industrialists and merchants will be decisive. They rely on an abundance of resources to accomplish this: Money, a lot of money, an international organization, and well-proven methods of squeezing the juice out of unsuspecting and happy countries. And, above all, they rely on popular politicians to help them enforce their social legislation or

---

[285] *Arriba*, no. 2, March 28th, 1935, 2.

write their own regulations on a daily basis . . . . Only a small number of people may be unaware of the fact that Nestlé products are controlled by a multinational corporation.

In the fourth issue, a report was included of the meeting of Falange Española de las JONS, held in Jaén, on Sunday, April 7th, 1935, with Francisco Rodríguez Acosta, Manuel Valdés, Manuel Mateo, Raimundo Fernández-Cuesta, and José Antonio as speakers. His intervention was highlighted in the summary of the speeches:

> "Fight the great international and Jewish capitalism that is invading our fatherland at the expense of industry and commerce." He then uses the example of a list of companies that exist in Spain which have enslaved the national economy to foreign capital.
>
> "It is not true," he adds, "as is often claimed with a certain air of lightness, that all revolutionary movements fail; they fail when, as it has happened in Greece, they lack popular roots; but, on the other hand, there are the examples of Italy and Germany, with their triumphant revolutions. Therefore, what must be opposed to the bloody and fruitless revolution is not the counter-revolution but another national and constructive one; for this purpose, it is necessary that the youth of Spain stand up to build a great fatherland that unites all Spaniards in a common syndicalist and national destiny."[286]

In the fifth issue, the article by Alvaro Cruzat entitled "Mando Único" ["Unified Command"] concluded with the following paragraphs:

> We admire the patriotic German movement and have learned lessons from it for Spain . . . . The international Judeo-Masonic order, which created the two great evils that have befallen humanity, capitalism and Marxism, is on its way to its demise. The monster has grown so much that even in its agony, it will bring us hardship. But we must not forget that when social democracy ruled in Germany, its people suffered, and that today, with a unified command, it has succeeded in uniting everyone to achieve victory.

Ernesto Giménez Caballero, in that same issue, wrote an article that appeared on the last page, entitled "El miedo al Estado" ["Fear of the State"], in which he addressed the Jewish question in the following terms:

> According to the liberaloids, the state should only be concerned with what

---

[286] *Arriba*, no. 4, April 11th, 1935, 3.

represents our society's life and sustenance: The famous economy—which, when put like that, seems to be something of importance. But when this is stated by the little newspapers of the liberaloids, it means "the sustenance of certain companies—the railroads—and of certain Jewish bankers." In other words, "The sustenance of their (Anonymous) Society . . . . What disgusts us is the endless farce of those who continue to sustain themselves—like Jews and crows do—upon the unburied corpses of popular fighters.

In the sixth issue, the editorial article discussed the "Esquema de una política de aldea" ["Outline of a Rural Policy"], explaining how "the countryside is a victim of the city's and the banking system's gamblers." It also included the complete text of the conference "Economy, Work, Class Struggle," held on April 15th at the local premises of the Falange by the Secretary General Raimundo Fernandez-Cuesta, in which he stated:

We are enemies of big financial capitalism, which should not be confused with private property, which consists of a direct relationship between a man and a thing; it is an extension of the human personality. Financial capitalism is the opposite: anonymous, anti-human, selfish, and calculating. It is the capitalism of stock market speculation, usurious loans, bank runs, and large boards of directors. The one that has made money the world's pivot and capital the primary concern of the economy, believing that the latter exists solely to generate profits, yields, and interests at the cost of whatever abuses are necessary. It is the actual hangman of the laborer, as well as the small-scale farmer, business owner, or industrialist. That is, it is the executioner of all those who, rather than using capital as a tool of dominance, use it to the benefit of labor and production.

The Jewish question is dealt with most directly in an article by Emilio Alvargonzález in the seventh issue, dated May 2nd, with the title "Ante un posible futuro" ["Before a Possible Future"], which, because of its importance, will be reproduced below:

Slavery used to be employed for labor. Today, slaves are used for war. With the old slavery the masters grew their wealth. Modern capitalism aims to have a wider range of action and faster development.

Judaic capitalism made every possible profit from the Great War, but in order to prepare for the future, it devised a Machiavellian strategy. It conceived the idea that, just as a mineral deposit is exploited, a country can be exploited in order to extract a certain amount of production. And so it did, and the chosen country was Russia, and the Russians were the human mine from which a new commodity was to be extracted: the slave-soldier. The Russians were subjected to the greatest misery and the most refined barbarism, then presented to them as a prospect for a better life, to become soldiers, and thus many of them were enlisted under an unprecedented degree of military rigidity. The unyielding whip was in command, and the Russians became what was planned: slave-warriors, led by equally brutalized and degraded people, guided by cruelty as their only principle. Acts of vandalism were and continue to be their finest accomplishments. Russia now appears on the international stage with several million of these slaves.

The truth is that the preparation of this business must have been very expensive, but the perpetrators had already calculated their potential profits. The capitalism that made Russia such an inhuman mine and that implanted there its mechanism for producing and exploiting man in such a peculiar form has seen, from the first moment, how the nations have increased the production of materials for war, of which they are the main interventionists. In the face of the unrest in which they have enveloped the lives of the majority of countries, they have devalued and continue to devalue the sources of wealth of which they took and are taking possession in magnificent economic conditions, and they know that by extending their financial domains, they are extending their tentacles, and by making the world economy and politics subservient to them, they will have succeeded with their soldier-slaves in making mankind the slaves of their ambitions.

Nations dialogue and decide. Some of them expel the Jews. Others outlaw Freemasonry. In Spain, about twenty thousand of the exiled Jews have recently returned and have settled, preferably, on the Catalan coasts and in other Mediterranean towns. Masonic lodges have sprouted up as if by magic, and the villages of the Moroccan coast and some of the Levant have been chosen as strategic points.

It is necessary to consider the possible future, with Jews entering, Masons emerging, and separatists gaining a foothold, all keeping an eye on the quiet Mediterranean . . . . The Catalan Statute is being reconsidered.

Spain, be alert. Spanish Lion, get your claws ready if you don't want them to put your neck in the noose.

The seventh issue contained on its last page, prominently placed and written in capital letters, as if it were a warning message, an article titled "Financial Invasion":

The financial monster is sinking its claws into the national economy. Every day, S.E.P.U., the big Jewish company, exploits employees and drives small businesses further into ruin. Nestlé, with its international capital, is poised to monopolize the milk industry, bringing more than ten thousand peasants to their knees. The Catalan textile industry has also been targeted by international banks. And all of this is being perpetrated with the support of the political parties, which act as lawyers for these corporations.

We know their names and surnames, and we will shout them out in every corner of Spain to unmask them. The destruction of the national economy and the corruption of Spain by international capitalism are only possible because of the collaboration of the political parties. It is time to destroy the parties!

The topic of the Jewish financial invasion was also covered by other media outlets of the Falange. For example, in its fourth issue, published on March 31st, 1935, *Patria*, an irregularly published publication edited in Granada, stated that "the ruin of the economy in Madrid is imminent" if the closure of "the warehouses of the Jewish capitalism of S.E.P.U." would not take place, and that "small and even big Spanish capital cannot compete with those big Jewish trusts that have all of world commerce in their hands."

In the eighth issue of *Arriba*—May 9th, on page 3—there is a list of "Nuestra constante preocupación" ["Our Constant Concerns"], which was summarized in "Los manejos del capitalismo internacional" ["The Schemes of International Capitalism"]:

The financial invasion. S.E.P.U. Nestlé. Unemployment. The hunger of millions of Spaniards. The agony of the peasants. The tyranny. The usurers. The corrupt political parties. The right. The left. The ruckuses of the socialists. All the internationals.

In the ninth issue—May 16th, on page 4—a new article by Emilio Alvargonzález was published with an eloquent and clear headline: "El mundo comienza a desenmascarar al enemigo común" ["The World Begins to Expose the Common Enemy"], which we reproduce here in its entirety for its exceptional documentary value:

In Nuremberg, the universal anti-Jewish league held an event that was of great importance and will be of great significance if the citizens of all nations open their eyes to reality by understanding what took shape there.

Mr. Streicher, a German, pointed out and declared that the Jew is the world's enemy, with no homeland and gold as his only god.

Jean Boissel, a French writer who was maimed in war, stated: "I have come before you as a Frenchman, as a former combatant, and as a crippled man of war to reveal both our and your enemy: Judas. We fought on the battlefields for four and a half years, and in the end, we were all deceived because this war was not fought for a noble purpose, and it will conclude with a tremendous defeat for the entire world."

Here, the French patriot is a little naive, because the defeat of the world did not end with the conclusion of the war; rather, it continued, allowing the Jew without a nation to continue amassing gold and gaining as much power as they could at the expense of the collapse of trade, industry, and other nations' sources of wealth, even if this meant that the majority of the population would suffer hunger.

However, this calculating capitalism, full of deception and astuteness, would not be as powerful and imperious if it did not work with its unpatriotic henchmen: Freemasons, socialists, and communists—a collaboration that is truly effective in achieving its goals.

Reality teaches us that the Masonic element, which has infiltrated the justice system, politics, public administration, and the army, is a slave to his international obligations and subordinates his country's duty to orders he receives. Could there be a scandalous affair? Politicians, magistrates, and judges with Masonic ties are distorting the facts in order to avoid punishment for the true perpetrators. Is there a need to demolish sources of wealth: industry, commerce, railroads, sea transport? Thus, the Freemasons proceed to impose laws that prevent them from developing and that subject them to an overwhelming and deadly competition. The socialists then lead the workers into convenient struggles to prevent the productive capital from surviving and to make them more easily manageable due to their forced unemployment. Should this plan fail to materialize fully, the communists, with their terrorist attacks, would finalize such a Machiavellian plan.

In order to oppose this plan, we must attack all of its elements, and since the most fundamental ones in this Jewish plan are, as reality shows us, Freemasonry, socialism, and communism, the nations will have to extirpate them without any regard, and the Jewish capitalists and the like will have to face the fact that if their god is gold, our God has created man to live happily and not to increase his wealth with his blood, his life, and his wounds.

A large number of Jews have settled in Spain. Freemasons can be found in all of the state's fundamental institutions, including political magistracy, public administration, and the army. There are many socialist and communist parasites. The situation is alarming. We Spaniards must confront it with firmness and vigor, expelling Jews and Freemasons and neutralizing the others radically, even driving them out of national territory if necessary.

Ah! Then, may the Jews subsidize them.

In the twelfth issue of *Arriba*—June 6th, on page 5—once again, there is emphasis on a recurring theme: "¡Siempre S.E.P.U.!" ["It Is Always the S.E.P.U.!"], an article in which one can read:

These Jews of the S.E.P.U. are giving us reason to deal with them on a daily basis because of what they are doing with the employees they exploit.

If their mere existence was not enough to enrage anyone, the outrages they subject their employees to would make even the most composed person revolt. It is not enough for them to compete unfairly with small businesses or to perpetrate a thousand abuses through their exploitation methods; their cold greed and eagerness to monopolize profits drive them to dish out unspeakable treatment.

According to our reports, when auditing the cash register, some amount is always mysteriously missing. What a coincidence, huh? They are missing some money, but you should not expect them to sue the cashier, not really. Adopting a quicker procedure, they take the law into their own hands, thus freeing themselves from dangerous inspections, and they summon the women and oblige them to sign salary advances equal to the differences that they have "found out." And if they don't sign, off they go.

We ask: Does S.E.P.U. have a free pass? Who is protecting S.E.P.U.? Do courts not hear cases involving S.E.P.U.? Is the representative of labor aware of S.E.P.U.'s practices?.

In the fifteenth issue—June 27th, on page 3—*Arriba* published a "Manifiesto de la Central Obrera Nacionalsindicalista" ["Manifesto of the National Syndicalist Workers Union"] addressed "to all the workers," following the brilliant success of the rally at the Cinema Madrid, which resulted in a widespread hate campaign by the press against the Falangist movement. Therefore, the manifesto states:

But what is the reason behind such a hostile attitude from the general press? To put it simply, almost all newspapers, both left-wing and right-wing, survive and thrive due to financial support from banks and large companies. It is a huge lie to claim that they are independent organs of opinion. They use whatever rhetoric suits them best to deceive the workers, but they always do so in the interests of the big businessmen who pay them.

Thus, *Ahora* may profess to be democratic or not, but above all, it is a defender of the big capitalist Montiel; *Diario de Madrid* is under the protection of the Jewish banks; *El Sol* is subsidized by the Catalan plutocracy; *Heraldo* and *El Liberal* are at the service of the big business of the Busquets brothers; thus, the right-wing newspapers turn their backs on popular anguish. All the newspapers, those of the right and those of the left, ostracize us for no other reason than because of our anti-capitalist stance.

The right-wing newspapers cover and devote significant space to the activities of the left. Naturally, left-wing newspapers cover right-wing events in a similar manner. And both manifest their hostility toward our movement in the same way. We do not have a press. They undermine all of our efforts. This is the reaction of big finance capitalism to our resolute offensive against its privileges!

Workers!

Action over words.

We have no press because we are the enemies of big capitalism, which uses its newspapers to sow confusion.

The Central Obrera Nacionalsindicalista, supported by the masses of enthusiastic workers, will wage battle against the financial monster and will organize production by ridding it of parasites.

Worker! You will find your liberation by joining us in this struggle.

The subsequent issue of the weekly featured an editorial with a resounding title, "Falsedad" ["Falsehood"], and it made use of the following powerful rhetorical images:

> On one side we have that scoundrel Barabbas, who calls for the crucifixion of Spain and the division of his clothes, the bad thief and also the good thief, and the Longinus of the spear thrust, while, on the other side, we have the Pilates, who wash their hands in the governmental basins, the Pharisees, the braggarts of religiosity and patriotism within the boundaries of law, the money changers of the temple, the fools, and the innumerable liars. "Woe unto you, scribes and Pharisees, hypocrites!" Jesus said, "for ye compass sea and land to make one proselyte." The Pharisee pursues the numbers of proselytes; he wants to defend himself with the numbers, while the apostle and the prophet seek the quality of the souls because they know that ten righteous men can save the city.

A sinister and macabre illustration on the third page of the publication featured a skeleton that symbolized the Spanish worker, national trade, and small businesses. It sat atop the capitalist gallows, looking down from its Golgotha at the S.E.P.U. storefronts, which advertise themselves as "cheaper than anyone else," along with a big coin showing the price of ninety-five pesetas on it.

In 1936, in the twenty-ninth issue of *Arriba*, the Falange continued to commit itself to the "nationalization of credit against Jewish manipulations" as an alternative to financial capitalism.

15.

Haz: University Students Contribute to the Movement

On March 26th, 1935, five days after *Arriba* hit the streets, the first issue of a university magazine with a Fascist-sounding masthead appeared: *Haz*, whose lifespan lasted until the eve of the February 1936 elections—that is, nearly a year, during which fourteen issues were published. Alejandro Salazar was the soul of the youth university publication linked to the Falangist movement, with its registered office at the Falange headquarters at 3 Cuesta de Santo Domingo in Madrid, though, as David Jato tells us, the actual editorial office was located in the boarding house where Alejandro Salazar lived, taking charge of the newspaper's direction with great enthusiasm and commitment. Salazar's boarding house was, in fact, another Falangist center. A large red and black flag covered one of the walls of the room where he received his comrades.

The emblem of the SEU was based on another imperial insignia, the coat of arms of Cardinal Cisneros, the architect of the Complutense University of Alcalá, to which the yoke and the five arrows were added.

The editors of *Haz* were the students themselves, although a few alumni also collaborated by sending their own submissions to this youthful and revolutionary publication that sprung out of the classrooms and faculty lounges.

Despite its academic and cultural orientation, there was no lack of allusions and works on Fascism in the weekly, such as the articles written by Arturo Ormeti published, one on July 29th, 1935, with the title "La juventud fascista italiana"

["The Italian Fascist Youth"], or the one that appears in the issue corresponding to October 12th, Day of Hispanity and Race, by the same author on "El fascismo de Mussolini" ["Mussolini's Fascism"], praising the Duce and his Italian cultural and social effort.

Fascism received much attention in *Haz*, which even published a serial entitled "Diario de un escuadrista,"[287] by Fernando Bernabini, a Fascist intellectual and editor of the Italian magazine *Conquista*, from its tenth to its final, fourteenth issue. The text of the series was a translation of *Diario di uno squadrista qualunque*, which achieved notable success in Italy. An offprint of that Fascist literary work would also be published in the form of a small booklet.

Among the fundamental points of the syndicate was the aspiration for unified and obligatory unionization. Sport was a major theme in *Haz*, as well.

On three occasions, specifically in the sixth through the eighth issue—all of which appeared during the second half of July 1935—*Haz* had to compensate for the silence of its brotherly political weekly *Arriba*, which was suspended by government order. In that trilogy of extraordinary issues, the publication became the Falange's voice.

---

[287] [Translator: "Diary of a Squadrista," a member of an Italian Fascist squad.]

16.

Mussolini's Aid to José Antonio

From June 1935 onwards, Italian Fascism provided its Spanish counterpart with a subsidy. Fascism's inherent characteristics were resource scarcity and economic hardship, which were made worse in 1935 when Francisco Moreno Herrera, Marquis of Eliseda, one of the Falange's financial backers, openly left the movement in the pages of *ABC* and joined the National Bloc as a deputy. Galeazzo Ciano, a prominent member of the Italian Fascist regime and Mussolini's son-in-law, authorized, in agreement with the Duce, a monthly allowance in favor of José Antonio to be sent to the Italian embassy in Paris. The financial assistance validates the theory of political communicating vessels. The amount, which was generous in comparison to other aid sent to European Fascist movements, such as Bucard's Francism, helped to mitigate some shortcomings. The amount allocated to support the Falange's political activities was fifty thousand lire per month, which was equivalent to four thousand dollars at the time.

Note the accordance of dates between José Antonio's visit to Rome—May 1935, the reception of the Fascist aid—the order for payment to José Antonio was issued by Ciano on June 3rd, 1935, and the secret meeting of the Junta Suprema de Mando Falangista in the Parador Nacional de Gredos—June 16th, 1935—where José Antonio submitted to the consideration of his commanders the need to resort to armed insurrection. José Antonio acknowledged in his declarations in the trial begun by the special court of Alicante on November 10th, 1936, that he "did not hide the fact that he had been in Italy several times, the last one at the beginning of the summer of 1935."

Mussolini was aware of the monetary assistance provided to José Antonio. This act of solidarity among comrades was kept under strict confidentiality. Even within the Falange, the reception of aid was kept secret. It was also unreported to the Italian embassy in Madrid, which had Orazio Pedrazzi as its ambassador since autumn 1934. This forty-five-year-old lawyer and Nationalist journalist, who had served in the Fiume government from 1919 to 1920 and later was director of *Il Regno*, did not pursue a diplomatic career but was a man of Mussolini's trust and was aware of the monthly transfers of funds which Italian Fascism was contributing to the Falange's difficult and dangerous march. The task of delivering the money was extremely delicate. It would have represented an irrefutable argument for the antifascists and the other enemies of the movement led by José Antonio, who was personally responsible for withdrawing the funds in Paris. No precaution and discretion was enough.

The historian Max Gallo was the first to mention the existence of these transactions in his 1969 book, *Histoire de l'Espagne franquiste*. As with everything new, it was more a general historical piece of news than a thorough investigation of the subject. In his new book *Cinquiéme Colonne* [*Fifth Column*], he further elaborated on the subject.

In Spain in the 1970s, a heated debate erupted between negationists and those who claimed the payments were true. The documents were beginning to surface and evidence gave way to certainty.

It was an operation carried out with care and meticulousness. Amadeo Landini, a diplomat at the Italian embassy in Paris, was the person in charge of conducting the money transfer order. It was envisioned as a collaboration to spread Fascist propaganda abroad. Amadeo Landini, the Italian consul and press attaché in Paris, was a dynamic, active man who was deeply committed to Fascism. He maintained contact with journalists and intellectuals and worked tirelessly on information dissemination. Landini was in charge of delivering the subsidy ordered by the Italian Fascist regime to José Antonio. In the same letter-order of payment, another economic compensation was included in favor of Marcel Bucard, leader of the French Francists. The funds for both leaders, José Antonio and Bucard, were drawn from the budget of the Italian Ministry of Press and Propaganda.

Amadeo Landini received the following payment order via confidential mail on June 3rd, 1935:

Dear Landini,

I hereby notify you that on this date I have arranged for the following amounts to be charged to your current account:

Three thousand lire for the "journalistic services" for the month of June; ten thousand lire to be transferred to Mr. Marcello Bucard at the current exchange rate in local currency; fifty thousand lire to be handed over to Primo de Rivera.

Similar amounts will be paid in the following months, with the aforementioned amount due monthly. Furthermore, you must contact the aforementioned individuals so that they can establish contact with you in order to arrange for the withdrawal of the funds that have been assigned to them.

I respectfully request that you send me the corresponding receipts in due time, properly signed by the interested parties. I thank you and send you my best regards.

Ciano

Landini had to justify the expenditure to Prefect Celso Luciano, who presided over the cabinet of the Fascist Ministry of Press and Propaganda in Rome. The transfer orders and funds arrived at the Banque Française et Italienne pour L'Amerique du Sud, which is located in Paris at 12 Rue Halévy.

In June 1935, José Antonio received the first payment from the Fascist fund intended for the dissemination of the ideology outside of Italy. In a letter dated June 25th, Landini justified the money transfer to his superior by mentioning this possibility proposed by José Antonio: "Estella had also suggested that I make the successive deliveries through a Parisian bank of his confidence." It was eventually agreed to withdraw the sums in francs personally rather than through a financial institution.

The payments for July and August would be merged. On the eleventh of that month, it was reported that José Antonio had not received the money for the previous or current month, but he would actually end up collecting them both in August. There exists a letter dated August 21st, 1935, which reads:

I am sending you the receipts for July and August of the current year. I have instructed him [José Antonio] to write a report on the political situation in his country, which I will send you in the next parcel.

Three days later, on August 24th, Landini forwarded to Rome the political report prepared by José Antonio.

The secret and confidential report written by José Antonio for the Italian Fascist government at the request of Amadeo Landini was first published in Spain in the magazine *Actualidad Económica*, issue number 871, dated November 23rd, 1974. It was leaked by historian Ángel Viñas, who presented it on the front page without including a reference or signature as an "exceptional unpublished document" containing the analysis of the Spanish political forces in the summer of 1935. The report examines José Antonio's reputation and the Falange Española, which is referred to as "the only Fascist movement in Spain."

According to the journal that revealed the document to the Spanish public, the document focuses on the following points:

a) A distinctive emphasis on the decisive role of the army, on the importance of the infiltration into it, and on the pre-existing links between the Falange and certain sectors within it.

b) A reaffirmation of the socialist and radical currents' inevitable overflow onto the bourgeois left, as previously noted in June, as well as their electoral prospects.

c) A new observation on the historical role and political significance of Mr. Manuel Azaña.

d) The Falange's clear orientation toward a specific course of subversion, along with a reaffirmation of the intriguing theory of insurrection.[288]

In the report, the demeaning depiction of the Spanish monarchist forces stands out, and there is no mention—it is intentionally omitted—of Calvo Sotelo's National Bloc.

The document is held in the archives of the Italian Ministry of Press and Propaganda of Mussolini and today can be found microfilmed in the National Archives in Washington, D.C.[289] The original report is written in French—though with some grammatical errors—because it came from the Italian Embassy in France, via the intermediation of Amadeo Landini, passing through Galeazzo Ciano, who eventually delivered it to Benito Mussolini.

Landini's message to his superior on December 11th indicated the possibility of reducing the allowance to José Antonio and Bucard in order to cut expenses, pointing out the following arguments:

> We discussed the possibility of pulling the brakes. I will hint to Bucard and Primo about this so they can be prepared. Don't you believe it would be wise to warn Count Ciano, since such subsidies must have been decreed by him? Perhaps he has some special plans regarding the matter. In any case, please notify me within the month of December. Primo's subsidy, I believe, could be reduced by half.

This proposal was put forward by the public official Landini, who was unaware of the goal pursued by Count Ciano with this aid, which was supposed to be part of the general policy of propaganda and support for allied Fascist organizations in other countries.

On January 3rd, 1936, Luciano sent the following letter to Amadeo Landini:

---

[288] *Actualidad Económica*, no. 871, November 23rd, 1974, 71.

[289] Microfilm from series T-586, reel 417, consisting of five pages numbered sequentially by the allied microfilming services with frame numbers 008361 to 008365.

Dear Landini,

I am writing to inform you that yesterday I ordered the following amounts to be transferred to your current account: Four thousand lire for the transalpine to give to Mirko Giobbe;[290] three thousand lire for the journalistic services in January; ten thousand lire that you can deliver to Mr. Marcello Bucard in the corresponding local value; fifty thousand lire to be handed over to Primo de Rivera.

I kindly request that you send me in due time the receipts for the amounts received, properly signed by the individuals in question, and I send you my thanks and best regards.

Luciano[291]

If we consider the actions that Italy had to take during those months as a result of the sharp decline in the gold reserves of the Italian banking system, the adjustments proposed to regulate the payments become understandable and justified.

In the correspondence of January, a reduction was once again requested, and finally found an answer in Celso Luciano's letter of January 20th, in which he informed Landini that:

in relation to your letter of the 14th of this month, I wish to inform you that what you suggest to me regarding Messrs. Bucard and Primo de Rivera is correct, and consequently, starting from February 1st, the monthly payments assigned to them will be reduced by half.

The next day, Ciano issued new instructions to Police Chief Bocchini, reducing the amount to 25,000 lire per month as of February 1st.

On February 1st, Landini's letter to his superior, Luciano, stated:

I am forwarding to you Primo de Rivera's receipts for the months of November and December of last year. I have hinted to him about the reduction: since he is a gentleman, it seems to me that he has acknowledged it with a great deal of grace.[292]

---

[290] [Translator: An Italian journalist and foreign correspondent, mainly in France, for *Critica Fascista* and *La Nazione* from 1925 to 1940.]

[291] Microfilm from series T.586, reel 472 frame 042128. Available at the National Archives in Washington, D.C.

[292] February 1st, 1936, letter from Amadeo Landini to Celso Luciano. Central State Archive (Italy), Ministry of Popular Culture, b-171.

José Antonio was imprisoned on March 14th along with the other Falange officials following a government order. Because of this, he could no longer withdraw the funds that continued to accumulate in the embassy at the rate of 25,000 lire per month until he was released from prison, as can be read in the letters dated May 15th: "To Primo de Rivera: I am waiting for you to be released from prison. As a precaution, given the uncertain situation of the French franc, I considered converting the quota to British pounds: this would also dispel any suspicion." On July 17th, this followed: "As I have already reiterated more than once, regarding Primo de Rivera, I am waiting for him to get out of prison." Landini was instructed not to transfer the funds to any other Falangist representative since their delivery, according to the orders received, was destined solely and exclusively for Primo de Rivera.

On July 14th, while the Falange leadership was imprisoned and the rest were operating clandestinely, Landini wrote a letter to Luciano that read:

Dear Luciano,

As I have already informed you, Primo de Rivera's monthly funds are available to you. I refrained from sending them (as I told you) to one of his trustees for reasons of basic precaution; after all, we are always in time to pay. We have no further information. If possible—within my means—I will try to obtain British pounds in the event of a devaluation of the franc; however, restrictive measures prevent such currency exchange at the moment.

If you need to close the books, I can send you the receipts I signed (while I await further decisions from you), with the exception of the ones I am waiting for from Primo de Rivera, as soon as he puts them into circulation. In short, I'm looking forward to receiving your instructions and would be glad to be relieved of this hassle.

I believe that the subsidy should be suspended. The available funds are already quite substantial (though, as you know, they have been reduced by half compared to previous allocations), and their staggering size may make liquidation easier. Primo de Rivera is a gentleman and does understand.

Things in Spain are going from bad to worse; it will not be our modest help that will make Fascism triumph; if it does, it will unavoidably have to rely inevitably on us.

Landini[293]

---

[293] National Archives, Washington, D.C. T-586, Reel 416, frame 007667, and Reel 418, frames 008749 and 008667.

According to the records, José Antonio would personally receive the amounts from June to December 1935, including both. The total sum was 350,000 lire, or about 250,000 pesetas at the time. It was delivered to him in French francs, which amounted to approximately 530 francs per month. The entire amount received, based on 2002 exchange rates, would have come to approximately seven million pesetas, or 42,000 euros in round numbers. José Antonio used to travel to Paris every two months to collect the money, as we can infer from the correspondence that has been preserved. Due to the imprisonment of the Falange's leader, the amounts corresponding to January through August 1936, the last month in which funds were transferred to Paris in order to fulfill the commitment, remained uncollected. In November, in Rome, the payment orders would officially and definitively be halted. The uncollected sum, which, despite the 50% reduction applied at the start of February, amounted to a total of 250,000 lire, was returned to Italian Chief of Police Bocchini on November 16th, 1936.

On May 14th, 1936, from the Cárcel Modelo where he was jailed, José Antonio sent Amadeo Landini a personal letter written in French, a language he spoke perfectly, signing it with the pseudonym of "E. Andrés" for safety reasons. It is intended to be interpreted in the context of the particular circumstances. The document, which is preserved in the Central Archives of the Italian State, reads as follows:

Dear friend,

The illness I am suffering caused by the change in temperature, which we have suffered, has kept me sick for two months. I hope that you will see me free again in a month, but I cannot assure you of this.

It would be best if you could wait. However, if our arrangements do not allow for any delays, I could send you a person of complete trust. So, I look forward to hearing from you.

Despite the crisis, our situation here is improving more than ever.

I wish to express to you my most distinguished regards.

E. Andrés

The name "Primo de Rivera" can be read, written in parentheses, below the signature. Landini was unwilling to take any risks, particularly given the delicate political situation at the time and the brutal repression that the Falange was facing. He chose the first of the two options suggested by José Antonio, that of waiting for direct and personal delivery rather than through an intermediary, no matter how trustworthy he was.

The level of caution was raised when rumors of possible executions by firing squad were spread in July 1936, when José Antonio was transferred to the prison in Alicante, which would be his final destination.

17.

A Recommendation from José Antonio: La Riqueza en el Régimen Liberal, Comunista y Fascista [Wealth in the Liberal, Communist, and Fascist Regimes]

On June 24th, the fourteenth issue of *Arriba* was released. On the third page, in the lower right corner, one could find a suggestion:

> We recommend the E. Álvarez de Perán's new book *Wealth in the Liberal, Communist, and Fascist Regimes*, which scientifically defends the programmatic points of the Falange, as the only solution to current issues which are rooted in an unsustainable position associated with the incompatibility between liberal politics and the common good.

The manner in which Álvarez de Perán's work is promoted as being consistent with the programmatic tenets of the Falange is worth noting. It is not stated that the reading of this text is recommended for its general interest, but for its scientific and rigorous conformity to the essential postulates of Falange Española.

Álvarez de Perán was an economist who, prior to the publication of this book, had already written a volume on the stock exchange. He was an expert in economic science and a good analyst.

This was not the only time that such an ideological recommendation was published in *Arriba*. Half a year later, on February 13th, 1936, in the run-up to the elections, an identical advertisement was inserted with the same wording and placement, except that the author's address had changed from the one given seven months earlier in Barcelona to 14 Calle Ventura de la Vega, Madrid. The following issue, number 33, which was published after the February 16th elections and would be the final, farewell issue, featured yet another strong recommendation for this work on the bottom of the second page.

We are no longer in the early stages of the Falangist movement, but rather in the decisive moment, the battle for the freedom of the Falangist leadership. We find ourselves in February 1936, only a few days after the imprisonment of the Falange Board of Command, with José Antonio at the head, the period of persecution without mercy and of the brutal repression to which the Spanish movement of redemption was subjected. In those moments of agony, prior to the period of clandestine operation and on the verge of the armed insurrection, Álvarez de Perán's book was still being promoted by the official press organ, *Arriba*, to its readers, militants, and the general public as a book that provided a scientific—that is, exact and rigorous—defense of the program of the Falange from an economic and financial perspective. It was considered a mandatory and formative read, necessary to acquire an orthodox interpretation of the Falangist ideal.

The book is a compact 315-page volume that was published in Barcelona in 1935, edited by the author, and printed in the workshops of Horta S.A. It consists of an introductory chapter and three distinct sections. The first section, divided into twelve chapters, begins with an exposition and sharp critique of liberalism that leaves nothing to chance, both in terms of doctrine and political line. The second section of the book, organized into eleven chapters, examines communism, and, after presenting its theory, the author delivers a devastating and irrefutable critique. The third and final section of the text, which is composed of fourteen chapters, provides an exhaustive analysis of Fascism, a praise of its doctrine, and a laud of its political line, refuting any criticisms leveled at the economic and social solutions advocated by this ideology. This is the structure of the book that José Antonio heartily endorsed in *Arriba*.

The first statement that opens the section on Fascism eliminates any uncertainty on how the scientific defense of the Falangist program would begin: "Fascism is a spiritualist doctrine," because it establishes the spirit as the fundamental basis of its entire doctrine. In this section, we find the following:

> Fascism is the work of the will under the protection of the intelligence to achieve the common good; it is social improvement and individual improvement at the same time: it is Christian socialism. It could not be communism, which accepts historical materialism, or liberalism, which, although it does not dissent from the spirit, rejects it with its acts to satisfy the unjust ambitions of the capitalism that sustains and perpetuates it.

Fascism and liberalism are not on the same rational plane because an unmistakable boundary separates one doctrine from the other; the first subjects freedom to justice, whereas the latter offers such an excess of freedom that justice is left unguarded. And, since justice is the fruit of reason and reason is that of spirit, here lies the cause of the denaturalization of the spiritual function of liberalism . . . . The false formula that is used, entailing unrestricted freedom of action, is concentrated in a symbol; this symbol is money, and thus the absurd case can occur—and does occur—of one population being at the mercy of another, of international capitalism, which is the absolute owner of that miraculous formula. Fascism represents the path to emancipation from this perverse predominance, and to demonstrate the falsity of the formula, it tells the people: "Your life can only be sustained by the Fatherland, so let your heart be open to the Fatherland. Produce for yourself: work and live." In these words, the new doctrine is condensed, which is nothing more than the old traditional doctrine that comes to rescue society from the misery that currently pervades it all around.[294]

Emilio Castelar once said that the term "revolution" did not imply the disorderly movement of force but rather the logical and necessary transformation of ideas.

Álvarez de Perán defined the syllogism of replacement as follows: "The triumphant Marxism punishes capitalism at the cost of its own punishment; the triumphant Fascism punishes capitalism and redeems, at the same time, the people."

The book includes extensive excerpts from recent speeches given by the chancellor of the Reich, Adolf Hitler, as supporting proof of the claims being made. It also includes entire paragraphs from José Antonio Primo de Rivera's most important speeches.

According to the author, Fascism was "intensive production and equitable distribution," which is to say, "social harmony."[295] He illustrates Ramiro de Maeztu's thoughts on Fascism when he writes:

I believe that a fasces, a true patriotic union, or a temporary union of parties will be necessary to put an end to class struggle; what really pleases me in Fascism is the corporative spirit that is invoked in its program. I believe that the solution consists in restoring an authoritarian state, which will once again govern economic life according to the rules of justice.[296]

---

[294] E. Álvarez de Perán, *La Riqueza en el régimen liberal, comunista y fascista* (Barcelona, 1935), 198–199.

[295] Ibid., 208.

[296] Ibid., 217.

One of the most convincing statements about Fascism is that which lends itself to being the title of the fourth chapter in the third section of the book:

> To sustain the well-being of the nation, the Fascist state does not rest; it remains vigilant, organizing the production of ideas—spiritual material—and the production of labor—tangible material. From the production of ideas, duties and rights emerge, which harmoniously give impulse to wealth . . . . The Fascist state it is not built on new ideas; it is built on just ideas. The Truth is a spotlight—as broad as the world and as narrow as the atom—which channels ideas and can only contain those that are just, when they are righteous, exact, conforming. Scientific. Reason cannot reject science.
>
> If the determining values of the nation are driven by the idea, the Fascist state incorporates that national idea—from which the common good emanates—to put it into harmonious activity in order to achieve maximum benefit. The individual needs society, but society also needs individuality. The individuality of the nation is the state because a nation without a state would be a nation without a spirit. The spirit of the Fascist state embraces all of the values that define the nation in order to give them life and propel them into orderly activity.
>
> Thus, it is necessary to discipline the product of intelligence, the idea, to guide it uniformly toward the truth. A fragmentary, divergent idea cannot propagate the national spirit, nor can it favor social welfare. The Fascist state does not remain indifferent to the idea; it establishes norms and obligations based on the force of talent. The force of talent must be the force of social welfare. The cooperation of the idea leads to the cooperation of the matter.[297]

That is why out of the Fascist organization, of corporative character, a leader emerges who is capable of organizing and defending the life of the people:

> The leader, then, soul of the people, is exalted by the same people who already experience the fruits of the new situation—welfare, love—and in this way are born, automatically, the rules of justice, the new regulation of a gratifying social coexistence.[298]

According to the author, Fascism is not a normative doctrine; it is a realist doctrine because the power of the spirit over the idea generates the power of the idea over the action:

---

[297] Ibid., 222–223.

[298] Ibid., 227.

The essential characteristic of Fascism is the eradication of class struggle, which is accomplished through the forced, all-encompassing unionization of all tasks in order to harmonize among themselves all the productive forces with sufficient margin of individual freedom not to deprive life of its superior, rational qualities, not to constrain the wings of intelligence that set the course of progress.

Unionization requires order; order requires technique, and technique requires leadership. Hierarchy is unavoidable; unionization without hierarchy would be a seedless, fruitless tree doomed to die without meaning or succession. If institutions were to perish, life itself would perish. The worker who reaches the level of technician or manager climbs to higher ranks, and his technique, the fruit of his intelligence—talent driven by will —can be used freely (in this lies his freedom) for his own benefit, as long as this principle does not conflict with that of the social body from which, in the material aspect, he must necessarily come. Fascism raises its banner only against capitalism, which lurks in the shadow of the large enterprise and disproportionately monopolizes its profits, not against any other characteristic of the small businesses that acts as a regulator of the large enterprise.[299]

The author reaches the conclusion that the Fascist state brings into harmony with its authority the faculties of labor and intelligence so that they may occupy the hierarchical positions that rightfully belong to them.

One of the guiding principles of Fascism is the fair distribution of wealth, on which he reflects:

If the valuation estimate becomes inexact, the distribution will never be equitable or just. And when the valuation estimate reaches the possibility of unlimited expansion—the state's capacity of absorption, overcapitalization, and inflation with absorption capacity—it subjects the real wealth— production—to its arbitrary will, assigning to labor values that may seem apparently great but that are derisory or worthless in reality. This inexactitude is characteristic of capitalism, whose unrestricted action is safeguarded by the liberal regime. Action proceeds in the opposite direction under the communist regime: individual property is suppressed and the individual is valued according to his consumptive force, which is, if we understand correctly, even more precise than the value capitalism bestows upon him. This implies that the individual may be reduced to the extent of slavery, if not completely nullified. Between these two perfectly defined

---

[299] Ibid., 243.

positions—one without limitations of power and the other without any power—there is the position that occupies the intermediate—capital—zone of rightful valuation, the zone of Fascism.[300]

That is why a fair and social state:

> must rely on the Fascist doctrine in order to prevent the selfishness of capitalism from competing with the interests of the people when distributing wealth. That is the reason why Fascism arose in various nations; because the people, who constantly aspire to the good, seek, tirelessly, the formula destined to fulfill their righteous aspirations. . . [301]
>
> The Fascist regime considers banking an instrument of the state rather than an instrument of capitalism, with more influence on the distributive order of wealth than the liberal state itself. That is why the Fascist state's authority over banking institutions is as a regulator, ensuring that the national value as a means of exchange—distribution of wealth—and propellant of the vitality that nourishes and articulates the activities required by production is not degraded to a mere bastardly profit.[302]

He concludes that, in these circumstances of unrealizable reasoning and challenging solutions, if the Fascist doctrine represents social harmony, which is the fruit of justice under the protection of juridical equality, he can only support his thesis by openly and fearlessly adhering to this very doctrine.

Fascism is the doctrine for a civilizing action. It must be underlined that the work in question, which José Antonio and the Falange recommend for being "the orthodox interpretation of the Falangist ideal," only refers to Fascism in general without making any reference in its pages to the Falange in particular, neither as a movement nor as a doctrine; therefore, there is a comparison, in terms of equivalence, between Fascism—which is what Álvarez de Perán's work defends and justifies—and Falange Española, which sees in this writing the reliable representation of its own principles, endorsing its content that confirms and ratifies its condition of identity.

---

[300] Ibid., 254–255.

[301] Ibid., 265.

[302] Ibid., 285.

18.

José Antonio and the European Fascist Leaders

José Antonio did not keep himself sheltered within the boundaries of Spain. He quickly broadened his international horizons. Falange Española is a movement that was born in the era of Fascist movements, among its analogs, its contemporaries. In 1933, Adolf Hitler reached legitimately, democratically, the chancellery of the German Reich. National Socialism triumphed, giving a decisive boost to Fascist currents in both Europe and the New World. At the time of the rise of the Falange, Mussolini was celebrating the eleventh anniversary of the Fascist era, which began in October 1922 with the March on Rome. In every nation, the dream bore the name of Fascism; the revitalizing hope was seeping into the most intimate fibers of the peoples of the old continent. Spain was no exception to the general trend. History has its own cycles, its trends, its common denominators, progress, and ideological overcoming. The Spanish Nationalist and revolutionary impulse is related to its European counterparts and consanguineous movements. It was the Europe of camaraderie, of idealism, of traditional nationalisms, and of the righteous social revolution that wanted to put an end to both stateless Jewish Bolshevism and Jewish liberalism, which proved corrupt, outdated, and obsolete.

The two great European leaders, the two political entities of light, were the German Führer Adolf Hitler and the Duce of Italy, Benito Mussolini. José Antonio kept in personal contact with both of them.

Mussolini was already a friend of José Antonio's father, who paid him a formal visit, resulting in a long-lasting friendship. Through their eyes, their affection, their minds, their personal empathy, and their hearts, they understood each other.

José Antonio met Mussolini, the father of Fascism, several times. Their very first encounter occurred in November 1923, when General Primo de Rivera and his son José Antonio accompanied King Alfonso XIII on his official visit to Rome. The king, during that visit, said to his colleague Victor Manuel, referring to Don Miguel Primo de Rivera: "This is my Mussolini"; Mussolini, for his part, greeted Primo de Rivera as "the head of Spanish Fascism" and the general in return called the Duce his inspirer and teacher.[303] In an interview that the general granted to the Fascist newspaper *Impero*, he declared that "Spain will ultimately follow the footsteps of Italian Fascism . . . . Fascism is a universal phenomenon that shall conquer all nations . . . . Fascism is a living gospel." Several years later, José Antonio had a brief conversation with the Duce during an audience granted to a group consisting of his fellow students of law from the Complutense University of Madrid, who were visiting Rome in 1926, shortly after his father assumed the highest responsibilities of government in Spain. His biographer, Felipe Ximénez de Sandoval, describes their first meeting as follows: "Mussolini's genius has instilled into the turbulent Italian blood the Fascist 'way of being.' By accompanying the kings of Spain and the head of the government, José Antonio went to Rome, observed, and listened to the Duce and his people."[304] In 1929, he allegedly accompanied his father again on an official visit to Italy, where he had the opportunity to become more acquainted with Mussolini. However, the most significant meeting between José Antonio and Mussolini occurred on October 19th, 1933, ten days before the speech at the Comedia, which marked the birth of the new Spanish Fascist movement.

Pilar Primo de Rivera, José Antonio's sister, a few years later, in her role as national delegate of the Women's Section of the Falange in Spain, would visit Mussolini at Palazzo Venezia, accompanied by Carmen Werner, the writer Carmen de Icaza, and the poet Dionisio Ridruejo. In her visit to Italy she was accompanied by the Marquise Medici del Vascello, President of the Fascist women's section. Eugenio Montes, Director of the Casa de España in Rome at that time, a "Falangist since the beginning and an intellectual of the highest order," showed her the secrets of the eternal and imperial Rome that had been redeemed under the aegis of Fascism.

In 1935, Francisco Bravo spent a few days on vacation with José Antonio in San Sebastián. There, in a bar in Fuenterrabía, as they were gazing at the French land from a terrace overlooking the estuary,

José Antonio expressed his concerns to us regarding the outcome of the undertaking that Mussolini's Italy intended to carry out in Abyssinia.

---

[303] Payne, *Fascism in Spain*, 28.

[304] Ximénez de Sandoval, *José Antonio*, 54.

There was no doubt; the Duce's failure would have marked the downfall of Fascism in the West. And for us—Italy's only allies at the time of that undertaking—it was critical that Mussolini and his Caesarean genius emerge victorious, even if all the military experts in the world disagreed.

The conversation eventually led us to Caesar . . . . Then, José Antonio shared once more with us his captivating recollections of the visits he had paid to Mussolini. And again he would reaffirm his admiration for his figure of leader, man, and statesman with a praise we had heard on other occasions: "What magnetizes me most is his voice; a dominating, caressing, inexorable voice. An unparalleled voice, like that of no other man."[305]

José Antonio would return to Italy once more, at the invitation from the CAUR—the Committees of Action for the Universality of Rome—in May 1935. General Coselschi, the chairman of these Committees, would be his host. His meetings with Count Ciano are of particular relevance. Ciano, as we have already seen, played a key role in granting José Antonio financial assistance to fund the Falange's activities.

On April 30th, 1934, José Antonio was granted a personal appointment with Adolf Hitler. On the occasion of his visit, which was made possible by the official invitation of the National Socialist authorities, he also had an interview with the ideologist Alfred Rosenberg. He took advantage of his visit to observe and learn about the institutions that defined the new German Reich. During that journey, his host and companion was the loyal National Socialist Arnold von Engelbrechten, who was general secretary of the Deutscher Auslands-Club, a group related to the Third Reich's Ministry of Propaganda.

As for interactions with members of the National Socialist Party in Spain, we can mention the friendship that José Antonio held with Count Welczeck, German ambassador in Spain, with whom he shared many evenings, and who shared his passion for hunting, besides being the one who prepared the visit for him as official guest to his country in May 1934. Somewhat more discreet were his connections with Walter Zuchristian, head of the National Socialist Party and founder of the Madrid group in 1929; he also met the German *chargé d'affaires* in Spain, Hans Hermann Völckers, and the representative in Madrid of the Lufthansa company, Ludwig von Winterfeldt, who would be the person tasked with handling the logistics of José Antonio's visit to Germany.

---

[305] Francisco Bravo, *José Antonio, el hombre, el jefe, el camarada*, 105–106.

Rolão Preto, Leader of the
Portuguese National Syndicalist Movement

On November 26th, 1934, José Antonio received Rolão Preto, the Fascist leader of Portuguese National Syndicalism, in Madrid.

The ideological foundation of Portuguese National Syndicalism is based on Lusitanian Integralism, a current of thought and action that began in Louvain (Belgium) in 1913, centered on a monarchist magazine founded in exile as a spiritual and doctrinal response to Portugal's demagogic republic, which was established in 1910. The Lusitanian Integralists were a youthful group of intellectuals who possessed a realist, restless, bold, and original character, while also being deeply rooted in the old Lusitanian traditions. The director of the publication *Alma Portuguesa* was Domingos de Gusmao Araujo, but the most notable ideologue was the great philosopher, poet, and writer Antonio Sardinha. The secretary of the editorial staff of that magazine was the very young Francisco Rolão Preto, who, years later, at the height of his political maturity and intellectual vigor, founded in Portugal, in 1932, the most important and fierce Fascist movement of the Peninsular neighboring country: National Syndicalism.

The Integralist program, which was published in the first issue of the magazine *Naçao Portuguesa*, was inspired by Antonio Sardinha and preceded the more radicalized National Syndicalism, which was characterized by a greater and strict Fascist observance. The program manifestly and openly declared its anti-parliamentary, anti-liberal, decentralizing, municipalist, and corporative principles.

Rolão Preto collaborated actively with the Integralist nucleus, writing articles for *Naçao Portuguesa* and for the first newspaper of Integralism, which first appeared in 1917 and whose masthead was *A monarquía*, under the direction of Sardinha. Rolão Preto took over the direction of the newspaper in 1920, when its previous director, Hipólito Raposo, was imprisoned after being accused of thought crimes by the censorship.

Rolão Preto was born in a small town in Alentejo called Gaviao. His grandfather, Antonio Maria, was an academician from Coimbra who was hanged for defending freedom and justice. Rolão Preto enlisted in the troops of Henrique Paiva Couceiro in Galicia in 1912 while still in law school, which meant he had to experience the pain and bitterness of exile from his youth, leaving for the Belgian city of Louvain, where he graduated in social sciences in 1917. He went on to earn a law degree from the University of Toulouse. In Paris, he met Charles Maurras, who invited him to his office on Rue de Rome, where he also became acquainted with Léon Daudet.

He later joined the General Board of Lusitanian Integralism, alongside Sardinha, Rebelo, Raposo, and Monsaraz.

Rolão Preto took an active and committed role in the uprising of General Gomes da Costa on May 28th, 1926, writing the short manifesto composed of twelve lines that was placed on the walls of the Portuguese city of Braga, calling on the Portuguese people to take up arms "for the freedom and honor of the nation."

Following General Gomes da Costa's victory, Rolão Preto rose to the position of leading intellectual of the new political scene, in charge of establishing ideological guidelines through editorial articles in the official organ *Revolução Nacional*, where he also wrote prolifically, signing his articles with the pseudonyms "Plures" and "Pluribus." General Carmona y Salazar would assume command in place of Gomes da Costa.

On February 15th, Rolão Preto's new newspaper, *Revolução*, was launched. Thus began the march of the National Syndicalist movement, the purest exponent of Lusitanian Fascism, which "emerged from the anxieties and concerns of the new generations and in the face of the outdated liberal democracy."[306]

The Portuguese National Syndicalism of Rolão Preto called for a revolutionary mystique and promoted unity among the various forces of production. His purpose was to establish a "great spiritual movement, for it is a mistake, a tragic mistake, on the part of those who believe they can change the conditions of the world around us, without first creating a new spirit. Official bulletins and decrees alone are not enough to carry out a revolution."[307]

The movement's motto was: "It is necessary for the very rich to become less rich, so that the very poor can become less poor." *Ni contra las izquierdas, ni contra las derechas: ¡Adelante!* ["Not against the left, nor against the right: Forward!"]. Lusitanian National Syndicalism does not argue for any type of regime. The denomination adopted in 1932 by Rolão Preto justifies this, according to his own words:

> "National" does not mean to us "in opposition, exclusive," nor could that be in line with the principles of a truly Portuguese thought, which is, naturally, "universalist" and "humanist," being the heirs of the civilization of Rome . . . . It is syndicalist in that it regards the union as an economic and social unit. The union, freely organized and legitimately representative of the values of technical education, labor, and capital.[308]

The National Syndicalist party of the Portuguese Blueshirts was revolutionary, justicialist, municipalist, decentralizing, organic, and syndicalist, oriented toward corporatism. Its tenets were: a) family; b) tradition; c) municipality; d) trade union; e) corporation; f) nation. *Todo para el hombre* ["Anything for the man"] is the only

---

[306] José Placido Machado Barbosa, *Para alem da revolução . . . la revolução*. Interview with Rolão Preto (Oporto, 1940), 19.

[307] Ibid., 25.

[308] Ibid., 20–21

acceptable formula, the only one that the history of civilization justifies and which is the supreme essence of our personality, made in God's image.

Soon came several other publications, in addition to *Revoluçao*. In Algarve, south of Portugal, in the city of Faro, the newspaper *O Nacional-Sindicalista* was already being published before the end of 1932, and in Lisbon, from January 1933, the weekly newspaper *La Revoluçao dos trabalhadores* began to be distributed as a supplement to the official organ.

Portuguese National Syndicalism gained recognition in Spain thanks to the magazine *Acción Española*, directed by Ramiro de Maeztu, through the publication of a series of articles under the title "The Portuguese National Syndicalist Movement," written by Rolão Preto, which appeared between October 16th, 1933, and April 1st, 1934, in issues 39, 45, 46, 47, 49, and 50 of the magazine. In issue 45 of *Acción Española*, the published collaborative article featured the "12 Principios de la Producción" ["12 Principles of Production"], which define the fundamental rules of the Lusitanian Fascist movement. Preto's collaboration with the intellectual publication *Acción Española* led to a heated polemic with Onésimo Redondo, which was solved nobly and chivalrously after both ideologues clarified their misunderstandings on terminological details.

In April 1934, at the end of his series of doctrinal articles on his movement in the Spanish press, Rolão Preto concluded that:

> a revolutionary and nationalist era in Europe is before us. Revolution, like a bayonet, does not allow anyone to sit on top of it. Salazar must take revolutionary action in order to carry out his work. Only because of that he truly relies on us. The National Syndicalists are the organized and fiery militias of the workers' national revolution.[309]

Thousands of new supporters joined the newly formed party. A series of rallies would follow, such as the banquet that took place on February 18th, 1933, in Eduardo VII Park in Lisbon, which was attended by more than seven hundred fifty guests, many of them already wearing the blue shirt that was adopted as the party's uniform. As the leaders made their entrance, all of the attendees raised their arms in a Roman salute. On May 7th, 1933, another rally was held in Oporto's Palacio de Cristal, following a parade attended by over 6,200 people. On May 28th, a parade was held in Braga to commemorate the anniversary of the military uprising, with over three thousand participants.

On July 5th, Rolão Preto, acclaimed by the Fascist masses, was received in Portugal by General Carmona, President of the Republic, at his official residence in the Palace of Belém. On the 16th, he gave his final public speech at the San Carlos

---

[309] Rolão Preto, *Acción Española* (April 1st, 1934), 172.

Theater, where he spoke against "stale financial theories, absurd economic concepts, in the name of which man is a slave of plutocracy, usury, and the state," placing his trust in the family, union, and municipal frameworks, genuine areas of freedom, which are the archetypes of the nation and the things that truly protect man from the arbitrary will of tyrants.

The Portuguese government, which was more moderate and conservative, viewed with great suspicion the rapid rise of Fascism in the original line advocated by Rolão Preto. As a matter of fact, a covert persecution was already in the works. In June, the party newspaper published in Faro and the magazine from Lisbon were ultimately silenced, and after 418 published issues in which the essence of Portuguese Fascism was aligned with Italian Fascism and German National Socialism, it would be the turn of the main organ of the party. In Rolão Preto's view, Mussolini governed with the support and collaboration of the people, explaining: "The special temperament of a Mussolini, passionate, imaginative, and enlightened, is necessary to achieve the miracles of *souplesse* and variety that render the current Italian state a permanent focal point of polarization and renewal of enthusiasm."[310] The newspaper *Revoluçao* was forced to close on September 23rd, 1933.

With no press, its activities of public propaganda outlawed, and under a sort of monitored freedom, the last congress of the Portuguese National Syndicalists was held in November, during which the question of maintaining the *hard line* was debated, to keep the unequivocally Fascist and independent approach to the government undertaken and upheld by Rolão Preto, as opposed to the reorientation toward obedience and submission to the directives of the Salazarist government, by adopting a lighter, less revolutionary, patriotic tone free of any conflict, as proposed by the *dissident line.* Faced with a schism, the party was weakened by the collaboration of dissidents with the National Union, the ruling party of the Estado Novo.

When Rolão Preto refused to follow Salazar's call for moderation, his radical wing was judged disruptive and incompatible with the state and, as a result, he was sent into exile for the second time, this time to Spain, where he remained until February of the following year. Upon his return, he attempted to rebuild his previous militant organization by taking part in the attempted coup of the monarchist commander Mendez Norton on September 10th, 1935, which failed, forcing him to return to exile once more within our country.

Rolão Preto considered his Portuguese National Syndicalist Movement the predecessor of José Antonio's analogous movement, Falange Española, which he referred to as "our spiritual daughter."[311] Both were ideologically united by doctrine, symbols, signs, camaraderie, faith, and style, bundled into the same fasces. The blue

---

[310] Machado Barbosa, *Para alem da revoluçao*, 86.

[311] Ibid., 135.

color of the Portuguese shirt was quite similar to the blue of their fellow Falangists. When asked, "What is the attitude of the Portuguese National Syndicalists toward the Spanish National Syndicalists?" he answered:

> That of most warm sympathy and fervent hope for their revolutionary aspirations. If the Falange is successful in overcoming, as I hope, all the attacks of certain reactionary sectors, it shall carry out in its country the monumental task of the National Syndicalist revolution: the conciliation of freedom with authority, the conquest of bread and justice. We trust in the courage of our comrades, and we believe in the Falange, with high hopes for revolutionary accomplishments.[312]

Rolão Preto did not hesitate to recognize that "Mussolini and Italy currently hold a central position in the century we are living in . . . . Fascism harbors a stable and healthy climate of optimism at the service of order and, therefore, peace."[313]

Rolão Preto, according to his own testimony, closely worked with José Antonio in 1934, when, after the First Council of Falange Española de las JONS, its Political Board was commissioned to draft the *Norma Programática* of the Falange, which would encapsulate in the *Twenty-Seven Points* its ideology. There is photographic evidence of his visit at the office of José Antonio on November 26th, when he was already working on the final touches to the text of the draft for its conversion into a definite program, giving him suggestions and opinions on certain social aspects.[314] His assistance was greatly appreciated by the Falangist leader, who presented him with a dedicated photograph as a memento of their meeting and thanked him for his collaboration and sound advice during the final revision of the Falange's fundamental program. Rolão Preto and Primo de Rivera conversed amicably and at length:

> We had a long conversation. In a few hours, we put in a lot of work. Perhaps among so many friends who received his generous thought each day, few have, like me, felt so much the true projection of his beautiful soul.[315]

Rolão Preto recalled about José Antonio that he led his political battle as an apostolate and that:

---

[312] Ibid., 134.

[313] Rolão Preto, *Revoluçao Espanhola* (1938), 108 and 113.

[314] Ibid., 182.

[315] Machado Barbosa, *Para alem da revoluçao*, 35.

He loved ideas in the true sense of the word "love," that is, giving himself totally. He was more than a soldier; he was a faithful believer. He was a character. A nobleman. A Great of Spain.[316] . . . Restless, spiritual, and cultured, José Antonio could magnetize from the first contact through the charm that he emanated, through his personality, confidence, and faith, and through his higher intellectual concepts of the purest European and revolutionary lineage.[317] . . . His thought always appears as if permeated by a powerful mysticism, illuminated by the inner reflections of his admirable sensibility . . . . Never ever will the lean, virile, triumphant figure of José Antonio be erased from my memory.[318] . . . José Antonio understood and experienced the full breadth and variety of revolutionary thought, as few others did at the time. Thus, indeed, through his words, the profile of the revolution, hard but righteous, outlines and clearly etches itself in the mental retina of all men of good will.[319]

Rolão Preto translated into Portuguese and published the entire text of the *Twenty-Seven Points* of Falange Española, as well as several selected paragraphs from the most outstanding speeches of the national leader of the Falange, in his book *Revoluçao Espanhola*. In addition to his personal relationship with José Antonio, he also maintained contact with Sancho Dávila, Onésimo Redondo Ortega, Ernesto Giménez Caballero, and Julio Ruiz de Alda.

In 1939, he published a book titled *O Fascismo*. In the copy of this work that he offered to the Italian ambassador in Rome, he left the following handwritten dedication: "To His Excellency the Minister of Italy, with the greatest admiration for his country, and for the Duce, the author offers this work with the most vivid Portuguese and Fascist yearnings."[320] The book was a collection of articles he wrote about Italian Fascism in the newspaper *A Epoca*, prior to the March on Rome. In those articles, he was already anticipating and hoping for Mussolini's triumph, as well as that of the newly formed Fascism. In the introduction of the book, Preto wrote:

Mussolini succeeded in the miracle of giving Italy a new soul through him, while Hitler reforged the sword of Siegfried for the Third Reich; both broadened their empires and put an end to unemployment, misery, and crisis . . . . Every great historical shift begins with an act of faith, a deep

---

[316] Rolão Preto, *Revoluçao Espanhola*, 132.

[317] Ibid., 181.

[318] Ibid., 182.

[319] Ibid., 186.

[320] Private archive of the author.

breath of poetry. Imagination is the most productive and limitless source of dynamism . . . . This is not a characteristic of reality; it is not the conditioning of reality that pulls and leads men to decide they want to push forward, but their longings! And for that very reason, the Duce establishes the foundations of the empire, by sending heroic vibrations through history with the cry: *Rome!* [321]

José Antonio sought to establish relations with his Iberian brothers right from his earliest political days. At the end of 1933, he was interviewed by Portuguese journalist Oscar Pacheco, who was intrigued and thrilled to hear that General Primo de Rivera's son would be leading a Fascist movement in Spain. This encounter is narrated in great detail by Pacheco in an article published in the Lisbon newspaper *Diario da Manha*, on November 20th, 1943, the seventh anniversary of José Antonio's assassination. As a memento of their meeting, José Antonio offered him an autographed note.

Léon Degrelle, Leader of Belgian Rexism and Card Number 1 of the Falange Exterior

Léon Degrelle was the embodiment of eloquence and loyalty. A natural leader, he was born in Bouillon, Belgium, on June 15th, 1906, in the heart of the Ardennes, beneath the shadow of the fortress of the mythical warrior of the medieval Crusades, Godfrey of Bouillon. His family had deep Catholic roots. He earned his law degree from the University of Louvain. In his youth, he grew fascinated by Charles Maurras' doctrines. He spent several months in Mexico during the Cristero War.

Endowed with great dynamism and privileged intelligence, he rose to the position of young propagandist for Catholic Action's media outlets, where he was assigned various responsibilities.

In a few lines, we could describe Léon Degrelle's extraordinary personality as embodying the following traits and qualities: he was a man of deep and intense faith, a mystic and civil apostle among the people of the twentieth century; he was a poet imbued with inspiration and wit, author of a vast poetic work full of feeling, tenderness, a lover of art and beauty, integrity, and spirituality who, through stanzas and rhymes, sought the revolution of the burning souls devoted to the ideal; he was a heroic, charismatic leader, with a captivating aura, who gave himself to his people with generous and total dedication; as a warrior he challenged the standards of courage in the noble, brave, reckless fights on the Eastern Front, during the Second World War, beginning as a private and reaching the rank of general for his war

---

[321] Rolão Preto, *O Fascismo* (Guimaraes, 1939), VII.

merits, decorated for his deeds and his bravery in the face of risk; an orator and speaker of the most excellent breed; his words were warm, his rhetoric vibrant, his speech moving, his gesture revolutionary and poignant; a vivid and complete writer, rigorous and plastic, who could turn a real scene into fantasy and fantasy into reality; a Fascist of word and deed, of honor and fidelity, of good judgment and action, of style and thought, to whom Hitler said, "If I were to have a son, I would want him to be like you."

José Antonio recognized all of Léon Degrelle's exceptional human and political qualities. For this reason, in 1934, he awarded him, by personal and direct concession, honorarily but eloquently, given his status as a foreigner, card number one of the Falange Exterior. Degrelle wore on his chest, alongside the highest European decorations for merit, valor, and dignity—the Iron Cross, the Blood Order, the Cross of Burgundy, the War Merit Cross, the Wound Badge, the Infantry Assault Badge, the Close Combat Clasp, the Knight's Cross of the Iron Cross with Oak Leaves—the Old Guard Medal of the Falange.

Léon Degrelle proudly wore the medal of the star constellation, with its white chevron on the clip, decorated with the embroidered yoke and arrows, and on the golden back of the award, his concession number, 35,214. The date on the card issued to him by the Inspectorate of the Brotherhood of the Old Guard of the Falange demonstrated his seniority within the movement: 1934.

In his book of memoirs, *Hitler for a Thousand Years*, Degrelle insists on the unity and collaboration of the two national movements in the following terms: "The Phalange [sic], with a Catholic basis, was very close to Rexism, politically and spiritually. I myself had been named, in 1934, by José Antonio Primo de Rivera, the leader of the Phalange [sic] abroad."[322]

José Antonio and Degrelle shared significant similarities that made him deserving of such high recognition. Poetry, more than anything else, moved, inspired, and imbued them both. José Antonio stated this point clearly at his founding meeting on October 29th at the Comedia in Madrid:

> None but the poets have ever moved a people, and woe to those who know not how to counter the poetry of destruction with the poetry of promise! In a poetic movement we shall raise high that fervent concern about Spain.

Léon Degrelle was a poet in the most mystical and spiritual sense of the word. His written work is rich in verses, stanzas, rhymes, and inspiration. In 1946, while bedridden and recovering from his wounds in the military hospital General Mola in San Sebastian, he wrote *Je te bénis, ó belle mort*, a collection of poems inspired by the work of St. Teresa of Ávila. He leaves us with testimony of his poetic sense in the

---

322 Léon Degrelle, *Hitler for a Thousand Years* (Ostara Publications: 2019), 57.

foreword of the work when, struggling between life and death, he traces his thoughts in these brief, intense, and emotive words: "As I write these poems, death stands before me. She is the one who suggests I follow the pulse of the heart over anything else: in poetry, as in everything else, only love counts."[323]

In his delightful book *The Burning Souls*, a breviary of Fascist morals and conduct, which we owe to Dr. Marañón for translating into Spanish, even Léon's prose turns into poetry, poetic sentiment.[324]

However, José Antonio and Léon Degrelle were not only poets, minstrels of politics, troubadours, and heralds of the "good news"; they were also warriors, and this is how the Falange's leader wanted his comrades to be: "half monks, half soldiers." Léon achieved a service record unmatched by any other soldier in the Second World War, during the fighting on the Eastern Front, in the midst of intense combat.

Their similarities extended beyond their lyrical aptitudes and military prowess. They were also both leaders, heads of youth movements, Nationalists, revolutionaries, and Fascists. They were speakers and debaters; they fought with the word and with the pen, with both thought and action.

Léon and José Antonio shared a deep religious faith. The twenty-fifth point of the Falange's program states: "Our movement brings the Catholic sense—of glorious tradition and predominant in Spain—to national reconstruction." The name chosen by Léon Degrelle for his political movement, "Rex," was a word he borrowed from *Christus Rex*. Its labarum was the Cross of Burgundy.

José Antonio and Léon Degrelle had a strong social conscience. They fought for justice for the most disadvantaged and reclaimed human dignity from a transcendental standpoint. Their revolution was popular and social, confronting both intransigent and selfish capitalism and spiteful and vengeful Marxism.

Léon Degrelle has left us some writings on the Falange:

In 1933, José Antonio founded Falange Española. The Falange was, more than anything, youth and idealism. It was a wonderful group of people. Those boys had a bright gaze in their eyes, full of faith. They lived for the sake of their fatherland and their civilization. They did not belong to those masses that shambled through the streets of Madrid at that time. The Falangists were young men worthy of the Conquistadors, determined to give their souls to the Fatherland. They soon achieved considerable success. Because José Antonio was a prince. He was thirty years old at the time. He read tirelessly. He was wide awake. His ancestry was from Andalusia. He had a sense of humor and, most importantly, was a poet.

---

[323] León Degrelle, *Je te benis ô belle mort: Poemes d'apres Sainte Therese D Avila* (1991), 11.

[324] Léon Degrelle, *The Burning Souls* (Antelope Hill Publishing, 2020).

He captivated the masses. He founded a popular movement that was, at the same time, an exceptional elite.[325]

Léon and José Antonio fought in the same political trench, on the same front, with the same comrades, and against similar adversaries. José Antonio was the teacher and leader of the youth, who, on November 20th, 1936, surrendered his soul to God before a firing squad for the Fatherland and the National Syndicalist revolution. Léon, until his death on March 31st, 1994, made of his existence a living example of spiritual rebirth, austerity, nobility, and dignity.

José Antonio and Léon Degrelle sought a new Europe, one of art and culture, of tradition, of Fascist ideals, of sovereign peoples, and of a brighter future.

In his memoirs, Léon Degrelle writes about José Antonio:

José Antonio could have been the young Mussolini of Spain in 1936. This tall, splendid boy saw his dream ruined in that very year by an execution squad in Alicante. His ideas marked his country for a long time. They inspired hundreds of thousands of combatants and militants. They rebounded, revivified by the heroes of the Division Azul, even up to the bloody snows of the Russian Front, bringing their part to the creation of the new Europe of that time.[326]

When writing about Falange Española and Rex, Léon, pointing out their similarities, did not hesitate to proudly state that Rex was the Belgian contribution to the "common revolution."

When he founded the Rexist Party in Belgium on February 21st, 1936, his motto was "sweeping away the filth." He believed in Christian discipline, order, and social renewal, and he opposed Judaic usury, political corruption, and financial autocracy. He wrote in his book *The Burning Souls*:

The money, the honors, the mess of bodies, the eagerness to seize an earthly happiness that leaks between the fingers and always escapes, has made of the human herd a pitiful horde, ruining itself, tearing itself apart to find a liberation which does not exist.[327]

The appearance of Rex on the Belgian political scene was a reviving force in public life, bringing large segments of Catholics out of parliamentary apathy and denouncing the situation of corruption on which the political elites relied.

Forty-eight hours after the official foundation of the Fascist movement Rex, a rally

---

[325] Léon Degrelle, *Los movimientos fascistas*, part 3.

[326] Degrelle, *Hitler for a Thousand Years*, 32.

[327] Léon Degrelle, *The Burning Souls*.

was held in Namur where five thousand students attended, attracted by the strong, vigorous, and charismatic personality of Léon Degrelle, who in the general elections held on May 24th obtained a great triumph with 11.49% of the total votes counted, securing twenty-one deputies and twelve senators for his party.

During the Spanish Civil War, Léon Degrelle, together with the writer Juan Denis and the deputy Mathis, paid an official visit to Spain as a guest of honor of the Falange from February 2nd to the 14th, 1939, visiting several cities and war fronts, including San Sebastián, Burgos, Valladolid, Ávila, Toledo, the front of Madrid, Zaragoza, and the recently liberated—only a week had passed—Barcelona. It was not Degrelle's first trip to Spain. He had come during his childhood for a vacation and visited again during the dictatorship of Primo de Rivera and later during the Republic.

The national delegate of the Foreign Service of the Falange, José del Castaño, welcomed him with these warm words published in the national press:

> Léon Degrelle's trip to Spain will be received with the most lively sympathy by everyone, because the leader of the Belgian Rexist movement is an excellent and true friend of our country, and since the first days of our movement, he has lent us the support and help of his numerous supporters . . . . The popular, young, combative, and energetic figure of Léon Degrelle will be embraced during his stay in Spain by the unanimous affection of all of us . . . . Identifying his movement as Fascist, Léon Degrelle declares: "If Fascism is the recognition of authority with the consent of the people and with their support, if it means the reestablishment of order and morality, we have no objection to Rex being listed as a Fascist movement." Jean Denis, . . . besides his innumerable journalistic works, many of them translated and published by the press of the Falange, has edited the translation of the speeches of José Antonio . . . . He has recently finished writing a Falangist drama, which he will read aloud to the Spanish intelligentsia in San Sebastian.[328]

During his official visit, Léon Degrelle was received by Franco at the Términus, the place where he had located his general headquarters for the final offensive, and among the Falangist comrades who greeted him there were Deputy Secretaries General of the Falange Fanjul and Julián Pemartín, Undersecretary of Agriculture Dionisio Martín Sanz, Chief of the Cartographic Section Baz, Miguel Primo de Rivera, Undersecretary of Foreign Affairs General Espinosa de los Monteros, Minister of the Interior Ramón Serrano Suñer, Correa Veglison, Ribas Seba, Pilar Primo de Rivera, and Sancho Dávila.

During an interview in Burgos with journalist José Cano of the agency Logos, which was published in a large number of newspapers in Spain, he stated:

---

[328] *Amanecer* (Zaragoza, February 2nd, 1939). Article by José Castaño.

No other revolutionary movement in the world is as similar to the Falange Española Tradicionalista y de las JONS as Rex. As a matter of fact, Rex is a revolutionary youth movement. It shares the same program as the Falange, the same ideals, the same way of being, and the same fundamental principles, and although the nature of its struggle is not the same, it is in its daily hardships, dynamism, and the goal it seeks to achieve.[329]

On February 6th, 1939, he was interviewed in Zaragoza by the journalist R. Garza, who welcomed him and greeted him with the following words:

We pay homage to Léon Degrelle, a champion of noble causes, the first Belgian Falangist, and a friend of Spain from the early moments of the civil war, to whose service he put enthusiasm and youth.

Among his Falangist comrades and friends of the early days were Eugenio Montes, José Finat, Count of Mayalde, Roberto Reyes, José Antonio Girón, Mariano Sanchez Covisa, and José Utrera Molina.

Sir Oswald Mosley, Leader of the British Fascists

He was a distinguished Englishman with refined manners and a noble demeanor, despite his political origins in the radical wing of Labourism, where he rose to the position of minister of labor. He created a Fascist movement because he concluded, on the basis of his initial socialist views, that Fascism was the sole ideology that could provide a just and dignified solution to the workers' question, distancing himself from the ideas of class struggle and fierce demands on the one hand and showing himself hostile to capitalist exploitation on the other.

He had a gaze as bright as a constellation of stars. He was farsighted. He believed that a rapprochement between England and Germany, as well as an alliance of Germanic peoples, was an exigence, necessary for Europe. He agreed with Hitler's vision of an Anglo-German alliance.

He was the man who, for a brief moment, seemed to form, with Mussolini and Hitler, the European triumvirate. He was the only Englishman who could have been prime minister with support from both the Conservatives and the Labour Party. He was the best orator in the House of Commons and has been considered by many historians to be the most extraordinary English politician of his generation. In 1919, he was a Conservative MP before joining the Independent Labour Party, the Labour Party's fiercest wing. He left the party in 1931 and formed the British Union of

---

[329] *Unidad* (San Sebastián, February 8th, 1939), 1.

Fascists a year later. In July 1939, approximately forty thousand people attended the Fascist rallies in London, and Fascism appeared to many Englishmen as the only possible alternative to communism. From 1932 to 1936, he met with Mussolini about twelve times. In October 1936, Hitler was a guest at his wedding, which was celebrated in Berlin. He had previously met with Hitler in Munich in April 1935 and again in October 1936, in the Reich's capital. English Jewry soon declared war on his party, and the large outdoor rallies of the Blackshirts were banned by the Public Order Act in 1936, which likewise prohibited the wearing of their uniforms and denied them the right to maintain order in public open-air assemblies. The indoor rallies were able to continue with increasing attendance and enthusiasm, culminating in the Earl's Court Exhibition in July 1939, which was then regarded as the largest indoor rally in history. He was imprisoned in 1940 for opposing the war against Germany, since, according to his analysis, "The declaration of war in 1939 risked three consequences: the disaster of defeat, the triumph of communism, the loss of the British Empire despite victory. The only power which could in no circumstances benefit from that war was Great Britain."[330] He could only regain freedom at the end of the war.

Essentially, Mosley believed that Fascism "was a national creed, and therefore by definition took an entirely different form in different countries." The strength of Fascism stemmed from its intensely nationalist ideology. He adopted the black shirt as the uniform of his militant movement.

José Antonio had published in the seventh issue of *F.E.* a long article written by the Viscount Rothermere on Fascism in England, whose title was "Hurrah for the Blackshirts!" and it featured a photograph in which Mosley can be seen leading the parade of his units behind the English flag, saluted by the public with raised arms. The article included an introductory statement that read, among other things:

> It is not surprising, then, that the parades of the Blackshirts excite men and women in England who are tired of the party system, liberalism, and their inaction. They see a strong and vigorous organization that is modern and, most importantly, young. It is not in the hands of the timid dodderers who dominate all the organs of English public life. The motto of the Blackshirts is "action," rather than "drift" and, as Goethe said, doing is the most important of human activities.

To refute the accusations of plagiarism of English Fascism with respect to Italian Fascism, the author presented the following argument: "The socialists especially, who jeer at the principles and uniform of the Blackshirts as being of foreign origin, forget that the founder and high priest of their own creed was the German Jew Karl Marx."

---

[330] Oswald Mosley, *My Life* (Black House Publishing, 2012).

José Antonio paid a visit to Sir Oswald Mosley in London, and this would be recounted in the memoirs of the head of the British Union of Fascists, published in London in 1968, translated into Spanish, and published in 1973 by the publisher Luis de Caralt, a long-time member of the JONS Mosley would visit Spain for the first time only at the end of the Second World War, after being released from prison. His first stop was José Antonio's tomb, which was then located at the base of the main altar of the Monastery of El Escorial. This is how he recorded that moment in his memoirs:

> We stood alone in the awe of that somber splendour. The purpose of the visit was to stand for a few moments by the tomb of José Antonio Primo de Rivera, founder of the Falange. I had seen him only once, when in the thirties he had visited me in London at our headquarters in Chelsea. He had made a deep impression on me, and his assassination seemed to me always one of the saddest of the individual tragedies of Europe. I was deeply moved as we stood beside the sepulchre of this young and glittering presence I remembered so vividly, and was reminded of the initial line of Macaulay's memorable tribute to Byron: "When the grave closed over the thirty-seventh year of so much sorrow, so much glory."[331]

When asked by the judge during the summary trial held by the Special Court of Alicante on November 10th, 1936, José Antonio stated:

> That the only meeting he has referred to before is the one he held with Hitler in Germany; that no act or rally was held in Germany in which the declarant or Mosley took part, given that he was also not acquainted with the aforementioned gentleman.

Through deceptive political questions, they sought to portray José Antonio as part of an intricate network of high-level contacts, and to defend himself, he refuted the information that, if confirmed, could have had a serious negative impact on his trial.

Henry Coston

On Thursday, April 19th, 1934, *F.E.* dedicated a full page to the main French Fascist movement: Francism.

At that time in France, the list of Fascist parties, according to the summary given in the weekly, consisted of the following atomized groups: 1) Solidarité

---

[331] Ibid.

Française; 2) Croix-de-Feu; 3) Le Socialisme National; 4) Action Française; 5) Néo-socialisme; and 6) Mouvement Franciste (Francism).

According to the information provided by *F.E.*, the Francist movement was split into two different leaderships. One was Bucard's faction, to whom the CAUR's magazine *Roma Universa* granted editorial space in its pages, in which he declared that "Francism is Fascism in the French style, applied to our character, our temperament, and our homeland's methods."

The other original leader of Francism, with whom José Antonio interacted, was Henry Coston, who led the "young phalanxes" of the French Fascist movement. He was an active writer and directed, at that time, two notable publications: *La Libre Parole*, which was a doctrinal magazine, and *La Libre Parole Populaire*, a militant newspaper.

Coston recognized at a very early age—in 1934, when his photographs appeared in the weekly magazine *F.E.*, he was only twenty-five years old—the threat posed by the Jewish spirit to the peoples because of its harmful socio-economic influence. He was deeply concerned with exposing the Jewish lobbies that pulled the strings of world politics from behind the scenes. He was well aware of the secret plans that were simmering in the minds of the Jews. *F.E.* emphasized the attention he dedicated to the Jewish question: "It could be said that his main, almost obsessive, concern is the Jewish question. According to Coston and his friends the Jews are the cause of all the ills of France."

In the words of José Antonio: "Coston's magazine and newspaper carry great anger and nerve. It is the authentic Fascist pamphlet." That is why, after the analysis of the two currents within Francism—those represented by Bucard and by Henry Coston—in *F.E.* José Antonio chose and bet:

> We hope that the Francism of our young friend Coston will find fortune and a bright future. He is generous and likable. *But we also hope* that our national party and this small party will establish in France a deep, serious, and sacred union.[332]

Coston and José Antonio met in Paris, during one of his regular trips to the French capital. They communicated with one another through letters. Henry Coston kept three letters from José Antonio in his archive, which were seized during one of the several raids conducted by the French police, along with many other documents from his organization.

---

[332] *F.E.*, no. 11, March 19th, 1934, 8.

Pierre Drieu La Rochelle

Jean Marot published, in 1960, an essay entitled "Face au soleil (L'Espagne de José Antonio)" ["Facing the Sun (The Spain of José Antonio)"], in which he wrote:

> Although he spoke English and French as fluently as Spanish, José Antonio never qualified as what is called a cosmopolitan. He was a Spanish nationalist his entire life, and nothing else . . . . He was an admirer of our culture, but absolutely not of the ideological atrocities of 1789 and 1848. José Antonio had a profound knowledge of France. He visited Paris frequently and had the pleasure of meeting some literary celebrities, particularly Pierre Drieu La Rochelle. When one reads today the comments he wrote in his weekly regarding some of our politicians, from Marcel Déat to Léon Blum and from Charles Maurras to Colonel de la Rocque, one is tempted to attribute him the gift of prophetic vision.[333]

Drieu de La Rochelle was, according to historian Jean Mabire, "a Fascist until the very end," and Armin Mohler considers him "the most important figure of the French Fascist generation."

He was born in Paris in 1893 to a Norman family from the petite bourgeoisie. He fought heroically in the Great War, as attested by his awards and wounds. After the war was over, he maintained contact with some members of Action Française. He was an avid reader of Barrés and Maurras, Céline, and D'Annunzio. According to Tarmo Kunnas, Drieu de La Rochelle can be classified as a "left-wing Fascist." He soon joined the most representative party of French Fascism, the Parti Populaire Français of Jacques Doriot. In the eyes of the French writer, Fascism was the only solution that would bring salvation. On this matter, Drieu himself is clear: "I came to Fascism because I witnessed the progress of decadence within Europe, and having rejected the intrusions of the foreign empires of Russia and America, I saw in the genius of Hitler and Nazism the only salvation."[334]

When Germany occupied France, Drieu became one of the most ardent supporters of collaboration with the National Socialist power as a means of achieving the European unity he longed for, based on National Socialism; however, he did so always from a position of independence, and not without criticism when he saw fit. He advocated for a federation of European states in which capitalism would have been eradicated. Drieu saw the Second World War

---

[333] Jean Marot, *Face au Soleil. L'Espagne de José Antonio* (Paris: La Librairie Francaise, 1960), 36.

[334] Drieu de La Rochelle, *Thule, La cultura de la otra Europa* (Barcelona: Ediciones Bausp., 1979), 70.

as a revolutionary conflict that would give birth to a new order.

Just like José Antonio, he cultivated a poetic sense of life and wrote that it is only poetry that moves and inspires men because, as Mabire points out, "poets are the worst enemies of merchants."

According to Drieu de La Rochelle, it was necessary:

> from now on to take our thinking beyond capitalism and communism. And this beyond has a name: *Fascism*. What is Fascism, after all? The name associated in our century to the eternal human need: to live faster, to live more intensely; today this is called being Fascist. Totalitarianism offers the possibility of a double restoration, corporal and spiritual, of the man of the twentieth century.[335]

He believed in the rebirth of the European man, which is why he embraced Fascism and joined the French Popular Party. He declared himself both a French patriot and a European patriot.

For his part, Robert Brasillach, the young journalist, poet, and great lover of Spain who was executed by firing squad in the democratic "euphoria of liberation" of 1945, left a record of his admiration for José Antonio by describing him as the "Young Caesar"—as he would be called in Nationalist Spain, which was rekindled by the heat of his words—as the greatest and purest hero of Fascism, this *mal du siécle*, which he himself has defined as "the poetry of the twentieth century."[336]

Corneliu Zelea Codreanu

He was the founder and captain of the Romanian Iron Guard. The foundation of the Legionnaires took place on June 24th, 1927, and it succeeded the nationalist student movement that emerged in Romanian universities at the end of the Great War.

There was no personal contact between José Antonio and Codreanu, nor did they have the opportunity to influence each other, but Codreanu's successor at the head of the Iron Guard, Major Horia Sima, noted that:

> From the first contact with the works of José Antonio and Cornelio Codreanu, we will be surprised to discover extraordinary similarities in their thinking . . . . These movements have not imitated each other, but

---

[335] Ibid., 71.

[336] Antonio Medrano, "José Antonio Primo de Rivera: Fondateur de la Phalange," in *Totalité*, no. 13 (October 1981), 55.

each one answered the call that history has addressed to all nations, according to the peculiarities of their people."[337]

Horia Sima observed that one country can reach its national truths faster than another through the path of inner search, as Italy did. "Furthermore: the Fascist experience could serve as an example for other peoples to attempt the same spiritual adventure, the search for their historical being."[338]

Despite the absence of personal contact, "both have approached the problems of their nations independently, and, in spite of the isolation in which they have lived and have expressed themselves publicly, they have reached very similar conclusions."[339] Horia Sima reminds us that for both José Antonio and Codreanu, the real joys of life were those of struggle, and their only satisfaction was to know that their sacrifice would serve their own countries.

Both were assassinated, and in their "last speeches," the enduring nature of their work is demonstrated. Both of them "were martyrs of the Christian and nationalist faith."

The Falange and the Iron Guard were not parties, but "movements" of national integrity stemming from spiritual concerns, and precisely, as Sima reminds us, they were called movements "because it is the result of a 'movement,' of a vibration of the soul."[340] José Antonio and Codreanu appeared in analogous historical contexts. Fate summoned each one of them to resolve a revolutionary situation in their fatherlands, and each one has performed this historic role with unquestionable loyalty.

---

[337] Horia Sima, *Dos Movimientos Nacionales. José Antonio Primo de Rivera y Corneliu Zelea Codreanu* (Madrid: Ediciones Europa, 1960), 7 and 16.

[338] Ibid., 21.

[339] Ibid., 8.

[340] Ibid., 13.

19.

No Importa: "The Fascist is not the one who has the desire, but the one who has the ability"

Under the masthead *No Importa*, three issues of the *Boletín de los días de persecución* [*Bulletin of the Days of Persecution*] would be published. It was the clandestine newspaper of the Falange after the triumph of the left-wing coalition on February 16th, 1936. In the first issue, it was reported that "since February 16th, forty comrades of the Falange have been assassinated and more than one hundred have been wounded; not a single one of the aggressors has been arrested or brought to trial,"[341] and the honor roll included the name of José Urra Goñi, a construction worker who was the first to be killed by the "jubilant" bullets, by the "democratic" inebriation that broke out after the leftist triumph. He was assassinated as he left his workplace on March 6th. Ramón Faisán, who was accompanying Urra, was also shot in the back.

In March 1936, under the accusation of illicit possession of weapons, all the centers of Falange Española de las JONS in Spain were closed and, on the 14th of that same month, the whole leadership of the organization, including its national leader, was arrested. According to the official letter issued by the inspector on duty of the Social Division of the General Directorate of Security, which is preserved in José Antonio's police file, the charge was that of being "Fascists." He was initially

---

341 *No Importa*, no. 1, May 20th, 1936, 1.

brought to the cells of the General Directorate of Security and, later, to the Cárcel Modelo in Madrid and the Provincial Prison in Alicante; however, he would never regain his freedom, as he was assassinated on November 20th, 1936.

After being stripped of his freedom, José Antonio named his brother Miguel as the Falange's supreme leader, temporarily and indefinitely, as long as the entire Junta de Mando remained in prison.[342] One of the first actions taken by José Antonio from the cell of the Cárcel Modelo in Madrid was to try to arrange a personal meeting between his brother Miguel and Benito Mussolini in order to inform him of the delicate situation the Spanish Fascist movement was going through and the plan regarding the internal situation in Spain. The mediation of an Italian attaché in the Italian Air Force was sought for this purpose, and the meeting was requested on March 19th, less than a week after José Antonio's arrest.

The head secretary of the Italian Embassy in Madrid sent, on March 25th, a telegram to his government in which the following was stated:

> Primo de Rivera, who is still detained, has made a confidential request of the most absolute secrecy to this air attaché, with whom he maintains personal and friendly relations, requesting that his brother Miguel be received by Your Excellency to explain his plan in relation to Spain's internal situation.
>
> The air attaché telegraphed directly to His Excellency Valle and, after receiving no response, informed me of the request today.
>
> I would have asked the air attaché to solicit further details from the person who put forward the request in order to enable Your Excellency to decide on the course to be taken in response to his request; given, however, the uncertainty of the internal situation, which could worsen unexpectedly, I have thought that it is my duty to let Your Excellency know quickly the preceding information, asking you to telegraph me if you consider it appropriate and possible to hold the hearing in question.[343]

The appointment could not take place due to the turbulent internal situation in Spain.

The Falangist leadership was accused of "illicit association," and the allegations were founded on points 2, 3, 4, and 26 of their program, which had been in effect since November 1934. The Emergency Court of Madrid ruled in favor of Falange Española on April 30th, issuing the following sentence:

> Given the evidence presented, it is impossible to conclude that the

---

342 [Translator: The Falange's leadership.]

343 Reproduced in Ismael Saz Campos, *Mussolini contra la II República*, 164–165.

defendants committed the crime charged by the Public Prosecutor's Office because the Association's political ideology, which is contained in the legally accepted statutes, has not been altered in essence, orientation, or procedure by the printed document on page six of the summary . . . . We rule: that we must acquit and thus do acquit the defendants Mr. José Antonio Primo de Rivera, Mr. Augusto Barrado, Mr. Julio Ruiz de Alda, Mr. Raimundo Fernández Cuesta, Mr. Alejandro Salazar Salvador, Mr. José Guitarte Irigaray, and Mr. Manuel Valdés Larrañaga of the crime of which they are accused . . . . Likewise, by virtue of the previous sentence, we must declare and thus we do declare that the dissolution of the Association Falange Española de las JONS shall not take place.[344]

The ruling of the Emergency Court was confirmed and ratified by the verdict of the Second Chamber of the Supreme Court, following the hearing held on June 5th of the appeal filed by the Public Prosecutor's Office based on an alleged breach of form. The verdict regarding the legality of the Falange became final and unchallengeable.

Despite all the above, from March 14th, the Falange had its centers closed, its organs of expression silenced—the weekly magazine *Arriba* was arbitrarily suspended with its last issue, number 34, dated March 5th, 1936—its militants persecuted, its leadership imprisoned, and members of its upper hierarchy imprisoned. A brutal campaign of political repression was carried out. The most severe clandestineness became mandatory. In those days of oppression and relentless persecution, there was no other alternative other than flyers and a bulletin that appeared in Madrid with the title *No Importa (Bulletin of the Days of Persecution)*, which, on May 20th, reported on its front page, in the headline, that "Falange Española de las JONS, declared lawful by the courts, continues to endure the government's attacks."

No Importa thus became the official underground publication of the Falange. In the midst of such dark clandestinity, the bulletin was launched as a strangled cry for freedom. It was edited, published, and distributed by trade unionist and Political Board member Manuel Mateo, who managed to elude arrest and carry on with the resistance. The administrator and person in charge of the distribution was Mariano García—card number 29 of the Falange—who had also been in charge of *Arriba* and who was the one who received from José Antonio himself, from behind the bars of the Cárcel Modelo, the order to secretly publish the bulletin. Its editors were mostly the same as those who collaborated on the weekly *Arriba*.

No Importa "was edited by José Antonio, and when he left for Alicante he

---

[344] *No Importa*, no. 1, May 20th, 1936, 2.

entrusted Raimundo with the task of revising and censoring all the originals."[345]
The places of meeting and gathering were the cafés, cinemas, and museums of
Madrid, such as the Museo de Reproducciones Artísticas [Museum of Artistic
Reproductions]. This was the militia headquarters, as Luis Aguilar had suggested
to José Antonio.

The now decimated editorial staff was joined by the illustrious thinker Manuel
Bueno and the writer Tomás Borrás, whose contributions should have been included
in the fourth issue, which never saw the light of day. *No Importa* featured articles by
José Antonio, Juan Aparicio, José María Alfaro, Raimundo Fernández Cuesta,
Ismael Herráiz, the vice director of *Ya* Joaquín Arrarás, and Andrés Gamboa.

The procedure for its preparation was the following: the news that was
considered interesting was gathered from *Agencia Logos*; those that were crossed out
by the censorship were then elaborated by José María Cía, Manuel Vázquez de
Prada, and Ismael Herráiz, who would ultimately deliver them to Alfaro. José
Antonio submitted his articles during the visits he received in prison.

To collect the originals, Alfaro or Mariano García would meet the authors in
the middle of Calle de Alcalá, on the Gran Vía, or in one of the cafés in the
surrounding area. The handwritten or typed originals were delivered concealed
between the pages of a daily copy of *El Heraldo* or *El Socialista* so as not to arouse
the slightest suspicion.

Furtively and covertly, it evaded the surveillance of the henchmen of Alonso
Mallol, who was then director-general of security.

Amelia Azaróla, Julio Ruiz de Alda's wife, supplied the six thousand pesetas
needed for the publication of each issue. The printing house Zoila Ascasibar—
known as "Doña Zoila's printing house"—located in Calle Martín de los Heros,
whose manager was a Falangist affiliated to the Syndicate of Graphic Arts, took over
the task of printing the copies, risking everything in order to do so, given the
vigilance to which the Falange activists who had not yet been arrested were
subjected. The Falange leadership had already hired that printing house before, and
there, for example, the pamphlet *Economía, Trabajo y Lucha de clases* by Raimundo
Fernández Cuesta was printed in 1935, as well as various leaflets for the Sindicato
Español Universitario. To print *No Importa*, work was done at night with a very
small staff—a linotypist, a typesetter, and a machinist—and in complete secrecy.
The procedure was carried out over two nights; the first was dedicated to
composition and correction, and the second to printing the copy. "José Antonio had
the most determined interest in keeping only Raimundo, another comrade, and
myself aware of the printing house. Keeping the police away was essential."[346] In
that same printing house, curiously enough, a professional publication of the police

---

[345] Ximénez de Sandoval, *José Antonio (Biografía Apasionada)*, 7th ed. (Madrid: Fuerza
Nueva Editorial, 1976), 485.

[346] Bravo, *José Antonio*, 195.

force was published, the same agency that was being mobilized all over Spain to prevent the distribution of *No Importa*.

The name of the masthead, *No Importa*, was not made up on the spot. José Antonio had already utilized this expression in the first meeting of the newly formed Falange Española de las JONS in the town of Carpió de Tajo, near Toledo, celebrated on February 23rd, 1934, when, addressing the farmers, he said: "They attack us from many sides: five of our people have fallen dead because of treachery; perhaps the same fate awaits some of us. *¡No importa!* [It does not matter!]. Life is not worth living unless it is burned in the service of a great cause."[347] In the eighteenth edition of *Arriba*, dated November 7th, 1935, Commander Emilio Alvargonzález, first provincial chief since the foundational days of 1933, who assiduously collaborated with articles and commentaries in this Falangist weekly, published one with the allegorical title "No Importa" ("It Does Not Matter"). This very caption could be found on a sculpture located in the Centro Cultural del Ejército y de la Armada [Cultural Center of the Army and Navy] that represented a flag-bearer who, while raising a waving flag with his right arm, lifts up with the left one the lying body of an officer, fallen on the field of honor; hence, to give one's own life for a just cause, to die for the Fatherland, "does not matter," as long as the flag is kept raised with dignity. During the clandestine period, the publication represented the banner of war that keeps waving in the face of adversity.

In the twentieth issue of *Arriba*, dated November 21st, 1935, Emilio Alvargonzález again used the expression "*no importa*" as the headline of a short article, commenting:

> In the previous issue, when we dedicated a solemn remembrance to those who died to save Spain, under the flag of the Falange Española de las JONS, we announced *twenty-two dead*! It does not matter. More will die.
>
> And, on the 6th, in Seville, two more have fallen as a result of a vicious attack in the back . . . . Two more died! One was a great worker, while the other was a brilliant student. It does not matter. More will die. But they will all die with their hearts filled with patriotic love and holding on their lips as their last cry our sacred motto: *¡Arriba España!*[348]

While the editing of the newspaper was fraught with danger, its distribution was almost an impossible mission. The packages that were sent throughout the provinces were disguised as being from specific companies or bearing labels from academies. The packages were prepared in a room of the printing house by the manager and Mariano García. Alfaro and Dávila would then handle their distribution through

---

[347] *F.E.*, no. 8, 7.

[348] *Arriba*, November 21st, 1935, 4.

mail. Pursuing every possible loophole, the four-page bulletin reached the army's hubs and served as a morale booster for members of the movement who were going through hardships and mortifications. Firstly, the batches destined for the different provincial centers were dispatched, while those destined for distribution in Madrid —some three thousand copies—were not sent out until a day after the provincial ones were issued—some more than seven thousand bulletins. A safety protocol for bulletin distribution was put in place from the very first issue:

1. Anyone who obtains a copy of *No Importa* and wishes to receive subsequent issues must order them from the person who gave him the first one. This person will pass on the new name to the person who, in turn, gave him bulletin issues, and so on until the order reaches the secret printing house where *No Importa* is edited.
2. Nobody will reveal who gave them the issue of *No Importa*. When recruiting new readers, the names of these readers will be transmitted to the previous middleman, but the reverse must not happen; that is, the names of the previous middlemen will never be told to the new readers.[349]

The number of copies printed did not exceed twelve thousand. The girls of the women's section collaborated very diligently to carry out the concealed distribution. Some even carried them around in baby strollers.[350]

No Importa was, despite the modesty of its composition and the very small number of pages, a far-reaching, revolutionary publication, which, in the face of the unjust violence unleashed against the Falange, called for rebellion. It was neither a literary journal nor a florist's newsletter. It was the Falange's mouthpiece during the period in which it was arbitrarily declared illegal, with its headquarters sealed up and its leaders imprisoned, if not assassinated. It embodied the response from the hideout, sheets recklessly prepared among dangers, in defiance, to proclaim the revolutionary principles of National Syndicalism right from the first issue, which made clear the position and doctrine of the Falange, even during its most difficult hours. A worthy example is the article published on the third page of the first issue under the title "¿Un fascismo de Azaña y Prieto?" ["A Fascism of Azaña and Prieto?"], which we reproduce here due to its importance:

Indalecio Prieto has proposed to create in Spain a National Socialist party, which would very soon come to power, protected from the Plaza de Oriente by the brand-new president of the workers' republic and the

---

[349] *No Importa*, no. 1, May 20th, 1936, 3.

[350] Ximénez de Sandoval, *José Antonio*, 485.

presidential guard. The name National Socialism, which is not definitive, is a circumvention to avoid the word Fascism, since it causes so much outrage in Spain.

We do not trust Indalecio Prieto nor that kind of Fascism so distorted and falsified that they want to call it left-leaning, as if Fascism, which is totalitarian, could admit partisan designations such as any "mesocracy" that is pushed by the presidential chamber would.

And we do not trust it, because Fascism is born in the streets. It emerges between anarchy and democracy. It rises from the banners of the ideals trampled by the red mob; it is strengthened by the warm flow of the young blood of those who die for this ideal. It grows while imprisoned and persecuted, among resentment and hatred. Fascism is a movement of generosity, not of vainglory, in which each individual of the fasces stakes all his blood and all his freedom for the glory of the fatherland.

And if this is what Fascism is, where will Prieto get all of the wealth of selflessness and sacrifice that make up the Fascist substance? Relying on the support of the powers that be is not enough. An intelligent and skillful leader is not enough. An indifferent crowd and militias wearing colored shirts are not enough. (These militias of Prieto, which are recruited among members of cultural associations and favorite disciples of Asúa, wear cute little rosy shirts and parade around singing a little song by Alberti to the sibylline commanding voice of Rivas Cherif.) A spirit, a faith, an asceticism, and a manly will are required that would lead with the same joy to triumph as they would to death or imprisonment. And who will be able to smile before death for Prieto or for Azaña, and for what they represent? The workers? The same applies to Figols, Batas, and Casas Viejas. Or the Asturian and Catalan revolutionaries who remember Prieto's escape to Paris and Azaña's "coffee and balcony heroism" in Barcelona? October has not yet been forgotten. Or maybe the intellectuals of the Human Rights Leagues and other of Ateneo's swine, enemies of Fascism, and enthusiasts of the Negus? The army, targeted by Azaña throughout every phase of his government? What about the "jubilant" arsonists and murderers of poor nuns and ladies?

Where will Prieto find the human components required to "fascistize" Spain through their word? Can the Spanish people believe in a genuine national sentiment coming from those who have defended the Statute of Catalonia and advocated for those of the other regions?

It is very convenient, once the positions achieved by crawling to lick the revolutionary beast's hooves are lost, to attempt to replace the tongue with a whip, and to switch sides, from being anti-national to adopting a cliché patriotism. It is very convenient if the country is nothing more than a hysterical mass that swings from one side to the other to the sound of whatever is played. Perhaps Prieto's warning signal will elicit a sigh of relief from the shady people who only seek their safe little dividend. But it will surely not move the Spanish youth, who can see through the false and hollow meaning of the cheers for an agonizing Spain that is now in a puddle of blood and festering pus, launched amid the belching of a succulent dinner in a luxury restaurant. The Spanish youth know that the Fascism of Azaña and Prieto would lead to another wave of rottenness that would bury Spain in a cesspool even deeper than that of the liberal pseudo-democracy.

Spain must be pulled out of this disgusting situation. It must be elevated toward the unity of destiny spanning its lands and skies. It must be cleansed of misery and filth. It must be liberated from fat bellies, warts, and capitalism. It must be cleaned, groomed, and placed into the ranks of the uniforms of the National Syndicates. Spain cannot accept Marxism, even if it is labeled as "national." Spain cannot bend to the will of Azaña and Prieto, who, even when dressed as Fascists, remain monkeys, like the monkey dressed in silk. The national revolution is made in the streets, with the chest against the bullets, falling facing the sun, with blood that boils in harmony with its ideals.

Desiring Fascism is not as simple, Mr. Manuel and Mr. Inda, as ordering fish. It is more difficult, more complicated, more heroic. Do not bother, it is not for you. *The Fascist is not the one who has the desire, but the one who has the ability.* And your past proves that you cannot be anything other than what you are. Prieto's wonderwork could turn him from a shoeshine boy into a stenographer and from a stenographer into a millionaire. Azaña's has been transformed, in the blink of an eye, from a pen-pusher and mediocre intellectual, a coffeehouse circle habitué, to a guest in the rooms of Queen Maria Cristina in the Palacio de Oriente. All these picaresque transformations are possible in the grotesque Spain of Valle Inclán. But it is not possible for a picaresque story to become an epic. And Fascism, as well as National Socialism, are nourished by a feeling for that which is epic that could never belong to the columns of *El Liberal* or to the dull scenes of *La Corona*.[351]

In the three issues of *No Importa* that have been published, the use of violence as a legitimate defense against governmental harassment and intimidation is justified. Julio Ruiz de Alda did this in his article "Justificación de la violencia" ["Justification of Violence"], published in the second issue of *No Importa*, dated June 6th, 1936:

---

[351] *No Importa*, no. 1, May 20th, 1936, 3.

Because it is indecent to attempt to narcotize a people with the deception of peaceful solutions, *there are no peaceful solutions anymore.* War has been declared and the government has been the first to proclaim its belligerence . . . . We are at war. That is why the hostile government has little concern for the dossiers of the secessionists and the conservative press. The government does not waste its time killing flies: it rushes to annihilate everything that could serve as a bulwark for Spanish civilization and for the historical continuity of the Fatherland: the Army, The Navy, The Civil Guard—and the Falange.

It is not us, then, who have chosen violence. It is the law of war that imposes it. The assassinations, the arson, the acts of violence were not started by us. Now, without a doubt—and in this lies our glory— our fighting spirit, our holy violence, was the first obstacle against which the criminal violence of the men of October stumbled. That is why they have confronted us with such sudden wrath. They expected that everything was going to be golden, as in the other biennium of Azaña. They believed they could cause harm and injury, as they did back then. Then, lo and behold, the Falange stood in their way. It has proven futile to escalate the persecutions: the Falange stands here, firm, in place.

Let there come this violence, this war, in which we defend not only the existence of the Falange, at the expense of the most worthy lives, but also the very existence of Spain, which is being attacked by its enemies! Fight on, comrades, alone or with others. Close your ranks, hone your techniques. Tomorrow, when brighter days shall dawn, the fresh laurels of supremacy in this holy crusade of violence will belong to the Falange.[352]

On June 6th, 1936, the second issue *No Importa* reported on its front page that "The national leader of Falange Española and five other comrades were violently dragged out of the Cárcel Modelo in Madrid and transferred to an unknown location." The transfer took place on Friday, June 5th, at half past nine in the evening.

This second issue was distributed in Madrid by Mariano García using Dr. Vaquero's vehicle, in which were loaded the ten packages to be delivered to each of the Falange's district chiefs.

In the third and last issue of *No Importa*, a full-page article by José Antonio was

---

[352] *No Importa*, no. 2, June 6th, 1936. When the article mentions the "criminal violence of the men of October," it refers to the Asturias Revolution of October 1934. The article, mistakenly attributed to José Antonio and included in his *Escritos*, is actually by Julio Ruiz de Alda, also collected in his *Obra completa*, 262–264.

published: "Vista a la Derecha. Aviso a los 'madrugadores,' la Falange no es una fuerza cipaya" ["Eye on the Right-Wing: Warning to the 'Early Birds,' the Falange Is Not a Mercenary Force"] in which, after stating that "the Falange is one and indivisible, militia and party," a warning was given not to be fooled by obscure right-wing machinations. In this article, José Antonio centered his attention on the possibility that Calvo Sotelo—the *madrugador* or "early bird"—could be the indirect beneficiary of the spectacular growth experienced by the Falange. Calvo Sotelo:

> had extraordinarily radicalized his discourse and did not hesitate now to declare himself "Fascist" in the middle of parliament and to make public appeals to the armed forces to rise up against the government. This greatly irritated the Falangists, who, despite avoiding publicly assuming the status of Fascists, did not want to share their doctrinal space with a politician they regarded as deeply reactionary.[353]

As José Antonio wrote:

> You will never see the *madrugador* during the rough days. In times of persecution, he would never dare cross the border into his fatherland without some form of parliamentary immunity to shield himself. He would never go out on the street without at least three or four police officers watching his back. His body will know neither prison nor deprivation.
>
> But—that's for sure—if others, at the cost of the most worthy lives— the dead men of the Falange!—succeed in making an idea or a behavior respectable, then the early bird will not hesitate to impersonate it. Thus, in our days, when the Falange, after three years of effort, obtains its first public recognition—so expensively watered with blood!—the early bird will come out saying: "What the Falange thinks is what I think! I also want a corporatist and totalitarian state! I do not even have any objection to declaring myself a Fascist."[354]

The police would intercept this last issue at the Madrid Post Office after it had already been dispatched by Alfaro. In Madrid, the distribution was carried out in the car of comrade Ara, the chief of the Buenavista District, accompanied by the tireless Mariano García, to avoid causing any suspicion. Because of the ongoing persecution, this third issue was poorly produced, presenting repetitions and typographical errors. Given the severity of the noticeable flaws in form, José Antonio sent a handwritten reproach from Alicante to those in charge of preparing

---

[353] Gil Pecharromán, *José Antonio Primo de Rivera*, 479–480.

[354] *No Importa*, no. 3, June 20th, 1936, 1.

that clandestine newspaper, threatening to suspend it outright "to the shame," the note said, "of everyone," if such errors occurred again.

José Antonio, four days before the release of the third and last issue of *No Importa*—June 20th, 1936—assessed, from the Provincial Prison of Alicante, the situation of the Falange in those tragic moments by answering the questionnaire of eleven questions that the journalist Ramón Blardony had formulated and sent him through the intermediation of Agustín Peláez. The Falange leader answered the questions almost militarily, in a brief and concise manner:

"Approximate number of members?"

"One hundred and fifty thousand."

"Approximate number of imprisoned members?"

"About two thousand. There have been more than six thousand during the months of March and April. Except for thirty or forty, the rest of them are imprisoned without trial. Many of them remain in jail by government order, even after the judges have ruled that they must be released."

"How is the Falange organized?"

"National leader. National Council (forty-eight members; fifteen elected by the local organizations and the other members elected by the national leader); political board (permanent delegation of the twelve members of the National Council); provincial chiefs (one for each province); JONS (this is the name given to the organization within each city or town). Within each JONS, all members are organized into groups of eight to fifteen elements, each with its own chief. These coordinated groups form the higher units, which are variable."

"Distinctive signs, and adopted emblems?"

"The yoke and arrows (sewn as a badge). This badge is common to all members. The members of the National Council wear a red and black aiguillette, with gold tassels. The territorial and provincial chiefs wear the same aiguillette but with red and black tassels. The shirt is dark blue, with the arrows and yoke embroidered in red on the left side. A yoke and three arrows, two or one for those commanding front-line units, are displayed beneath the emblem, which is embroidered in silver or red (depending on whether they are chiefs or vice-chiefs)."

"Number of dead and wounded in encounters between members of the Falange and those of a different ideology?"

"Dead, forty-eight. Wounded, about five hundred."

"Did the Falange adopt some of the methods and systems of German Fascism?"

"In the choice of methods, Falange has not been fixated on any specific model. It has simply tried, at each moment, to select those most suitable to the achievement of its goals."

"Having acknowledged that the Falange, as a Spanish organization, has a distinctly Spanish style, etc., which Fascism is it closer to, Italian or German?"

"It coincides with the essential concerns of both: the destruction brought by the liberal capitalist regime and the urgency of avoiding it from leading irremediably to the communist catastrophe, of anti-Western and anti-Christian nature. In its search for a way to avoid this catastrophe, the Falange has reached doctrinal positions of lively originality; thus, in the national aspect, it considers Spain to be a unity of destiny, compatible with regional variations, but adopting a policy that, with the preservation of this unity as its primary duty, overcomes party and class opinions. In the economic field, the Falange tends toward total syndicalism; that is to say, that the surplus value of the production remains entirely in the power of the organic, vertical syndicate of producers, so that its own economic force would procure the necessary credit for production, without need to borrow it—expensively—from the banks. Perhaps these economic guidelines bear more resemblance to the German program than to the Italian one."[355]

There was talk of the existence of a fourth issue in preparation of *No Importa* that would have been published by another printing house, located on Calle Ventura Rodríguez, which could no longer be published due to the final outcome of the events. The change in printing location was caused by the graphic arts workshop's refusal to continue working on the newspaper after the police conducted a search and arrested the manager. The police discovered the printing shop because, together with issue number three of *No Importa*, was included the pamphlet of Raimundo's conference *Economía, Trabajo y Lucha de clases*, which had been produced the previous year in the same graphic workshops and of which there were still copies in existence, containing the publisher's signature.

That same night, the police raided the facility and seized all existing copies, arresting the manager and a Falangist militant who was assisting him.

It was extremely difficult to find a new printing house for such a task, but this did not discourage the organizer, Mariano García. Some of the workshops that were contacted were offered payment in advance, but they declined due to fear and a lack of a valid compromise. Finally, in the small printing house Ferga, at 26 Calle Ventura Rodríguez, near the Cuartel de la Montaña, a printer affiliated with the Falange bravely defied the terrible consequences he could have faced if he were found out. The fourth issue was supposed to be dated July 16th. Following the assassination of Calvo Sotelo on July 13th, José Antonio ordered a postponement so that he could publish his article condemning the heinous state crime on the front

---

[355] Primo de Rivera, *Escritos y Discursos. Obras completas*, vol. II, 1005–1006.

page, requesting that a panel for the mourning section be reserved. The next day, José Antonio sent a very harsh condemnatory piece in his own handwriting. As the printing process was taking place, a new messenger arrived from Alicante with a manifesto dated July 17th, coinciding with the army's uprising in Africa, which stated: "The Falange and the military have launched a movement to overthrow the factious and cowardly government."

Since it was not possible to print both the newspaper and the manifesto during the night shift, Mariano García consulted with Rafael Aznar to determine the order of priorities, and the decision was made to publish the manifesto as it was the most urgent, collaborating that night with the owner of the printing house, his wife, Manuel Mateo, and Mariano García in its preparation. 170,000 copies were printed during the twenty-four hours that followed. They were cut off from communication when the Alzamiento broke out, and the person in charge of collecting the copies was unable to reach the facility. The Falangists gathered at the Cuartel de la Montaña to join the revolt. In the printing press, they would remain isolated until the 20th, listening to the bursts of gunfire against the heroes of the Cuartel de la Montaña, where the Falange of Madrid sacrificed their lives. Mateo planned to leave the printing press with false documentation and sunglasses to avoid being arrested in the establishment that was known as "Fascist" in the political circles of Madrid because of the printing of pamphlets and graphic material for the Falange, therefore expecting the assault of the militiamen and mobs.

On the 21st, the graphic arts workshop and the owner's apartment situated in the building where Mateo and Mariano García were also staying were searched, as expected. In the workshops, still with the ink half-dried, José Antonio's manifesto was packed into 170 packages among bank forms; therefore, no suspicions were raised. As the armed militiamen left, everyone in the workshop began to destroy the copies, dumping them in the sewage system.

On July 23rd, Mariano García left the printing house in search of his family.

20.

German Logistical Support
for the Liberation of José Antonio

José Antonio was arrested, along with the upper echelons of the Falange, on March 14th, 1936. His pre-trial detention was imposed. A series of trials ordered that the Falange's leader remain in prison. There were fears of an uprising. The social and political climate became tense and heated. The army was on alert. The situation was chaotic. The prisons were brimming with young nationalists. They were chased down like wounded prey in an unprecedented hunt.

Some authors, such as Álvarez del Vayo, in 1940 first and later in his book *Les batailles de la liberté* (Paris, 1963), and Werner Orlowsky, in his work *Das Vorpiel zum Kriege. Zum zwanzigsten. Jahrestag des spanischen Bürgerkrieges* (1956), support the thesis that, on the occasion of the Winter Games held in Germany in 1936, the white prelude to the Berlin Olympics, José Antonio and General Sanjurjo were at the Kaiserhof Hotel in the capital of the Reich, a building that served as a reception for the official guests, where they came into contact with National Socialist leaders. Their theory is corroborated by the brief mention of the trip in General Sanjurjo's letter to José Antonio dated March 21st, when José Antonio was already detained in Madrid, and by the fact that he would bring up the subject once more in a letter dated April 23rd. The Republican government would intercept these letters and use them during the trial in Alicante as incriminating evidence against the Falange national leader, who refuted the facts when questioned about them during the preliminary interrogation.

José Antonio was transferred from the Cárcel Modelo in Madrid to the prison of

Alicante to isolate him from his comrades, with whom he shared the cell, prison block, and courtyard. The reputation of José Antonio was not irrelevant to the Republican authorities. The righteous youth of Spain followed him, acclaimed him, obeyed him. In spite of the reclusion of the Falange leaders, the movement continued to grow, membership increased, and the party spread across Spain. It was an uncontrollable and unbridled phenomenon that the number of members and new Falangist comrades during the imprisonment increased.

Following the Uprising of July 18th, the Falangists strived to free their leader. The National Socialists also mobilized to provide logistical support to their Spanish comrades in the dangerous and difficult task of freeing José Antonio.

The work of Falangists, militiamen, and soldiers in the early days and weeks of the National Uprising caused chaos on the front lines, which had not yet been consolidated. Rumors were, during those days, more reliable than news. Conjecture arose from whatever information was available. Things happened in a contradictory way. Everything was rather unpredictable.

Adolf Hitler had decided to support the national cause in his anti-communist crusade, though direct German intervention was initially ruled out.

José Antonio remained isolated in the Spanish Levant, whose borders and city remained under communist control. His young Falangists, mostly boys, stepped forward, picked up their rifles, and charged into the fray, willing to give their lives for Spain's liberation.

In the first days of September, Deputy Chief of the Wehrmacht High Command Walter Warlimont, traveled to Spain to assess the situation on the field and report back to the Chancellery. On the 19th of that month, he sent a dispatch in which, after an examination of the scope of the conflict, he stated:

> It is especially appreciated here that, following our recommendation, the commander of the light squadron of the fleet has immediately and with the best will rendered all his help so that the Falangist volunteers could approach the supreme leader of the Falange, who is imprisoned in Alicante.

On September 5th, the unofficial representative of the Nationalist Spain in Lisbon reached the German embassy there, asking it to allow the embarkation of a delegate of the Falange, secretly and with absolute confidentiality, on a ship of the German squadron that was anchored in Alicante, so that negotiations could be undertaken to free José Antonio. On September 14th, the naval fleet commanders issued the following orders:

> It is absolutely necessary to quickly transfer two delegates from the white government, who are currently in Lisbon, to Alicante in support of the action to be taken for the prisoner there. Attempts to employ a Portuguese warship have yielded no results. It is urgently necessary that the transfer be carried out

by German warship. The presence of the delegates onboard must be kept secret.[356]

On the same day, another telegram clarified the National Socialist navy's involvement in the liberation efforts: "The boarding can be carried out in Lisbon, Gibraltar, or in accordance with the proposal of the light squadron. The delegation in Lisbon and the *chargé d'affaires*, Volckers, are aware of the matter."

Hermann Boehm was the commander of the German naval units in Spanish waters, including the light squadron of those ships.

The torpedo boat *Litis* reached land in Bonanza on September 16th to transport the Falangist delegates tasked with negotiating the liberation of the national leader.

For his part, the honorary consul of National Socialist Germany in Alicante, Joaquin von Knobloch, who had been appointed in August of that same year, went into action. Alicante was designated to serve as an evacuation zone for the German nationals, and the Reich's squadron approached its port for the evacuation of the German colony and of the nationals of non-belligerent neutral countries. The embassies of the friendly countries of Nationalist Spain established themselves in Alicante in order to move away from the Madrid front. Ships from Italy, Germany, and Portugal were frequently seen anchored at the port dock or off the coast of Alicante.

Consul von Knobloch, a loyal National Socialist, had the highest human interest in releasing José Antonio from prison. After taking the first steps, he reasoned that he might be able to get his release through economic bribery. On September 15th, the commander of the German fleet wrote about these ideas in his journal:

> In the meantime the *chargé d'affaires* has tried to obtain, by means of bribery, the prisoner's freedom. Details have been agreed upon with him. The prisoners will be transported by boat to the bay, where they will be gathered by a launch with its lights turned off, coming from the cruiser *Nuremberg*, in return for a payment of 100,000 pesetas.

The High Command of the Navy in Berlin approved of the operation as long as secrecy was maintained to avoid directly involving the German squadron.

In his book *Guerra, Dinero, Dictadura*,[357] professor Angel Viñas reconstructed the "operation bribery" carried out to free José Antonio with the help of the Third Reich Navy and the German consul in Alicante, relying on official documentation.

On September 16th, Boehm, the commander of the German fleet, was informed that the representatives of the Falange, a total of eleven Falangists had

---

[356] Boehm's Operations Journal, AMAF, file M Box 1405/80.837, vol. 1, 81.

[357] Angel Viñas, *Guerra, Dinero, Dictadura (Ayuda fascista y autarquía en la España de Franco)* (Barcelona: Grupo Editorial Grijalbo, 1984), 72ff.

embarked on the German torpedo boat *Litis*, crewed by Lieutenant Commander Hans Schottky, headed for Alicante. They had clearance from the German naval authorities with the concise approval to "execute the operation" granted to them. On the 17th, the torpedo boat arrived in the waters of Alicante with two squadrons of Falangists, ready for anything and armed with considerable weaponry and ammunition supplied by the Germans. The commander of the Falangist expedition embarked on the German torpedo boat *Litis* was the national militia chief of Falange Española, Agustín Aznar Gener. José Antonio's assistant, Rafael Garcerán, was among those in that operative group. Garcerán had been evacuated to Nationalist territory a month prior via Alicante and with the assistance of the National Socialists.

The mission of the Falangist group, as described in Boehm's journal, was, "in the first place, to obtain the liberation by means of bribes; but in the case of not obtaining it, it would be carried out by means of a surprise attack."

Agustín Aznar was in charge of attempting the bribe to exchange the prisoner for money. The German consul, von Knobloch, landed the commissioner with the false documents provided by the German services. The German consul in Alicante, who knew well the terrain he was working on, actively collaborated to introduce and put Agustín Aznar in contact with various elements of the FAI [Federación Anarquista Ibérica (Iberian Anarchist Federation)] and the CNT [Confederación Nacional del Trabajo (National Confederation of Labor)], who could have had influence over the jailers and who were suitable to receive the bribe.

Fate was against Agustín Aznar, as he was recognized in the middle of the street by a captain of the Assault Guards who had identified him on some occasion and knew of his energy and ardor in the student skirmishes in Madrid, thus leading immediately to his arrest. Aznar had the chance to get away solely due to the protection provided by the German consul. Aznar initially took refuge in one of the rooms that the Victoria Hotel kept reserved for the German delegation in the town. To evacuate the leader of the Falange militia, the consul requested the use of a German naval officer's uniform as a disguise, as well as the presence of several sailors to accompany and protect him if necessary. The commander of the torpedo boat *Litis* himself lent his parade uniform for this purpose, taking into account Aznar's corpulence.

A German officer arrived on shore with a suitcase containing the requested uniform and headed to the embassy. Dressed as a German lieutenant commander, Agustín Aznar left his refuge and was able to pass through any checkpoint without arousing suspicion until he boarded the German torpedo boat again. The bribery option failed due to the incident of the recognition of Aznar, and the attempt, despite German efforts, was ineffective.

The German consul had become so involved in the situation that he had to abandon his mission in the city after assisting the Falangists, but not before suffering a suspicious incident in his official vehicle when he was rammed for no apparent reason by a truck full of Red militiamen. The Madrid government, for its part, issued an order for von Knobloch's expulsion. The National Socialist consul was forced to seek refuge in the torpedo boat *Litis,* which was anchored in the dock, but not before encountering and overcoming some police resistance.

In the general report that Boehm submitted to his government in his role as commander of the light squadron and of the naval units stationed in Spain between August 19th and October 7th, the following is stated, among other things, about the situation in the Nationalist zone:

> First and foremost, there are two major factions here. In the North (General Mola) are situated the Carlists, of a monarchist and clerical orientation. In the Center and Southwest (Franco), there is the authentic zone of the Falange, a popular movement with ideas and a program similar to those of the National Socialist German Workers Party. The Falange advocates for radical social reforms and the abolition of class conflict.[358]

On October 5th, the German consul in Alicante and the Falangist expedition members were transported by sea to Bonanza aboard a German ship. Meanwhile, a command change occurred within the German naval forces, with Vice Admiral Rolf Caris, who was even more committed to Falangist ideals, appointed as the squadron's new commander in chief.

Another attempt to free José Antonio was made on October 6th, this time with the assistance and participation of German forces. That same day, von Knobloch, Agustín Aznar, and the rest of the commando arrived in Seville, where they studied the possibility of instructing a large and selected group of Falangists to carry out, once the instruction and training for the mission were completed, a surprise attack involving an assault on the Provincial Prison of Alicante for the liberation of the national leader. The Falange's territorial chiefs enthusiastically supported the Spanish-German plan, which was preceded by a new bribe attempt to save José Antonio without spilling blood and in a less dangerous way.

On this occasion, the head of the militias preparing for the assault on the prison was Agustín Aznar himself, and Manuel Mora-Figueroa would be appointed by General Franco as coordinator of the operation, in which the "elite of the Falange of Castile," that is, José Antonio Girón, Gumersindo García, Anselmo de la Iglesia, Luis González Vicén, and others, would take part. The mediator would be, according to the plans, Gabriel Ravello, an elderly man who walked supported by his cane because of his slight limping, who had been the head of the Ybarra shipping company in Alicante and who, last August, through the diplomatic offices of the German consul in that city, was allowed to flee to the Nationalist zone and since

---

[358] Ibid., 79.

then has been residing in the Sevillian town of Dos Hermanas. Despite their ideological differences, Ravello was a close personal friend of Alicante's civil governor. On behalf of Germany, Lieutenant Commander Wagner, also known as "Wenzel," would be in charge of providing logistical support for the operation.

Franco, through the mediation of Agustín Aznar and von Knobloch, was informed of the plans and intentions for the liberation project. He approved the operation once the details were known, and he wished them luck with the outcome.

On the same day, October 6th, the German coordinator Wagner asked the commander of the battleship *Admiral Scheer*, Captain Otto Ciliax, to keep him constantly updated on the situation of José Antonio, and three days later he officially informed him: "It is necessary to urgently transfer Consul von Knobloch to Alicante on October 10th by torpedo boat for a matter of the utmost importance. Telegraph the time and location of boarding."[359]

Once the vice admiral was informed of the mission, he arranged for the torpedo boat *Albatros* to pick up the consul, who informed Varlimont in a dispatch dated October 10th "that the new attempt he had begun to obtain the liberation of Primo de Rivera could only be carried out with the support of the German representation."[360] On the 10th, the torpedo boat *Albatros* docked in the port of Cádiz in order to take aboard the consul von Knobloch, the mediator Gabriel Ravello, and the Falangist Pedro Gamero del Castillo. Before sailing, the Falange militia chief, Agustín Aznar, awarded the German consul with the honorary title of "Jefe de Bandera." The only condition for German intervention was that the Reich's authorities not be compromised in the execution of the plan.

The three commissioners re-embarked on the 12th at Algeciras on the torpedo boat *Luchs*, which transferred them the next day to the tanker *Hansa*, and, subsequently, they boarded the ship *Deutschland*, where they met with Vice Admiral Rolf Caris, German embassy counselor Karl Schwendemann, and Consul von Knobloch to go over the details and gain some insight into the circumstances.

According to German navy documents:

Von Knobloch claims that he comes on behalf of Franco and the Fascist party to launch an attempt to free Primo, and devises two plans: a) an attempt to bribe the civil governor of Alicante. It shall be carried out by arranging a meeting aboard an Argentine cruiser or the battleship *Deutschland*. Duration of the attempt: up to three days; b) Liberation by force relying on a Spanish landing squad transported by ship with the support of two national cruisers.[361]

---

[359] Ibid., 82.

[360] Quoted in ibid.

[361] Viñas, *Guerra*, 83.

During that meeting, the consul argued that the liberation of Primo de Rivera was a critical issue for Spanish Fascism and that this was also the view of influential sectors of the National Socialist Party in Germany.

On the 21st, Ciliax paid a visit to the governor of Alicante on land.[362] The following day, the civil governor went on board the *Admiral Scheer* at half past six in the evening to hold a meeting with those responsible for the mediation, his friend the German consul, Ravello, and Gamero del Castillo, who were also transferred from the mother ship *Hansa*, where they had been staying, to the *Admiral Scheer*. The conversation was friendly, but no concrete solution was reached. Nevertheless, the governor confided to them his opinion that there was no danger to Primo de Rivera.

On October 26th, the torpedo boat *Luchs* approached the territorial waters of Alicante to retrieve the commissioners. In the meantime, the German embassy was also carrying out countless efforts toward liberation. On the morning of October 26th, Vice Admiral Caris sent Ciliax the following telegram: "I expect the matter of Primo to be settled this week, if at all."

When the second attempt to bribe the communist authorities failed, the German consul was relieved of his role as mediator for José Antonio's release and evacuation, which he had been carrying out with such tenacity, commitment, and camaraderie. The Germans sent the money back to Franco's headquarters. The only remaining option was to launch the surprise attack, involving Falangist militias landing on the ground to storm the Provincial Prison and free the national leader. This act of force was reconsidered and initially dismissed as impossible at that time. The Falangist landing was temporarily halted due to the high risk and uncertainty surrounding the possible outcome.

German collaboration was critical to José Antonio's rescue. M. Merkes, in his book *Die deutsche Politik gegenüber dem spanischen Bürgerkieg 1936–1939*, on page 60, wrote:

> The bribery attempts were unsuccessful. The *chargé d'affaires* of the German consulate in Alicante became so embroiled in the affair that he had to flee to a German warship for his own safety. A violent liberation appeared to the *chargé d'affaires* and the commanders of the German ships to be so dangerous to both the prisoner and the embassy that participation was denied.

On November 4th, a last attempt to make an exchange was studied by Franco, who told the Germans that he was willing to exchange José Antonio for the socialist deputy from Asturias, Graciano Antuña, plus the amount of three million pesetas

---

[362] [Translator: Otto Ciliax was a German naval officer.]

that the Germans had on deposit for that purpose. The proposal was being processed by the embassy when José Antonio was assassinated at dawn on November 20th, along with two Falangist boys and two militiamen who also died that morning while facing the rifles of the communists. José Antonio was mercilessly killed by Marxist hatred in the courtyard of the Provincial Prison of Alicante after a mock trial.

The Germans took advantage of the evacuation of foreign citizens to facilitate the departure of certain Spanish personalities who had aligned themselves with the patriotic cause prior to the Uprising of July 18th. The German consul facilitated the departure of several Falangists, among them the wife of Fernando Primo de Rivera, Rosario Urquijo, Lolita Primo de Rivera (who would later marry the Falange Militia Chief Agustín Aznar Gener), Pilar Primo de Rivera (National Delegate of the Women's Section of the Falange and sister of José Antonio, who, accompanied by a secretary of the German embassy, was able to leave the Red zone through Alicante thanks to the passport of the Third Reich that was provided to her, and from there set sail with a German identity on a ship of the same flag), and José Antonio's assistant, Rafael Garcerán. Several of the evacuated Falangists did so wearing the uniform of the German navy anchored in the Mediterranean, in the coastal area of Alicante.

Germany acted with great commitment in the liberation of José Antonio, placing part of its naval fleet at the disposal of the Falangists, providing them with German credentials and passports, giving them uniforms, and so on, bearing in mind that, officially, it had diplomatic relations with the Republican government, and any kind of indiscretion when providing assistance to the Nationalists could have been interpreted as interference and belligerence, especially in regard to the international context, in which the other countries were also preparing their own agendas and arguments for the intervention. On the other hand, if the important German collaboration with the Falangists had been discovered, the German émigré community in Spain and the country's businesses would have faced an extremely challenging situation.

The Germans did everything they could to assist the Falangists in their efforts to liberate José Antonio. Camaraderie motivated them to come to his aid. Fate put a tragic end to the life of the young José Antonio on November 20th, now and forever a day of sorrow.

The successor of José Antonio, as second national leader of the Falange, was Manuel Hedilla Larrey, who, as worthy and faithful heir of the founder, on September 26th, 1936, in Burgos, declared: "We are related in blood with Italian Fascism and with German National Socialism, and we declare our most open sympathy with these revolutions."

ENJOYED THIS BOOK?

TO READ MORE, VISIT US AT

ANTELOPEHILLPUBLISHING.COM

www.ingramcontent.com/pod-product-compliance
Lightning Source LLC
Chambersburg PA
CBHW021212130626
46554CB00004B/1186